In Potiphar's House

In Potiphar's House

The Interpretive Life of Biblical Texts

James L. Kugel

Harvard University Press
Cambridge, Massachusetts
London, England

First Harvard University Press paperback edition, 1994

This Harvard University Press paperback
is published by arrangement with
HarperSanFrancisco, a division of HarperCollins Publishers.

Library of Congress Cataloging-in-Publication Data

Kugel, James L.
    In Potiphar's house : the interpretive life of biblical texts /
    James L. Kugel.—2nd ed.
        p.   cm.
    Includes bibliographical references and index.
    ISBN 0-674-44563-5 (pbk.)
    1. Narration in the Bible.   2. Rabbinical literature—History and
criticism.   3. Bible.   O.T. Genesis XXXIX—Criticism,
interpretation, etc.   I. Title.
BS1171.2.K84   1994   93-44893
220.6'6—dc20   CIP

Contents

Preface to the Second Edition

In preparing this book for publication by Harvard University Press I have written a new introduction. My aim in the new introduction is to set out in brief the method of analyzing ancient biblical interpretation that I developed in the course of writing this book. I hope that this methodological introduction will make the book's ultimate concern somewhat more explicit. For, what began as an attempt to elucidate the origin and development of some interesting traditions about individual biblical verses ended up presenting, albeit indirectly, a method for analyzing passages of ancient biblical interpretation. I hope that this method (now set out a bit more directly in the present edition) may be of use to fellow scholars and students of biblical interpretation and that, in particular, it may prove of value in regard to the Dead Sea Scrolls and the biblical apocrypha and pseudepigrapha, whose store of ancient exegesis is only now undergoing systematic investigation.

In Potiphar's House

Introduction

Judaism and Christianity have not only a book in common, the Hebrew Bible, but also a common set of traditions about what that book means. For although these two religions ultimately diverged on many issues—including the interpretation of Scripture—Christianity at its origin was a Jewish sect, and from the beginning it had adopted a number of Jewish assumptions about how to go about interpreting the Bible, as well as a substantial body of Jewish traditions about the meaning of specific biblical passages. This common store of biblical interpretations and the assumptions that underlie them are a subject of no small importance; perhaps even more than the words of the Bible itself, they have helped to shape the very character of Judaism and Christianity.

When did these traditions about how to read and interpret the Hebrew Bible originate? Some of them had apparently been in existence for quite some time before the rise of Christianity: we possess an extensive body of biblical interpretations in documents that go back two or three centuries before the common era (B.C.E.), and there are scattered written reflections of interpretive activity that go back even earlier than this. (Indeed, the oldest evidence of biblical interpretation is to be found within the Hebrew Bible itself—passages from later books of the Bible that seek to interpret verses from earlier books, glosses that were inserted into the biblical text by later copyists or editors, and so forth.) Nor should the fact that biblical interpretation began so long ago be particularly suprising: there are several factors that combined to make interpretation, or *exegesis*, a central Jewish concern in the centuries before the common era.

To begin with, certain biblical texts—and especially the Pentateuch (Hebrew *Torah*), the first five books of the Bible—were of great importance to Jews during this period. These texts exercised a central role in daily life, and were discussed and commented upon in public assembly. It was thus natural that determining their precise significance should become a major concern. But often the sense of such texts was far from clear. Many of them contained words whose meanings were no longer understood, or references to people or places or customs no longer known. Moreover, sometimes one passage in the Bible seemed to contradict another, and so required some explanation if the contradition was to be resolved. Elsewhere it was simply a question of filling in the details. For many biblical histories seemed here and there to lack a crucial detail: Why did X do what he did? What was Y thinking at the time? And how does it all relate to this or that fact told to us elsewhere? Faced with such questions, ancient Jewish interpreters—scholars and ordinary folk, individuals or groups—had set out to provide explanations, and these explanations, known in Hebrew as *midrash* ("interpretation"), were apparently passed on orally for some time, communicated from scholar to scholar, from teacher to student, or from a preacher to his listeners. Midrash is not just dry biblical commentary: it is clever, inventive, quite down-to-earth, sometimes humorous, often moving, and always full of fresh insights with regard to the biblical text. Little wonder, then, that it was passed on so widely and so eagerly, not only among Jews of different sects and persuasions in late antiquity, but, as noted, in the nascent Christian churches as well.

Ultimately, much of this early biblical interpretation was committed to writing by various schools or individual authors, and these writings now comprise a library that is dauntingly large and varied. Students of Judaism are of course aware of the classical corpus of rabbinic learning, including the Jerusalem and Babylonian Talmuds, as well as various individual compendia of midrash such as *Genesis Rabba, Midrash Tanḥuma,* and the like. But this is only part of the library of early exegesis— and not the earliest part, either. Indeed, this library comprises works written from the third or second century B.C.E. on through the Middle Ages, and includes, in addition to biblical commentaries as such, retellings of biblical stories in the authors' own words (such as are found abundantly in books written in the centuries just before and after the start of the common era), as well as interpretive translations, sermons prepared for synagogue or church, plus devotional poems, prayers, legal compendia, apocalyptic visions, and yet other works, all of which in some way or another pass on traditions about the meaning of particular biblical texts. Some of the books that set forth or echo these early exegetical traditions are, as stated, relatively well known: rabbinic works, or the writings of the first-century Jewish historian Flavius Josephus, or, for that matter, the New Testament, which is full of traditional Jewish interpretations of stories and prophecies from the Hebrew Bible. But other works in this library are more obscure. In some cases, the original commentaries or retellings, written in Hebrew or Aramaic or Greek, now survive only in translation, preserved for centuries in dusty tomes in such languages as Ethiopic, Armenian, Coptic, and Slavonic.

Because so many of the interpretations found in this library are *traditional*—that is, the author of a given text does not make up the explanation himself, but simply passes on something that he has heard or read—many of the same exegetical traditions tend to recur again and again within this library. But, since human beings are both fallible and inventive, the traditions are rarely absolutely identical: authors often make a mistake in copying from their sources, or may not understand their sources, or may simply feel that they can do a better job by putting things in their own words. The result is that a single exegetical tradition may survive in five or ten different forms, and sometimes the most assiduous detective work is required in order to trace their interrelationship and development.

Purpose of This Book

This book seeks (among other things) to present a methodological model for reading early biblical interpretation. I did not start out with this purpose in mind. My initial aim was simply to study a group of early interpretations of the biblical story of Joseph. (Later, I expanded the book to include interpretations of other parts of the Bible as well.) As I proceeded, however, I noticed that the same basic set of questions kept presenting itself to me in different contexts: How did a particular piece of biblical interpretation originate? Indeed, how can one sift out *interpretations* from works (such as those found among the biblical apocrypha and pseudepigrapha) that are not biblical commentaries at all—works which seem mostly devoted to imaginative, often polemical reworkings of biblical material? And when a particular piece of interpretation is found in more than one ancient text, how can one determine which ancient author borrowed from the other or if the two had a common source?

As time went on, I developed a method for dealing with these issues—although "method" may be too grandiose a term to use here, since what is involved is more in the nature of a simple set of steps and a standard agenda of questions. (Nor, for that matter, is the approach that I arrived at entirely of my own devising: it has benefited greatly from the work of previous scholars, in particular Louis Ginzberg and Victor Aptowitzer and, in more recent times, Joseph Heinemann and Geza Vermes.)

The workings of this method will be clear enough from the chapters that follow, but it might be appropriate to present it in schematic form at the outset.

And so, to begin with, a basic postulate of this book: some traditions about the meaning of individual verses or sections of the Hebrew Bible, as well as general ideas about *how* to interpret Scripture, are very, very old. The oldest books in the library of ancient interpretation date back to the second or third century B.C.E. But does this mean that biblical interpretation as an ongoing activity did not exist much before that time? I do not think so. It is not only that traces of interpretive activity can be found here and there within the Bible itself; the quantity and nature of this biblical material would not on its own persuade us that interpretation was a central, ongoing concern. But there is another, simpler argument to be made, one that has to do with the transmission of biblical texts. For, even the most hard-nosed modern biblical scholar would concede that large sections of the Hebrew Bible are extremely old; they were apparently committed to writing in the eighth, ninth, tenth, and still earlier centuries before the common era. If such texts have come down to us, it is not because they were written down once and then painstakingly preserved in vacuum cases for hundreds of years, only to be reopened in the second century in time for the earliest of our surviving commentaries to be written about them. If they have come down to us, it is because they were, *almost from the time of their composition,* copied and recopied in every century—and, in all likelihood, not by mindless scribes bent only on preserving them, but by people who had some use for these texts, sages and priests, court officials and teachers. Such figures doubtless did more than preserve the texts: they read and referred to them, explained them to others, sought to apply them to new situations or to extend their meaning—in short, they *interpreted* them.

Thus, it seems reasonable to suppose that some of the bits of biblical interpretation that we find in the Dead Sea Scrolls or the biblical apocrypha and pseudepigrapha, although appearing in texts of the first, second, or third centuries B.C.E., may belong to a still earlier age. More important, the activity that such works exemplify, commenting on Scripture, was something that had, by the late Second Temple period, probably been going on in one form or another for some centuries.

This brings us to the heart of our postulate. Many of the books written in late Second Temple times—the Enoch literature, the book of Judith, Ben Sira, *The Testaments of the Twelve Patriarchs,* and so forth— contain references to Scripture and even full-scale retellings of biblical tales. Curiously, however, such books frequently do not present the biblical material exactly as it appears in the Bible: when quoting a verse, they often change a word or two, and in retelling a story, they not infrequently add details, sometimes whole incidents, not found in the biblical original. (Sometimes, they also delete things that *are* in the original story.)

These modifications are potentially misleading to modern readers. Our natural tendency is to regard slight changes as not particularly significant, and even major additions sometimes appear to us as merely imaginative flourishes. Scholars who deal with this material are of course keenly aware of the modifications and do not often dismiss them outright. But more often than not such divergences from the biblical text are explained by scholars as references to the various theological-political conflicts that raged in the Second Temple period; the changes constitute an attempt to "update" the biblical material to make it match the later author's ideology or politics. Deletions from the biblical original are often explained as acts of simplification or oversights on the part of the later author.

None of these explanations is necessarily wrong: imagination, politics, simplification, and even oversights do sometimes play a role in a later author's retelling of a biblical story or the restating of a biblical verse. But to say only this is to miss the point of a good many of these modifications, indeed, the vast majority. They are a form—and, in late antiquity, a rather common form—of biblical *interpretation*. That is, instead of saying "By word X the Bible really means Y," an ancient interpreter might simply rewrite the biblical verse in question by substituting Y for X. Similarly, instead of saying "I deduce, from such-and-such evidence, that a particular incident, or conversation, or other detail not found in the biblical account must actually have taken place in order for this story to make sense," the author simply inserts the "missing" item in his retelling.

I am hardly the first to suggest this, and yet it seems to me that the implications of this insight have not been fully appreciated. And so I come to the first step in my set of procedures for analyzing any ancient text that talks about, retells, or alludes to something from the Bible:

1. **Identify potential interpretations by closely comparing the secondary text with the biblical original.** If, as suggested by our first postulate, there was indeed a considerable store of early biblical interpretation circulating in Israel throughout the Second Temple period, then one might well expect to find reflections of this interpretive material in a broad variety of texts written during that time. For that reason, careful consideration of all Scriptural references, no matter how slight, in this literature might indeed help us to reconstruct some of this ancient store

of biblical interpretation. (Obviously, this must be done with some caution and reserve. I discuss some of the issues and dangers involved here in the first of the "nine theses" presented in the closing chapter of this book.) The surest way to turn up potential reflections of this interpretive store is through close comparison of the secondary text with the biblical original. One ought therefore to read all ancient retellings, translations, sermons, prayers, and even commentaries *with Bible in hand*; any deviation from the biblical account is potentially (though, to be sure, not automatically) a piece of interpretation.

As noted, exegetical additions can involve something as slight as an inserted new word or something as big as a whole new episode. But here it may be useful to comment on a particularly characteristic phenomenon of the early interpretation of biblical *stories*. As with the rest of the Bible, biblical stories were viewed by ancient interpreters as fundamentally elliptical: the narrative was believed to say much in a few words and often to omit essentials, leaving a number of details to be filled in by the interpreter. But biblical stories in particular seem to have generated an extraordinary amount of "filling in" on the part of early interpreters. Any little item in the biblical story—an apparently unnecessary repetition, a logical inconsistency, an unusual grammatical form, a no longer understood word or phrase—could generate a wealth of additions to the narrative, for interpreters tended to regard all such things as opportunities, nay, *invitations*, issued by the Bible itself, to create some new bit of action or dialogue. Once the additional material was created, it was, as I have said, simply inserted in the new author's retelling of the biblical story. The chapters that follow are thus full of such specially created additions to the narrative—accounts of how the young Joseph primped and preened to cultivate his good looks, or how his bones were secretly hidden away after his death in Egypt.

It seemed to me that this phenomenon, so common in the retelling of biblical stories, ought to be referred to in distinctive and consistent fashion, and so I have decided in this study to speak of such additions to biblical stories as **narrative expansions.** A narrative expansion can consist of anything not found in the original biblical story—generally, an additional action performed by one or more of the people in the story or additional words spoken in the course of the events. (Indeed, I might have, somewhat more awkwardly, referred to them as *exegetical* narrative expansions since, as noted, such expansions tend to be aimed at explaining something that *is* in the story, the unusual word or grammatical oddity or unnecessary repetition mentioned above.) The distinguishing characteristic of the narrative expansion is that it proceeds by actually *expanding the narrative content* of the biblical text, boldly asserting that, in addition to what is explicitly related in the Bible, other words or actions not specified in the text actually accompanied what is specified.

The name narrative expansion may be rather colorless, but I have used it because it says exactly what it means and may thus avoid some of the not inconsiderable problems associated with terms used by other students of biblical interpretation. Thus, narrative expansions have in the past been referred to as "stories" (Hebrew *sippurim*), "legends" (*aggadot*), or "homilies" (*derashot*), but each of these terms is somewhat problematic. Narrative expansions are often less than "stories"—they sometimes consist only of a single action inserted into the narrative flow[1]—and to call them "legends" is to distort the fundamentally ad hoc and exegetical character of most.[2] As for "homily," this term is hopelessly vague and regularly includes materials (parables, *petihta'ot*, extended textual comparisons, and so forth) that are not narrative expansions at all.

Narrative expansions are easily identified; if one reads the retelling, restatement, or translation of a particular biblical story with Bible in hand, the little additions will be spotted without difficulty. But that is only the first step: there is a second, complementary act of analysis that must accompany any reading of ancient interpretation.

2. Isolate individual pieces of interpretation and identify the exegetical idea that each embodies. Biblical interpretations traveled far and wide; as noted, they passed from scholar to student and from one student to another, indeed, from one ordinary person to another. In the process, they also passed from place to place, traveling through different geographical locations and crossing the lines of different groups and sects and social divisions. As they traveled, interpretations (especially narrative expansions) tended to change: new details were added, and, not infrequently, two or more originally separate interpretations were combined.

As a result, it is sometimes difficult to spot the fundamental similarity underlying two now quite different narrative expansions, or to pry apart two originally distinct interpretations that have been skillfully welded together by an ancient author. As I struggled with this problem, it became clear to me that the key to it lay once again in referring back to the Bible itself. In order to spot underlying resemblances or various sorts of combinations of material, one ought first to determine what it was in the biblical text itself that had originally caused an ancient author to create a particular narrative expansion. This will often make it possible to understand how two apparently different texts nonetheless embody one and the same "solution" to a particular biblical problem, or how two quite distinct solutions may have been combined in a single interpretive text.

In order to do all this, however, I had to be able to deal with exegetical material at a somewhat higher level of abstraction: in addition to talking about individual narrative expansions themselves, I had to be able to talk about the exegetical ideas underlying them. This involved another basic definition, the **exegetical motif:** an exegetical motif is the underlying idea about how to explain a biblical text that becomes the basis, or part of the basis, of a narrative expansion. It is an ancient interpreter's hypothesis about what a particular detail in the Bible may be intending to imply. Thus, as we shall see in Chapter 2, an unusual turn of phrase in the Joseph story caused an ancient interpreter to suppose that, at a certain point in the story, the wife of Joseph's master in Egypt convened a meeting of the ladies of her household in order to talk about Joseph. This exegetical motif, "The Assembly of Ladies," came to be embodied in various narrative expansions found in different forms in a number of ancient texts.

It sometimes happens that an exegetical motif itself acquires further modifications, engendering new narrative expansions. In such cases, the new narrative expansions may themselves be identified as embodying distinctive exegetical motifs, "variant motifs" of the original or "basic" motif. Thus, the "Assembly of Ladies" motif, a basic motif, developed the variant motifs "Forgot Their Wine" and "Cut Their Hands." Similarly, "Tombs of the Egyptian Kings" and "Treasure Houses of the Palace," two motifs which underlie narrative expansions connected with the exodus story, are both variants of the basic motif "Inaccessible Bones." (Exegetical motifs in this study are always identified by taglines, capitalized, and put in quotation marks—"Assembly of Ladies," "Levites Mutilate Fingers," "Buried by One Greater.")

3. **Treat each exegetical motif separately.** Once individual exegetical motifs are isolated, one can then go on to treat each separately—that is, to focus on motif X as embodied in texts A, B, and C, or to analyze text A as embodying three separate exegetical motifs, X, Y, and Z. To treat each motif *separately* is simple enough, but it is nonetheless immensely important; numerous studies have gone astray precisely because they fail to isolate each individual motif.

Separating motifs is crucial for one simple reason. Because with the passage of time biblical interpretations tended to acquire a certain authority of their own (either because they had been attributed to this or that respected teacher or had been included in this or that authoritative document), later writers not infrequently found themselves in the uncomfortable position of having to include two rival bits of interpretation of the same verse in their own retellings. Such authors consequently developed the most ingenious ways of reconciling and combining rival interpretations into a single retelling. In so doing they nonetheless usually left traces of this work of combination—bits of evidence such as **overkill, midrashic doublets,** and **narrative resumptions** (all of which will be defined and illustrated in the chapters that follow). Focusing on the underlying motifs separately is the surest way of sorting through an ancient text or group of texts and reconstructing the steps underlying any one particular narrative expansion.

In the course of this study, a few further terms and refinements will be introduced. In particular, something I eventually came to call **reverse-engineering**—a way of assessing the relationship of a particular motif to its apparent biblical source—will be presented. But it seems best to allow these further refinements to be presented in the course of analyzing actual ancient texts. At the end of this study, I have set out nine "theses" concerning the workings of ancient biblical interpretation. These theses are the conclusions suggested by the method of analysis outlined here and ought therefore to be read in the light of this introduction.

A note on transcriptions: for the sake of simplicity, I have generally cited Hebrew words and short texts in transliteration. The letters *ḥet*, *ṭet*, and *ṣade* have been transcribed with diacritical dots as indicated; *'aleph* and *'ayin* are indicated by different slanting apostrophes, likewise as indicated; other equivalences should be clear.

Biblical verses are as a rule quoted as they appear in the Revised Standard Version, though I have not infrequently resorted to my own translations in order to bring out a particular nuance being highlighted by an exegete. The works of Philo of Alexandria and Josephus are cited from the well-known editions of F. H. Colson and H. St. J. Thackery in the *Loeb Classical Library*, though again I have sometimes decided to translate from the Greek afresh. With regard to *Genesis Rabba*, I have generally cited from the Vatican manuscript found in the critical apparatus of J. Theodor and Ch. Albeck, *Genesis Rabba* (Jerusalem: Wahrmann, 1965). For other rabbinic texts, I have used such modern critical editions as are available; for works unavailable in a critical text, such as *Midrash Tanḥuma*, I have cited commonly used editions, though noting, where appropriate, variants that appear in manuscript.

"Why Was Lamech Blind?" appeared in *Hebrew Annual Review* 1990. The first half of chapter 8 appeared in somewhat different form as "On Hidden Hatred and Open Reproach," *Harvard Theological Review 80* (1987): 43–61. My thanks to these journals for allowing me to reuse the material of these articles here.

This book was completed with the aid of grant from the National Endowment for the Humanities. Much of the work was done in Jerusalem, where I was a guest of the Bible Department of the Hebrew University, and where I was likewise able to avail myself of the resources of the Israel National Library. My thanks are offered to all these institutions and their staffs. I am further indebted to two who took the trouble to read my manuscript and offer suggestions, Profs. Daniel Boyarin and Chaim Milikowsky of Bar Ilan University. I am grateful as well to John Loudon and Georgia Hughes of Harper & Row for their help. My greatest measure of gratitude belongs to my wife, Rachel, to whom this book is dedicated.

Notes

1. I believe that the weakness of the "story" approach is evident in a recent, and valiant, attempt to deal with the issue of terminology, O. Meir's *The Darshanic Story in Genesis Rabba* (Jerusalem: ʿAm Oved, 1987). Starting off with a modern literary-critical definition of "story," the author ends up being ill-served by it, since it causes her both to eliminate on formal grounds a goodly number of the exegetical narrative expansions of *Genesis Rabba* (because they do not contain the minimum number of "actions" to fit the definition of story) and, equally strikingly, to include "stories" that are not expansions of the biblical narrative at all, but little narratives about the rabbinic exegetes who comment on the text. Clearly "story" was the wrong point of departure for this study, which otherwise shows such devotion to clarity and systematic analysis.
2. This, alas, was something of a failing in L. Ginzberg's masterwork, *The Legends of the Jews* (Philadelphia: Jewish Publication Society, 1909–38), which, as a matter of policy, sought to submerge utterly the exegetical character of these expansions (confining occasional remarks on this subject to the voluminous notes—the true heart of the work). The great work of generations and centuries of Jewish exegetes was thus fundamentally distorted into being what it certainly was not, popular "legends" that simply sprang up in the minds of the commonfolk just as the "legends" of ancient Greece or the folklore of other civilizations.

Part I

1.

Joseph in the Bible

Before we turn, in succeeding chapters, to some of the exegetical traditions that sprang up about the Joseph story, we might do well to begin by considering that story itself (Genesis, 37–50), and ask what can be said about it in the light of modern biblical scholarship, as well as what it might reveal about the historical reality of its principal personage. Who was Joseph in ancient Israel?

Certainly one of the striking features of the Joseph narrative is its *literary* quality. Unlike other narratives from the lives of Israel's patriarchs, this one is rather long and complicated (it is, in fact, by far the longest single narrative in Genesis), and it is very story-like. That is, for all the complications, it has a beginning, a middle, and an end, and the various strands of the narrative ultimately unite to form a neat and satisfying whole. The dreams that Joseph had dreamt as a youth—foretelling that his brothers would come and bow down before him—are eventually realized (in a way that Joseph himself had not understood) in the subsequent twists and turns of the story: Sold by his jealous brothers as a slave, Joseph is brought down to Egypt and eventually rises to prominence there, first by correctly interpreting the dreams of Pharaoh's ousted butler and baker, and then by interpreting Pharaoh's own dream of an impending famine in Egypt. Pharaoh puts Joseph in charge of storing up grain against the coming shortage, and when the famine strikes, his brothers come down from Canaan in order to buy grain, bowing before an Egyptian official whom they do not recognize to be their own flesh and blood.

In all this, the motifs of dreaming and dream-interpretation, truth and dissembling, divine foreknowledge and human ignorance, all weave through a story in which justice ultimately triumphs and no one really ends up the loser. Joseph's virtue is rewarded and, if he does arrange things so as to give his brothers a scare or two along the way—well, a reader most likely feels that this is only justified in view of their earlier misconduct. And surely there are few moments in the Bible (or anywhere else) more affecting than the one in which, at the story's denouement, after having played his brothers along and now holding the threat of imprisonment over the youngest of them, Joseph, suddenly unable to conceal or hold himself back any longer, finally bursts into tears and exclaims to his stupefied listeners: "I am Joseph."

It is this very dramatic power of the story that has caused some modern biblical critics to view it as something other than a recitation of the facts of the "historical Joseph's" life. Some have suggested that, before it became the biblical story of Joseph, a tale of this sort must have existed in schematic form, a folktale, which was only later "tacked on" to fit the family and circumstances of the biblical Joseph.[1] Others have been struck in particular by the role that *wisdom* plays in the story: for wisdom in the ancient Near East was more than simply a good trait of character—it was more like a philosophical outlook or understanding of the world, one whose principal tenets are set out didactically in wisdom collections like the book of Proverbs in the Bible. Now Joseph appears in his story to be the very embodiment of this "wisdom" outlook, illustrating all the virtues of the biblical *ḥakham* (sage or wise man). He interprets dreams and can foretell the future (the sage's activity *par excellence*), meets adversity with patient confidence (again, the great sagely virtue), refrains from sexual dalliance, eschews revenge and hatred, and in all other ways conforms to the values inculcated in the sagely texts of the ancient Near East. If the wisdom philosophy had one single message or underlying theme in ancient Israel, it was that a divine plan underlies all the vicissitudes of human existence—and in this too, Joseph's story is an embodiment of sagely teachings. For his is a tale in which the divine plan and its wisdom only emerge at the end (Gen. 45:5–8; and again 50:19–20), and the unfolding of this divine plan through Joseph's ups-and-downs thus essentially seems to serve as an embodiment of wisdom's great message in narrative form. In the view of some scholars, then, the Joseph of this story is something of an idealized figure, one whose life is meant to mirror the virtues of the wisdom philosophy.[2]

Whatever one chooses to make of the Genesis narrative and its associations, it is in any case striking that the "Joseph" one encounters elsewhere in the Bible has little to do with this literary hero or the sagely virtues he embodies. For the fact is that, save for a passing reference to Joseph being sold into slavery in Psalm 105 (see below) and a somewhat more obscure reference to Joseph in Egypt in Psalm 81, there is scarcely the slightest allusion to the events of Joseph's life recounted in Genesis anywhere else in the Hebrew Bible.[3] This is not to say, of course, that the name "Joseph" does not appear. It does, but in a radically different sense: Joseph is the great founder, the ancestor and progenitor, of the tribes of Ephraim and Manasseh who lived in the North of Israel during much of the biblical period.

The birth of Ephraim and Manasseh to their father Joseph is only a passing detail in the Genesis account (Gen. 41:50–52), but the existence of these two tribes was, after all, a present, palpable fact during much of the biblical period. And so the name "Joseph" (or: "the house of Joseph," "the sons of Joseph") represents, outside of the Genesis story, largely this geopolitical reality—a place, the North, and the people of these two tribes (and sometimes others) who dwelt there. In the texts that speak of Joseph in this fashion, we can sometimes sense a further bit of underlying geopolitical reality, the relative lushness and fruitfulness of the land that was Joseph's inheritance. This aspect is clear, for example, in the "Blessings of Jacob" (a series of sayings about each of the twelve sons, that is, the twelve tribes of Israel, in Genesis 49), where Joseph's blessing is rivaled in length only by that of Judah— and Joseph even appears to come out on top of Judah, at least in a material sense. For while Judah is here praised for his fighting strength and political sovereignty ("The scepter shall not depart from Judah . . ." [Gen. 49:10]), Joseph's blessing stresses the fruitfulness of his land and people, the physical bounty, apparently, that was the lot of the Northerners. A related text, the "Blessings of Moses" (Deuteronomy 33), is still more explicit about Joseph's well-being: here he clearly stands out as first—he is endowed with the "choicest gifts of Heaven . . . the choicest fruits of the sun . . . the best gifts of the earth and its fullness" in a blessing conspicuously longer than those of his siblings—and is explicitly described as "prince among his brothers" (Deut. 33:16). Then:

> Ah, majestic is the firstborn bull, whose twin horns are like those of a wild ox! With them he will butt other peoples, yea, all of them to the ends of the earth. These are the myriads of Ephraim, and these are the thousands of Manasseh.

Here we encounter the symbolism of the bull that was associated with the North,[4] and in this particular text, at least, that symbolism receives a further gloss: the bull's "twin horns" are the two tribes of Ephraim and Manasseh. Via these two he is to eliminate other peoples from the region and extend his own power and influence "to the ends of the earth." Again, this presents a striking picture of the political situation, wherein the two great Northern tribes exercise dominion and enjoy its rich fruits.

Sometimes the name Joseph seems to include more than specifically those two tribes said to descend from him. Thus it may be that Ps. 80:2–3,

> Give ear, O Shepherd of Israel, you who lead Joseph like a flock!
> You who are enthroned on the cherubim, shine forth!
> Before Ephraim and Benjamin and Manasseh, raise up your might
>   and bring about our salvation, . . .

"generalizes" Joseph's name so as to include all three tribes named, that is, not only Ephraim and Manasseh, but Benjamin as well (like the other two, a "Rachel tribe"—one whose descent from the patriarch Jacob comes via Jacob's second wife, Rachel). Some have even suggested that the references to Joseph in Pss. 80:2 and 81:6 represent an early form of referring to the people of Israel in general.[5] In any case, it is clear that after the great schism during the reign of Rehoboam, when the previously united monarchy of David and Solomon divided into Northern (Israel) and Southern (Judah) Kingdoms, Joseph's name came to be used more or less synonymously with the North as a whole, and many of its appearances come in contexts dealing with North-South relations or describing the conditions and events leading up to the Northern Kingdom's ultimate fall to the invading Assyrian armies in the eighth century B.C.E. The latter is the "ruin of Joseph" (Amos 6:6). The book of Hosea dwells much on the North in this period, and here, although the name of Joseph is not mentioned, some of the same bull/ calf imagery is encountered as representative of the North (e.g., Hosea 4:16, 8:5–6, 10:5, 11; etc.), perhaps, as has been suggested, echoing the sayings in Genesis 49 and Deuteronomy 33 mentioned above.

As noted, one text, Ps. 105:17–22, does present a picture of Joseph that is somewhat reminiscent of that seen in the Genesis narrative, the wise and patient hero who overcomes all obstacles in order to rise to leadership in Egypt. Here are its words:

> He [God] called down famine upon the land, He broke the staff of
>   bread.
> But He sent before them [the Israelites] a man, one sold as a slave,
>   Joseph.
> They forced his feet into fetters, and iron around his neck, until
>   such time as his word came to pass, and the word of the Lord
>   justified him.
> Then the king had him unbound, the ruler of peoples had him set
>   free.
> He made him lord of his house, and ruler over all his possessions,
>   to instruct his princes at his will, and teach his elders wisdom.

The date of this particular excerpt is far from certain. Many scholars have asserted that this psalm as a whole belongs to the preexilic period (on the basis, *inter alia*, of its being partially cited in 1 Chron. 16:8–22), and this may be so, although a postexilic date is equally possible. In any case, it is interesting that, while this passage alludes to the same basic events as those contained in the Genesis narrative, here there is nothing of the motif of dreaming nor of the brothers' relations with Joseph—only Joseph's rise to success and, in particular, the suffering out of which that success had emerged, iron shackles on feet and neck. The great divine plan could hardly have seemed evident to Joseph at such a moment, yet he trusted in "the word of the Lord" and his situation was reversed; this was certainly, in the eyes of the Psalmist, a lesson worth stressing. Joseph's wisdom in the face of adversity certainly vouchsafed his ability to rule others wisely too, but more than that, a man of such character had something to teach even the king's vaunted wise men. None of this is particularly helpful in the situating of Ps. 105:17–22 within our developmental history of Joseph's "image"—for such a picture might well be appropriate in various periods of Israel's history. But it is to be stressed that, wherever it may precisely belong, this passage is quite unique: nowhere else in the Hebrew Bible outside of Genesis do we encounter Joseph as the individual hero of the events in Egypt.

Indeed, relatively early in the biblical period, the figure of Joseph came to be profoundly affected by political change. For with the fall of the Northern Kingdom to the Assyrians, the name of Joseph began a steady decline: if there nevertheless remained the hope that "the Lord, the God of hosts, may be gracious to the remnant of Joseph" (Amos 5:15), this hope became dimmer and dimmer with the passing decades and centuries, and Joseph—in the sense of the Northerners' ancestor—is mentioned with corresponding infrequency. Long after, the book of Ezekiel still records a vision in which Joseph and Judah are to be joined as two sticks and bound into one (Ezek. 37:15–22), that is, North and South restored into a single mighty kingdom, and Zech. 10:6 similarly holds out the hope for Joseph's salvation and return; but these were not to be.

The Postexilic Period

Judah itself fell to the Babylonians in 587 B.C.E., and the flower of its citizenry was deported to Babylonian exile. After the return from exile half a century later, Jewish society underwent many significant changes, including, apparently, a renewed interest in the ancient writings of bygone days and the men and women whose deeds they celebrated. And so, with the geopolitical Joseph as remote as ever, one might think that Joseph the individual, the distinguished figure of ancient narrative, might now undergo something of a rehabilitation in the popular imagination, especially in the period immediately following the Babylonian exile. For surely the story of Joseph's forcible removal from his homeland to Egypt must have resonated with the Jews' own experience of captivity and exile in Babylon and, in a more general way, with the sufferings of foreign domination that they experienced after their return, first under Persian rule, then under successive foreign regimes centered in Hellenistic Egypt and Syria.

Yet there is scant biblical evidence for such a rehabilitation. That the story of Joseph, along with the entire account of the Exodus from Egypt, is omitted from the (postexilic) book of Chronicles may simply be the result of a conscious effort on the Chronicler's part to stress Israel's continuous connection to the land and eliminate any mention of exile or absence.[6] Still, the absence of reference to Joseph elsewhere is harder to explain. Perhaps it was the fact that he was, after all, still so pointedly not "our" ancestor—that is, his descendents had become the Northern Kingdom, Israel, while "we," the South, were connected principally with Joseph's brother Judah—that he does not play any significant role as a representative figure or model in the other biblical books belonging to the postexilic period (although, for example, the narrative of the book of Esther seems in many particulars to be modeled after the Genesis account of Joseph in Pharaoh's court). In any case, it is truly only in the corpus of extrabiblical Jewish writings known as the apocrypha and pseudepigrapha of the Hebrew Bible that one encounters such a "rehabilitated" Joseph. But if the change was long in coming, it was nonetheless striking.

The last parts of what was to become the Hebrew Bible were probably written in the second century before the common era. Even before that time, however, texts had begun to be written which in one way or another sought to interpret and explain points in Israel's sacred literature, and it is in these works that the figure of Joseph attains a new prominence. For, with the "geopolitical" associations of Joseph now a distant memory—and, along with them, the regional issues that his name had represented[7]—what was foremost was the Joseph of the Genesis narrative. Here, among all of Israel's illustrious ancestors, Abraham, Isaac, Jacob and the rest, it was Joseph who had received the lion's share of attention; and what figure in that book might better serve as the raw material for a lesson in virtue?

This "lesson in virtue" is very much to the point: for by, say, the third or second centuries B.C.E., the historical reality of such texts—as records of actual people and events way back in Israel's past—had been increasingly eclipsed by a new way of reading them, one that saw these stories as essentially bits of divine instruction, imparting lessons relevant to today. Here is not the place to go over in detail the various political and social factors that led up to this change in the way Scripture was approached,[8] but we can at least observe that such a change did occur. Consider, for example, the book of Ben Sira. (This book, also known as "Sirach" or "Ecclesiasticus," was written in Hebrew sometime around 180 B.C.E. Although ultimately excluded from the Jewish Bible, it was nonetheless considered sacred by earlier Christians and preserved in translation among the apocrypha or "deuterocanonical" literature of the Christian Old Testament.) Ben Sira was a champion of the wisdom philosophy seen above, and in his book he collected many wise sayings in the manner of earlier wisdom teachers, such as the authors of the biblical books of Proverbs and Ecclesiastes. Unlike these, however, Ben Sira's book also contains many overt references to Scripture, including one long catalogue of biblical heroes ("Let us now praise famous men . . .", [Sirach 44–49]). In it, we can see clearly what the accounts of Genesis and other books had become by Ben Sira's time. Here, for example, is his description of Abraham:

> Abraham was the great father of a multitude of nations, and no one
>   has been found like him in glory.
> He kept the law of the Most High, and was taken into covenant
>   with him;
> he established the covenant in his flesh, and when he was tested
>   he was found faithful.
> Therefore the Lord assured him by an oath that the nations would
>   be blessed through his posterity;
> that he would multiply him like the dust of the earth, and exalt his
>   posterity like the stars,
> and cause them to inherit from sea to sea, and from the River to
>   the ends of the earth.

This neat little summary of Abraham's importance should remind us a bit of the treatment of Joseph in Psalm 105: here too, a complex story is collapsed into a few lines, and all the salient points are touched. But unlike the former, this passage's relationship to the corresponding Genesis narrative is unmistakable. Abraham is the "father of a multitude of nations," an allusion to Gen. 17:5, "I have made you the father of a multitude of nations"; he is granted God's covenant because he "kept the law of the Most High" (a reference to the covenant enacted in Genesis 15, this passage being, apparently, quite consciously conflated with Gen. 26:5, which attributes the granting of that covenant to the fact that "Abraham obeyed my voice and kept my charge, my commandments, my statutes, and my laws"); the "covenant in his flesh" alludes to circumcision (Gen. 17:10–14), and "when he was tested he was found faithful" is an allusion to Gen. 22:1 ("After these things, God tested Abraham"); "Therefore the Lord assured him by an oath," etc. is a collection of references to different passages, respectively, Gen. 26:4 and possibly 12:3, Gen.22:17, and Deut. 11:24. All this in four lines! These verbal cues back to the biblical narrative eloquently attest to the fact that, for Ben Sira and his contemporaries, Abraham and the other major figures of Genesis were no longer viewed so much as men as chapters of *Scripture*, a sacred text whose main purpose was not to record the past but to teach things of interest to the present, and whose main points (it was presumed) were well known to all and, therefore, could be captured in an allusive phrase or two.

Interestingly, Ben Sira has very little to say about Joseph (nor, for that matter, does he include much about Isaac or Jacob): he only alludes in passing to the story of Joseph's bones (Sir. 49:15; see below, chapter 5), and this in a separate section, after he has already traced the major heroes of Israel from patriarchal times down to Nehemiah in the postexilic period.[9] But other sources from the same period or slightly later are less reticent. Consider, for example, 1 Maccabees, a book written only a few decades after Ben Sira and recounting the Jews' successful struggle for independence from their Seleucid rulers. At the book's beginning, Mattathias, the old patriarch, is about to die; he charges his sons to "remember the deeds of the fathers," and proceeds to list what these were:

> Was not Abraham found faithful when tested, and it was reckoned to him as righteousness? Joseph in the time of his distress kept a commandment, and became lord of Egypt. Phineas our father, because he was deeply zealous, received the covenant of everlasting priesthood.
>
> (1 Macc. 2:53)

Here Joseph is in somewhat exclusive company; he is one of the "fathers" whose great deeds are memorialized in Scripture (note, by the way, the absence of Isaac and Jacob from this list). It may not be absolutely clear what "commandment" Joseph had kept in time of distress, but his whole subsequent rise to power is attributed to this apparent instance of zeal for divine law, the same trait which Mattathias had stressed in his opening words ("Now my children, show zeal for the law . . ." [1 Macc. 2:50]). If the list is short on details, we are at least made to feel that Joseph is, like the other figures mentioned, a scriptural *example*, and that the inclusion of his story in Scripture is—

like everything else—intended to impart a lesson for use in everyday life.

Joseph and Potiphar's Wife

But what lesson? Trust not your brothers? Keep your dreams to yourself? There is so much detail in the story, so many different ways in which Joseph embodies the canons of wisdom, that a reader nowadays might be hard pressed to name *one* lesson that the story was meant to impart. And yet there *was* one particular virtue that Joseph came frequently to be connected with. It may even be that the "commandment" kept in time of distress in the passage from 1 Maccabees cited above was an instance of this virtue; in any case it is openly the importance of Joseph in another, slightly later, text:

> It is for this reason, certainly, that the temperate Joseph is praised, because by mental effort he overcame sexual desire. For when he was young and in his prime, by his reason he nullified the frenzy of his passions. Not only is reason proved to rule over the frenzied urge of sexual desire, but also over every desire.
>
> (4 Macc. 2:1–4)

This passage alludes, of course, to a famous episode that occurs after Joseph has been sold as slave in Egypt. Bought by Potiphar, "an officer of Pharaoh, captain of the guard," Joseph apparently rises rapidly through the ranks of household servants, until his master puts him in charge and makes him overseer of all the household. The text continues:

> Now Joseph was comely of form and comely of appearance. And it happened after these things that his master's wife cast her eyes upon Joseph, and said, "Lie with me." But he refused and said to his master's wife, "Lo, having me my master has no concern about anything in the house, and he has put everything that he has in my hand; there is no one greater in this house than I am; nor has he kept back anything from me except yourself, because you are his wife; how then can I do this great wickedness, and sin against God?" And although she spoke to Joseph day after day, he would not listen to her, to lie with her or to be with her. But one day, when he went into the house to do his work and none of the men of the house was in the house, she caught him by his garment saying, "Lie with me." But he left his garment in her hand, and fled and went outside.

This brief episode serves an important function within the narrative. First, it is the incident that lands Joseph in jail (because, having refused his mistress's favors, he ends up being accused by her of attempted rape), and this is what allows him to encounter Pharaoh's ousted butler and baker, also jailed, and thus ultimately to come to the attention of Pharaoh and interpret his dreams. Beyond this, the incident sharpens the picture of Joseph's character and his sage-like behavior. We see, first, the managerial skills that lead to his elevation to supervisor of the household (and foreshadow those same abilities when he is put in charge of Egypt's grain); then, his temperate refusal of his mistress's adulterous proposals; and finally, his steadfastness in the face of adversity when, wrongly accused, he plummets from a position of some power and authority to the depths of a dreary prison cell.

Yet for all that, it is only one incident among many. In surveying the various narrative high points of the story—Joseph the spoiled child, dressed in his "coat of many colors"; his brothers' jealousy and treachery; Joseph in prison, interpreting his cellmates' dreams; Joseph in Pharaoh's court, in charge of all of Egypt; the visit of his brothers, and Joseph's intrigue with their grain sacks; troubled times in Canaan, and disputes between Jacob and his sons; the return to Egypt, and the banquet in Joseph's house; the denouement with Judah, and Joseph's startling revelation; finally, Joseph's reunion with his aged father—when one considers these principal elements of the story as a whole, the incident with Potiphar's wife is certainly something of an aside, interesting and relevant, but hardly the whole point of the story. In fact, if a modern reader were asked to extract some overriding moral message from the story, would it not most likely be something like: accept what comes your way with equanimity and trust in God, for everything will work out for the best?

Yet it is interesting that, for ancient readers of the Joseph story, the adulterous proposal of Potiphar's wife, and Joseph's virtuous refusal to cooperate, came to loom larger and larger in the imagination. Something of this process can be observed even in the *Book of Jubilees*, a retelling of the book of Genesis and part of Exodus that goes back to the second century B.C.E. The story of Joseph is apparently not of great interest to the author of *Jubilees*—he collapses much of the narrative, eliminating, for example, the whole opening section, from Joseph's childhood dreams through and including his being sold as a slave by his brothers' treachery. Yet the incident with Potiphar's wife is there, indeed, expanded a bit. Here is the beginning:

> And Joseph was good-looking and very handsome. And the wife of
> his master lifted up her eyes and saw Joseph and desired him. And
> she begged him to lie with her. And he did not surrender himself but
> remembered the Lord and the words which Jacob, his father, used to

read, which were from the words of Abraham, that there is no man who [may] fornicate with a woman who has a husband [and] that there is a judgment of death which is decreed for him in heaven before the Lord Most High. And the sin is written [on high] concerning him in the eternal books always before the Lord. And Joseph remembered these words and he did not want to lie with her. And she begged him [for] one year. And he turned away and refused to listen to her.[10]

The excursus on "the words which Jacob, his father, used to read" is necessitated in *Jubilees* by the fact that the revelation of divine law at Sinai, with its prohibition of adultery (Exod. 20:14), has not taken place yet: in order to make Joseph's conduct not just good behavior based on fear or common sense, *Jubilees* here (as elsewhere) posits a pre-Sinaitic revelation of divine law, one that is passed on to Joseph by his father Jacob. But note as well that in this account, Joseph's steadfastness apparently exceeds that of the biblical text itself: the latter has Mrs. Potiphar's request repeated to Joseph "day after day" (Gen. 39:10), but this expression is apparently interpreted here to mean that her solicitations continued over the course of an entire year! Still, Joseph resists. Later on in the narrative, when he encounters Mrs. Potiphar alone in the house, she locks the door behind him, so that, in making his escape, Joseph is obliged to "break the door" in order to get out. This too seems an embellishment designed to augment our appreciation of Joseph's piety.

Still more striking is the picture of Joseph that emerges in another early text, *The Testaments of the Twelve Patriarchs*. (Again, the exact date of this text cannot be determined: it has gone through various stages of editing and is in its final form a Christian book. Still, there are clear indications that it was originally a Jewish composition, a collection of imaginary testaments of a sort apparently popular in the last pre-Christian centuries; scholars generally date this earlier, Jewish form of the *Testaments* to the first or even second century B.C.E.). Joseph is the great moral exemplar of the *Testaments*:[11] although each individual testament is spoken by a different brother, Joseph's name comes up again and again, until he comes finally to speak for himself in his own testament. Here the incident with Potiphar's wife is the main—virtually the only—item on the agenda: Joseph narrates it in some detail, then returns to it again afterwards with more particulars. Needless to say, his behavior in the face of temptation is exemplary—so much so that one might even say he was *not* tempted!

How often the Egyptian woman threatened me with death! How often after turning me over to the tormentors would she call me back and threaten me! But since I was unwilling to have intercourse with her, she kept saying to me, "You will be master over me and all my household if you will only give yourself over to me; then you will be our ruler."[12]

None of this avails in the *Testaments;* the lady flatters, wheedles, and offers to convert (herself and her husband) from idolatry to the true religion if Joseph will but oblige her, then threatens suicide if he does not; she also tries aphrodisiacs and charms—likewise to no avail. Joseph is simply unmoved. As he himself notes toward the end of his testament:

> Not even in my mind did I yield to her, for God loves more the one who is faithful in self-control in a dark cistern than the one who in royal chambers feasts on delicacies with excess. . . . For when I had been with her in her house, she would bare her arms and thighs so that I might lie with her. For she was wholly beautiful and splendidly decked out to entice me, but the Lord protected me from her manipulations.[13]

What made Joseph's resistance to an adulterous proposal such a central episode in his life, not only in the *Testaments* but in the other sources seen? The answer to this question is no doubt complex. The subject of adultery, as we know from sources contemporaneous to, or slightly later than, the *Testaments* (including, prominently, the New Testament), was one that was very much in the air, and so this relatively minor part of the Joseph story might become correspondingly emphasized. What is more, there were few other possibilities in the Hebrew Bible that one might turn to in order to illustrate the virtues of chastity and resistance to temptation, whereas Joseph's *other* virtues— trust in God, lack of vindictiveness, and so forth, or indeed his special abilities as seer and dream-interpreter—were shared by other biblical figures such as Abraham or Jacob or Daniel. It might therefore be only natural that Joseph's uniqueness receive special emphasis. Beyond this, the incident with Potiphar's wife certainly was a simple, self-contained unit; notwithstanding its role in moving the plot forward, was it not likely to be perceived as, first and foremost, an example, a depiction in sacred Scripture of the way a pious man ought to behave?

Whatever the reason, the fact is that Joseph's "image" did come to be associated specifically with his behavior in this incident. If, as noted, the text of 1 Macc. 2:53 sounds ambiguous about which commandment it was that Joseph kept "in time of distress," there can be little doubt in the light of all we have seen that, in the author's eyes, that commandment was, "Thou shalt not commit adultery." Soon enough, Joseph, like so many biblical figures, developed a particular title or appellation that was paired with his name in rabbinic exegesis, comparable to "Abraham our Father," "Moses our Teacher," "Balaam the Wicked," etc.; in his case it was "Joseph the Righteous" or "the Virtuous," *Yosef ha-ṣaddiq*, and there can be little doubt that this name, too, was based on the incident with Potiphar's wife.[14] Among the earliest evidence of the conferral of this title may be the above cited passage from 4 Maccabees, where "the temperate Joseph" (ὁ σώφρων Ἰωσήφ) may be an attempt to render the Hebrew appellation into Greek.[15] Joseph is referred to obliquely as "a righteous man" (δίκαιος) in the *Wisdom of Solomon*, a pseudonymous Jewish work written in Greek sometime around the turn of the era. This may tell us something about the development of such oblique references in general (witnessed so abundantly in later Hebrew liturgical poetry), but it can say little about the title "Joseph the Righteous" in particular, since the substantive δίκαιος is likewise applied to Abraham, Lot, Jacob, and others in the same fashion elsewhere in that book. Nevertheless the passage may be of some interest in what it shows further about our theme:

> When a righteous man was sold, Wisdom did not desert him, but delivered him from sin. She [Wisdom] descended with him into the dungeon, and when he was in prison she did not leave him, until she brought him the scepter of a kingdom and authority over his masters. Those who accused him she showed to be false, and she gave him everlasting honor. (Wisd. 10:13–14)

At first this may look like a somewhat more well-rounded summary of the biblical Joseph than that found in the *Testaments*. Still, it should not escape our attention that the little incident in Potiphar's house is alluded to twice in these scant lines: Wisdom "delivered [Joseph] from sin," that is, from the clutches of his master's wife, and later "those who accused him she showed to be false." The latter likewise refers to our incident—for there certainly is no accusation brought against Joseph in his whole story other than Mrs. Potiphar's claim of attempted rape. The sense of our text is thus: Wisdom (meaning the great divine plan) showed by subsequent events (that is, by the reward that Joseph received in being elevated over Egypt) that Joseph was indeed a righteous man[16] and, therefore, that the accusations against Joseph by Mrs. Potiphar were retrospectively proven to have been false. In this way was Joseph's reputation saved, and he received "everlasting honor." Note likewise what is *not* said in this summary: no brothers, no Joseph the dreamer, no Pharaoh, and so on and so forth. Thus, despite first appearances, this passage too seems to be one in which the adulterous proposal by his master's wife looms as the central episode in the whole story of Joseph.

The evolution in the significance of "Joseph" that we have been following might therefore be seen as a gradual crystallization: from the somewhat shadowy and inchoate "geopolitical" Joseph, the ancestor of the tribes of Ephraim and Manasseh (or, still more broadly, the *genius loci* of the North in general); to a Joseph increasingly dissociated from geography and viewed more and more as, simply, the virtuous hero of the narrative in the latter part of the book of Genesis; and thence to, specifically, "Joseph the Righteous," the Scriptural example of resistance to temptation, whose heroic struggle against the advances of his master's wife might serve as a model to later generations.

But what actually happened in Potiphar's house? The narrative of those events is not, as we have seen, extraordinarily cryptic by biblical standards, nor does it seem to contradict or call into question things stated elsewhere. Yet, as we began by observing, early biblical exegetes, those who transmitted biblical texts from generation to generation, were fond of looking deeply into such narratives, sometimes asking questions about the "plot" of a story or the motivation of its various figures, and sometimes looking only into an unusual word or turn of phrase in order to discover some hidden, theretofore undiscovered, aspect of what went on. So in the case of Joseph, exegetes were not content with the bare biblical recitation of events cited above, but wished to discover, through close examination of the words of the text itself, just what it was that went on in Potiphar's house. Let us now consider some of their findings.

Notes

1. See for this argument, D. B. Redford, *A Study of the Biblical Story of Joseph (Genesis 37–50)*, Supplements to *Vetus Testamentum* 20 (Leiden: Brill, 1970).
2. See G. von Rad, *Die Josephsgeschichte* (Neukirchen-Vluyn: Neukirchener Verlag, 1956); also his *Wisdom in Israel*, translated by J. D. Martin, (London: SCM Press, 1972).
3. Joseph is mentioned at the beginning of the book of Exodus, but this is basically an articulation of the continuation between the Genesis account and the exodus narrative.
4. Cf. 1 Kings 22:11. On the bull iconography, see in particular F. M. Cross, *Canaanite Myth and Hebrew Epic* (Cambridge: Harvard University Press, 1973). The association of Joseph with the bull/ox was in turn to influence the interpretation of various other biblical passages. Particularly interesting is the case of Deut. 22:10, "You shall not plow with an ox and ass together." Perhaps because of the overtones attached to "plow," this biblical law had

already acquired a metaphorical dimension by the time of Ben Sira: "Happy the man who marries a wise woman, and does not plow as an ox and an ass together" (Sir. 25:12). But since Joseph was the "ox" *par excellence*, and Mrs. Potiphar was one of those lustful Egyptians whose symbol, via Ezek. 23:20, was the ass, then the connection of this verse with, specifically, that particular incident in the Joseph story must have seemed inevitable. So, for example, Joseph refuses Mrs. Potiphar's advances in an Aramaic poem discussed below (chapter 2) by saying: "I will not plow with an ox and a she-ass together."

5. See in particular Y. M. Grintz, "Psalm 80" in his *Biblical Studies* (in Hebrew) (Jerusalem: Y. Marcus, 1979), 109–27.

6. See S. Japhet, "Conquest and Settlement in Chronicles," *Journal of Biblical Literature* 98 (1979): 205–18.

7. The "geopolitical" Joseph was, of course, to reemerge in Samaritan biblical exegesis; these Northerners identified Joseph as their ancestor and gloried specifically in the geographical connections. See chapter 5.

8. I have dealt with this theme at some length in J. Kugel and R. Greer, *Early Biblical Interpretation* (Philadelphia: Westminster Press, 1986).

9. See the discussion in M. H. Segal *The Complete Book of Ben Sira* (Jerusalem: Mosad Bialik, 1972), 240. Surely the omission of Joseph from the first survey of biblical heroes is no accident, and reflects, in my view, the persistence of Joseph's "foreignness" in some quarters even down to the second century B.C.E.

10. Jubilees 39:5–8, translated by O. S. Wintermute, in J. H. Charlesworth, *The Old Testament Pseudepigrapha*, vol. 2 (Garden City, NY: Doubleday, 1985), 128–29.

11. H. W. Hollander, *Joseph as an Ethical Model in the Testaments of the Twelve Patriarchs* (Leiden: Brill, 1981).

12. "Testaments of the Twelve Patriarchs," trans. H. C. Kee, in Charlesworth, *Old Testament Pseudepigrapha*, 1:819–20.

13. "Testament of Joseph" 9:2–5, in Charlesworth, *Old Testament Pseudepigrapha*, 1:821.

14. See L. Ginzberg, *Legends of the Jews*, vol. 5 (Philadelphia: Jewish Publication Society, 1925), 325: "There can be no doubt that this title was conferred on Joseph on account of his virtuous victory over the wiles of his master's wife."

15. Ibid.

16. Note that 1 Macc. 2:53 had likewise seemed to connect Joseph's virtue under duress with his subsequent rise to power—he "in time of distress kept a commandment and became lord of Egypt."

2.

The Assembly of Ladies

The first narrative expansion[1] that we will examine in connection with the story of Joseph is apparently a rather late one. It does not appear in any of the earliest postbiblical sources—sources like Ben Sira or *Jubilees* or *The Testaments of the Twelve Patriarchs*—nor can it be found in Hellenistic Jewish writers like Philo of Alexandria or Flavius Josephus (who lived, respectively, at the turn of the common era and in the latter part of the first century c.e.). Nor, for that matter, is it present even in the earliest level of rabbinic exegesis—the writings of the *tanna'im* ("teachers") who flourished until the end of the second century c.e. Rather, it appears only in a variety of later sources, in Hebrew, Aramaic, Arabic, and other languages. This is rather disappointing from one standpoint, because certainly one thing scholars hope for in examining exegetical traditions such as these is to be able to trace their development back to an early source in order to understand, therefore, their origins and subsequent development.

But if, in chronological terms, this narrative expansion appears somewhat disappointing, in terms of its content it could not be more exciting. For it tells of an incident not only absent from the biblical narrative of Joseph, but for which in fact there appears to be not the slightest justification in our Genesis text. There, it will be recalled, Mrs. Potiphar sets her eyes on Joseph and, unable to seduce him despite her repeated entreaties, finally waits until such time as there will be no one in the house in order to seize him physically and press her desires upon him. The fact of her waiting until the house is deserted bespeaks a certain restraint, or at least fear of gossip, in the woman. And indeed, we have the feeling that, throughout the narrative, Joseph is Mrs. Potiphar's *secret* obsession: she whispers her urgent desires into his ear, but takes care to let no one else know; then, when Joseph runs away, leaving his telltale garment behind, she is obliged to reverse reality and accuse him of attempted rape—is this not in part because, fearing that the evidence of the garment now threatens to turn her private infatuation into a public scandal, she seeks to combat the truth with a, so to speak, preemptive lie? Here too, apparently, is a Mrs. Potiphar conscious of shame, a woman anxious that her obsession with Joseph remain secret.

Not so, it seems, with the expansion in question, where her feelings for her servant have apparently become common knowledge in the Egyptian court, a subject of gossip among the ladies of the court. As mentioned, the expansion exists in different texts. The following is from the standard text of *Midrash Tanḥuma*, a medieval midrashic collection extant in various different forms;[2] its approximate time of compilation is unknown (though a guess of seventh–eighth century C.E. might not be far off):

> No one can find a person of greater faithfulness than Joseph, for he was in Egypt, of whose people it is written "whose flesh is the flesh of donkeys" [Ezek. 23:20; interpreted to mean that they are a people plunged in wantonness][3] and he was seventeen years old; yet he did not succumb to adultery. What is more, his mistress was with him in the house and sought to entice him with words day after day, and she used to change her clothes three times a day, day after day—the clothes that she wore in the morning she did not wear at noon, and those that she wore at noon she did not wear in the evening—and to what purpose? Only that he desire her. Said the Rabbis of blessed memory: On one occasion the Egyptian women gathered and went to behold Joseph's beauty. What did Potiphar's wife do? She took citrons [= Heb. *'etrogim,* a citrus fruit] and gave them to each of them and gave each a knife and then called to Joseph and stood him before them. When they beheld how handsome Joseph was, they cut their hands. She said to them: If you do thus after one moment, I who see him at every moment, am I not all the more so [justified in being smitten]? And day after day she sought to entice him with words, but he overcame his desires. How do we know this? From what we read next, "And after these things the wife of his master set her eyes upon Joseph." (Gen. 39:7)

We shall return presently to some of the less obvious features of this passage, but for now, the essential: contrary to what we are led to understand in the Genesis narrative, Mrs. Potiphar's attraction to Joseph is apparently not a strictly private matter. To begin with, the fame of his physical attractiveness has spread to the ladies of Egypt (is she herself their source of information about Joseph?), and they come to see for themselves how handsome he is. When they arrive, Mrs. Potiphar's own deeds are revealing: one might guess that she had been the subject of some gossip, for the whole scenario she creates—the fruit and knives, the sudden appearance of Joseph, the cut hands as testimony that, in her place, these same women would likewise lose all self-control—all this seems to be some enormous act of self-justification. And this is explicitly the case with the words she speaks to them, for what she says, essentially, is: "If you were in my position you would not act differently!"

The gossip about Joseph and Mrs. Potiphar, perhaps implied in the *Tanḥuma* text, is stated more directly in other versions of this story. The following is from *Midrash ha-Gadol*, a medieval anthology of midrashic comments on the Pentateuch. (While this collection, of Yemenite origin, is relatively late even within the period we are discussing, it often contains material from far earlier periods, and sometimes in comparatively pristine form.) Here, in commenting on the verse "And she called out to the members of her household . . ." (Gen. 39:14), *Midrash ha-Gadol* remarks:

> She put the righteous one [Joseph] in the mouths of all of them. It is related:[4] When the queens and noble-women returned from worshipping idols,[5] they all went to visit her [Mrs. Potiphar]. They said to her: Why is it that you look so badly? Have you perchance been fancying that servant of yours? Whereupon she gave[6] them bread and meat and knives, and brought in Joseph and stood him before them. And when they lifted their eyes [from their food] to Joseph, they cut their hands as they ate. She said to them: If you, before whom he has stood for but a moment, were unable to endure it, how much less able am I, who see him each and every day. They said to her: You have no remedy other than to say to his master [Potiphar] to lock him up in prison and he will be entirely yours. She said to them: If I am the only one to speak against him to my husband, he will not believe me. But if each one of you tells her husband, "Joseph seized me," then I will tell my husband that Joseph seized me as well and he will put him in prison.

Here too we have the suggestion that Mrs. Potiphar's behavior has already become a public scandal, for when the ladies of the court arrive, they immediately suspect by her countenance that Joseph is the cause of her distress. Moreover, her remark at the end of the passage—to the effect that if she alone accuses Joseph, her husband will not believe her—may further indicate that the woman's lovesick condition, and its cause, were known even to her husband. As for the actual details, it is true that what is served to the ladies in this version is somewhat different (bread and meat vs. fruit in the *Tanḥuma* narrative), but that is a minor matter—certainly when compared to the questions raised by their common features. For, after all, whence cometh this story? Why the assembly of ladies—nowhere, to repeat, even hinted at in

Genesis—and why further the weird detail of the knives and inadvertant bloodshed?

It is a striking fact that this same story is found in another text, one in itself not an insubstantial repository of early exegetical motifs, the Qur'an (Koran). For, as is well known, Islamic Scripture contains not only references to figures and events found in the Bible, but even a fair number of incidents and details dependent not, or not only, on the biblical text itself, but on early Jewish and Christian traditions about its proper interpretation. In the case of Joseph, an entire *sura* of the Qur'an is given over to his story—with, as we might suspect, a great deal of attention devoted to the story of Joseph and Potiphar's wife. It is after the failed physical confrontation in Potiphar's house that we meet up with this same peculiar tale:

> Then said the ladies in the city: The wife of the nobleman [= Potiphar] is trying to seduce her own slave! He must indeed have smitten her with love. How foolish her conduct seems to us! When she heard of their gossiping, she sent to them and prepared for them a feast, and gave each of them a knife, and said [to Joseph]: Now go out in front of them. And when they saw him they praised him, and they cut their hands. They said: God protect us! This is no mortal, this is nought but a noble angel! She said: Yes, this is the one about whom you did blame me. And I did indeed try to seduce him away, but he remained guiltless. But now, if he does not do my bidding, he will be put in prison, and he will be among the base ones.
>
> (Sura XII 30–32)

Of course Joseph refuses her advances in the Qur'anic version as well, and lands in jail a few lines later.

This same basic story appears frequently thereafter—understandably elaborated among later Muslim poets and exegetes, for whom the tale of Yusuf (Joseph) and Zulaikha[7] was nothing less than revealed Scripture; but it is also found among later Jewish writers. The variations, however, are generally minor. The *Chronicles of Yerahme'el*, a collection of midrashic material assembled in the late thirteenth or early fourteenth century, repeats the same material; though here the food brought to the ladies is a dish of apples, the result is no different— "when they started peeling their apples they all cut their hands, since they were so much captivated with Joseph's beauty that they could not take their eyes off him."[8] *Sefer ha-Yashar*, a midrashic collection written in pseudobiblical style and whose origins are probably to be located in Italy no earlier than the thirteenth century, also presents a version of our story. In characteristic fashion it adds a few details: in its version, the lovesickness of Mrs. Potiphar (she is here, in keeping with post-Qur'anic tradition, known by the name Zulaikha) has real physical manifestations—she is ill—and that is why the ladies go to visit her. When they ask the cause of her disease, she promises to show them, then orders her servant girls to bring food for a feast and, presumably for desert, citrons with knives to peel them. Meanwhile, she orders Joseph dressed in his finest clothes and, at the crucial moment, dramatically produces him before their eyes, whereupon they all cut their hands. Then she says, "Did this thing not happen to you the very moment that you saw him, yet you were unable to restrain yourselves? So I, in whose house he resides, and who see him day after day coming and going in my house—how could I not fall sick and die from this?!"[9]

One version somewhat different from the others is a poem, an alphabetical acrostic of uncertain date, written in Aramaic; it was incorporated in the liturgy for the holiday of Shavuot and has survived in a number of ancient prayer manuscripts and books, the best known of which is the medieval *Maḥzor Vitry*. In keeping with the holiday's theme of the giving of the law on Mt. Sinai, this poem was recited to celebrate Joseph's virtuousness with regard to the seventh law of the Decalogue, the prohibition of adultery. The event it recounts, however, is slightly different from the one we have seen. Here, after Joseph's refusal to submit to her advances, Mrs. Potiphar "convene[s] all the neighboring ladies" to tell them of her handsome servant Joseph. She relates his attractions in great detail, and then further recounts her frustrations in seducing him. "Though I ask him to plow in my garden, he does not wish to. . . ." Although she has threatened Joseph with expulsion, then wheedled and cajoled him,[10] he has remained uninterested. Having related all this to her friends, Mrs. Potiphar then invites them to see for themselves. She brings them to her palace and sits them down, then calls to Joseph to put on his finery and serve the ladies:

> With serving-bowls in his hand, he went and mixed their wine;
> They held their cups, but took no taste of them;
> For when they beheld him, their faces grew quite pale.
> Yet though his face was toward his mistress, his heart was to his
>   Heavenly Father.[11]

Here there are no knives and the women do not cut their hands, as in all our others sources, nor is there any remonstrating "I told you so" from Mrs. Potiphar; all this may suggest that this Aramaic version represents a somewhat separate tradition of our story. (If we wished to be precise in our terminology, we might refer here to two **variant motifs,** the first, "Cut Their Hands" embodied in various forms in our previous sources, the second, "Forgot Their Wine," embodied here in the Aramaic poem. Both of these motifs are, as the term implies, variants of the same overall or **basic motif,** "Assembly of Ladies.") Despite the differences, the fundamental connection of this variant to the previous versions is clear: for here too, the ladies of the court are informed of Mrs. Potiphar's indiscretions, and she invites them to see for themselves; and at Joseph's appearance they react with such astonishment that they neglect what has been served to them (in this case, wine), thus bearing sincere testimony to Joseph's striking good looks.

Which Came First?

Having surveyed briefly these various versions, we may proceed to ask: what does it all mean? Which of these is the oldest version, and why? Particularly intriguing is the relationship between the Qur'an and the other (Jewish) sources. For while it is true that Qur'an contains a number of early Jewish exegetical motifs, it is likewise true that Qur'anic passages, and even their later interpretation, did sometimes penetrate later Jewish writings (this certainly seems the case with *Sefer ha-Yashar* cited above, whose adoption of the name "Zulaikha" for Mrs. Potiphar seems to have come via post-Qur'anic Moslem sources).[12] But what stemmed from what? Did the *Midrash ha-Gadol* version serve as a source for the (very similar) version of the Qur'an, or vice versa? Moreover, *why* did this whole story originate? As we have seen briefly, the very idea of Mrs. Potiphar sharing her feelings about Joseph with outsiders is not only absent from the biblical text, but even seems to belie her behavior elsewhere in the story. If so, why should this motif have been created?

These various questions are not unrelated, but let us start with the first issue: which version came first? It is to be noted that the relation between the Qur'anic story and various Jewish sources has been a subject of interest to scholars for some time, but at present no consensus has yet been found. In the nineteenth century, Abraham Geiger had argued that the Qur'anic version was based on the account found in *Sefer ha-Yashar* (which he believed to be an ancient work predating the Qur'an).[13] Somewhat later, however, Max Grünbaum took up the opposite position, arguing that the various Jewish sources containing our motif had ultimately all derived it from the Qur'an or later Islamic sources.[14] More recently, the great scholar of midrash Louis Ginzberg claimed that the Jewish origin of the story in, at least, *Midrash Tanḥuma* was "beyond dispute,"[15] but he has been opposed in this by other scholars, including the equally perceptive student of the relationship between midrash and Qur'anic motifs, Bernard Heller.[16] In a recent review of the current state of the question, H. Schwarzbaum has apparently sided with the latter, arguing that Ginzberg "overlooked the important fact that this Midrash belongs to a later age than the Qur'an."[17]

The actual date of composition or compilation of the various collections cited is, of course, of great relevance, though it may not in itself be decisive, since any midrashic work is by definition a gathering together of different bits of exegesis created by different authors, often in different times and historical circumstances. Among the various collections seen, *Midrash Tanhuma* might be a good candidate for precedence, since much of its constituent material is demonstrably very old and even its own compilation may belong, as stated, to a relatively early period. But, in the case of this particular text in *Tanhuma*, what is especially intriguing is the manner in which the story is introduced, that is, with the formula, "the Rabbis of blessed memory said. . . ." Ginzberg saw in this formulation a sign of the material's antiquity: it "indicates that an old source was made use of."[18] Alas, that argument could be turned on its head: for cannot this vague formula of introduction simply be an attempt to cover origins that are either simply unknown or best left undisclosed?

One thing in any case becomes clear about the *Midrash Tanhuma* passage upon closer inspection: the story of ladies and the knives has actually been stuck into it after the fact.[19] This is apparent from what may be called the **narrative resumption** in the *Tanhuma* text. For it happens not infrequently with midrashic texts that a later author or editor will seek to introduce some new material or excursus into the text that he has inherited. If the new material can be introduced without disturbing the flow of things, all well and good; but if not, the author or editor will often go to the trouble of arranging things in order to repeat a sentence or phrase that came just before he started his new digression. By repeating the old sentence or phrase at the end of the new material, he in essence returns things to where they were before, so that the text can then flow smoothly on to the next thing as if no interruption had taken place. Now in the *Tanhuma* text cited above, it will be noticed that the brief remark "she sought to entice him with words day after day" is *resumed* later on in the passage in the words, "And day after day she sought to entice him with words." Between the first remark and its resumption come the observation about Mrs.

Potiphar changing her clothes three times a day and, afterwards, our story. The inevitable conclusion is that some editor did indeed introduce this "digression" into a preexistent text. This still does not quite condemn our *Tanḥuma* version to being particularly late, of course. The story may have been introduced at some very early stage of our *Tanḥuma*'s compilation; and in any case, the underlying motif, though not presently attested in earlier collections, may nonetheless have come to the *Tanḥuma* from some very ancient source. (It is to be noted that the style of the *Tanḥuma* version is quite terse when compared to the Qur'an or the other sources, and this is often a sign of priority.) Still, the narrative resumption in our text does lend credence to the idea that this particular retelling of the "Assembly of Ladies" was not present in an earlier version but, being something of an afterthought, had to be encased in the manner that we have seen.

Differences

It is common for scholars trying to establish the priority of one version among many to fix on *differences* between them—differences in wording, narrative details, and the like—in order to try to establish which is the earliest, or to reconstruct a composite "original version." Although this can be a highly speculative endeavor, it is sometimes possible to prove definitively that text A contained a remark that was misunderstood in text B, or that B elaborated something in A, or the like. With regard to the variants that we have been examining, there are two telltale sets of differences, either or both of which might prove useful in establishing the relative priority of the different versions.

The first set of differences concerns what is actually served to the ladies: "citrons" in both *Tanḥuma* and *Sefer ha-Yashar*, "bread and meat" in *Midrash ha-Gadol*, a non-specific "feast" in the Qur'an, "apples" in *Yeraḥme'el*, and "wine" in the Aramaic poem. Can these differences shed any light on our question? One interesting, though not unequivocal, bit of evidence in this connection is the fact that some of these different traditions about what was served eventually came to overlap with one another in a later period. Thus, for example, the word for "feast" used in the Qur'anic account came to be the subject of some considerable speculation by Muslim commentators during the Middle Ages. For not only is the term *muttaka'* rather rare in Arabic, but, because of the vagaries of the Arabic writing system, it was capable of being understood in different ways—that is, its consonants could be associated with one of several different verbal roots and, consequently, given different meanings. It is interesting, therefore, to note how the medieval Qur'anic commentator 'Abdallah ibn 'Umar al-Baiḍawi wrestles with the question of this term's meaning:

> muttaka'an [so Baiḍawi understands it, deriving it from the verb waka'a, "to lean, recline"]: cushions on which they would recline . . . in order that they might recline with the knives in their hands, and when Joseph came out to them they would be astonished and forget themselves, so that their hands [holding the knives] would fall on each other's hands and cut them, and they would stand rebuked by the proof. . . . It is also said that mutaka'an here means "food" or "feast" since people used to recline to eat and drink, out of luxuriousness, which is why this practice has been forbidden. . . . It is also said that muttaka' is "food which is cut," because the carver "leans over" it with a knife. There is a reading muttakkan with suppression of the hamzah, and muttaka'an with lengthening of the a . . .; **and mutkan, which means either "citrus fruit" or "that which is cut."**[20]

The implications of this last part of Baiḍawi's statement are not negligible for our study. For apparently, in struggling with the meaning of muttaka', Baiḍawi had come into contact with some tradition to the effect that this word's real meaning was connected with citrus fruit. Now in fact neither muttaka' nor any of the variants Baiḍawi proposes has such a meaning in Arabic: these represent an attempt to explain a rare term for "banquet" that was not readily understandable to many Arabic speakers.[21] But if so, Baiḍawi's words suggest that he was aware of some "oral tradition" that indeed stipulated what the account in the Qur'an did not, namely the kind of food served to the ladies. And that kind of food, according to this tradition, was citrus fruit (or elsewhere, specifically "citrons")—so he suggests such a meaning for muttaka'. Indeed, apart from Baiḍawi's statement, there is ample evidence from other Muslim sources of a post-Qur'anic tradition that oranges or citrons were served by Mrs. Potiphar.[22]

Now this hardly proves that the "citron" version of our story is either older or younger than the "banquet" version reflected in the Qur'an. Indeed, what it seems to show is that, whichever came first, both versions circulated independently for a time—the former in texts like our Midrash Tanḥuma, the latter in the Qur'an—but that, at a certain point, people like Baiḍawi, who by one means or another had become aware of the "citron" version, then sought to combine the two traditions by attaching the meaning "citron" (or, later, "orange") to the difficult word muttaka'.

However, if one had to guess which of these two versions is the more primitive, one would not be entirely without clues. For it would be quite normal to suppose that the relatively colorless version reflected in the Qur'an, in which an unspecified "banquet" is set, ultimately represents a more primitive form of our motif, and that the detail of the "citrons" only came in later. For this is often what happens in the popular transmission of stories: a concrete detail comes in at some point to fill in for something general or colorless, and that detail is ever afterwards repeated in retellings of the story—even when, as sometimes happens, the detail itself had originated in some popular misunderstanding, or simply came about as an irrelevant flight of fancy on the part of one reteller of the tale. So it might well have been with the "citrons": for reasons not clear, the food served came at a certain point to be represented as, specifically, citrons, and these citrons then survived in all (or most) subsequent retellings. Indeed, when one stops to consider it, the role of the fruit in our story is somewhat puzzling: not only are citrons alone a rather odd thing for Mrs. Potiphar to be serving, but it is rather odd of the story to specify what was served at all, since this has no bearing on the subsequent events (and the proof is the fact that, in our other versions of the "Cut their Hands" variant, the elements "bread and meat" in *Midrash ha-Gadol* or "banquet" in the Qur'an version seem to work just as well). In fact, "prepared a banquet" or "prepared food" could have engendered *all* the variants we have seen—bread and meat, nothing specific, wine, and citrons (this last perhaps later transformed into the more pedestrian "apples" of *Yerahme'el*)—whereas the opposite process, that is, having an original "citrons" end up in all these different permutations, seems highly unlikely.

The hypothesis that the element "citrons" came to elaborate an originally simpler story may find some support in an interesting bit of evidence connected with the Aramaic alphabetical poem cited above. For in fact that poem exists in various forms, having been preserved in a number of early prayer books belonging to different Jewish communities. The one cited above, from *Mahzor Vitry*, mentioned only "wine" being served. But other versions speak of *both* wine and citrons! Here, for example, is a version contained in another old manuscript:[23]

> With serving-bowls in his hand, he went and mixed their wine;
> They held their cups, but took no taste of them,
> When they beheld him, in their hands were knives and citrons,
> The citron they did not cut, and their hands were full of blood.

This version, while presenting the same text of the first two lines as that cited from *Mahzor Vitry* above, has a radically different version of the next two lines (*Mahzor Vitry*'s had read: "For when they beheld him, their faces grew quite pale./Yet though his face was toward his mistress, his heart was to his Heavenly Father.") To complicate things still further, there is another manuscript tradition which puts the mention of the citrons a little later in the poem. It reads:

> With serving-bowls in his hand, he went and mixed their wine;
> They held their cups, but took no taste of them;
> When they beheld him, their faces grew quite pale;
> His face blanched, but his heart was to his Heavenly Father.
> They all arose and kissed him on his head and said to him,
> "Kingship, oh lad, befits you well."
> They looked at him, and in their hands were knife and citron,
> And they did not taste the citron, and their hands were full of
>   blood.[24]

What is one to make of all of this? The evidence is not unequivocal, yet it seems that we may have before us a snapshot of the "citron" tradition invading the Aramaic poem. For it is clear that these two versions suffer from the common midrashic disease of **overkill.** Overkill comes about when the author of a particular text is aware of two separate versions of a story or two different explanations for some phenomenon and, unable or unwilling to decide between them, he seeks to incorporate both in his own retelling. In so doing, he frequently ends up "overkilling" something in the story, giving two reasons for why something happened or two different ways in which it took place. So here, apparently, the authors of these other versions of the Aramaic poem seem each to be in possession of two different traditions about what was served, the one specifying "wine," the other "citrons." And so they seek to include both in their retelling: Joseph comes and serves the wine, and the ladies are so taken with him that they fail to taste their cups; but in the meantime, they also seem to have citrons and knives in their hands, and so cut themselves à la *Midrash Tanḥuma,* etc.

One might of course ask: is it not possible that the original version of this story had two things being served, and later versions, in the interest of simplicity, reduced the food to one sort? Such a possibility is highly unlikely. To begin with, the whole purpose of our story is evidently to demonstrate in some graphic way how strikingly handsome Joseph was, and each of the things served has been included in the story in order to illustrate how this was so. On the one hand, the women are so captivated by Joseph that they forget to taste their wine; or, on the other, the women are so captivated that they cut their hands instead of their citrons. This being the case, it is virtually impossible that the original version of the story had both—there simply was no need, and to have both in the same story is extremely awkward. Furthermore, any student of midrash knows that the combination of two motifs or elements is usually a sign of lateness: complication, rather than simplification, is what later development almost inevitably brings about, because later sources want to give each separate tradition its due.

Moreover, it should be obvious from the above versions which of the two "food elements" has been added in later on. It is not only the fact that there exists a text-tradition—the one originally cited above from *Maḥzor Vitry*—in which wine alone is served. But the very fact that the two different families of versions represented in the two subsequent citations should add the "citron" element in different places (the first adding it in the verse starting with the letter *ṣade*, the second in the verse starting with the letter *resh*, two lines later) suggests that the idea of adding the "citron" element somewhere into an originally citronless poem has achieved two separate realizations. Finally, one might note how each of the two wine-plus-citrons versions cited is something of a dramatic flop, and this because the citrons come in *after* the mention of the wine. It is not only that overkill has made the mention of the citrons somewhat anticlimactic: it is also that the necessity of mentioning the citrons after the wine and in a relatively short space has obligated the poet to undercut somewhat the dramatic force of the incident. For ideally, he should have done what the author of *Midrash Tanḥuma* did, and have the citrons and knives distributed first, then have Joseph make his appearance, and then have the ladies cut their hands in reaction to seeing him (perhaps adding after this—since the two traditions are to be included—that although the ladies had been served wine, they did not touch their cups, so taken were they with Joseph's beauty). But since Joseph appears first with the wine in the poem, there can be no mention of the distribution of citrons and knives: and so these are just said to be "in their hands"—how they got there we are not told. Moreover, the very point of the presence of the "citron" element of the story, the dramatic climax when the ladies cut their hands, is skipped over entirely in the poem. At no point is it said that the ladies cut their hands, and this ellipsis should be most striking for us. Instead, all that is said is that they did *not* cut their citrons, and that "their hands were full of blood," the latter a throwaway line from the Targum of Isa. 1:15. For all these reasons, the presentation of the "citron" element looks very much like an afterthought, something stuck in in order to make the poem's account of things agree with that contained in, for example, *Midrash Tanḥuma*.

This of course still does not tell us anything for certain about the overall development of our motif. But considered together, the foregoing observations do suggest that a number of versions of our story without citrons—a nonspecific "banquet," a meal of "bread and meat," a serving of "wine"—did circulate independently for a time, and that, in the case of both the Qur'anic version and the Aramaic poem, the element "citrons" eventually overtook these originally citronless versions and at a certain point came to be incorporated into them, either via commentaries like Baiḍawi's or in actual rewritings such as those apparently performed in the versions of the Aramaic poem cited above. Moreover, the relative colorlessness of the "banquet" or "wine" versions (a colorlessness dramatically illustrated in the way the "citron" version came to invade both, as we have seen) may suggest that at an early stage of the "Assembly of Ladies" motif, there was simply no particular importance attached to stipulating what was served, only that *something* was served and that the ladies reacted to it (by not touching their food/drinks, or by cutting their hands instead of their food, etc.) in such a way as to indicate how captivated they were with Joseph's beauty.

When Did It Happen?

To this question of the food served we shall return presently, but let us now turn to the other difference between the various versions seen. It is one that is hardly so striking, indeed, it might normally escape our notice entirely, since it involves not something within the stories themselves, but rather *when*, in the opinion of our different authors, the incident of the ladies and the knives is alleged to have taken place. That is, at what point in the whole sequence of actions involving Joseph and Mrs. Potiphar did the assembly of ladies occur? Let us examine each of our sources on this question in the order in which we have treated them.

Midrash Tanḥuma is not specific about the time, but if one looks carefully into the words surrounding our incident, the sequence of events will nonetheless be clear. For convenience, let us reexamine just the "frame" of our story:

> What is more, his mistress was with him in the house and sought to entice him with words day after day, and she used to change her clothes three times a day, day after day—the clothes that she wore in the morning she did not wear at noon, and those that she wore at noon she did not wear in the evening—and to what purpose? Only that he desire her. Said the Rabbis of blessed memory: On one occasion the Egyptian women gathered . . . [etc.]. She said to them: If you do thus after one moment, I who see him at every moment, am I not

all the more so [justified in being smitten]? And day after day she sought to entice him with words, but he overcame his desires. How do we know this? From what we read next, "And it came to pass after these things that his master's wife set her eyes upon Joseph." (Gen. 39:7)

In order to understand this framing midrash's purpose, it is necessary to consider closely the biblical text it is seeking to explain. For in Genesis the words introducing the incident with Mrs. Potiphar seem slightly out of order:

> So he [Potiphar] left all that he had in Joseph's charge, and had no concern for anything but the food that he ate; and Joseph was comely in form and comely in appearance. And it came to pass **after these things** that his master's wife set her eyes on Joseph.
>
> (Gen. 39:6–7)

"After what things?" our exegete asks. For the statement just preceding recounts no "things" at all, but rather a simple circumstance, the fact that Joseph was "comely in form and comely in appearance." Now obviously, the "things" being referred to here are not this circumstance, but Joseph's elevation to the head of Potiphar's staff (recounted just previously)—and so it was that after Joseph's promotion, Mrs. Potiphar set her eyes upon him. Yet if so, an ancient exegete could not but wonder why it was that the Sacred Writ had arranged things as it had. For if the element of Joseph's handsome bearing had to be introduced somewhere (as preparation for Mrs. Potiphar's entreaties), it should logically have come somewhere other than just before the words "And it came to pass after these things . . ." (For example: Joseph is put in charge of the household, then "And it came to pass after these things that his master's wife set her eyes on Joseph, for he was exceedingly handsome.") Here then is a small irregularity in the text, but one that nevertheless seemed to require explanation.

Midrash Tanḥuma provides not one explanation, but two. The first takes the Hebrew word *debarim* in our biblical text (". . . after these *things*") not as "things" at all, but as "words" (an equally common meaning of the Hebrew term). What "words"? Why, words of Mrs. Potiphar—idle chatter, perhaps, or suggestive phrases, or little terms of endearment—anything to get him to desire her. This is how *Midrash Tanḥuma* interprets "after these words/things"—the words themselves are not cited in the Bible, but their existence is hinted at in this phrase; and so, *Tanḥuma* says, she "enticed him with *words*," and it was, therefore, "after these words" had been spoken that the rest of the story ensued. The other explanation put forward in *Tanḥuma* is quite separate from this one and in fact incompatible with it, since it goes back to the other meaning of *debarim*, "things." What things? Things again unreported in the biblical text, but whose existence is being hinted at in the phrase "after these things," things designed to get Joseph to desire her. And so, in the absence of specifics in the Bible, our midrashist supplies them: Mrs. Potiphar kept changing her clothes, three times a day in fact, one spectacular dress after the next—"and to what purpose? Only that he desire her."[25]

While they are quite different, both these explanations have an underlying similarity. They both refuse to take the anomalous order of items in the biblical sentence as a mistake or something not to be taken too literally, and so feel a necessity to read *debarim* as referring to something other that Joseph's promotion to head of Potiphar's household; this requires them to invent the words/things in question. But moreover they also have a shared, and rather subtle, sense of the phrase that follows, that is, the observation that Mrs. Potiphar "set her eyes" upon Joseph. This does not mean, according to our midrashist, that she simply *noticed* him; she had noticed him long before! Indeed, the entire sentence in the Bible reads, "And after these things, his master's wife set her eyes upon Joseph and said 'Lie with me.' " Are these the words of a woman who catches sight of a handsome slave for the first time? Obviously not. And so, our midrashist reasons, long ago she had begun trying different words/things to get him to desire her, conversations or changes of clothing, and it was only "after these words/things" had failed that she actually took the initiative. That is the meaning of "set her eyes": despairing of Joseph "setting his eyes" on her, that is, taking the initiative, she sets her eyes on him.

This is marvelous exegesis, but we ought not to lose sight of our initial question regarding the sequence of actions, a question that we are now prepared to answer. For the story of the ladies and their knives appears, in *Tanḥuma*, just between the first "enticed him with words" and its narrative resumption at the end. In the opinion of the editor of *Midrash Tanḥuma*, then, what happened was this: Joseph gets promoted; Mrs. Potiphar tries to arouse his interest with words and/or dresses; *then* the Egyptian women come to admire Joseph's good looks and, to demonstrate her plight, Mrs. Potiphar serves them the citrons, etc.; then, *en désespoir de cause*, she finally seizes the initiative herself and says, "Lie with me."

This is quite different from the sequence found in *Midrash ha-Gadol*. Let us look now at how our incident is introduced there:

She put the righteous one [Joseph] in the mouths of all of them. It is related: When the queens and noble-women returned from worshipping idols, they all went to visit her [Mrs. Potiphar]. They said to her: Why is it that you look so badly? Have you perchance been fancying that servant of yours?

All one needs to know in order to situate our incident in *Midrash ha-Gadol* is precisely when the "queens and noble-women" returned from worshipping idols. But this is not hard to discover: for the reference here is to an ancient exegetical motif, first attested in the writings of Josephus and found frequently thereafter in rabbinic texts,[26] to the effect that the day on which Mrs. Potiphar finally confronted Joseph was actually a religious holiday, a festival of the Nile, and everyone in Potiphar's household had gone down to the Nile to celebrate—all except Mrs. Potiphar, who saw in the occasion of this festival a once-in-a-lifetime opportunity to seduce Joseph. Josephus writes: "So, on the approach of a public festival, when it was customary for women also to join the general assembly, she made illness an excuse to her husband, in quest of solitude and leisure to solicit Joseph; and, having obtained her opportunity, she addressed him even more importunately than before."[27] (The reason for this ancient exegetical flight, by the way, is to account for the fact that the biblical texts notes that, on the day of Mrs. Potiphar's intiative, "none of the people of the house was in the house" [Gen. 39:11]—where could they all have been, if not at some such public ceremony?) Now, according to *Midrash ha-Gadol*, it was only after the ladies had come back from the festival that—worried, after all, about Mrs. Potiphar's health, since she had missed this great event— they come to visit her and, seeing her face, diagnose her illness without further reflection: "Why is it that you look so badly? Have you perchance been fancying that servant of yours?" And so we can reconstruct the very different sequence of events according to *Midrash ha-Gadol:* Joseph is put in charge of the household; Mrs. Potiphar says "Lie with me" but Joseph still refuses; then, one festival day, when the house is empty, she seizes him and he flees; the other ladies come back to the house to visit her; she summons Joseph while they are eating and they cut their hands.

What about our other sources? The Qur'an, as in other ways, is in agreement with *Midrash ha-Gadol* here: the physical confrontation in which Mrs. Potiphar seizes Joseph by his garment (which we might now refer to, for convenience, as the "garment scene") takes place before the incident of the knives. In fact, the Qur'an has Joseph fully exonerated after the garment scene—the fact that his garment is ripped from the back indicates that he was fleeing Mrs. Potiphar rather than attacking her, and Potiphar orders her to apologize to Joseph (Sura 12:29). *After that* comes the incident of the knives, and Mrs. Potiphar,

finding her friends in agreement as to her servant's beauty, is embold-
ened to say out loud that she will have Joseph imprisoned if he does
not cooperate. He still does not, and does indeed end up in prison
(12:35). *Sefer ha-Yashar*, although it shows Moslem influence in its use
of the name Zulaikha for Mrs. Potiphar, follows the same order as
Midrash Tanḥuma here: first the assembly of the ladies, and only afterwards the "garment scene" with Mrs. Potiphar and Joseph. The sequence of actions in the two remaining sources that we have been
examining is not entirely clear. *Yeraḥme'el* does not even report Mrs.
Potiphar's seizing Joseph, and so the sequence can only be guessed at.
But it is noteworthy that the assembly of the ladies in *Yeraḥme'el* follows
the observation that Mrs. Potiphar "used to entice him every day by her
conversation, and used to bedeck herself with all kinds of ornaments
and array herself in many dresses in order to find favor in his eyes"[28]—
another indication[29] that *Yeraḥme'el*'s source was none other than *Tanḥuma* itself. As for the Aramaic poem, it gives one clue in its opening
line (or at least a line that came to precede the poem proper in some
versions):

> Joseph overcame his impulse when his mistress sought him out,
> And refused to lie with her, to be with her in the World to Come.

This is a restatement of an exegetical remark found frequently in
rabbinic texts, one which was designed to explain the apparent pleo-
nasm of Gen. 39:10, "And although she spoke to Joseph day after day,
he would not listen to her, to lie with her, to be with her." As *Genesis
Rabba* remarks: "He would not listen to her, to lie with her in this
world, so that he not be with her in hell in the world to come."[30] If, in
some versions of the poem, the assembly of ladies comes *after* this
explanation of Gen. 39:10, then there may be some grounds for saying
that, in the opinion of the poem's author or editors, the assembly of the
ladies also came after that verse, that is, long after Mrs. Potiphar's
desperate "Lie with me!" Indeed the poet may be situating the assembly, in the manner of the Qur'an and *Midrash ha-Gadol*, even after the
garment scene (for the opening line, "Joseph overcame his impulse
when his mistress sought him out," could be a general statement sum-
ming up all of Mrs. Potiphar's temptations).

To summarize: The various sources that we have seen disagree
both on what was served to the ladies, and on the sequence of events
into which the incident is to be fitted. We can summarize their differences with the following chart:

Source	Kind of Food Served	Before (B) or After (A) Garment Scene
Midrash Tanḥuma	citrons	(B)
Midrash ha-Gadol	bread and meat	(A)
Qur'an	not specified	(A)
Sefer ha-Yashar	citrons	(B)
Yeraḥme'el	apples	(B?)
Aramaic poem	wine	(A?)

It is interesting that, in the above diagram, the very same sources that have citrons (and their likely derivative, "apples") also seem to agree that the assembly of the ladies took place before the garment scene in which Mrs. Potiphar seizes Joseph. This may well indicate that all three are related—most likely the later two used *Midrash Tanḥuma* as their source for the story. But does it also indicate that these three sources are *wrong* in placing the incident where they do, before rather than after the "garment scene"?

One might be inclined to argue just the opposite. For in dramatic terms, it makes little sense to have the story work up to its crisis, the physical confrontation between Mrs. Potiphar and Joseph ending in the seized garment, and then have the interlude with the ladies (in which Joseph appears tranquilly before the ladies and before Mrs. Potiphar, apparently as if nothing had happened), only to have Joseph subsequently thrown into jail for the alleged crime that occurred two scenes earlier! Certainly if one were going to create a smooth-flowing and dramatic sequence of events, it would be thus: Joseph is made head of Potiphar's household; Mrs. Potiphar falls in love with him, but Joseph is uninterested; as she pines away, her friends come to visit her, or she gathers her friends there to see the cause of her suffering; finally, she loses all control and seizes Joseph; he flees, and she accuses him of attempted rape.

And it is apparently because of just such dramatic considerations that *Midrash Tanḥuma* and the other two sources have placed the incident where they have. But this is only one more indication of their relative lateness. For the truth of which *Tanḥuma* and, in fact, all the other sources save one are ignorant is that this story was not created out of thin air, but was an attempt to make sense of one difficult sentence in the biblical narrative. The sentence occurs at the end of the "garment scene," after Joseph has fled outside.

> And when she saw that he had left his garment in her hand and fled outside, she called out to the members of her household and said to them, "See! He brought to us a Hebrew man to 'sport' with us; he came in to lie with me, but I cried out with a loud cry."
>
> (Gen. 39:13–14)

There are many things in this verse that might deserve comment, but the one aspect that apparently most directly troubled early exegetes was a simple matter, the fact that, when Mrs. Potiphar cries out, she suddenly switches into the first person plural, "He brought to *us* a Hebrew man to 'sport' with *us.*" What could this mean?

The earliest source to comment on this switch to the plural is Philo of Alexandria. For in his retelling of the Joseph story, he has Mrs. Potiphar inform her husband of Joseph's "attack" in the following words:

> "You have brought to us," she said, "a Hebrew boy as a house-servant, who not only led you astray when you casually and without inquiry set him over your household, but now has had the audacity to dishonor my body. For not satisfied **to have availed himself merely of the women among his fellow slaves,** he has become utterly lustful and lascivious and has sought to lay his hands upon me, the mistress of the house, as well, and to take me by force."[31]

The words indicated above are not to be found in Mrs. Potiphar's actual accusation of Joseph to her husband in Gen. 39:17. Rather, they seem to be a reflection of the "to sport *with us*" in Gen. 39:14.[32] For what had Mrs. Potiphar meant there by saying "us"? Philo apparently saw in this plural a hint that Mrs. Potiphar wished to include the other ladies of the household among the victims of Joseph's lust. For that reason he has Mrs. Potiphar say, somewhat more explicitly in his own account, that Joseph was "not satisfied to have availed himself merely of the women among his fellow slaves."

A similar, but nonetheless distinct, reading lies at the origin of the exegetical tradition that we have been tracing. It begins with a remark found in *Genesis Rabba,* a terse comment that is virtually the same as the one that occurs at the beginning of the passage from *Midrash ha-Gadol* that we have been examining: "She put the righteous one [Joseph] in the mouths of all of them."[33] At first glance, this might seem to mean something like "She put the righteous one in *their* mouths as well," that is, Mrs. Potiphar spoke in such a way as to include them, the other members of the household, in her accusation (just as we saw happen in Philo's retelling). By saying, in effect, "Look, this Hebrew slave was brought to *us* to molest *us*, and it so happened that I was his first victim," she craftily sought from the first to have the other ladies of the household identify with her plight.

But the observation of these anomalous plurals, once made, seems to have been combined with another element in the verse in order to create a somewhat different understanding of it. That element is the apparently innocuous Hebrew term *le'mor* (lit., "to say"). This word is frequently used in narrative texts in the Bible to introduce direct quotation, and is usually left untranslated (as I have done throughout), since quotation marks serve the same function in modern English. But the fact is that in the above-cited verse, the Hebrew actually says, ". . . she called out to the people of her household and said to them *le'mor*, 'See! He brought to us a Hebrew man.' " Now the reason why this is of interest here is that rabbinic exegesis regularly (or at least when, as above, the *le'mor* can be construed as unnecessary, pleonastic) seeks to treat the word *le'mor* as if it were more than, in effect, punctuation, but understands it as a further command. The *locus classicus* of this very common midrashic reading is the rabbinic explanation of the introduction to the Ten Commandments, "And God spoke all these words, *le'mor*" (Exod. 20:1):

> The word *le'mor* teaches us that [as God spoke the commandments, the Israelites] would say "yes" after every positive commandment and "no" after every negative one—this is the tradition of R. Ishma'el. But R. Akiba said: "yes" after every positive one and "yes" after every negative one. Another explanation of *le'mor*: [God said to Moses:] Go and tell [the commandments to] them and tell me their words.[34]

In all of the explanations put forward here, *le'mor* is understood as an additional proviso: God spoke these words *to say*, in order that someone else say something in addition. According to R. Ishma'el and R. Akiba, that additional "saying" was to be done by the Israelites: after each commandment they were to indicate their acceptance by saying, according to R. Ishma'el, "yes" to the "Thou shalts" and "no" to the "Thou shalt nots," while according to R. Akiba it was "yes" after every commandment, whether positive injunction or prohibition. The second (anonymous) opinion cited holds that the additional "saying" was to be done by Moses: God spoke the words and Moses was then "to say" (*le'mor*) them to the Israelites and bring back their response. Now this is but one small example of the way *le'mor* is frequently treated in rabbinic texts: when the rabbis found it (as above) apparently unnecessary and could give it some additional significance by clever exegesis, they did.

So in our story, when Mrs. Potiphar cries out to the people of her household and says to them *le'mor*, a rabbinic exegete might automatically be inclined to seek some additional significance in this word. Was it not that Mrs. Potiphar was really commanding the ladies (whose presence now seemed to be implied by the fact that she uses the first person plural) *to say* something, that is, to say (presumably to their husbands) the rest of the sentence, "Look! This Hebrew man has been brought to *us* to molest all of *us*," and in this way start a mass movement among the members of the household against Joseph? This seems to be the full intent of the terse remark of *Genesis Rabba.* "She put [Joseph] in the mouths of all of them" means that Mrs. Potiphar told the ladies of her household to talk about Joseph to their husbands, repeating the same accusation in their own names. In fact, the idea that a *group* of people jointly accused Joseph goes back even before *Genesis Rabba* to the very start of the common era. For above (chapter 1), we saw in passing that Wisd. 10:14 speaks in the plural of "those who accused him [Joseph]." Although one ought not to place too much weight on such scant evidence, the fact that this text does speak of more than one accuser might well indicate that the rabbinic tradition of reading *le'mor* as a command stretches back to the beginning of the first century C.E. or even earlier. In any event, this exegetical connection is set out explicitly in later sources. Thus, for example, *Midrash Sekhel Ṭob* observes " 'And she called out to the members of her household and she said to them *le'mor*': What does *le'mor* mean? That she put him in the mouths of all."[35]

The Missing Link

Thus, Mrs. Potiphar's cry has been slightly transformed. In the biblical text, Joseph runs from the room, leaving his garment behind, and (presumably only a few seconds or minutes thereafter), Mrs. Potiphar comes running out, crying to anyone around, "Look! This Hebrew slave tried to molest me! Here is his garment!" But in our new understanding, Mrs. Potiphar's words need not have been spoken in the heat of the moment. An hour, perhaps longer, after the fact, she calmly "called out to [that is, summoned] the [lady] members of her household and told them to say [to their husbands], 'This Hebrew slave came to "sport" with us.' "

Indeed, delaying Mrs. Potiphar's "calling out" and turning it into a summoning of the members of her household will likewise answer another minor difficulty in the text. For, as remarked above, the incident begins with the observation that on the particular day in question "none of the members of the household was there in the house" (Gen. 39:11). But if so, then how could Mrs. Potiphar come running out immediately afterwards and call out "to the members of her household"? How did they suddenly materialize? Note that the biblical text does seem to imply that her "calling out" occurred immediately afterwards: "And when she saw that he had left his garment in her hand and had fled outside, she called out . . ."—that is, apparently at the time when she saw these things, in other words, right away. Yet perhaps the text can be taken a bit more loosely, interpreting "when she saw" here more as "since she saw," or even "in view of the fact that he had left his garment. . . ." If so, then there is no need to assume Mrs. Potiphar's "calling out" occurred at once—and delaying it somewhat could help resolve the apparent contradiction between this verse and the earlier assertion that no one was in the house. Indeed, no one was in the house at the time of the incident; but later, after the ladies had returned from the festival, Mrs. Potiphar "called out" to them and instructed them as to what to tell their husbands.

From such an understanding of this verse comes much of our motif of the assembly of ladies. Her "calling out" is now not a cry of distress, but a *summoning* of the ladies, one intended to solicit their help in accusing Joseph. And so, an exegete with no concern other than to explain the various problems cited—the anomalous plurals and the word *le'mor*, as well as the apparent discrepancy with regard to the presence or absence of the other members of the household—might indeed come up with the beginnings of our story: a summoning of the ladies of the court to Mrs. Potiphar's room, where they are told to (*le'mor*) tell their husbands about Joseph's advances to them. Indeed, such a primitive form of our legend is not entirely a hypothetical construct—it exists! For the following version—without Joseph, without knives—is preserved in the medieval midrashic anthology *Yalquṭ Shim'oni:*[36]

On that particular day, they all went to idolatrous rites, but she made herself out to be sick. When her friends came back they went to visit her. They said to her: What is wrong that your face is thus? She told them the entire episode. They said to her: You have no remedy other than to tell your husband thus and so, so that he will shut him [Joseph] up in prison. She said to them: I beg of you—each of you say that he also sought the same from you. And so they did. Then all the princes entered Potiphar's courtyard and told him. He wished to kill him [Joseph], but she said to him: Do not kill him and lose your money, but imprison him.

In order to understand this text, we will have to clear our minds of all that we have seen thus far. For what does it mean when it says that Mrs. Potiphar "told them the entire episode"? Probably not that she told the truth about her infatuation with Joseph (as she does in our other sources). No, here it seems that she tells them (as in the biblical account) the great lie, that Joseph tried to attack her. Only then would the reaction of the ladies make sense: "They said to her: You have no remedy save to tell your husband thus and so, so that he will shut him [Joseph] up in prison." Whereupon she asks their support (for she knows her story is a lie): her own accusation against Joseph will not carry as much weight as multiple accusations, so she asks them to say the same thing to their husbands, and they agree. Now all this, it will be noted, perfectly accounts for our biblical text's irregularities, the anomalous plurals and the apparently pleonastic le'mor—and it does so without having recourse to any reappearance of Joseph, citrons, knives, and the rest. This *Yalqut Shim'oni* text thus looks like the "missing link" between the biblical account itself and our legend of the ladies and knives.

But how does one get from the *Yalqut* account to these other versions, in which Joseph is present at the assembly—indeed, in which he becomes the whole point and so dazzles the ladies that they neglect their food? For, as noted, the presence of Joseph at this assembly is quite problematic: presumably only a short while before, he had fled the house—yet now here he is back again, waiting on Mrs. Potiphar and her friends as if nothing had happened. The only way this aspect of our story could come into existence is if it, too, had originally served some exegetical purpose. Let us look again at our troublesome verse:

> And when she saw that he had left his garment in her hand and fled outside, she called out to the members of her household and said to them, "See! He brought to us a Hebrew man to 'sport' with us; he came in to lie with me, but I cried out with a loud cry."
>
> (Gen. 39:13–14)

The exclamation "See!" in biblical texts is almost as innocent as *le'mor*, yet it too has a history of homiletical explanation. For example, when God says to the Israelites (Deut. 1:8), "*See*, I am granting you the land; go in and take possession . . .," a tannaitic midrash comments: " 'See . . .': [God] said to them: I am not telling you [to believe] from supposition or hearsay, but only what you can see with your own eyes."[37] (This explanation is all the more remarkable in that the biblical verse refers to a time when the Israelites were still at Mt. Sinai, and hence much too far to be able to "see" anything of their future homeland!) Similarly, when God says to Israel, "*See*, I have begun to set before you Sihon and his land" (Deut. 2:31), *Genesis Rabba* takes this as indicating that God actually caused them to *see* the Amorites' guardian angel (*sar*) falling from the heavens, a sign of the Amorites' future downfall. "See, the Lord has given you the Sabbath" (Exod. 17:29) is understood in the tannaitic *Mekhilta deR. Yishma'el* as: "Moses said to the Israelites, beware [that is, let your eyes be on the lookout], for God has given you the Sabbath so that you keep it."[38] In all these and dozens of other instances, the little imperative "See," which we might describe as a minor bit of emphasis in biblical Hebrew, is taken quite literally as referring to some visual phenomenon.

Against this background, it is not difficult to understand how Mrs. Potiphar's exclamation, "See! He brought to us a Hebrew man to 'sport' with us" could seem to imply that the ladies being so addressed were actually *seeing* the Hebrew man in question, Joseph, standing right in front of them. But how could they be seeing Joseph, and why? The only possible explanation was that (sometime perhaps long after Joseph's flight *and return*), Mrs. Potiphar had convened this meeting of ladies in order to show Joseph to them; and it required very little further imagination to supply the reason—in order to show them how handsome Joseph was so as to be able then to confide in them the passions to which Mrs. Potiphar had been prey since his arrival, and so to enlist their aid in reversing the truth and trumping up the charge of attempted rape against him. Thus it is clear that not only Joseph's appearance at the assembly of ladies, but, consequently, the whole story of their amazement at Joseph's beauty, and Mrs. Potiphar's seizing on their reaction in order to confess her infatuation—*all* of this was generated by an original attempt to give added significance to the harmless "See!" in the biblical text.[39]

Prison

It was said above that there is only one text among those cited that seems to have any awareness of the exegetical function of this story, and that is *Midrash ha-Gadol*. It alone specifically connects the story with the verse "And she called out . . ." (Gen. 39:14), and immediately comments (in the same words as *Genesis Rabba*) "She put the righteous one in the mouths of all of them." The story then comes to fill in the details of how this happened: the assembly of women, the presentation of

Joseph, the conspiracy to accuse Joseph of attempted rape. The fact that *Midrash ha-Gadol*'s version is so uniquely aware of the exegetical basis for this story argues in favor of its closeness to the original version of our story in other details as well. Indeed, one can easily imagine how this exegetical story, more or less as it now appears in *Midrash ha-Gadol*, could be the ancestor of various other "Cut Their Hands" versions. It is of course possible that the *Tanhuma* version, which seems so schematic and brief, also represents a relatively early branching-off of the original tradition. But if so, one thing is clear: in the form in which we encounter it, at least, it has been inserted into an earlier text of the *Tanhuma* that lacked this incident (this is proven by the narrative resumption discussed above), and, in fact, the editor has inserted the story in the wrong place—before the "garment scene," a position more satisfactory from a dramatic point of view but quite wrong in terms of the story's original exegetical function (of which he is thus apparently unaware).

But what of the relationship of *Midrash ha-Gadol* to the Qur'an? The *Midrash ha-Gadol* version, it has been noted, is rather similar to the Qur'an's; nevertheless, there is one striking difference between them, the matter of prison. Can this provide a clue as to which came first? In the Qur'an, prison is a threat that Mrs. Potiphar holds over Joseph's head: "But now," she says to the ladies, "if he does not do my bidding, he will be put in prison, and he will be among the base ones." In *Midrash ha-Gadol*, by contrast, prison is apparently Mrs. Potiphar's way of holding on to Joseph: "They [the ladies] said to her: You have no remedy other than to say to his master [Potiphar] to lock him up in prison and he will be entirely yours." The latter seems extremely awkward: one would have to imagine that Potiphar's house comes with its own little private dungeon in the basement, to which Mrs. Potiphar will now repair from time to time in order to be with the object of her desire. And even so, how would such an arrangement advance Mrs. Potiphar's aims? The Qur'an's version, on the other hand, is not only more natural, but has traditional support; the same use of prison as a threat is attested in an early midrash that interweaves different verses of Ps. 146:

> When that wicked woman [Mrs. Potiphar] came, she would torture him with her words. She would say to him, "I will have you put in prison [if you do not cooperate]." He said to her, "The Lord frees those that are bound up" (Ps. 146:7). She said to him, "I will pluck out your eyes." He said, "The Lord gives sight to the blind" (Ps. 146:8). She said, "I will bring low your posture." He said, "The Lord straightens those bent low" (Ps. 146:8; and so forth).[40]

Moreover, as we have seen, even as early as the *Testaments of the Twelve Patriarchs*, the idea that Mrs. Potiphar threatened Joseph in order to secure his compliance had some currency, although prison itself is not among the threats specified there.[41]

Why then the version found in *Midrash ha-Gadol?* The reason is, once again, the overall context and sequence of events. For the problem is that Joseph *must* eventually be jailed, since he ends up in jail in the biblical story; and he must be jailed on the charge of attempted rape, again, as in the biblical story. But if the "Assembly of the Ladies" motif is to come in its proper exegetical place, that is, *after* the garment scene, then this assembly necessarily intervenes between the time of the alleged crime and the time of Joseph's being accused and imprisoned. Therefore, there should be something in the assembly story itself that leads to the next event in the narrative, Joseph's accusation and imprisonment. Now in the Qur'an, this is handled very awkwardly: Mrs. Potiphar seizes Joseph in the garment scene, and he flees; *then* comes the accusation of attempted rape, which is immediately, and publicly, disproved; then comes the assembly of ladies; then Joseph, as something of an afterthought, is jailed in spite of the fact that he has been proven innocent. The *Midrash ha-Gadol* version is exegetically much better, because—improbable as the "private little dungeon" scenario might appear—it at least gets Joseph into prison *as a result* of what is said at the assembly of ladies, namely, "They said to her: You have no better remedy than to say to his master [Potiphar] to lock him up in prison and he will be entirely yours." Not only that, but Joseph's imprisonment could not, according to the *Midrash ha-Gadol* version, have been accomplished without the ladies' cooperation ("She said to them: If I am the only one to speak against him to my husband, he will not believe me. But if each one of you tells her husband, 'Joseph seized me,' then I will tell my husband that Joseph seized me as well and he will put him in prison"). And so again, what happens at the assembly—Mrs. Potiphar's securing the ladies' cooperation in accusing Joseph—leads directly and smoothly into what happens next, Joseph's being successfully accused and put in prison. So, in spite of its apparent improbability, the "private little dungeon" motive for Mrs. Potiphar's actions actually works much better than the Qur'an's mention of prison as a threat. (And, it must be said that the idea of Mrs. Potiphar continuing to pursue Joseph even after he has been put into prison is, after all, apparently not so improbable: this motif is found in the same *Testaments of the Twelve Patriarchs* as well as in *Genesis Rabba*.)[42]

Understanding these considerations, we may now further penetrate the precise development of the "prison" theme among our various sources. For the fact is that, upon close inspection, the ladies' words in the *Midrash ha-Gadol* version actually appear to be a reworking of the ladies' words in *Yalquṭ Shim'oni* version. Compare:

> They said to her: What is wrong that your face is thus? She told them the entire episode. **They said to her: You have no remedy other than to tell your husband thus and so, so that he will shut him [Joseph] up in prison.** She said to them: I beg of you—each of you say that he also sought the same from you . . . [etc.].
>
> *(Yalquṭ Shim'oni)*

> She said to them: If you, before whom he has stood but for a moment, were unable to endure it, how much less able am I, who see him each and every day. **They said to her: You have no remedy other than to say to his master [Potiphar] to lock him up in prison and he will be entirely yours.** She said to them: If I am the only one to speak against him to my husband, he will not believe me. But if each one of you tells her husband . . .
>
> *(Midrash ha-Gadol)*

It will be noticed that the two sentences indicated above are quite similar. But what a difference in context! For the *Yalquṭ Shim'oni* version is still fairly close to the biblical narrative—Mrs. Potiphar has just told the ladies that Joseph tried to attack her, and their reaction (utterly consistent with what happens in the biblical account) is: Report what has happened to your husband and he will have Joseph thrown into prison. But in the *Midrash ha-Gadol* version—where, in order to explain the word "See!", the midrashist now has Joseph actually present at the assembly of ladies, and where, as a consequence, Mrs. Potiphar now no longer lies but tells the truth, confessing her infatuation—the old reaction of the ladies, "Throw him into prison," no longer makes sense on its own. And so our midrashist in *Midrash ha-Gadol* has cleverly added an explanatory phrase to the ladies' reaction as cited in *Yalquṭ Shim'oni*. Here they say, "You have no remedy other than to say to his master [Potiphar] to lock him up in prison *and he will be entirely yours.*" The last few words were tacked on in order to provide the now-necessary rationale.

And just as the sentence about prison in *Yalquṭ Shim'oni* was reworked in *Midrash ha-Gadol*, so it seems that the *Midrash ha-Gadol* version (or something like it) was in turn reworked in the Qur'an version. For the latter was not content with the "private little dungeon" scenario implied by *Midrash ha-Gadol*: instead, it substituted the psychologically more satisfying notion that prison was used as a threat by Mrs. Potiphar. Unfortunately, in so doing it broke the logical sequence of events in the story. For what had worked so well in the Bible (garment scene, accusation, imprisonment) and in *Yalquṭ Shim'oni* (garment scene; assembly of ladies ending in joint accusation; imprisonment), and worked even tolerably well in *Midrash ha-Gadol* (garment scene; assembly of ladies with Joseph present, "private little dungeon" proposed as solution; joint accusation of Joseph; imprisonment) now fell apart entirely in the Qur'an (garment scene; assembly of ladies with Joseph present, prison mentioned by Mrs. Potiphar as a threat; eventual imprisonment despite Joseph's having previously been proven innocent).

It should by now be clear that, as Ginzberg noted, the Jewish origin of this story is "beyond dispute" (though he was somewhat off the mark, as we have seen, in saying this specifically about the *Tanḥuma* version). For it is, from start to finish, an *exegetical* creation, one aimed at explaining peculiarities in a particular verse. In that respect, it is indisputable that the Qur'an, which has no interest in biblical exegesis *as such*, has thus simply taken over a bit of traditional exegesis that was also a good story, and woven it into its retelling of the doings of the hero Yusuf. It is certainly not irrelevant to emphasize here the provenance of our *Midrash ha-Gadol*: as noted, it comes from Yemen, that is, the Arabian peninsula. What could better explain the resemblance between its version and that of the Qur'an than that this story had come into the possession of the Arabic-speaking Jews of the peninsula, where it was, eventually, both committed to writing in the form it is in in *Midrash ha-Gadol* and, also, passed on orally (in Arabic) until it found its way, along with a good deal more Jewish exegetical material, into the Qur'an. As is so often the case with Qur'anic recycling of biblical stories, there is no indication that that book's author sought (or was even able) to distinguish biblical text from exegetical elaboration, or to distinguish both of these from later flourishes that had been added for no exegetical reason at all.

Knives

This last brings us to the matter of the knives; why the knives? I am unable to find any exegetical reason for the knives, and so am inclined to regard them as just such a flourish, something added on in the story's transmission for no other reason than that it made for a livelier, more memorable narrative. And it is very easy to see how this touch came about: the evidence is before us in the Aramaic poem. There, it will be recalled, the ladies are served wine by Joseph, but "They held their cups, but took no taste of them/ For when they beheld him, their faces grew quite pale." No doubt this is an early form of our motif: whatever they were served—wine, meat and bread, or nothing specific—they *did not pay attention* to their food, so captivated were they by the sight of Joseph. This "not paying attention" serves a useful purpose in the narrative, it dramatizes the extent to which the women are captivated by Joseph. And yet, one might say, it does not dramatize very well. After all, "not pay attention"?! But that is so passive, such a nonaction! One would like something to happen, something decisive: Joseph walks in and at once they all drop their wine cups, or their knives and forks all fall to the table, or to the floor! It would not be at all surprising if somewhere, in some as yet undiscovered source, some such variant on the Aramaic poem's underlying story were to be found, for such an "improvement" would be irresistible. And so it was too with the knives and cut hands. Whatever its origins,[43] once this element entered the tradition it could scarcely be dispensed with, for it is one of those scintillating details (like the "glass" of Cinderella's slippers)[44] which, wherever they come from, seize the imagination and make a tale far more vivid. And for just this reason, given the evidence of the Aramaic poem, it seems to me that the knives cannot be original in the story. An earlier version contained a passing remark, like that of the Aramaic poem, to the effect that the women were so struck by Joseph's beauty that they did not even eat their food (or drink their drinks). But having been incorporated into the story, this passing remark was found to be insufficiently dramatic or decisive, and so, eventually, the knives and cut hands came to replace it. Once there, they became a central focus of the story, and never left it.

The "Vienna Genesis"

This last hypothesis may find support in a final piece of evidence, one that comes not from a written source, but from a picture. The picture is found in an ancient illustrated book known as the *Vienna Genesis*, which has been dated to sixth century c.e.[45] It was probably made somewhere in the Eastern region of the Byzantine world—scholarly opinion is divided as to its likely place of origin between Constantinople, Antioch, and Jerusalem. In any case, among the illustrations contained in it are two concerned with the episode of Joseph and Mrs. Potiphar. As is characteristic of many such ancient illustrations,[46] these each contain a succession of different "scenes" within a single illustration. Thus, the first illustration shows, in the upper left, Joseph fleeing from Mrs. Potiphar through an open door as she seizes his garment (here, a purple outer cloak). To the right of this scene stands Joseph, now outside, staring back through the same open door; with him are two ladies, one of whom is bathing a baby. The third scene, below the first two, shows three women, one of whom now holds the baby. The next illustration is similarly divided, depicting, successively, the return of Potiphar to the house, the accusation of Joseph, and corroboration by members of the household, who point at the telltale garment.

One must be careful in using evidence such as this, especially since exegetical motifs can sometimes become garbled when translated to a visual medium. And yet it seems likely that exegetical traditions are at least part of the basis of this depiction of the incident of Joseph and Mrs. Potiphar: the illustrations are derived from more than simply a reading of the biblical text. Thus, for example, the baby in the picture, who in reality is probably none other than Aseneth, Joseph's future wife: she is presented in this depiction because of a particular exegetical motif that had placed her at the scene of Joseph's flight in order to allow her subsequently to tell Potiphar that Joseph is innocent.[47] Similarly striking in the picture, and of greater relevance to us, is the fact that members of the household join in accusing Joseph and pointing at the garment. This is nowhere stated in the biblical text: it was generated, as we have seen, by the anomalous plurals and the word le'mor in Gen. 39:14. So our artist seems to be familiar with at least that part of the exegetical tradition.

Most intriguing, however, is the fact that he has followed up the "garment scene" in the first illustration with a subsequent moment in the story, a moment not contained in the biblical account itself. For in the Bible, the "garment scene" is the climax of the whole episode: after it, Mrs. Potiphar simply tells her husband her version of the events and Joseph is imprisoned forthwith. Here on the other hand, *something else* happens in-between, something that involves Joseph standing among some other ladies of Potiphar's household in a scene of idyllic tranquillity. Might this be a reflection of something like the "Assembly" story in a garbled and (in any case) very primitive stage—one that places Joseph among the ladies of the household, but in which there is no visual reference to food or drink being consumed? If so, then this illustration might be seen to correspond to a stage in the development of our motif roughly equivalent to that of the Aramaic poem—a stage in which, Mrs. Potiphar's "See!" having been interpreted as referring to Joseph himself, the assembly of ladies now requires Joseph's presence, but in which there is as yet no firm tradition of what in particular was served, if anything. In any case, the fact that the household members join in accusing Joseph indicates, as noted, that at least the beginnings of the "Assembly" motif have been transmitted; it was to remain to later generations to refine them and produce the succession of elaborations that we have seen.

How the "Assembly" Developed

And so we now have a fairly complete picture of our story's evolution. It began (Stage I) with the simple observation of the anomalous plurals in Mrs. Potiphar's cry, "See! He brought to us a Hebrew man to 'sport' with us. . . ." This observation inspired Philo to have Mrs. Potiphar mention the female slaves of her household as the previous objects of Joseph's lust, and logically stands as well at the beginning of the rabbinic tradition we have been tracing, although it is not attested in this form there. Stage II occurred when the observation of the anomalous plurals was combined with the fanciful exegesis of *le'mor* in order to create the story of Mrs. Potiphar getting the other ladies together for the purpose of having them tell their husbands that Joseph had likewise sought to molest them. This early stage may be reflected in Wisd. 10:14, "*Those* who accused him," and in any case appears in the remark found in *Genesis Rabba*, "She put [Joseph] in the mouths of all of them," as well as in the somewhat fuller narrative cited above from *Yalquṭ Shim'oni*. Stage III came about when this story of the assembly of the ladies was combined with creative exegesis of the word "See!" in Mrs. Potiphar's cry, which seemed to imply that Joseph was actually present at the time. This introduced an interesting wrinkle into the story—the wonderment of the ladies at Joseph's beauty—but, as we have seen, it posed difficulties as well, namely, Joseph's business-as-usual presence at the assembly *after* the time when (according to Mrs. Potiphar's later accusation) he was supposed to have attempted to rape her. The purpose of the assembly thus could no longer be to *accuse* Joseph and solicit the ladies' cooperation in having him imprisoned. With Joseph present, the purpose now had to become that of having Mrs. Potiphar show the ladies how handsome her servant was, confessing her infatuation, and, as well, having something said at the assembly which might then logically lead into the next episode of the story, Joseph's imprisonment. If this last item bothered the author of the Aramaic poem, there is no indication of it in the text: no transition to Joseph's imprisonment is provided or even suggested. What is more, the version of our legend that stands behind this poem seems to be rather primitive with regard to dramatizing the ladies' awe at Joseph's beauty (wine cups untouched vs. knives and cut hands in the other versions). For both these reasons, the poem's account appears to be the earliest form of the story incorporating the creative exegesis of the word "See!" in Gen. 39:14. And, as we have just seen, the illustration in the *Vienna Genesis* may likewise correspond to this same stage of development.

In Stage IV, the element of the knives and cut hands is introduced—a highly dramatic touch that will appear ever after. This element is present in both *Midrash Tanḥuma* (with "citrons") and *Midrash ha-Gadol* (with "bread and meat"), and one cannot decide, on the basis of the food, which of the versions underlying these sources was created first—or whether indeed both represent a development of something less specific, a "banquet" as in the Qur'an, at which the ladies cut their hands instead of their (unspecified) food. In any case, the versions underlying our *Tanḥuma* text and *Midrash ha-Gadol* both belong, in terms of development, to Stage IV, and both circulate independently for a time.

Although they both thus belong to the same stage of development, it is nonetheless to be stressed that the *Midrash ha-Gadol* version, as we have seen, is uniquely aware of the exegetical function of the story, and its faithfulness in this regard may suggest that it is closer in other respects as well to an original narrative expansion specifically designed to account for some irregularities in the biblical text. Moreover, we have seen that the opening words of this text go all the way back to Stage II in our history, the remark in *Genesis Rabba* ("She put [Joseph] in the mouths of all of them"), while one of its later sentences ("You have no remedy other than to say . . .") is a direct echo of our other Stage II text, *Yalquṭ Shim'oni*. For all these reasons, then, the *Midrash ha-Gadol* version seems to stand in a close developmental line with the preceding sources. By contrast, the *Tanḥuma* text bears all the marks of a free, popular reworking of the same basic motif, with the pungent (but exegetically pointless) specification that "citrons" were served, and without any apparent awareness of the exegetical function of the story. In whatever form it may have circulated, a story of the "citrons" type eventually acquired a certain cachet and authority of its own, even causing some versions of the Aramaic poem to be rewritten in such a way as to now include both wine and citrons.

A form of the story very similar to that of *Midrash ha-Gadol* must have served as the basis for the Qur'an version, which is Stage V. The two differ, as we have seen, in the way they handle the matter of the transition from our story to Joseph's imprisonment (a problem that had apparently not bothered anyone in Stage III). *Midrash ha-Gadol*'s solu-tion, as we have seen, was to have the women at the assembly explic-itly suggest imprisonment as a means of holding on to Joseph (for the midrashist here had picked up on the sentence about prison in the earlier, *Yalquṭ Shim'oni* version), and Mrs. Potiphar secures their coop-eration in accusing him. The Qur'an, by contrast, transforms the ele-ment of prison from a way of holding on to Joseph to a threat in order to secure his cooperation. This was obviously done because it was psy-chologically more satisfying, as we have seen, but this change also seriously flawed the sequence of events, particularly if one puts it alongside the biblical narrative. But the fact that this form of the story is found in the Qur'an, where clearly the biblical narrative itself is no longer relevant, suggests that it is indeed a later swerve from the Stage IV versions, one more interested in psychological motivation (prison as a threat) than in illuminating the biblical text. It thus constitutes a sep-arate stage of development, Stage V.

As we have seen, the editor of one manuscript tradition of *Midrash Tanḥuma*, apparently unaware of the proper placement of the assembly of ladies incident (for he no longer understood its exegetical purpose), switched the sequence of actions so as to have the assembly precede, rather than follow, the garment scene. And placing it there, he no longer needed any reference to prison, either as a threat or as a way of holding on to Joseph; and so that part of the story does not appear. In placing the story where he did and in passing over the element of prison, he in effect created a new stage, Stage VI, wherein the assembly is now an incident that leads up to, rather than follows, the garment scene. Widely disseminated in this form, the *Tanḥuma* version is sub-sequently retold and elaborated in still later Jewish sources—Stage VII—either with relatively few variants (as in *Yeraḥme'el*), or greatly reworked and joined with motifs from the Qur'anic version and later traditions (*Sefer ha-Yashar*).

The story of the Assembly of the Ladies is instructive, not only about the way that motifs travel, but about how an originally *exegetical* story can quickly lose its exegetical character, so that later tradents are even unaware of it and so introduce elements that obscure or confound its original purpose. At the same time, it is to be stressed that, despite its existence in primitive form in *Genesis Rabba*, this story is still a rel-atively late elaboration of the exegetical picture of Joseph. The begin-nings of that picture, and specifically the handling of certain other crucial aspects of the incident with Mrs. Potiphar, are to be found in earlier texts, and it is to these that we now turn.

Notes

1. For the precise sense of this term, please see Introduction.
2. The various forms of this text are known by two different names, *Tanḥuma* and *Yelammedenu*. Despite the efforts of past researchers, it is unlikely that any of the extant forms of the text can be shown to be the "original": our various texts do all seem to derive ultimately from a common source, a Palestinian midrash on the Torah that achieved wide circulation and, in the process, acquired many additions, rewritings, and deletions. See below.
3. See the brief discussion in J. Heinemann, *Aggadot vetoldoteihen* (Jerusalem: Keter, 1974), 124, and above, chapter 1, note 4.
4. Literally, "they said"; I have translated this as a passive to avoid confusion, since the "they" is an impersonal "they" and not the "all of them" in the previous sentence.
5. Where they were during the confrontation between Joseph and Mrs. Potiphar. For the origins of this particular tradition, see below.
6. Heb. *qiddemah*. This looks like an Arabism, but cf. the Hebrew idiom in Deut. 23:5, Isa. 21:14, Neh. 13:2.
7. The name Zulaikha for Mrs. Potiphar does not appear in early Jewish sources, nor even in the Qur'an. It is apparently of Persian origin and was popularized by post-Qur'anic Muslim writers. See L. Ginzberg, *The Legends of the Jews*, vol. 5 (Philadelphia: Jewish Publication Society, 1925), 339 n. 113; also J. Macdonald, "Joseph in the Qur'an and Muslim Commentary: A Comparative Study," *The Muslim World* 46 (1956): 113–31, 207–24; esp. p. 124.
8. M. Gaster, *The Chronicles of Jerahmeel,* reprinted with a prolegomenon by Haim Schwarzbaum (New York: KTAV, 1971), 94.
9. L. Goldschmidt, ed., *Sefer ha-Yashar* (Berlin: Benjamin Harz, 1923), 159–60.
10. All this is extraordinarily reminiscent of the picture of Mrs. Potiphar that emerges in the "Testament of Joseph" among the *Testaments of the Twelve Patriarchs*. For the threats, see 3:1; for her treatment of Joseph as the son she never had, 3:7.
11. See the edition of S. Horowitz, *Maḥzor Vitry* (Nürnburg, 1923), 342, as well as the version of this poem presented in the (unpublished) thesis of A. Rosenthal (Tal), "The Aramaic Poems of Shavuot" (Hebrew University, 1966), 94–102. Tal's text was used by M. Schmeltzer in his edition of a medieval commentary to the poem published in H. Z. Dimitrovsky, *Meḥqarim umqorot* (New York: Jewish Theological Seminary, 1978), 169–238. Prof. Joseph Yahalom of the Hebrew University is preparing a new critical edition of this and other Aramaic poems in collaboration with M. Sokolov, to be entitled *Shirei benei ma'arava*. I am grateful to Prof. Yahalom for sharing with me some of his preliminary findings.
12. On other Arabic elements in *Sefer ha-Yashar*'s version, see M. Grünbaum, "Zu 'Jussuf und Suleicha' " in his *Gesammelte Aufsätze zur Sprach- und Sagenkunde* (Berlin: S. Calvary & Co., 1901), 524.
13. A. Geiger, *Was hat Mohammed aus dem Judenthume aufgenommen?* (Bonn, 1833), 143.
14. M. Grünbaum, "Zu 'Jussuf und Suleicha,' " 515–51.
15. Ginzberg, *Legends,* 5:339–40, n. 118.

16. See the discussion and bibliography in H. Schwarzbaum's prolegomenon to Gaster, *Jerahmeel*, 14–15; 50–51.
17. Ibid., 14–15.
18. Ginzberg, *Legends*, 5:339.
19. Ginzberg himself noted this. See his *Ginzei Schechter*, vol. 1 (New York: Jewish Theological Seminary, 1928), 466.
20. See A. F. L. Beeston, *Baiḍawi's Commentary on Surah 12 of the Qur'an* (Oxford: Clarendon Press, 1963), 18.
21. The whole question of the word *muttaka'* and its origins has been discussed by A. Yahuda, "A Contribution to Qur'an and Hadith Interpretation," in *I. Goldziher Memorial Volume*, vol. 1 (Budapest: Globus, 1948), 294–95. Yahuda argues that the use of this word in the Qur'anic account reflects an attempt to retell in Arabic a midrashic tale that reflected a characteristically Jewish, but not Arabic, custom. For he points out that while the institution of eating while leaning on cushions was "generally unknown to the Arabs," this custom—and indeed, the idiom "to lean" or "recline" in the sense of "to share a meal"—was well known to Jews. He concludes: "It is evident that *muttaka'* was used by the Jews of Medina for these cushions offered to the guest at meals and was extended to [mean] 'banquet,' " in which meaning it was used in a Jewish story which found its way into the Qur'an.
22. For Tabari, ibn al-Athir, and others see Grünbaum, "Zu 'Jussuf und Suleicha,' " 524–25. Note also Beeston's remark (note 20) on the Muslim iconographic tradition of this incident, which depicts the ladies eating oranges or citrons. See also, for example, the medieval poetic retelling of Sura 12 published by R. Y. Ebied and M. J. L. Young, *The Story of Joseph in Arabic Verse: The Leeds Arabic Manuscript 347* (supplement 3 to the Annual of the Leeds Oriental Society, 1975), p. 39: "She brought citrons to each of the women and knives to them also./She said: If Joseph comes here give him the citron to eat; cut a slice for him."
23. Oxford Ms. 2501, p. 52. This is the manuscript used by J. Yahalom in his forthcoming edition (above, note 11); see below.
24. Oxford Ms. 2895/4, pp. 165–66.
25. It is to be noted that this motif of Mrs. Potiphar adorning herself in order to seduce Joseph—an exegetical motif originally created to supply a possible referent for *debarim*—eventually received wide exposure in Syriac and Arabic sources. For the former, see the "Fourth Homily on Joseph" attributed to Ephraem [in *Sancti Ephraem Syri Hymni et Sermones*, ed. T. J. Lamy (Louvain, 1889), 3:354–55]; for Narsai's Joseph Poem, see H. Näf, *Syrische Josef-Gedichte* . . . (Ph.D. diss., University of Zurich, 1923), 97; cf. *idem*, p. 69 for Romanos and Firdusi. The same motif appears as well in a separate work, Pseudo-Ephraem's *Life of Joseph*. This book, written in Greek (though probably based on the series of Syrian Joseph homilies attributed to Ephraem and mentioned above), was probably completed in Syria in the fifth or sixth century. The iconographic tradition accompanying the extant manuscripts includes specifically this motif. See thus G. Vikan, "Illustrated Manuscripts of Pseudo-Ephraem's *Life of Joseph*" (Ph.D. diss., Princeton University, 1976), 97, "Illustration 25: The wife of Pentephres [= Potiphar] adorns herself in order to tempt Joseph." See on these sources in general D. Gerson, "Die Kommentare des Ephräem Syrus im Verhältnis zur jüdi-

schen Exegese" *MGWJ* 17 (1868): 15–33, 64–72, 98–107, 141–49; and Sten Hedal, *Interpretatio Syrica: Die Kommentare des Heiligen Ephräm des Syrers zu Genesis* (Lund, Sweden: CWK Gleerup, 1974); cf. T. Jansma, "Investigations into the Earily Syrian Fathers on Genesis," *Oudtestamentische Studien* 12 (1958): 69–181. For Arabic sources, see Grünbaum, "Zu 'Jussuf und Suleicha,' " 526.

26. For *Genesis Rabba* and parallels, see J. Theodor and Ch. Albeck, *Bereshit Rabba* (Jerusalem: Wahrmann Books, 1965), 1071–72.

27. Josephus, *The Jewish Antiquities*, trans. H. St.-J. Thackeray, vol. 4 (Cambridge: Harvard University, 1978), 188–91 (= II, 50).

28. Gaster, *Jerahmeel*, 94.

29. That is, in addition to the basic similarity of the "knives" stories in each— the only significant divergence there being on the kind of fruit served.

30. *Genesis Rabba* 87:6; see Theodor-Albeck edition for notes and parallels, p. 1070.

31. Philo, "On Joseph," 51.

32. Note that Mrs. Potiphar's words in Gen. 39:14, when she cries out immediately following the incident, are "He brought to *us* a Hebrew man to 'sport' with *us* . . ." whereas in repeating the accusation to her husband in Gen. 39:17 she says, "The Hebrew slave whom you brought to us came to sport with *me*." Philo's restatement of the latter verse thus seems to conflate it with the former.

33. *Genesis Rabba* 87:8 and 88:1.

34. *Mekhilta de R. Yishma'el*, ed. H. Horovitz and Y. Rabin (Jerusalem: Wahrmann, 1970), 219.

35. *Midrash Sekhel Tob*, ed. S. Buber (Berlin: Z. H. Izakowsky, 1910), 244.

36. Attributed there to the no longer extant *Midrash Abkir*; see *Yalqut Shim'oni* I: 146.

37. *Sifrei Debarim* 7; see the edition of M. Friedmann (Vienna, 1864), 66b, note 7.

38. *Mekhilta de R. Yishma'el*, ed. Horovitz and Rabin, 170.

39. The biblical story itself, as well as later exegetical traditions, supply other possible direct objects for Mrs. Potiphar's "See!" The most obvious candidate is the garment itself that Joseph has left behind: when Mrs. Potiphar says "See!", is she not holding the garment before her listeners? From this hypothesis develops another motif, "Examine the Garment." It is first attested in Philo, who says that Potiphar misunderstood the significance of Joseph's torn garment, which was actually "proof of violence not employed by him but done at her hands" ("On Joseph," 52). The fact that the garment is torn in the back rather than in the front is likewise proof of Joseph's innocence in a widely circulated motif found in the Qur'an (Sura 12:25–29) as well as in Jewish sources; see Ginzberg, *Legends* 5:362 n. 340. Yet another exegetical motif has Mrs. Potiphar put egg white on her bed as "evidence"; she then summon her servants and says, "See!" This motif is contained in Targum Pseudo-Jonathan 39:14 (later, in v. 20, the Egyptian priests tell Potiphar that it is a ruse); it is also found in *Midrash Sekhel Tob*, ed. S. Buber, 240. A similar story is recounted in b. *Gittin* 57a of a certain man who wished to divorce his wife. *Midrash ha-Gadol* cites the *Gittin* story in connection with Joseph, *ad* v. 22. Given these various possibilities, one might

ask why exegetes ever developed the idea that Joseph, rather than these other things, was the intended direct object of Mrs. Potiphar's "See!" The answer is simply that the words immediately following—namely, "See! He brought to us a Hebrew man to 'sport' with us . . ."—seemed to suggest that Mrs. Potiphar was indeed pointing to the Hebrew man in question.

40. *Abot deR. Natan,* version A, chapter 16; ed. S. Schechter (New York: Feldheim, 1967), 63.

41. See above and n. 10.

42. "Testament of Joseph," 8:4–9:5; *Genesis Rabba,* 87:10. See Theodor-Albeck, *Genesis Rabba,* 3:1075.

43. See Schwarzbaum's "Prolegomena," in Gaster, *Jerahmeel,* p. 51 for a hypothesis about the "folk-motif" from which the knives might originally stem, and cf. R. Köhler, "In die Hand, nicht in die Speisen schneiden," in his *Kleinere Schriften zur Erzählenden Dichtung des Mittelalters,* vol. 2 (Weimar: E Felber, 1900), 83–87. I am inclined not to accept the universal and inevitable character of many such folk-motifs, and so am disturbed in this case that all of these sources cited are relatively late; are they not simply reflections of the Qur'anic legend and/or Jewish texts as they penetrated Europe?

44. Apparently originally "fur" slippers, transformed into glass via the Old French homonyms *vair* and *verre.*

45. See on this E. Wellesz, *The Vienna Genesis* (London: Faber and Faber, 1960); also J. Gutmann, "Joseph Legends in the Vienna Genesis," *Proceedings of the Fifth World Congress of Jewish Studies,* vol. 4 (Jerusalem: World Union of Jewish Students, 1973), 181–84.

46. That is, Wickoff's "continuous style" common to classical and early Christian art. See W. Lowrie, *Art in the Early Church* (New York: Harper & Row, 1965), 165.

47. This motif in only one of several rival motifs that were all originally created in order to assert that Potiphar in fact knew that Joseph was innocent and for this reason did not have him killed, as would have only been appropriate, but merely imprisoned (and that only in order to save face). For other motifs proving Joseph's innocence, see above, n. 39. Apart from these, Mrs. Potiphar's words to her husband in the *Yalquṭ Shim'oni* version, "Do not kill him and lose your money, but imprison him," constitute yet another motif aimed at explaining why Joseph was not killed. As for Aseneth testifying to Joseph's innocence, this motif probably developed in the following manner: originally an anonymous someone, probably a child (because a child's testimony would clearly be disinterested and pure), told Potiphar of Joseph's innocence and hence his life was spared. But given the fact that ancient exegetes at least since the Septuagint had identified the "Potiphera" of Gen. 41:45, who is the father of Joseph's bride Aseneth, with our "Potiphar" (see below, chapter 3), it seemed likely that this same Aseneth was present in the household as a girl or infant at the time when Joseph was brought there as a slave. Therefore, having the anonymous witness to Joseph's innocence be none other than Aseneth would not only supply a handy identity for this witness, but would also help explain why, among all the available brides, Joseph chose one from the very household in which he had served as a slave. We find the motif in this form in the continuation of our *Yalquṭ Shim'oni* passage, which recounts that Aseneth

"came in secret" to Potiphar and told him the truth, whereupon God declares: "By your life, since you have argued in his [Joseph's] favor, the tribes that I am to establish from him will come from you." A similar story of an *anonymous* child who testifies on Joseph's behalf is found in Origen *ad* Gen. 41:45 (see Aptowitzer, "Asenath," 256–57); this may represent an earlier version of our motif, or simply an abbreviated one. In *Sefer ha-Yashar*, in any case, it is not Aseneth who testifies but an eleven-month-old (male) child, who is miraculously given the gift of speech for that purpose. This version seems to have been influenced by various Muslim accounts that likewise speak of the witness being an an infant; see Grünbaum, "Zu 'Jussuf und Suleicha,' " 525.

3.

Joseph's Beauty

In the "Assembly of Ladies" midrash, the focus of our attention is on Joseph's extraordinary good looks: this is what was originally responsible for Mrs. Potiphar's infatuation with him, and it is what, in its final form, is highlighted by the "Assembly" story itself—so dazzling is Joseph that the ladies cut their hands at the mere sight of him. Now as we have seen, the actual scriptural source for this tradition of Joseph's physical beauty is Gen. 39:6, "And Joseph was comely of form and comely of appearance," a somewhat emphatic turn of phrase which, to early exegetes, suggested that he was indeed extraordinarily handsome. Yet it would be wrong to suppose that the "Assembly" story therefore developed solely out of a contemplation of this and the other biblical verses from the Joseph story cited in the last chapter. For one tradition often feeds off another, and it is characteristic of early Jewish exegesis that, however much a midrashic motif may have been generated by a particular problem or point of interest in the biblical text, once launched on its career it will be modified in contemplation of other motifs, and sometimes its very nature will be profoundly altered by exegetical themes originally quite separate from it. This, as we shall see presently, was indeed the case with the "Assembly of Ladies"—for at the time it came into existence, there was already current another exegetical motif that involved awestruck ladies admiring Joseph's beauty. But in order to trace *this* motif's development, we must begin with some of the basic building blocks, various bits of ancient exegesis that touched on the theme of Joseph's beauty.

Popularity of the Theme

We might begin by observing just how popular this theme itself was among some of the earliest sources of postbiblical exegesis. Part of this popularity, especially in Hellenistic Jewish writings, has to do with the Greek association of physical beauty and inner virtue. Thus, for example, the "Testament of Simeon" in the *Testaments of the Twelve Patriarchs* (which contains reflections of many Greek ideas and themes) observes: "Therefore Joseph was comely in appearance and beautiful to look upon, because no wickedness dwelt in him—for the face makes manifest some of the trouble of the spirit" (5:1). Similarly, the first-century historian Josephus writes: "When Jacob had begotten Joseph by Rachel, he loved him more than the other sons, both because of the beauty of his body and the virtue of his mind, for he excelled in intelligence" (*Jewish Antiquities* II 9).[1] The idea that beauty of body and beauty of mind go together no doubt helped Greek-influenced readers of the Bible to see in the emphatic phrase of Gen. 39:6 ("comely of form and comely of appearance") an allusion to this biblical hero's mental and spiritual, as well as physical, qualities, and they therefore gave this description some prominence in their overall presentation of Joseph.

But the same phrase suggested something quite different to rabbinic exegetes. For it so happens that this particular combination of adjectives is used of only one other person in the whole of the Hebrew Bible, and that is Joseph's mother Rachel: she is likewise described (Gen 29:17) as "comely of form and comely of appearance" (in contrast to her sister Leah, of whom the best Scripture can report is that she had "nice eyes.") To a midrashist the conclusion is obvious, Joseph's beauty must have been inherited: "Said R. Isaac: Toss a stick into the air and it will fall to the same spot" (*Genesis Rabba* 86:6)—or, as we might say, "The apple never falls far from the tree." Thus, this phrase seemed to suggest to rabbinic exegetes that Scripture was not only seeking to tell us that Joseph was handsome, but to hint at where this quality had come from (his mother, Rachel); and, understood in this fashion, the verse received further prominence in early Jewish exegesis.

Joseph and Jacob

Yet there is another, apparently contradictory, tradition concerning Joseph's physical appearance: it holds that he resembled not his mother, Rachel, but his father, Jacob. This tradition is to be found as early as the "Testament of Joseph": there Joseph is said to observe about himself, "And He [God] gave me also beauty as a flower, beyond the beautiful ones of Israel; and he preserved me unto old age in strength and in beauty, *for I was like Jacob in all things*" (18:4). This text apparently intends to assert that it was Joseph's resemblance to Jacob "in all things" that was responsible for his beauty, and not his descendance from Rachel. Rabbinic sources likewise assert that Joseph and Jacob resembled one another, and specifically that Joseph's "countenance was similar to his [Jacob's]" (*Genesis Rabba* 84:8).

The existence of this apparent countertradition of Jacob's beauty deriving from his father is a good example of the way different motifs can come to overlap. For the fact is that this midrashic explanation for

Joseph's beauty is of an entirely different provenance: while the Joseph-resembled-Rachel motif sought to understand the apparently emphatic combination of adjectives "comely of form and comely of appearance" by pointing to its use in elsewhere in Scripture (in regard to Rachel), the second aimed at explaining a difficulty—or, rather, two—in quite a different passage, the opening exposition of the Joseph story. There we read:

> These are the generations of Jacob: Joseph, being seventeen years old, was shepherding the flock with his brothers. . . . And Israel [= Jacob] loved Joseph more than his other sons, for he was a child of his old age.
>
> (Gen. 37:2–3)

Why, one might ask, should Scripture announce "These are the generations of Jacob" and then pass immediately to the story of Joseph? Did not Jacob have twelve sons, and would we not therefore expect such a statement to be followed by a list of descendants, starting with Jacob's firstborn, Reuben, then Simeon, and so on, and only afterwards to begin the story of Joseph proper? Or, on the other hand, if the purpose here were simply to introduce the story of Joseph, would it not have been better simply to start right in, "And it came to pass, when Jacob's son Joseph was seventeen . . .", and say nothing about the "generations of Jacob"?

The answer, for Jewish exegetes, was that this blunt juxtaposition of "Joseph" with the "generations of Jacob" was intended to show us that Joseph was somehow Jacob's son *par excellence*—for example, in the sense that "these other generations [i.e., Joseph's brothers] only came because of Joseph's merits" (*Genesis Rabba* 84:5). Another possibility (and here is the verse's relevance for us) was that Joseph was in some striking way *similar* to his father: he was Jacob's son *par excellence* because he was the one who was most like him. This line of argument thus interprets the Bible's blunt "These are the generations of Jacob: Joseph . . ." as something like a mathematical equation, Jacob = Joseph, that is, an assertion of their resemblance in (as the "Testament" says) *all things*, of which physical appearance is only one. We only encounter this tradition fully articulated in rabbinic sources (though its prior existence may be implied by the passage just cited from the "Testament of Joseph," perhaps going back to the first or even second century B.C.E.). Thus, R. Samuel b. Naḥman, a Palestinian *amora* of the late third or early fourth century C.E., is credited with adducing the following exhaustive catalogue of similarities between Jacob and Joseph:

Just as Jacob was born circumcised, so was Joseph;[2] just as the one's
mother [Rebecca] had been barren, so was the other's [Rachel] ; just as
the one's mother had difficulty at the moment of giving birth,[3] so did
the other's; just as the one's mother had two children [Jacob and
Esau], so did the other's [Joseph and Benjamin]; just as the one's
brother hated him, so did the other's brothers; just as the one's brother
tried to kill him, so did the other's brothers; just as the one was a
shepherd, so was the other; the one was accused [by Laban, Gen.
31:26 ff.] and the other was accused [by Potiphar's wife]; the one was
stolen twice [Gen 31:39] and the other was stolen twice [Gen. 40:15];[4]
the one was blessed with ten [blessings] and the other was blessed
with ten;[5] the one left the land [of Israel] and the other left the land;
the one married outside of the land [Rachel and Leah] and the other
married outside of the land [Aseneth]; the one had children outside of
the land and the other had children outside of the land; the one was
accompanied by angels and the other was accompanied by angels;[6] the
one was made great by a dream [i.e., at Bethel] and the other was
made great by a dream [i.e., Pharaoh's]; the one's father-in-law's
house was blessed because of him, and the other's father-in-law's
house was blessed because of him;[7] the one went down to Egypt and
the other went down to Egypt; the one brought the famine to an end
and the other brought the famine to an end; the one caused an oath
to be sworn [that he would not be buried in Egypt, Gen. 47:31], and
the other caused an oath to be sworn [Gen. 50:25]; the one commanded [at his death, Gen. 49:29] and the other commanded [Gen.
50:2]; the one died in Egypt and the other died in Egypt; the one was
embalmed and the other was embalmed; the one's bones went up [to
the land of Israel] and the other's bones went up.

(Genesis Rabba, 84:6)

Although this catalogue may ultimately represent the collective wisdom
of generations that had speculated on the resemblances between Jacob
and Joseph, the textual starting point of that speculation was doubtless
the verse "These are the generations of Jacob: Joseph. . . ." And so,
strange as it may seem, this exhaustive list and the brief mention of
Joseph's resemblance to Jacob "in all things" in the "Testament of Joseph" are apparently two stages in the development of the same midrashic motif.

Joseph's "Countenance"

What then of the tradition, cited above from *Genesis Rabba*, that Joseph's
"countenance was similar to his [Jacob's]" (84:8)? This idea, that Joseph
physically resembled his father, might seem to be part and parcel of the

tradition just examined. And yet it is not. It comes from another minor trouble-spot in the same introduction to the Joseph story, just one verse away. There we read: "And Israel [= Jacob] loved Joseph more than all his other sons, *for he was a child of his old age.* . . ." (Gen. 37:3). The last phrase must have seemed problematical—for did not Jacob ultimately have a son younger than Joseph, Benjamin, born to him by the same beloved Rachel? What then could the text mean by explaining Jacob's preference for Joseph over *all* his other sons with the phrase, "for he was a child of his old age"?! Now one might seek to explain the anomaly by saying that Jacob loved Joseph *at his birth,* and perhaps for a time after that, because he then was a "child of his old age," and that even after Benjamin was born (truly *the* child of his old age), this pattern of preferential treatment continued. Still, the blunt scriptural statement that Jacob loved Joseph more than all the others *because* "he was a child of his old age" must certainly have troubled exegetes since it seemed so unconcerned with the problem of Benjamin.

And so it became necessary to understand "child of his old age" (more literally: "a son of old age to him") in some way other than the obvious one. One possibility was to read "old age" (here: *zequnim*) in the light of its standard association with, specifically, wisdom: for "old man" (*zaqen*) is practically a synonym in biblical Hebrew for "sage" or "wise man," and this association of age and wisdom had carried through directly to postbiblical times. What could appear more natural, then, than to understand the cryptic assertion that Jacob loved Joseph more than his other sons "because he was a son of old age" as meaning that he was a particularly intelligent child, a "son-of-wisdom"? And thus, for example, the Aramaic Targum of Onkelos (first–second century C.E.) renders our verse, "And Jacob loved Joseph more than all his sons, *for he was a wise son to him.*"[8] This same tradition may also be behind Philo of Alexandria's expansive version of this verse: "So his father, observing in him a *noble spirit which rose above ordinary conditions,* rendered to him high admiration and respect, while his love for this child of his later years—and nothing conduces to affection more than this—exceeded his love for his other sons." Still earlier is the statement of Artapanus (cited by Eusebius) that seems to be dependent on the same exegetical tradition: "Because he excelled all the other sons of Jacob in wisdom and understanding, his brothers plotted against him."[9]

Another possibility existed, however, and that was to distort slightly the troublesome word *zequnim* into two words, *ziv 'iqonin,* "splendor of countenance." This sort of play on words[10] is common enough in rabbinic midrash, and, if (as here) it squeezes the clear and obvious meaning of the verse into something more than a little forced, no doubt this disadvantage was to be weighed against the benefit it provided. For, according to this interpretation, readers will no longer have to struggle with Joseph's being the child of Jacob's "old age": now Jacob loves Joseph more than all his children for a somewhat different reason, because "he was a child of his own splendor-of-countenance (*ziv 'iqonin*)," that is, *his face looked like his father's.* Thus the assertion of R. Yehuda in *Genesis Rabba* that "his countenance was similar to his [Jacob's]" is based on what is simply a punning interpretation of Gen. 37:3. Indeed, it is possible that the above-cited statement in the "Testament of Joseph" that "He [God] gave me also beauty as a flower, beyond the beautiful ones of Israel; and he preserved me . . . in beauty, for I was like Jacob in all things" may even represent a conflation of these two separate motifs, the first that Joseph's beauty-of-countenance was like that of father's (generated by Gen. 37:3), the second that he was indeed like his father "in all things" (generated by Gen. 37:2).

Abraham and Isaac

It is to be noted that the same option seen here with regard to "son of old age" was exercised in another bit of traditional exegesis. For it is said about the birth of Isaac, "And Sarah bore to Abraham a son of his old age" (Gen. 21:2). This assertion is not in itself troubling, but it might seem a bit superfluous, since at various points in the events leading up to Isaac's birth, Abraham's great age had already been mentioned several times (Gen. 17:1, 15–17, 24; 18:11–12), and, what is more, just after this description of Isaac as a "son of his old age" the text goes on to state specifically that Abraham's age at the time of Isaac's birth was one hundred years old (Gen. 21:5). If so, then why the apparently unnecessary mention here that Isaac was a "son of his old age"? In the light of the foregoing, the answer was obvious: "This teaches that his face was similar to his [Abraham's]" (*Genesis Rabba* 53:6). *Midrash Tanḥuma* explains at greater length:

> At the time when Sarah was brought from being in Pharaoh's possession to being in Abimelech's possession, and then [subsequently] became pregnant with Isaac, the nations of the world said, "Can a child be born to a man one hundred years old? She must have been made pregnant by Abimelech, or by Pharaoh." And there was suspicion in Abraham's heart because of these words. What did God do? He told the angel in charge of forming the fetus: "Make his entire coun-

tenance ('*iqonin*) in the image of his father so that everyone will be able to attest that he is the son of Abraham." And whence [in the Bible can we conclude that this was the case]? From [the Bible's wording] "These are the generations of Isaac the son of Abraham, *Abraham was the father of Isaac*" (Gen. 25:19). If it says "Isaac the son of Abraham," is it not obvious that Abraham was the father of Isaac? What then can be understood from [the additional] "Abraham was the father of Isaac"? That all who saw Abraham would say, "Of a certainty it is Abraham who engendered Isaac."[11]

Thus, in the case of Isaac as well, there was some advantage in interpreting "son of old age" in some way other than the literal. Here it is not so much an exegetical difficulty as the squelching of a nasty rumor that stands behind this creative reading of the phrase "son of his old age." For, as *Midrash Tanḥuma* explains, the fact is that Isaac's birth in Genesis 21 is immediately preceded by the account of Sarah's being taken by Abimelech, who believes she is Abraham's sister (Gen. 20:2) and only releases her after he has been told the truth. Might one not conclude then that she had in fact become pregrant during the time she was with Abimelech—or, for that matter, when she was with Pharaoh, who had similarly taken her from Abraham in Genesis 12? Therefore, the text goes out of its way to assert that Abraham truly was Isaac's progenitor—and that, according to our midrash, their remarkable physical resemblance testified to this fact.

In passing, one might ask which of these two came first—that is, was the reading of "old age" (*zequnim*) as "splendor-of-countenance" (*ziv 'iqonin*) first invented in order to explain Joseph's being a "child of old age" and only later transferred to a similar problem with regard to Isaac, or vice versa? This is usually a difficult sort of question to answer definitively, and in this instance there is no conclusive case to be made for one side or another. Nevertheless, there may be some indication that our motif was first originated to account for Joseph and only later transferred to Isaac. How so? To begin with, the *exegetical* problem in the case of Joseph—what to make of a "son of old age" who has a younger brother—is far more severe than the relatively minor exegetical difficulty in the case of Isaac (that is, the fact that the Bible elsewhere tells us in great detail about Abraham's being an old man at the time of Isaac's birth and "son of his old age" would thus appear to be superfluous). As for the "problem" of potential doubt about Isaac's true progenitor, it certainly seems that the same divine intervention that had given the aged Sarah her long-sought fertility might likewise have encountered little difficulty in enabling Abraham to father a child at the age of one hundred. In any case, there were many better ways of solving this problem than using the somewhat strained "splendor-of-countenance" reading in order to argue that Isaac looked just like his father, Abraham. In fact, as we just saw, *Midrash Tanḥuma*—although it started off by evoking the argument of Isaac's *'iqonin* being similar to Abraham's—then switched (starting with the words "And whence . . .") to an entirely different tactic: it adduced the apparent superfluity in Gen. 25:19—"These are the generations of Isaac the son of Abraham, Abraham was the father of Isaac"— in order to argue that Scripture had here specifically countered the claim that Isaac might not have been Abraham's son. For this refutation it really had no need of the "similar countenances" argument. What is more, the same sort of refutation could be, and was, tied to another apparent superfluity, as explained in *Genesis Rabba:* 53:6:

> "And she [Sarah] became pregnant and bore *to Abraham* a son of his old age" [Gen. 21:2]: [the phrase "to Abraham"] teaches that she did not secretly take seed from another place.

Certainly one or both of these arguments would be sufficient to provide scriptural warrant that Abraham was indeed Isaac's progenitor without having to get into the story of Isaac's "splendor-of-countenance" resembling that of Abraham. And so it seems somewhat more probable that that story has been "imported" from the case of Joseph and made to apply to Isaac than vice versa. We might in any case refer to such parallel motifs as **midrashic doublets,** the result of transferring a motif originally created to solve a problem in verse A over to verse B, where it is sometimes (as we shall see) strangely inappropriate.

"The Bread That He Ate"

To resume: Our biblical text says at one point that Joseph was "comely of form and comely of appearance," and early exegetes made much of this fact, asserting that Joseph was indeed strikingly handsome, deriving his good looks either from his mother, Rachel, or his father, Jacob. The latter theme actually originated in a quite separate exegetical matter, the significance of "These are the generations of Jacob: Joseph . . ." and "son of his old age," but the two, as we have seen, eventually became entwined with the Bible's assertion of Joseph's physical beauty. So various exegetical strands eventually combined to stress Joseph's striking physical appearance, and, as some of the foregoing material suggests, this had become a major part of Joseph's "image" as early as the first centuries B.C.E. or C.E.

But accounting via genetics for the Bible's assertion that Joseph was handsome did not necessarily suffice to explain the full import of the statement in its context. For the mention of Joseph's beauty, it will be recalled, came as follows:

> So he [Potiphar] left all that he had in Joseph's charge, and had no concern for anything but the bread that he ate; **and Joseph was comely of form and comely of appearance.** And it came to pass after these things that his master's wife set her eyes on Joseph.
>
> (Gen. 39:6–7)

Quite apart from the question of why the emphatic "comely of form and comely of appearance" was used, there were other questions that arose concerning this phrase's placement in the sentence. To begin with, what was one to make of its connection with the preceding observation that Potiphar "left all that he had in Joseph's charge, and had no concern for anything but the bread that he ate"? The presence of this observation here must have been particularly intriguing for exegetes in view of the fact that the same basic idea had just been stated, albeit in slightly different form, only a few verses earlier. For we read in verse 4 that "Joseph found favor in his [Potiphar's] eyes, and he became his servant; and he set him over his household, and *he gave everything that he had over to Joseph's charge.*" In fact, verse 5 goes on to reiterate (twice!) that Joseph had charge of "all that he [Potiphar] had," the second time adding that this included his possessions "in the house and in the field." Why then, in verse 6, should we be told yet again that Potiphar "left all he had in Joseph's charge" — and now suddenly encounter for the first time the qualification that Joseph's responsibilities covered everything of Potiphar's except "the bread that he ate"? Indeed, this is striking not only because this qualification was not mentioned in the previous statements (whose tendency, on the contrary, was to insist that *everything* of Potiphar's was given to Joseph's care, inside the house and outside as well), but for a more obvious reason as well: After all, what sort of an exception is this, "the bread that he ate"? Is one to understand that Joseph supervises the entire household, but Potiphar still has to see to his own lunch?! And so, without much difficulty, various rabbinic sources came up with a plausible answer: "a euphemism" is the terse comment of *Genesis Rabba* 86:6. That is to say, "the bread that he ate" is actually a reference to Mrs. Potiphar herself: everything that was Potiphar's was put in Joseph's care *save for Potiphar's own wife.*

Indeed, later exegetes were to find a parallel usage in another passage, that describing Moses' sojourn in Midian. There, it will be recalled, Moses helps out the daughters of Jethro at the well. When they hurry home after the incident to recount it to their father, the latter asks about Moses, "And where is he? Invite him here and let *him eat bread*" (Exod. 2:20). This, in view of the fact that the very next verse reports that Moses indeed marries one of Jethro's daughters, was interpreted as a veiled invitation to choose a bride: "let him eat bread" really meant "let him come here and take a wife."[12]

This is delightful exegesis. But one might still ask: why is the exception of "the bread that he ate" (meaning Mrs. Potiphar) stated at all? Surely one does not expect the master of the house to entrust his own wife to the "care" of the chief servant! And the answer seems to come, dramatically, at the end of the verse: "So he [Potiphar] left all that he had in Joseph's charge, and had no concern for anything but the bread that he ate; and Joseph was comely of form and comely of appearance." Was it not the fact that Joseph was "comely of form" and so forth that led Potiphar, after having given over "everything" to Joseph's care, to think twice and then state an important exclusion: "But keep your distance from my wife!" Scripture's mention of this exception in connection with the statement about Joseph's beauty could thus not be coincidental: it must have been that, seeing Joseph's extraordinary good looks, Potiphar could only too well imagine his effect on his own spouse, and set out as best he could to place a barrier between her and this potential object of her infatuation.

Potiphar the Eunuch

Indeed, beside Joseph's physical attractions there was another element in the story that might suggest why Mrs. Potiphar would be drawn to him. For Potiphar himself is first presented in the story as "an officer of Pharaoh, the captain of the guard, an Egyptian" (Gen. 39:1). Now the word for "officer" here, *saris,* has the particular meaning in some (but not all!) biblical texts (Isa. 56:3–4; Esther 2:3, 14–15; 4:4–5) of "eunuch," and this meaning carried through into later Hebrew. The word might therefore naturally suggest to readers of the story that Mrs. Potiphar's husband was incapable of normal marital relations.[13] This understanding was not without problems, however, since Potiphar is generally identified by early exegetes with "Potiphera" in Gen. 41:45, the father of Aseneth, Joseph's future wife:[14] how could a eunuch be the father of Aseneth? But various ways around this apparent contradiction were found: Potiphar had become a eunuch only after Aseneth's birth; Potiphar was called Potiphera because he had been punished with castration (again, after Aseneth's birth); Aseneth was not Potiphar's real child; etc.[15] Nor did *saris* necessarily suggest a total absence of sexual relations between Potiphar and his wife: it may simply have indicated a form of sterility or impotence on his part.[16] Indeed, there was one good reason to suppose that Potiphar and his wife still enjoyed marital relations at the time of the incident with Joseph. For when Mrs. Potiphar later tells her husband the story of Joseph's attempted rape, Scripture somewhat modestly omits the details of her report, simply having her say "such things as these did your servant do to me" (Gen. 39:19), without specifying what the "things" were. But rabbinic exegetes, in a witty reading of this vague reference, suggested that this turn of phrase in fact indicated the *circumstances* under which it was uttered: Mrs. Potiphar waited until later that evening, when her husband was about to enjoy her favors, whereupon she volunteered: "Such things as these [that you are about to do] did your servant do to me earlier today."[17] If so, of course, Potiphar was a *saris* capable of sex, but simply sterile. No matter: for even the inability to have children with her legal husband might have further served to push Mrs. Potiphar to adultery. In that case, one can well understand why Potiphar, in appointing Joseph over his household, should have made specific mention of "the bread that he ate": for the good-looking servant would likely prove a temptation to a woman even under normal circumstances, but to Mrs. Potiphar, unable to have children with her "eunuch" husband, Joseph's allure might indeed be irresistible.

Joseph the Dandy

Apart from this, however, there was another aspect to the statement about Joseph's beauty in its wider context that was likely to disturb early exegetes: its connection, or apparent lack of connection, to what follows it, "And it came to pass *after these things* that his master's wife set her eyes on Joseph. . . ." For we saw above, in regard to the "Assembly of the Ladies," that the phrase "after these things" appeared to be out of place in the narrative: the "things" in question might seem, by their placement, to refer back to their nearest neighbor, the statement that Joseph was "comely of form," etc. (but how could something be said to happen "after" such *things* as Joseph being handsome?), whereas in truth "after these things" obviously intends to refer to the fact of Joseph's having been put in charge of Potiphar's household. We also saw that, as a result of this difficulty, *Midrash Tanḥuma* then sought to invent a wholly new referent for the "things" mentioned, interpreting them either as Mrs. Potiphar's *words* ("words" and "things" both being acceptable understandings of the Hebrew *debarim*) spoken to Joseph in an attempt to seduce him, or "things" as an allusion to certain frequent changes of clothing on her part, again in an attempt to attract the attention of her handsome slave.

But these two hardly exhaust the possibilities for explaining the apparently anomalous "things" in this verse. Another option presented in *Genesis Rabba* is to see in the word "things" (or "words") an allusion to Joseph's own unspoken thoughts (*hirhurei debarim*) after his elevation to head of Potiphar's house—thoughts of self-congratulation on his newfound status:

> "And it came to pass after these things . . .": [the "things" in question] were unspoken thoughts. Who thought them? Joseph. He said: When I was in my father's house, when my father would see something good to eat and give it to me, my brothers would be jealous of me. But now I must admit I am really well off. Said God to him: You fool! I swear, I will set loose a bear against you [i.e., put you in a difficult spot].

Another version:

> [Said Joseph]: My father was sorely tried, and so was my grandfather, but I—I am not tried at all! Said God to him: I swear, I will try you more than I did them.[18]

Both of these explanations follow essentially the same tactic as that witnessed in *Midrash Tanḥuma:* since the "things" cannot refer to the nearest referent, Joseph's being handsome, they are alleged to refer to "things" otherwise unattested, here, unspoken *words* (*debarim*) of self-congratulation. And in both cases, "after these things" is really being understood as *as a result of these things:* as a result of Joseph's arrogance and self-congratulatory mood (brought about by his being elevated over Potiphar's household), there came about the terrible trial of Mrs. Potiphar's attempted seduction, that is, "*After* these things, it happened that his master's wife set her eyes on Joseph. . . ."

It will be noticed that while all of these explanations aim at clarifying the connection-forward, that is, why "after these things" (whatever they were) it happened that Mrs. Potiphar set her eyes upon Joseph, none of them addresses the immediate connection-backward, the relationship between the "things" mentioned and the earlier statement about Joseph being handsome. But another exegetical expansion seeks to do just this:

> What is written just preceding this? "And Joseph was comely of form and comely of appearance . . ." [after which it says] "And his master's wife set her eyes on Joseph . . ." He was like a man sitting in the

marketplace bedaubing his eyes and smoothing back his hair and lifting his heel; he says, "I am quite the man!" Said [God] to him: "If you
are quite the man, behold, there is a bear prancing before you!"[19]

Joseph's beauty, according to this reading, is no accident, but the result
of various "things," his bedaubing his eyes, smoothing his hair—in
short, some very conscious primping. Indeed, we might note that behind this reading stands a very subtle shift in the meaning of the word
vayhi—not "And Joseph *was* comely of form" but "And Joseph *became*
comely of form"; this is certainly a defensible reading, and one that
attempts to resolve the contextual difficulties mentioned above. For it is
as a result of his elevation to the top of Potiphar's staff that Joseph,
slave that he is, has found a measure of comfort and well-being, and for
the first time in his captivity can look once again to his physical appearance: he primps and straightens and smoothes—and *becomes* a
handsome man.[20] Not only do these hypothetical acts follow nicely
from the preceding narrative (that is, being promoted is what allows
him to look to his appearance), but they then also can lead directly into
the statement concerning Joseph's beauty and connect well with what
follows. For Joseph actively becomes handsome by his primping and
smoothing; and *after these things*, that is, after these acts in Joseph's
personal toilette, why *then* it was that his master's wife first set her eye
upon him. (The "bear" at the end of this passage, as in the previous
instance, is a symbol of imminent danger, but no doubt the Rabbis
could not help but relish here the overlap of tenor and vehicle, which
makes of this lady a panting, oversized beast of dangerous embrace.)

In the aforementioned passage from *Genesis Rabba*, Joseph is compared to a marketplace dandy, the symbol of foolishness and vanity.[21]
Now it is interesting that, in this case as well, we have an instance of
a **midrashic doublet,** for this same picture of Joseph is presented with
regard to Joseph in an entirely different context, Gen. 37:2. This verse,
partially cited above, states in full: "Joseph, being seventeen years old,
was shepherding the flock with his brothers; he was a *boy* with the sons
of Bilhah and Zilpah, his father's wives; and Joseph used to bring back
bad reports about them to his father." The problem here is the word
"boy" (*na'ar*): is this term, used even of the three-month-old Moses
(Exod. 2:6), appropriate for a young man of seventeen? Yes, answers an
anonymous remark in *Genesis Rabba*, for although seventeen, he did
"deeds of youthful foolishness: he bedaubed his eyes and smoothed
back his hair and raised his heel."[22]

Here again we might ask: which of the doublets came first? Was
this picture of Joseph the dandy first created to solve the problem of

"boy" in Gen. 37:2 and later transferred to explain the "things" in Gen. 39:7, or vice versa? And again, while it is difficult to be categorical in this regard, it certainly seems probable that this motif was first created to explain the "things" in Gen. 39:7, and only later came to be transferred back to Gen. 37:2. How so? To begin with, the motif, as we have seen, works extraordinarily well in the first context: it explains the connection between Joseph being put in charge of Potiphar's house and his being/becoming "comely of form," etc. What is more, its three actions, "bedaubing," "smoothing," and "lifting" then become the "things" being referred to in "after these things," and thus serve to explain the connection between this vague phrase and what follows, Mrs. Potiphar "setting her eye" on Joseph. None of this appropriateness characterizes the motif in its second context, Joseph's being a seventeen-year-old "boy." For are such "acts of youthful foolishness"—adolescent vanity, really—so inappropriate to a seventeen-year-old? Moreover, how do they in any way illuminate the problem of "boy" in its context (that is, why would such "boyish" behavior be alluded to by Scripture specifically here, where it is irrelevant)? If any childish action needed to be adduced to explain the biblical use of "boy," was not a ready candidate at hand, in the rest of verse: "and Joseph used to bring back bad reports about them to his father"? Certainly being a seventeen-year-old tattletale seems more boyish—and more worthy of condemnation—than merely being a dandy. And so, on all these counts, it appears that the "dandy" motif has been imported here: indeed, one can all too easily imagine how a midrashist, well acquainted with the "dandy" motif in its original context, might—if pressed to explain the anomalous "boy" in Gen. 37:2—simply transfer the motif backward. "Ah yes," he would say, "Joseph's besetting sin of vanity must have begun even back in his days as a shepherd—that is what Scripture wished to tell us by the word 'boy.' "

"Bad Reports"

In any case, if Joseph did indeed "bedaub," "smooth," etc. when he was in Potiphar's house, then it appears that he himself was at least in part responsible for the catastrophe that overtook him there. And that would be just fine as far as rabbinic exegesis is concerned. For (as we shall see in detail below) Joseph's guilt was a theme dear to the hearts of the rabbis, who held it as an article of faith that punishment comes about as a result of sin, and that if the story of Joseph presents its hero as being thrown into jail under false pretenses, then this ordeal must

nonetheless have come about as a result of some misdeed on his part.[23]
Even if Joseph was not guilty of what Mrs. Potiphar had accused him
of, acts such as the vain primping deduced from the word "things" in
our text make of Joseph less than a totally innocent victim in rabbinic
eyes, and hence in some way deserving of the divine punishment that
comes his way.

The same is true of that earlier reversal in Joseph's life, his being
sold as a slave by his brothers and brought down to Egypt. Here the
biblical narrative had supplied a reason for the brothers' hatred for
Joseph (apart from the jealousy which his dreams and fancy cloak inspired in them), and rabbinic exegetes seized upon it to justify, as it
were, the divine punishment that subsequently overtakes him: Joseph
used to "bring back bad reports" (Gen. 37:2) about his brothers to his
father Jacob. No doubt it was the fact of these bad reports that was
responsible for Joseph's subsequent difficulties. For the Genesis narrative here uses for "bad reports" an expression that was, at least for
rabbinic exegetes, something of a loaded term: *dibbatam ra'ah*. The word
dibbah in biblical Hebrew often has the force of "slander," and the transmitting of *dibbah* is unambiguously condemned in such biblical texts as
Num. 14:36 and Prov. 10:18, 25:10. Moreover, Palestinian Judaism was
notoriously concerned with such matters as speaking behind another's
back and similar offenses,[24] so that the very fact that Joseph is represented as telling on his brothers seemed a *prima facie* condemnation of
his behavior. Thus, Joseph was guilty of something in his "bad reports."

But it remained to be determined what the substance of these "bad
reports" was. Early exegetes naturally connected them to the other
words of the same verse which relate that Joseph was, as a "boy,"
shepherding with his brothers, the children of Bilhah and Zilpah. For
here, as so often in Jewish exegesis, the juxtaposition of two separate
bits of information in the Bible implies some substantive connection
between them: Joseph's bad reports must have had something to do
with his brothers' shepherding. According to one tradition—found in
the *Testaments of the Twelve Patriarchs*—Joseph reported that his brothers
were guilty of eating the animals they were supposed to be caring for.
In the "Testament of Gad" (1:6–7), Gad reports:

> "And Joseph said to his father, the sons of Zilpah and Bilhah are
> killing the best animals and eating them against the advice of Judah
> and Reuben. He saw that I had set free a lamb from the mouth of bear,
> which I then killed, but that I had killed the lamb when I was sad-
> dened to see that it was too weak to live; and we had eaten it."

In this version of things, Joseph's "bad reports" are actually the result of a misunderstanding: he saw his brothers eating a freshly killed lamb and assumed that they had specifically slaughtered it for that purpose. Not so for rabbinic exegesis which, in the following, is interested not only in the reports *per se* but also in their relationship to later mishaps in Joseph's life:

> "And Joseph would bring back bad reports . . ." Said R. Meir: [Joseph said:] Your sons are guilty of eating limbs taken from a living animal. Said R. Judah: they [the sons of Leah] are belittling the sons of the servant-women [Bilhah and Zilpah] and calling them slaves. Said R. Simeon: they are setting their sights upon the daughters of the land. R. Judah b. Simon said: On all three counts [it is said] "A just balance and scales are the Lord's" (Prov. 16:11). God said to Joseph: You say that they are guilty of eating limbs taken from a living animal? I swear to you, at the very hour of your downfall they will slaughter [as it says], "And they slaughtered a goat [and dipped Joseph's coat in the blood]" (Gen. 37:31). You say that they were calling them slaves? Why then, [they will pretend that you are a slave, as it says:] "as if a slave was Joseph sold" (Ps. 105:17). You say that they were setting their sights on the daughters of the land? I will set loose against you a bear, [as it says] "And his master's wife set her eyes upon Joseph."
>
> (Genesis Rabba 84:7)

This is another interesting example of how one midrashic motif can affect another. The first statement, attributed here to R. Meir, to the effect that Joseph's "bad reports" had to do with his brothers' shepherding, was no doubt generated, as we just saw, by the simple fact that the biblical sentence that mentions Joseph's "bad reports" also mentions the fact that he was shepherding the flock with his brothers. (Note, however, that unlike the "Testaments" version, this one has the brothers guilty of the crime of taking a limb from a living animal: this specification is intended to put the brothers' offense into an established judicial framework, for according to rabbinic tradition, the prohibition against this cruel practice goes back to the time of Noah, and hence was well known to all concerned.)[25]

But the syntax of the sentence in which the "bad reports" are mentioned is also somewhat strange, and it gave rise to the second interpretation cited above. For the biblical text says that Joseph, "being seventeen years old, was shepherding the flock with his brothers; he was a boy with the sons of Bilhah and Zilpah, his father's wives; and Joseph used to bring back bad reports about them to their father." The sentence thus first says that Joseph was shepherding with "his brothers"—presumably all of them—but then later specifically mentions the sons of Bilhah and Zilpah. Why are they being singled out? Now certainly one possibility would be that they specifically were the subject of his bad reports—and, in fact, this was how the "Testament of Gad" understood the text, for there we saw it stated that Joseph's bad reports specifically concerned the shepherding of these brothers in particular. But another possibility existed. For the fact is that the sons of Bilhah and Zilpah were of socially inferior status—they were the sons of handmaidens rather than the legal wives of Jacob. By mentioning these sons in particular, could not Scripture be hinting that their inferior status was somehow involved in the misconduct which Joseph reported to his father? But how? Perhaps, our midrashist surmises, the sons of Bilhah and Zilpah were in fact the *victims* of some misconduct on the part of the other brothers (mentioned at the beginning of the verse), misconduct that focused, specifically, on their socially inferior status—something like, obviously, demeaning these brothers and calling them slave-children. And if that were the case, why then there would even be some poetic justice in having Joseph's punishment for transmitting *dibbah* (slander) and reporting on the mockers turn out to be that he himself would be misrepresented as a slave and sold to passing caravaneers. And so our later midrashist, R. Judah b. Simon, has God say: "You say that they were calling them slaves? Why then, [they will pretend that you are a slave, as it says:] 'Joseph was sold as if a slave' (Ps. 105:17)."[26]

Beyond these two possibilities, our text proposes a third: that Joseph's "bad reports" concerned his brothers "setting their sights upon the daughters of the land." How might this be deduced? There is nothing in the verse that mentions Joseph's "bad reports" which might indicate that these reports had to do with accusations of sexual misconduct on the part of his brothers. Instead, this third possibility seems to have been motivated by a desire to have Joseph's punishment in the Potiphar affair fit some earlier crime. Now if the punishment there was that of being (wrongly) accused of improper sexual advances, then let the crime that caused it have been Joseph's accusing his brothers of similarly improper advances, "setting their sights upon" (that is, pursuing, seeking to seduce) the "daughters of the land."[27]

Such are the factors that make up the above passage in *Genesis Rabba*. If we look carefully into its words, however, we may glimpse something of its own prehistory. To begin with, the accusation attributed to Joseph by R. Meir, "Your sons are guilty of eating limbs taken from a living animal," is probably an elaboration of the one found in the "Testament of Gad," that is, that his brothers were slaughtering animals from the flock in order to eat them. Not only is the accusation in the "Testament of Gad" chronologically earlier than that of *Genesis Rabba*, but we can also understand logically how this simpler accusation might ultimately give way to that presented by R. Meir. For the latter, as noted above, was one of the prohibitions of the Noahide laws: changing Joseph's accusation to that would not only, as stated, serve to locate it within the judicial framework assumed to exist at the time of the patriarchs, but it would also nicely tie in one bit of exegesis (Joseph's "bad reports") with another (the Noahide laws) in a manner dear to rabbinic hearts. And so R. Meir's version of the accusation is found in most, if not all,[28] rabbinic sources, including this passage in *Genesis Rabba*.

But we should note that, even in this putative earlier form, this accusation (or, for that matter, the accusation about teasing the sons of Bilhah and Zilpah) does not truly establish the correspondence between crime and punishment proposed by R. Judah b. Simon: Joseph *reports* on a misdeed, but his punishment does not result from some misdeed being *reported* about him . . . except in the third case. We saw that the accusation attributed to Joseph by R. Simeon, that his brothers were pursuing the daughters of the land, had no basis in the biblical text. But it did have the virtue of fitting the crime-and-punishment sequence perfectly: Joseph accuses his brothers, and Joseph is accused of the same thing with regard to Mrs. Potiphar. And this points up another glaring asymmetry between the different explanations put forward in our midrash. For while the first two flesh out Joseph's "bad reports" in such a way as to find some divine justice in his later being sold as a slave by his brothers, the third apparently seeks to understand those "bad reports" in such a way as to justify Joseph's being accused by Mrs. Potiphar.

It appears, therefore, that behind the answers of the three *tannaim* cited in the above passage in *Genesis Rabba* lie two quite separate exegetical goals, now more or less successfully harmonized. First we have the attempt to supply the substance of Joseph's bad reports by looking elsewhere in the very verse that mentions them, Gen. 37:2. This approach then led off in two different directions. The one fixed on the verse's mention of "shepherding" in order to deduce that Joseph's bad reports somehow concerned his brothers' conduct with the flock (itself subdivided into the earlier motif, "Slaughtered Animals from the Flock," witnessed in the "Testament of Gad," and the later motif, "Limb from a Live Animal," witnessed in the saying of R. Meir). The second possibility led to connecting Joseph's "bad reports" with the

verse's specific mention of the "sons of Bilhah and the sons of Zilpah";
here the substance of Joseph's reports would have to do with mocking
the inferior status of the children of the handmaidens. Now as noted,
both of these approaches look to the verse itself to explain the substance of Joseph's bad reports: their initial desire is to flesh out this
missing information, and originally they need have had nothing to do
with the "crime-and-punishment" theme. Not so the third possibility
advanced, that Joseph accused them of misconduct vis-à-vis the
"daughters of the land." For the whole raison d'être of this explanation,
which has no connection with the rest of the verse in question, was to
supply the substance of Joseph's bad reports *in such a way as to make
crime fit punishment* and so justify the fact that God visits upon Joseph
the disaster of his later imprisonment on false charges in Egypt.

If so, then we can imagine that these two alternate approaches to
fleshing out Joseph's "bad reports" (the one looking to the verse itself,
the other to the "crime and punishment" motif) coexisted for some time
independently. But then it was realized that, specifically, the "mocking
the sons of Bilhah and Zilpah" motif also had some potential with
regard to the "crime and punishment" sequence: they were mocked (as
the sons of slaves, perhaps even as "slaves" themselves), and so Joseph
was sold as a slave.[29] The fit was not perfect, but it was at least plausible: "You say that they were calling them slaves? Why then, [they will
pretend that you are a slave, as it says:] 'as if a slave was Joseph sold.' "
And in the same spirit a connection was pursued even in the first case,
the "shepherding" motif. And it was found, albeit in somewhat
strained fashion: Joseph's accusation of slaughtering (or, alternately,
taking a "limb from a live animal") was paired with the later mention
of a slaughtered goat's blood. But in truth, neither of these two motifs
duplicates the straightforward crime-and-punishment relationship of
the model which they were supposed to imitate, nor do these two even
aim at justifying the same "punishment" as the third (that is, Joseph
being sold into slavery vs. Joseph being accused by Mrs. Potiphar).

"The Girls Climbed the Wall"

Thus, if Joseph was guilty of transmitting "bad reports" in his youth,
and this in turn led to the catastrophe of his being sold as a slave, then
perhaps it was similarly guilty conduct—his self-congratulatory "I'm
doing fine" after being elevated over Potiphar's house, or (and this is
the point) his dandy-like primping there that caused him to *become*
"comely of form and comely of appearance"—that ultimately brought

about the episode with Potiphar's wife. And so we have seen that the theme of Joseph's beauty, originally generated by the passing remark in Gen. 39:6 ("comely of form," etc.), came not only to be elaborated there (as pointing to Joseph's resemblance to Rachel; as stirring up Potiphar's forebodings about the "bread that he ate"; as hinting that Joseph was in fact something of a dandy), but to find other foci elsewhere in the narrative: the blunt juxtaposition "These are the generations of Jacob: Joseph . . ." (Gen. 37:2), the phrase "son of his old age" (Gen. 37:3), and the reference to Joseph's "boyish" behavior (Gen. 37:2) all came to be explained with reference to the theme of Joseph's beauty.

And yet one more connection with this theme was to be found in the book of Genesis. For quite apart from the actual narrative of Joseph's life in Genesis is a short statement about him uttered by Jacob in Gen. 49:22, the "blessing" Jacob grants him just before his death. The entire passage, in which Jacob blesses each of his sons in turn, is full of textual and other difficulties, but perhaps none is so challenging as the blessing of Joseph: modern exegetes are no less stymied than ancients doubtless were. The opening sentence, which is what concerns us here, reads in the traditional Hebrew text:

ben porat yosef, ben porat 'alei 'ayin, banot ṣa'adah 'alei shur

Most modern commentaries understand this as something like: "Joseph is a fruitful bough, a fruitful bough by a spring; his branches run over the wall" (Revised Standard Version). This particular approach to the words of this verse—essentially that adopted a thousand years earlier by R. Se'adya Ga'on in his Arabic translation of the Bible, itself based here on still earlier exegesis[30]—connects the difficult phrase *ben porat* with the Hebrew root *parah*, "be fruitful" hence, "fruitful bough." This is fine, if a bit too certain-sounding in English for an essentially incomprehensible Hebrew phrase. As for "his branches run over the wall," the branches here are apparently engendered, as it were, by the "fruitful bough" that precedes them: the Hebrew word *banot* (if this indeed is how the word is to be read) means simply "daughters" or "girls."

There are, however, other possibilities. The biblical scholar A. B. Ehrlich argued cogently that the apparent subject and verb in this sentence are really a single noun construct, which he compared to Arabic *banat ṣa'dat*, "wild asses," which occurs only in the plural.[31] E. A. Speiser, in his *Anchor Bible* commentary on Genesis, then suggested that *ben porat* be derived from *pere'* "wild donkey" (the same word is used of Ishmael in Gen. 16:12). Speiser thus translated the whole verse: "Joseph is a wild colt, a wild colt by a spring, wild asses on a hillside."[32] This translation has not won unanimous approval, however, and modifications continue to be put forward.[33]

Among the ancient versions, the Old Greek ("Septuagint") translation seems to have understood the phrase *ben porat* as "son of fruitfulness," hence its translation, "a son increased" (υἱὸς ηὐξημένος). "Increase" (αὐξάνω) is how the Old Greek Bible consistently renders the verb *parah*—yet one cannot but admire here how the translation connects well with another Hebrew root, that of the name of Joseph, that is, "to increase" (*yasaf*), perhaps suggesting in Greek that the whole blessing is an etymologizing play on Joseph's name, just like the etymologizing blessings of Judah, Dan, and Gad in the same chapter. In any case, the entire sentence in the Old Greek comes out: "Joseph is a son increased, my beloved son increased, my youngest son, turn to me." The Greek rendering of this last phrase (πρός με ἀνάστρεψον) construes roughly the same Hebrew consonants in radically different fashion, not *banot ṣaʿadah ʿalei shur* but *beni ṣeʿiri ʿelai sur*, a reading paralleled in the Samaritan Pentateuch.

The Aramaic biblical translation of Onkelos, as well as the other *targums* (Aramaic translations), follows the "fruitful bough" approach. Some early exegetes, anxious to see in this blessing an epitome of Joseph's personal fortunes, sought to connect it to the all-important fact that Joseph, unique among his brothers, inherits a double portion, that is, his sons Ephraim and Manasseh are numbered as separate tribes among the twelve (Gen. 48:5). Allusion to this can be seen in the plurality of the "daughters" in the third clause: these daughter-vines are Ephraim and Manasseh, who "climb a wall" in gaining equal status with their uncles. (Alternately, the repetition of the phrase *ben porat* can be understood as emphasizing the vine's fruitfulness in that *two* offspring inherit.)

There is, however, yet another reading of the third clause of this blessing, and it is the one relevant to our theme. It takes *banot* simply as "girls," "women," and reads this third clause entirely separately from the first two: "Girls walk [or: "climb"][34] upon a wall." What for? Why, to behold Joseph's beauty! In fact, the phrase translated "upon a wall" can without difficulty also be read as "in order to look,"[35] that is, the girls climbed up in order to look at Joseph, or in order that Joseph look at them. A double translation—incorporating both "upon the wall" and "in order to look" readings simultaneously—is embodied in the translation of Targum Pseudo-Jonathan:

> And when [the Egyptian sages] praised you [Joseph], the daughters of the rulers [of Egypt] would walk along the walls and cast down in

front of you bracelets and golden ornaments so that you might look at them.

Jerome was apparently aware of this same tradition, and adopted it in his Latin translation of the Bible, the Vulgate: "A growing son, Joseph, a growing son and handsome of mien; *the girls ran about upon the wall.*" In his *Hebraicae Quaestiones in Genesin* (composed ca. 389–92 C.E.), Jerome explained:

> And the sense of this section is: O Joseph, you who are thus called because the Lord added you to me, or because you are to be the greatest among your brothers (as in fact the tribe of Ephraim was, as we read in the books of Reigns and Chronicles), O Joseph, I say, you who are so handsome that the whole throng of Egyptian girls looked down from the walls and towers and windows . . .[36]

The same tradition is likewise witnessed in *Pirqei R. Eliʿezer,* an eighth century (?) Hebrew retelling of parts of the Bible:

> Moreover, Joseph rode in a chariot and crossed the whole territory of Egypt, and the Egyptian girls would climb up on the wall and cast down upon him golden rings that he might perchance look upon their beauty.[37]

The version presented in Targum Neophyti is somewhat different: here the daughters are said to look down from the "windows"[38] and cast various sorts of jewelry in front of Joseph in the hope that he might set his eye upon one of them. In vain!

The motif of the golden jewelry being cast down deserves a word of comment. Strange as it may seem, this too is generated by the words of Gen. 49:22. The word ṣaʿadah ("walked" or "climbed") is, if indeed a verbal form, a feminine singular, hence apparently inappropriate for a plural subject. Obviously this bothered exegetes of the girls-climbing-up school, and one solution, apparently, was to connect it to another word, a rare word that appears only twice in the Hebrew Bible: 'eṣʿadah is a kind of bracelet or ornament, worn on the leg or arm (Num. 31:50; 2 Sam. 1:10). If, as it seemed to some exegetes, the word ṣaʿadah *in our verse might be a stand-in for 'eṣʿadah,* then the text might actually be telling something more—albeit rather cryptically—about the girls along the wall: that they cast their own jewelry, their 'eṣʿadot, down in front of Joseph. It is to be noted that Pseudo-Jonathan and Neophyti here use the Aramaic word *shirin* for the jewelry being cast down—the same word they use to translate 'eṣʿadah in Num. 31:50.[39] This reading of the verse thus turns it into an extremely telegraphic, condensed, message: *banot*—the girls climbed up; ṣaʿadah—they threw down their 'eṣ'adot; and why? 'alei shur—so that he might look at them.

In fact this tradition about Joseph and the Egyptian women is apparently still older than any of the sources cited above. Its first attestation is in a romance written about Joseph in Greek (presumably by a Greek-speaking Jew) sometime in the early first century c.e., *Joseph and Aseneth*. There the motif is garbled somewhat, but nevertheless recognizable. Joseph, young ruler of Egypt, comes to the house of Potiphera (called here "Pentephres"), father of his future bride; as he arrives he sees the young Aseneth looking down at him from the upstairs window:

> Joseph said to Pentephres, "Who is this woman who is standing on the upper floor by the window? Let her leave this house," because Joseph was afraid, saying "This one must not molest me too." For all the wives and daughters of the noblemen and satraps of the whole land of Egypt used to molest him [wanting] to sleep with him, and all the wives and daughters of the Egyptians, when they saw Joseph, suffered badly because of his beauty. But Joseph despised them; and the messengers whom they sent to him with gold and silver and valuable presents Joseph sent back with threats and insults, because Joseph said, "I will not sin before the Lord God of my father Israel."[40]

Here we have both elements of the tradition seen, (1) the "women" (here: Aseneth) "looking down" —not from a wall, which was undoubtedly the earliest form of the tradition (generated by 'alei shur) but from an "upper story" ($\dot{v}\pi\epsilon\rho\hat{\omega}ov$) "by the window"—cf. Targum Neophyti's and *Genesis Rabba*'s "windows"; and (2) the jewelry cast down at Joseph, here "gold and silver and valuable presents" pressed upon him.

And so, thanks to this difficult verse in Genesis, Joseph's reputation for physical beauty received one more great boost: for did not the solemn blessing of Joseph's own father contain an allusion to the fact that the daughters of the Egyptian aristocracy were so utterly captivated by him that they even tossed their precious jewels and ornaments at his feet as he passed by, hoping against hope that he might set his eye upon them? Surely this was the capstone of the theme of Joseph's beauty, the proof that the passing remark in Gen. 39:6 indeed corresponded to Joseph's most striking characteristic.

At the risk of stating the obvious, we now may turn to see the relationship of all this early exegetical material to the theme of the "Assembly of Ladies" seen in the previous chapter. For there, as we have seen, Joseph's beauty was the whole point of the story, and it is most unlikely that a midrashist would have ever fixed on the innocuous word "See!" in Gen. 39:14 to concoct the full story of the "Assembly" were it not for the existence of a considerable body of earlier exegesis that turned on the fact of Joseph's extraordinary physical appearance. But moreover, we can see a direct carryover from the last motif investigated, "The Girls Climbed the Wall," and that of the "Assembly." For the former presents us with a picture of the Egyptian ladies standing, as it were, awestruck by Joseph's beauty: they take their own precious jewelry and throw it recklessly at his feet. It is not hard to see how this picture of awestruck ladies could create another, that of the ladies of Potiphar's house staring in amazement at the servant who has brought them their food. There can thus be little doubt that the "Assembly" midrash was composed, consciously or otherwise, in contemplation of this earlier motif.

And so we have one more example, of a somewhat subtler kind, of how midrashic motifs can migrate, and how details originally created to account for a peculiarity in one verse can come ultimately to influence the understanding of other verses or to aid in the creation of wholly new motifs. But having thus investigated the role of Joseph's beauty in the events of Potiphar's house, we are left finally to ask what in fact happened on that fateful day, and specifically to focus on a question that intrigued rabbinic exegetes, the extent of Joseph's cooperation in Mrs. Potiphar's plans.

Notes

1. The precise focus of Josephus' remark here is Gen. 37:3, on which see below.
2. That Jacob was born circumcised is deduced from the use of the word *tam* ("simple") in Gen. 25:27 (though the tradition is sometimes also connected to Gen. 25:23, interpreted as "the two nations will already be distinct as they come out of your womb"); see *Genesis Rabba* 63:7 and 9. That Joseph was born circumcised was apparently deduced from our verse, Gen. 37:2: the apposition "These are the generations of Jacob: Joseph" was interpreted to mean that Joseph resembled Jacob specifically in the matter of circumcision (see *Abot deR. Natan* version A, chapter 2).
3. In the case of Rebecca, the allusion is apparently to the difficulties of pregnancy described in Gen. 25:22, ". . . the children struggled together within her," and not to the birth itself. Rachel's death in childbirth is recounted in Gen. 35:16–19.
4. That Jacob was "stolen" (= robbed) twice is deduced from the repetition of "stolen" in Gen. 31:39; for Joseph it is the repetition of "stolen" in the emphatic *gunnob gunnabti* in Gen. 40:15, interpreted as referring to two separate thefts.
5. Jacob's "ten blessings" are arrived at by enumerating the separate items in Gen. 27:28–29 (when Isaac blesses him); Joseph's "ten blessings" come in

Deut. 33:13–16. On the version of this midrash that the two were blessed with "wealth" (i.e., 'osher instead of 'eser) see Theodor-Albeck, *Genesis Rabba*, p. 1009 n.

6. That Jacob was accompanied by angels was apparently first deduced from the fact that the angels on the ladder in his dream (Gen. 28:12) are said to be "ascending and descending"; Joseph's accompanying angels are understood from the three occurrences of the word "man" in Gen. 37:15–17; see *Genesis Rabba* 84:14, and below, chapter 4.

7. Jacob's father-in-law, Laban, says "I have learned by divination that the Lord has blessed me because of you" (Gen. 30:27), and about Potiphar (identified with Potiphera, Joseph's father-in-law) the text says, "And the Lord blessed the Egyptian's house because of Joseph" (Gen. 39:5).

8. Along the same lines: The text of Genesis recounts that, when he was made ruler over the land of Egypt, Joseph went about in a lordly chariot "and they cried out before him *'Abrekh!*" (Gen 41:43). This Egyptian word, unintelligible in later times, was understood by being broken down into two constituents, Heb. '*ab*, "father," and *rakh*, "tender": " 'And they cried out before him *'Abrekh': a father in wisdom [though but] tender in years" (*Genesis Rabba* 90:3).

9. Eusebius, *Preparatio Evangelica*, 9.23.1–4; see C. R. Holladay, *Fragments from Hellenistic Jewish Authors*, vol. 1 (Chico, CA: Scholars Press, 1983), 204–207.

10. Called in Hebrew *noṭarikon* (from the Hellenized Latin for "shorthand [writing]"), this interpretive device analyzes a word or phrase as if it were actually a bit of shorthand notation or abbreviation; for another instance, see note 8.

11. *Midrash Tanḥuma*, p. 34b.

12. See *Exodus Rabba* 1:32, *Midrash Tanḥuma, Shemot* 11; *Tanḥuma*, ed. S. Buber (Vilna 1899) *Shemot* 11.

13. It is to be noted that while the Septuagint translation understands *saris* as "eunuch," Targum Onkelos renders the phrase simply as "officer of Pharaoh." It seems likely that this was in response to the Potiphar-Potiphera problem (see next two notes).

14. Both are called Petephres in the Septuagint (and this is followed by Josephus in his *Jewish Antiquities*); the identity of Potiphar and Potiphera is assumed in *Jubilees* 40:10 and the "Testament of Joseph" 18:3. Note also the motif "Potiphar is Potiphera" in *Genesis Rabba* 86:3 (and notes in Theodor-Albeck edition, vol. 2, 1054).

15. That Potiphar had been castrated was suggested by his apparent change of name to Potiphera: the last element is reminiscent of the verbal root *para'* whose meanings include "destroy" or "disarrange," hence castrate. Rabbinic exegetes suggested that Potiphar had bought Joseph for immoral purposes and was castrated by God [or the angel Gabriel] as a result: see *Genesis Rabba* 86:3 and parallels. For the tradition of Aseneth as the daughter of Dinah and Shechem adopted by Potiphar, see V. Aptowitzer, "Asenath, the Wife of Joseph: A Haggadic Literary-Historical Study," *Hebrew Union College Annual* 1 (1924):239–306.

16. A *saris* need not necessarily be incapable of marital relations, and note the distinction between the *seris ḥammah* and the *seris 'adam* in M. *Yebamot* 8:4. Cf. *Hadar Zeqenim* (Livorno, 1840) 18b. Philo seems to understand the term

"eunuch" (in keeping with its relatively broad range in Greek) as meaning someone stricken with infertility or, possibly, impotence: "The purchaser [of Joseph] is said to be a eunuch; rightly so, for the multitude which purchases the statesman is in very truth a eunuch, possessing to all appearances the organs of generation but deprived of the power of using them, just as those who suffer from cataract have eyes but lack the active use of them and cannot see" ("De Josepho," 58). See similarly the commentary of Hizquni *ad loc.* (*Commentary on the Torah*, p. 154).

17. "Said R. Abbahu: [these words were said] at the time of sexual intercourse" (*Genesis Rabba* 87:19; cf. Theodor-Albeck, p. 1074 notes).

18. Ibid., 87:4. These motifs reflect a smugness on Joseph's part, and are thus related to a more general problem that bothered early exegetes, namely: why did not Joseph make some effort to contact his father once he was safely in Egypt and even put in charge of Potiphar's household? Indeed, the connection is made explicit in the combination of these motifs with "Bedaubed his Eyes," etc. that appears in *Midrash Tanḥuma, Vayyesheb* 8: "When Joseph found himself thus [promoted to supervisor of Potiphar's house], he began to eat and drink and curl [sic] his hair and said: 'Blessed is the Lord who has caused me to forget my father's house [that is, the pain of separation].' Said God to him: 'Your father is grieving for you in sack-cloth and ashes and you are eating and drinking and curling your hair?! Now your mistress will pair herself with you and will make your life miserable.' " This version of Joseph's smugness—and perhaps the others as well—appears in fact to have a biblical basis. For although chronologically out of sequence, Joseph's words in *Midrash Tanḥuma* strangely echo the words of the biblical Joseph in Gen. 41:51, when he names his firstborn son Manasseh "For God *has made me forget* all my hardship and *all my father's house.*" Perhaps the whole theme of Joseph's failure to contact his father first developed in contemplation of this verse, and was then transferred by midrashists to before the incident with Potiphar's wife, so that that episode and Joseph's subsequent imprisonment might seem to come as punishment for his thoughtlessness. In any event, if Joseph is found blameworthy by rabbinic sources for his failure to contact his father, an older and more apologetic tradition also exists. The third-century Hellenistic writer Demetrius reasons: "But though Joseph had good fortune for nine years, he did not send for his father because he was a shepherd as were his brothers too, and Egyptians consider it a disgrace to be a shepherd." (Cited in Eusebius, *Preparatio Evangelica,* 9.21.13; see Holladay, *Fragments from Hellenistic Jewish Authors,* 68–71.)

19. *Genesis Rabba*, 87:3.

20. The same understanding of *vayhi* may underly the passage in the "Testament of Joseph" 3:4, where Joseph's fasting and penitence has the effect of increasing his beauty, "for they that fast for God's sake receive beauty of face." Here too, Joseph *becomes* handsome in Potiphar's house.

21. Cf. *Genesis Rabba* on Gen. 4:7, Theodor and Albeck notes, p. 212.

22. *Genesis Rabba*, 84:7.

23. This contrasts somewhat with the "wisdom" message of the story as described above in chapter 1: for the "wisdom" ideology holds simply that pain and suffering in this world are simply part of an overall divine plan,

and are to be endured by the "wise" one confident in God's ultimate control of events and the justice of his ways.

24. See below, chapter 8.

25. See on this Theodor and Albeck, *Genesis Rabba* vol. 2, 1009 and notes. Note however that *Midrash Leqaḥ Ṭob* says simply: "[Joseph] told him that the children of Bilhah and Zilpah were slaughtering the flock" (Vilna: Romm Brothers, 1890, 94a = p.187). Cf. V. Aptowitzer, "Asenath, the Wife of Joseph" *Hebrew Union College Annual* 1 (1924):239–306.

26. This verse from Psalm 105 works better in context than anything in the Joseph story itself, since its wording seems succinctly to highlight the fact that Joseph was *not* a slave but only misrepresented as such by his brothers.

27. This in keeping with the well-known rabbinic principle that "By the measure that a man measures out with, so is it measured out to him" (see Mishnah *Soṭa* 1:7–9), on which see further below, chapter 5.

28. See above, note 25.

29. Logically, the mocking ought only to have to do with their inferior status, for they were by no account considered "slaves" themselves. And indeed, this element need only be introduced when the "crime and punishment" sequence was extended to fit this motif as well. This is well mirrored in the words of our passage: "Said R. Judah: they [the sons of Leah] are belittling the sons of the servant-women [Bilhah and Zilpah] and calling them slaves." "Belittling the sons of the servant-women" would have been quite sufficient as a fleshing-out of Joseph's "bad reports," and perhaps that was all there was to it, at least initially. But "and calling them slaves" became necessary in order to tie into the crime-and-punishment sequence.

30. See below.

31. A. B. Ehrlich, *Randglossen zur hebräischen Bibel,* vol. 1 (Genesis-Exodus) (Leipzig, 1908), 250.

32. E. A. Speiser, *Genesis* (*The Anchor Bible*) (Garden City, NY: Doubleday, 1964), 367–68.

33. See S. Gevirtz, "Of Patriarchs and Puns," *Hebrew Union College Annual* 46 (1975):33–54, for a review of Speiser and others; note also B. Vawter, "The Canaanite Background of Gen. 49" in *Catholic Bible Quarterly* 17 (1955):8–9; J. Coppens, "La Bénédiction de Jacob" in *Vetus Testamentum Supplements* 4 (1957):97–115; J. A. Emerton, "Some Difficult Words in Gen. 49," in P. R. Ackroyd, *Words and Meanings* (Cambridge: Cambridge University Press, 1968), 91–93; and many more.

34. That this can be the sense of the D-form of the verb in Aramaic is suggested by M. Jastrow, *A Dictionary of the Targumim* (New York: Jastrow, 1967), *ad loc.;* cf. the Arabic cognate *ṣaʿida* "rise, climb."

35. Taking *shur* in the sense of "see," as in, e.g., Num. 24:17. Cf. Rashi *ad loc.* Note that this reading sometimes reflects back on the previous part of the verse, *ben porat yosef, ben porat ʿalei ʿayin.* For the phrase *ʿalei ʿayin* was now taken not (or not only) as "upon a spring," as in the fruitful vine reading, but was read in keeping with the more common meaning of *ʿayin,* "eye." Thus Targum Neophyti, Pseudo-Jonathan, and *Pirqei R. Eliʿezer* all take the phrase as if it said *ʿoleh ʿayin* "overcoming the eye," that is, desire (cf. *Genesis Rabba* 97:22, "that the evil eye had no power over him"). Jerome (see

below) translates *'alei 'ayin* as *decorus aspectu* ("handsome in mien"), thus apparently also taking *'ayin* as "eye."

36. *S. Hieronymi Presbyteri Opera* (*Corpus Christianorum series latina*, vol. 72) (Turnholt: Brepols Ed., 1949), 56.

37. *Pirqei R. Eli'ezer* chapter 39 (p. 93a in the frequently reprinted Warsaw edition of 1852).

38. The version in *Targum Neophyti* thus seems to embrace only the second sense of *'alei shur*, "in order [that they] look," the "wall" (*shur*) being absent here. The same is true of *Genesis Rabba* 98 [= 99]:18 (Theodor and Albeck, 1268) and *Joseph and Aseneth* (see note 40 below). Cf. M. Sokoloff, *Geniza Fragments of Bereshit Rabba* (Jerusalem: Israel Academy of Sciences, 1982), 182, 191. Note also Jerome's apparent harmonization (cited above), whereby the "Egyptian girls looked down from the walls and towers and windows."

39. See the commentary of David Luria (1798–1855) to *Pirqei R. Eli'ezer* (above, n. 22), 93a; cf. Theodor and Albeck, *Genesis Rabba* notes, 1268–69.

40. "Joseph and Aseneth," trans. by C. Burchard, in J. Charlesworth, *The Old Testament Pseudepigrapha* (Garden City, NY: Doubleday, 1985), 2:210.

4.

Joseph's Change of Heart

Was Joseph entirely innocent in the events of that fateful day in Potiphar's house? We have already seen above (chapter 1) that the tendency of the earliest exegetes was to celebrate Joseph's virtue to almost superhuman proportions: he is "Joseph the Righteous" or "the Virtuous," and, according to 4 *Maccabees* or *Jubilees* or *Wisdom of Solomon*, his resistance to the temptation and wiles of Mrs. Potiphar was unambiguous and altogether exemplary. As we heard Joseph recollect in the *Testaments of the Twelve Patriarchs*,

> not even in my mind did I yield to her, for God loves more the one who is faithful in self-control in a dark cistern than the one who in royal chambers feasts on delicacies with excess. . . . For when I had been with her in her house, she would bare her arms and thighs so that I might lie with her. For she was wholly beautiful and splendidly decked out to entice me, but the Lord protected me from her manipulations.[1]

Joseph the Guilty

Yet we have likewise noted a certain tendency, specifically in our rabbinic sources, to fault Joseph on occasion. It was his tale-bearing that was responsible for the divine punishment that overtook him when he was sold as a slave down to Egypt, and it was his vanity, his dandy-like primping in Potiphar's house, that brought on the attentions of Mrs. Potiphar and, ultimately, her wrongful accusation and his imprisonment. It therefore ought not to be terribly surprising to find that, with regard to the events of that day in particular, Joseph was likewise found by rabbinic sources to be something other than entirely innocent. The following passage, from the Babylonian Talmud (*Soṭah* 36b), is a relatively late summary of some of the elements in this exegetical line. It takes as its point of departure Gen. 39:11, "And it came to pass on a certain day that he [Joseph] went to the house to do his work":

> R. Yoḥanan said: this [verse] teaches that the two of them [Joseph and Potiphar's wife] had planned to sin together. "He entered his house to *do his work*": Rab and Samuel [had disagreed on this phrase]: one said

it really means to do his work, the other said it [is a euphemism that] means "to satisfy his desires." He entered; [and then it says] "And not one of the members of the household was present in the house." Is it really possible that no one else was present in the large house of this wicked man [Potiphar]? It was taught in the School of R. Ishma'el: that particular day was their festival, and they had all gone to their idolatrous rites, but she told them that she was sick. She had said [to herself] that there was no day in which she might indulge herself with Joseph like this day! [The biblical text continues:] "And she seized him by his garment . . ." At that moment the image of his father entered and appeared to him in the window. He said to him: Joseph, your brothers are destined to have their names written on the priestly breastplate, and yours is amongst theirs. Do you want it to be erased, and yourself to be called a shepherd of prostitutes, as it says [Prov. 29:3] "A shepherd of prostitutes loses [his] wealth"? At once "his bow remained in strength" [i.e., he overcame his desires].

This passage presents us with a somewhat different view of Joseph on that fateful day—or, rather, "views," since there are two quite distinct ones here. The first takes the text of Genesis 39 at, as it were, face value: Joseph is in all respects innocent and blameless. But the second, represented in our passage by R. Yohanan and one half of the Rab-Samuel dispute, sees Joseph as something of a willing participant, a man who has given in to temptation. Now one support for this approach is adduced from the biblical narrative itself; it is the innocent-looking phrase in "Joseph went to the house *to do his work*"—which, this second school of thought holds, is merely a euphemism for "to satisfy his desires."

That such a reading had enjoyed some popularity may be confirmed by a look at the Aramaic translation of Onkelos. For while Onkelos usually translates narrative texts rather closely, generally deviating only for doctrinal reasons, here he has veered sharply from the Hebrew original: instead of "to do his work," he has "to check his account books." One cannot but feel that this translator has gone out of his way to scotch what was already a very popular, but to his mind calumnious, reading of the phrase: instead of rendering it, and its vagaries, literally, he has substituted a more specific act that is safely beyond all possibility of double-entendre.

The second argument adduced against Joseph is one that we saw mentioned in passing above, in the "Assembly of Ladies." For the biblical text recounts that on this particular day there was no one in the house when Joseph came to "do his work." With, it seems, laudable historical imagination, the tradition (attributed here to the "school of R.

Ishma'el") finds this detail strange: in the household of such an important fellow as Potiphar, a high official in the court of Pharaoh, is it conceivable that no one from among the whole household staff of cooks, butlers, slaves, and retainers—no one was at home? The same tradition's answer is still more satisfactory. It was "their festival"—or, in another version, the "festival of the Nile"[2]—on that day, and everyone had departed to participate in the festivities. All except for Mrs. Potiphar: she feigns illness. She sees in the occurrence of this festival a one-time opportunity to have Joseph all to herself (since he, either because of his Hebrew birth or because of his crucial role in the running of the household, will in any case be at his job as usual); she can thus make one last all-out attempt upon his chastity. In fact her words, as supplied by the Babylonian Talmud, take advantage of a peculiarity in the Bible's wording here. For the verse in question (Gen. 39:11) begins *vayhi kehayyom hazzeh*—"And so it was that on a certain day [Joseph went to the house to do his work . . .]." While this is the sense of the opening phrase, it is to be noted that the somewhat anomalous particle *ke-* in *kehayyom hazzeh* must have been troubling to some postbiblical readers—as if the text literally meant something like "And so it was *like this day* that Joseph went to the house." Our exegete, in an elegant and precise handling of this anomaly, encloses it in mental quotation marks, and sees it as the end of sentence uttered, or thought, by Potiphar's wife: "I'll never have another opportunity *like this day*." The somewhat strange wording of the biblical text is thus being made out to be an allusion to this thought of hers, as if it were really saying "And so it was [that Mrs. Potiphar said] '. . . like this day,' and Joseph entered the house *to do his work*."[3]

In view of all this, Joseph's behavior takes on a somewhat different coloring: perhaps he knew perfectly well what he was doing when he approached the deserted house on Nile Day; perhaps he, no less than Mrs. Potiphar, was intent on "doing his work" there. It was not, according to our passage from the Babylonian Talmud, until after Mrs. Potiphar "seized his garment" that Joseph began to have second thoughts, thoughts that ultimately caused him to change his mind and flee. In that case, one must regard Joseph as, at least initially, a willing participant.

Joseph's Garment

Some exegetes even went beyond what is suggested here in searching for signs of Joseph's complicity. For there is the matter of the garment itself that the fleeing Joseph leaves in her hand. To modern readers, the word "garment" might include all manner of expendables, from neckties to pocket handkerchiefs to vests or jackets, and Joseph's abandoning his garment therefore has less significance for us than it should. To an ancient exegete—not to speak of a biblical Israelite—the range of possibilities was narrower, and the resultant shame that would have been Joseph's, as well as the financial loss (unless the garment could be recovered), far greater. The Hebrew word here for "garment," *beged* (like the Aramaic *lebush*, which translates it in the targums), is a general term, capable of describing both an outer garment with closed seams that covered the whole body, or the tunic sometimes worn underneath it (though normally the latter was called *ḥaluq*). It is clear that Joseph's becoming separated from his whole *beged* could not but arouse doubts in the minds of some exegetes: how could it have happened? Surely it was not simply that, in her passion, Mrs. Potiphar ripped the whole thing off in one deft sweep! And here the biblical text leaves a slight opportunity for Joseph's accusers. For the text reads: "And she seized him by his garment, saying 'Lie with me'; and he left the garment in her hand, and fled and went outside." These actions are sequential, but do not necessarily follow each other immediately. Hence, for example, the nuanced reading found in *Midrash Tanḥuma:*

> R. Yehuda said: That day was the day of sacrificing to the Nile, and they all went out, and she alone was left, and he along with her, in the house. And she seized him by his garment, *and he went into bed with her.*[4]

Joseph willingly sheds his clothes. It is only afterwards—after (as we have seen in our passage from the Babylonian Talmud) Joseph has the vision of his father's "image" come to expostulate him—that he flees in haste, leaving (then!) his garment "in her hand." (According to another tradition, cited in *Genesis Rabba* in the name of R. Abbahu, so enamored of Joseph was the lady that she kept his garments—now in the plural, as they likewise appear in Targum Neophyti—and hugged and kissed them; this is an expansion of Gen. 39:16, "And she kept the garment with her.")

Moreover, there is a grammatical ambiguity connected with this "garment" that might further strengthen the case against Joseph. For the biblical text says that Mrs. Potiphar "seized him *bebigdo.*" While this Hebrew word does mean "by his garment," it so happens that this same form can also mean: "in his betrayal." In fact, this is the very form of the word used in Exod. 21:8 to describe a man's conduct in selling a female slave or concubine who does not please him: he does so *be-*

bigdo bah, "in his dealing faithlessly with her." And so a careful exegete might conclude that by using this term *beged* (rather than, say, *simlah,* "clothing," used in connection with Joseph in Gen. 41:14), Scripture wished further to imply something about Joseph's own attitude at this crucial moment with Mrs. Potiphar. She seized him not only "by his garment" but "in his faithlessness," that is, Joseph was at that moment already prepared to betray his earlier moral stance and the profession of loyalty to his master Potiphar that he had made in Gen. 39:8–9.[5]

Taken together, these considerations seem finally to clinch the case against Joseph: not only is it true that he had something to do with stirring up Mrs. Potiphar's interest in the first place—primping and *becoming* "comely of form," etc. in Potiphar's house—but on the day in question he went to the house knowing full well what he was doing, he in fact went there "to do his work," and to that end voluntarily shed his garment, betraying, by this willing act, his master, his religious instruction, and his previous steadfastness. It was only afterwards that he changed his mind and fled.

If this picture of Joseph shows us less than the paragon of virtue seen in the earlier texts cited, it should not be adjudged inferior for all that. For, Joseph the Guilty not only helps out with the rabbinic problem, seen above, of justifying the ordeal of his lengthy imprisonment (that is, although Joseph was not, in terms of strict justice, guilty of adultery, his initial willingness and intention to sin may have been sufficient to warrant, within the divine plan, his suffering the punishment of imprisonment, all the more so if it enables him to emerge, at the end of his sufferings, as the thoroughly virtuous Joseph we know in the rest of the story). But apart from this, presenting Joseph as sorely tempted by Mrs. Potiphar, indeed, bringing him to the brink of submission, offered an advantage to exegetes intent on using the Joseph story (as so many biblical narratives were used) as a model of ethical conduct. For to hold that Joseph was not tempted for a minute by Mrs. Potiphar is, as it were, to put him outside of the range of normal human emotion. But to say, on the contrary, that Joseph was indeed tempted, and that events indeed brought him to the very point of complying—this is to present a Joseph of flesh and blood with whom others can identify, and whose example of sudden repentance others might seek to emulate.

Jacob's Teachings

It remains for us to inquire, however, into what it was that caused Joseph to change his mind in the heat of passion. And here, interestingly, one finds not one, but two broad lines of approach adopted by early exegetes. The first, and what might rightly be called the "rationalistic" approach, is to have Joseph suddenly remember the divine prohibition against adultery. That Joseph knew of such a prohibition seems to be clearly stated in the biblical text itself, for there, when Mrs. Potiphar first "sets her eye" on Joseph and makes her proposal of adultery, Joseph invokes this prohibition in his refusal:

> But he refused and he said to his master's wife: "Lo, having me my master has no concern about anything in the house, and everything that he has, he has given over to my charge; there is no one greater in this house than I am, nor has he kept back anything from me, except for yourself, insofar as you are his wife. How then might I do this great wrong and sin against God?"

> (Gen. 39:8–9)

This is in all respects an interesting speech. Indeed, a reader fresh from the theme of Joseph's initial complicity might easily find in it the signs of a certain hesitation on the part of the young hero: "Well, perhaps . . . after all, I am not accountable to anyone else in the house, and besides, Potiphar did tell me that everything was given over to me . . . though he did, come to think of it, exclude you, since you are, after all, his wife—but besides, to do such a thing would be a terrible sin against God." But, the somewhat ambiguous tone aside, the passage in any case does give clear evidence that Joseph knows that compliance would be a "great wrong" and cause him to "sin against God."

The question is, *how* did he know? The revelation at Sinai, with its clear interdiction "Thou shalt not commit adultery," had yet to take place—so how could Joseph be so sure that adultery was a sin?[6] One answer already glimpsed above (chapter 1) is that he had received instruction to that effect from his father Jacob, who in turn had learned from Abraham: "And he [Joseph] did not surrender himself but remembered the Lord and the words which Jacob, his father, used to read, which were from the words of Abraham, that there is no man who [may] fornicate with a woman who has a husband [and] that there is a judgment of death which is decreed for him in heaven before the Lord Most High" (*Jubilees* 39:6). Similarly in the "Testament of Joseph": "But I recalled *my father's words*, went weeping into my quarters, and prayed to the Lord" (3:3).[7] And likewise the first-century romance *Joseph and Asaneth* observed (in explaining why Joseph had turned aside the gifts of silver and gold sent to him by the Egyptian ladies) that Joseph "always had the face of his father Jacob before his eyes, *and he remembered his father's commandments.*"

This same idea—that Jacob had instructed Joseph concerning the divine commandments—is also represented in some rabbinic texts, and here it is not infrequently combined with one or more of the midrashic motifs seen above. Thus, for example, the "son of his old age" motif has some obvious potential relevance: for if, as Targum Onkelos has it, Jacob loved Joseph most because he was a "wise son to him," then surely this must imply that Joseph had at one point acquired that which is "wisdom" *par excellence,* a knowledge of Torah. (The "anachronism" of the patriarchs and other early figures "studying Torah" is, as we shall see now, a rabbinic commonplace.)

But if so, how did Joseph come by his Torah education? A further hint is provided in a verse already investigated at length above, Gen. 37:2, "Joseph, being seventeen years old, was shepherding the flock with his brothers." We saw earlier that the mention of Joseph's age, seventeen, seemed to conflict with his subsequent description in the same verse as a "boy." But beyond this, the very mention of his precise age seems somehow suspicious: for what purpose should Scripture be telling us exactly how old Joseph was at the time? And does not this verse's wording imply that, for some reason or other, Joseph had not been shepherding with his brothers before he was seventeen? If not, why not? An answer is presented in *Targum Pseudo-Jonathan's* expansive translation of this verse: "Joseph, being seventeen years old *when he left the study-house (beit-midrash)."* In other words, unlike his brothers, Joseph, being the "wise son," had theretofore devoted himself to Torah study—in fact, he had done so in a rabbinic-style study-house—and it was only at the age of seventeen that he "graduated" and went (ever so briefly) into the family livestock business. A similar theme is found in *Genesis Rabba* (84:8) in connection with Jacob's loving Joseph "more than all his sons": "Said R. Nehemiah: Because all the *halakhot* that Shem and Eber had transmitted to Jacob, he transmitted to him [Joseph]." In this case, apparently Jacob too has had a Torah education, which he then passes on to his son.

But if so, then where did Jacob acquire this education? The mention of "Shem and Eber" is an allusion to the well known rabbinic tradition of a *beit-midrash* founded by these ancient figures (as well, occasionally, as others).[8] That Jacob was a student there can be derived in particular from the wording of Gen. 25:27, which contrasts him with his brother: "Now the boys grew up: and Esau became a man knowledgeable in hunting, a man of the field; but Jacob was a simple man, *dwelling in tents."* This last phrase in particular seems to have suggested a preference for "book learning": here is how *Jubilees* rewords the same verse:

And Jacob was a smooth and upright man, and Esau was fierce, a man
of the field, and hairy, and Jacob dwelt in tents. And the youths grew,
and Jacob learned to write; but Esau did not learn.

(Jub. 19:13)

An anonymous remark in *Genesis Rabba* elaborates on the same theme:
" 'A simple man dwelling in tents'—two tents, the study-house of
Shem and the study-house of Eber." Apparently here the anomalous
plural "tents" was the initial focus of this midrashic tradition. For if the
text had intended merely to contrast Esau, the "man of the field," with
Jacob the homebody, "dwelling in *his* [or "the"] *tent*" would have been
more appropriate—for certainly one does not inhabit more than one
tent at a time. Unless . . . unless one of the "tents" in question was
really a study-house. Apparently this basic idea eventually underwent
modification, for in the above-cited text the plural form, "tents," is
taken to indicate that Joseph (as was not uncommon in rabbinic times)
had in fact studied with two masters, here Shem and Eber (separately).[9]
In any case, it is to be observed that this particular motif is entangled
with numerous others of the same basic *Tendenz*, for it was, as noted,
a rabbinic commonplace to project back to the time of the patriarchs the
practice of the Torah's commandments in general[10] and the commandment to study Torah in particular. Two other textual foci for this effort
(that is, beside the "two tents" inhabited by Jacob) were the earlier
mention of Rebecca's going to "seek the Lord" in Gen. 25:22,[11] and the
observation that Abraham, "kept my charge, my commandments, my
statutes, and my teachings" (Gen. 26:5).[12] In addition, there were two
verses that specifically used the term "tent" in such a way as to imply
"study-house," Gen 9:27 ("May God enlarge Japhet, and let him dwell
in the tents of Shem")[13] and Deut. 33:18 ("Rejoice, Zebulun, in your
going out, and Issachar in your tents").[14] All of these certainly rein-
forced the understanding that Jacob's "dwelling in tents" was really a
reference to his study of Torah, and this in turn could only suggest that
Jacob had passed on his learning to his "wise son" Joseph.

In fact, there are grounds for believing that Joseph in turn tried to
teach his brothers what he had learned from his father. For back in
Gen. 37:2, when it says that Joseph was "shepherding with his brothers," the word used for "with" ('*et*) can also be read as a sign of the
direct object, that is, Joseph was "shepherding his brothers." How so?
"He would hear a *halakhah* from his father and then go and teach it to
his brothers."[15]

"Jacob Saw the Wagons . . ."

One last (and relatively late) entry into this theme concerns a verse that appears later on in the story of Joseph. For it is recounted that after Joseph has revealed himself to his brothers, he sends them back to Canaan to tell Jacob that Joseph is still alive, indeed, has risen to a position of prominence in Egypt, and commissions them to bring Jacob along with their own families back down to Egypt. To this end Joseph sends a convoy of wagons with them on the journey. The text then continues:

> So they went up out of Egypt, and came to the land of Canaan to their father Jacob. And they told him, "Joseph is still alive, and he is ruler over all the land of Egypt." And his heart fainted, for he did not believe them. But when they told him all the words of Joseph, which he had said to them, and when he saw the wagons which Joseph had sent to carry him, the spirit of their father Jacob revived, and Israel said, "It is enough, Joseph my son is still alive; I will go and see him before I die."
>
> (Gen. 45:25–28)

The meaning of the text seems clear enough: the news brought to Jacob was so fantastic that at first he dared not credit it. But as he heard his sons go over Joseph's story in detail, and especially seeing the multitude of wagons they had brought with them, he realized that his sons were indeed telling the truth. Yet one might well inquire: what was it about *seeing the wagons* that caused Jacob to change his mind? After all, if his sons were indeed intent on deceiving him once again about Joseph, how difficult would it be for them to secure a few wagons—or even a great many—to accomplish that deception?

In addition to this, there is a slight problem in the biblical text with regard to *who* actually was responsible for sending the wagons. The passage cited above says "the wagons *which Joseph had sent*." A little earlier in the story, however, it is Pharaoh who commands Joseph concerning the wagons, "Take for yourselves some wagons from the land of Egypt . . ." (Gen. 45:19), and later, after Jacob has been convinced that Joseph is indeed still alive, the biblical text specifically says that Jacob and his sons departed for Egypt "in the wagons which *Pharaoh* had sent to carry him" (Gen. 46:5). What then could be meant by our passage's referring to "the wagons which Joseph had sent"? One answer, presented in *Genesis Rabba*, is that in fact there were *two* sets of wagons: "Those wagons which Pharaoh had sent to carry him had idolatrous images engraved on them, so Judah burned them . . ." (94:3). But this is hardly a satisfactory solution, since we have just seen that the reference to riding in Pharaoh's wagons in Gen. 46:5 comes chronologically *after* the reference to Joseph's wagons in Gen. 45:19: if Judah burned Pharaoh's wagons and these were replaced with Joseph's, why should the text later say that Jacob departed "in the wagons which Pharaoh had sent to carry him"?

A far cleverer solution is found in an adjacent remark in *Genesis Rabba*:

> R. Levi, in the name of R. Yohanan b. Sha'ulah [said]: [Joseph] said to them, If he [Jacob] believes you [when you say I am still alive], well and good. But if not, then you say to him [on my behalf]: At the time when I left you, was I not studying the law of the heifer whose neck is broken (Deut. 21:1)? Hence it is said, "And he saw the wagons which Joseph had sent."

This remark turns on the fact that the word "wagons" in Hebrew (*'agalot*) happens to be a homonym for the word "heifers." The remark of R. Yohanan b. Sha'ulah[16] cited by R. Levi (a third generation Palestinian *'amora*) thus suggests that Gen. 45:19 in fact has nothing to do with wagons, but really means "And he [Jacob] 'saw' the *heifers* which Joseph had sent." ("Sent" here is understood as "sent word of," a common enough meaning in biblical Hebrew [Gen. 20:2, 31:4, 41:8, etc.], while "saw" is apparently being interpreted in keeping with its rabbinic meaning of "consider" or even "approve of.") In other words, Joseph sends his brothers with a message to Jacob that he would immediately recognize as containing something that only the real Joseph could know: that the very last chapter in the Torah that Jacob and Joseph had been studying together before he was sold as slave was the law of the heifer in Deuteronomy 21. Thus, when Jacob hears this talk of "heifers" that Joseph had sent to him via the brothers, he knows for sure that they are telling the truth: he "saw [= considered] the [message of] 'heifers' that Joseph had sent" and his spirit revived.

This understanding not only takes care of the apparent discrepency with regard to who sent the wagons, but it also fits rather nicely into the immediate context. For the biblical verse in question reads: "But when they told him all the words of Joseph, which he had said to them, and when he saw the wagons which Joseph had sent to carry him, the spirit of their father Jacob revived." One might have wondered why the "words of Joseph" and the wagons are spoken of together here, as if being of the same order; but according to R. Yohanan b. Sha'ulah's explanation, they are indeed of the same order. For the brothers tell Jacob "*all* the words of Joseph, which he had said to them" (that is, not only that he is still alive, but the proof thereof, the words about heifers) "and Jacob considered the [message about] heifers that Joseph had sent" and knew that Joseph truly was alive.[17]

But why had Jacob and Joseph been studying the law of the heifer in Deuteronomy 21? Perhaps this is simply where they happened to be in their studies at the time. Yet inherent, it seems, in R. Yoḥanan b. Sha'ulah's choice of the law of the heifer—for he could have claimed that Jacob and Joseph had been studying the wagons of the tabernacle, or even the sin of the golden calf[18]—was a connection between that law and the fact of Joseph's departure. This connection, if it was present from the start, only found written expression in later writings, and ultimately came to be popularized in Rashi's Torah commentary. But in order to understand it, we must first turn to the law of the heifer itself:

> If in the land which the Lord your God gives you to possess, anyone is found slain, lying in the open country, and it is not known who killed him, then . . . the elders of the city which is nearest to the slain man shall take a heifer which has never been worked and which has not pulled in the yoke. And the elders of that city shall bring the heifer down to a valley with running water, which is neither plowed nor sown, and shall break the heifer's neck there in the valley. . . . And all the elders of the city nearest to the slain man shall wash their hands over the heifer whose neck was broken in the valley, and they shall testify, "Our hands have not shed this blood, neither did our eyes see it shed. Forgive, O Lord, your people Israel, whom you have redeemed, and do not set the guilt of innocent blood in the midst of your people Israel."
>
> (Deut. 21:1–8)

The rites prescribed in this law are apparently intended to atone collectively for a murder whose perpetrator and cause are unknown, and presumably the statement of the elders, "Our hands have not shed this blood," is being uttered by them on behalf of all the inhabitants of the town. But to a rabbinic expositor, the fact that the elders are required to say, in their own name, as it were, "Our hands have not shed this blood," must have seemed a bit extreme—after all, would anyone expect these most venerable and honored community figures of being murderers? And so their statement was interpreted not as a denial of guilt with regard to the murder, but as an affirmation that they themselves had exercised all the duties owed to a traveler coming into their territory: "It did not happen that he came to us and we let him depart without food, nor did we see him and let him continue without accompanying him on the road."[19] Such is the true meaning of "Our hands have not shed this blood . . ."—we properly offered hospitality and escort. But if so, then the whole law of the heifer in Deuteronomy

21 can actually be read as a prescription of the duties owed to a traveler, any traveler—namely, he must be offered food and must be *accompanied* on his way. Therefore, it was hardly a coincidence that this law was the very last thing that Jacob and Joseph had been studying together on the day that Joseph left his father's house to rejoin his brothers at the herds. It all happened, a *Tanḥuma* text explains, in the following manner:

> When [Joseph] departed from him, they were occupied with studying the law of the heifer, for it is said, "And he sent him off from the valley of Hebron" (Gen. 37:14). But is not Hebron in the mountains, as it is said, "And they *went up* to the Negeb, and came to Hebron" [Num. 13:22]? This demonstrates that Hebron is in the mountains. But [the phrase "valley of Hebron"] is to be understood as implying that Jacob *accompanied* him from the mountains down to the valley, and the expression "And he sent him off . . ." means "and he accompanied him." Thereupon Joseph asked him concerning the divine commandment of accompanying a traveler, and he [Jacob] told him of the law of the heifer, whereby they [the elders of the city] say ["Our hands have not shed this blood," meaning:] "We did not take leave of him without accompanying him."[20]

In other words, Jacob himself was busily fulfilling the duties owed to a traveler—in this case, his own son Joseph: he accompanied him all the way from the mountains in which Hebron sits to the lowland, and on his way he explained to his son that he was going to this trouble in keeping with the provisions of the law of the heifer, which he then outlined. Thus, many years later, when Joseph finally sends word back to his father that he is still alive, he instructs his brothers to mention the *ʿagalot*, the "heifers," as a way of reminding Jacob of the last conversation the two had had on their way down from the mountains. "And when they told him all the words of Joseph, which he had said to them, and when he *considered the heifers* which Joseph had 'sent' . . . , the spirit of their father Jacob revived."

Here then is another proof that Jacob had instructed Joseph in divine law, indeed, in the Torah-that-was-yet-to-be-given. If so, he certainly had also instructed him concerning the injunction of the Decalogue, "Thou shalt not commit adultery," and it is to this teaching that Joseph alludes when he tells Mrs. Potiphar that what she proposes would cause him to "sin against God." And, quite reasonably, it is this same precept not to commit adultery that came into his mind on that fateful day in Potiphar's house: Joseph suddenly remembers "his father's teachings" and flees.

His Father's Countenance

In the passage from the Babylonian Talmud with which we began, however, a different explanation is presented for Joseph's change of heart. For there it was said:

> "And she seized him by his garment . . ." At that moment the image of his father entered and appeared to him in the window. He said to him: Joseph, your brothers are destined to have their names written on the priestly breastplate, and yours is amongst theirs. Do you want it to be erased, and yourself to be called a shepherd of prostitutes, as it says [Prov. 29:3] "A shepherd of prostitutes loses [his] wealth"? At once "his bow remained in strength" [Gen. 49:24, that is, he overcame his desires].

Here it is not the memory of Jacob's *teachings*, but a vision of Jacob himself that brings about Joseph's sudden repentance.[21] Now the speech that Jacob makes at this crucial moment, in the version of the Babylonian Talmud, concerns a verse in the biblical book of Proverbs. That verse, only cited partially above, reads in full: "A wisdom-loving man will please his father, but a shepherd of prostitutes loses [his] wealth." In a manner typical of the rabbinic use of citations from books like Psalms, Proverbs, and Ecclesiastes, the text here goes out of its way to identify the subject of this general maxim (that is, "the wisdom-loving man") with a specific figure from the Pentateuch, in this case, Joseph. And it is a good fit: Not only is Joseph (as we have seen) a "wisdom-loving man" in the story, but, given the scenario of his father's sudden visionary appearance, it is quite appropriate for Jacob to call his son back to his senses by citing a verse from Proverbs that says, in effect, "Do the right thing and you'll please your father." But more than this, the second half of the verse seems especially appropriate. After all, Mrs. Potiphar has, by her base proposal, "Lie with me!", announced herself to be a woman of meager virtue. And so, our midrashist feels, "a shepherd of prostitutes" is not too exaggerated a description of what Joseph will become if he submits to her proposal: instead, says Jacob, let the "wisdom-loving man" please his father and thus not become a "shepherd of prostitutes." But what of the whole expression, "a shepherd of prostitutes will lose his wealth"? The word "wealth" here might have suggested to another midrashist some scenario whereby Jacob would threaten to cut Joseph out of his will if he succumbs, saying, "A shepherd of prostitutes will lose his wealth." But *our* midrashist had a better idea, one that was both more biblical and more concrete: he has Jacob talk instead of the priestly breastplate (Exod. 28:15–21), which is to contain twelve precious stones corresponding to the twelve tribes of Israel (= Jacob's sons). If you become a "shepherd of prostitutes," says Jacob, then you will have to be excluded from those who get precious stones assigned to them on the breastplate—you will "lose wealth," that is, lose your precious stone. This speech is enough to bring Joseph to his senses, and, according to our passage, he resists Mrs. Potiphar's temptation.

All this seems perfectly natural. But in fact the whole connection with the priestly breastplate did not originate with our midrashist contemplating a verse from Proverbs. On the contrary, the "shepherd of prostitutes" motif was tacked on to the original starting-point of this line of exegesis. That starting-point does not get mentioned until a little later on in the Babylonian Talmud: it is a cryptic line—another one!—from Jacob's blessing of Joseph in Genesis 49 (whose words "the daughters climbed the wall," etc. were discussed above, chapter 3). Here, the line in question reads: "At the hands of the Mighty One of Jacob, from there the Shepherd, the Rock of Israel" (Gen. 49:24). This verse is what the whole "breastplate" motif presented in the Talmud was originally created to explain, as becomes clear in the continuation of our passage from the Babylonian Talmud:

> "At the hands of the Mighty One of Jacob"—Who was it that caused him [Joseph] to be inscribed on the priestly breastplate? The mighty one, Jacob. "From there the Shepherd, the Rock of Israel"—from there [that is, "because of that"] he was found worthy and was made a "shepherd" [of the rock of Israel].[22]

Let us try to understand these words. The phrase "the Shepherd, the Rock of Israel" in Gen. 49:24 certainly seems, at first glance, to be a reference to God. But as such its meaning in the larger context is somewhat obscure, to say the least. And so, forced to cast about for a different approach, our midrashist thinks: "Rock [or, more correctly, "stone"] of Israel" might be transformed from a metaphorical to an actual stone. But what actual stone could be meant? "Israel" of course is Jacob's other name (Gen. 32:29), and so the idea eventually might suggest itself that a "rock of Israel" might in fact be one of the twelve "rocks" of the priestly breastplate that represent the twelve tribes descended from Jacob. If so, the "shepherd *of a* rock of Israel" (an equally possible way of reading these Hebrew words in the Bible) might refer to someone who has his own stone on the priestly breastplate. Then the whole phrase, "from there, the shepherd of the rock of Israel" could be understood to mean "thanks to that, he [Joseph] became the shepherd [possessor] of a rock of Israel." But thanks to what? The whole line was: "At the hands of the Mighty One of Jacob, from there the

Shepherd, the Rock of Israel." Now if "the Mighty One of Jacob" (another apparent reference to God) is distorted into "the mighty one, Jacob" (again, this is a defensible reading of the Hebrew), then the picture is complete: Joseph loses his desire (i.e., "his bow remains in strength")[23] thanks to the miraculous apparition of his father Jacob. And if all this thus happens "at the hands of the mighty one, Jacob" then "from there," thence, as a result of his father's apparition, Joseph does indeed retain his precious stone on the breastplate and becomes "the shepherd of a rock of Israel."

The basic stages of development of our whole passage from the Babylonian Talmud should thus be clear. After having cited sources suggesting that Joseph had knowingly gone to Potiphar's house on Nile Day in order to "do his work," it then turned to some of the cryptic phrases found in Gen. 49:24, the "Blessing of Joseph," which it (and earlier exegetes) had interpreted as referring to Joseph's change of heart vis-à-vis Mrs. Potiphar. This verse's first clause, "his bow remained in strength," was read a statement of the cooling of Joseph's desires, just as the following clause, "his arms were made agile" was similarly found to relate Joseph's abstinence.[24] But if so, then what is one to make of the rest of the verse, "at the hands of the Mighty One of Jacob, from there the Shepherd, the Rock of Israel"? The Babylonian Talmud, as we have just seen, understood "from there" as "as a result of which"—presumably a reference to something Jacob had done in the previous clause—and then went on to take "Rock of Israel" as a reference to the priestly breastplate. Hence: as a result of Jacob's doings, Joseph became the "shepherd of a rock of Israel." It was only after these basic lines of approach had been established (for they appear in other texts as well)[25] that the author of our Talmudic text came up with his unique contribution, the happy connection between that verse and the one in Proverbs 29:3, "A wisdom-loving man will please his father, but a shepherd of prostitutes loses [his] wealth." The common term, "shepherd," suggested to him creating an exegesis that would contrast "shepherd of prostitutes" with "shepherd of the rock of Israel," and he elaborated this contrast in the form of a speech put in the mouth of Jacob at the time of his miraculous appearance.[26]

Where Did It Come From?

In sum, we have seen that some of our oldest texts suggest that it was a sudden attack of memory that caused Joseph to change his mind—he "remembered his father's teachings"—while the passage just studied in

the Babylonian Talmud, along with other rabbinic and later texts[27] —
including, interestingly, the Qur'an[28] — suggest that it was a vision of
his father's countenance that brought about Joseph's volte-face. It
seems likely that the former motif, "father's teachings," is the older: not
only have we seen it attested in such ancient sources as *Jubilees* and the
Testaments, but it has a certain obvious quality to it. After all, the biblical
text tells us that Joseph changed his mind, and even has Joseph evoke
in one speech the idea that adultery is a sin; it only remained to explain
how he knew this, and the idea of Torah study *avant la lettre* came to
the rescue. Joseph had learned of the prohibition of adultery from his
father, and remembered his father's teachings at this crucial moment.
Yet the second explanation, that it was a vision of Jacob's face that
caused him to change his mind, is hardly a rabbinic invention. We saw
it above in passing, in a sentence cited from the first-century *Joseph and
Aseneth:* Joseph refused the gifts of silver and gold sent to him by the
Egyptian ladies because he "always *had the face of his father Jacob before his
eyes,* and he remembered his father's commandments." Here, in other
words, in a document written around the turn of the era, are both our
motifs, "Saw Father's Countenance" and "Remembered Father's Teachings," put forward in a single elegant sentence.

But where did the "father's countenance" idea come from? Here we
may observe that while the passage cited from the Babylonian Talmud
asserted that Joseph had seen a vision of his father's face, it did not give
any textual justification for such a scenario. Of course, its reading of
Gen. 49:24, to the effect that Joseph's change of mind came "at the
hands of the mighty one, Jacob," certainly fits in with the notion that
Jacob's face suddenly appeared to Joseph. But, as a matter of fact, there
is nothing about this reading per se that would require the creation of
the "father's countenance" motif. On the contrary, "at the hands of the
mighty one, Jacob" might just as easily have been explained as "thanks
to the *teachings* of his father Jacob" —without having to have recourse to
any supernatural apparitions. In fact, this is precisely how Targum
Pseudo-Jonathan does translate this phrase: "from the mighty teaching
that he had received from Jacob." In other words, the "Remembered
Father's Teachings" motif could adequately explain Joseph's change of
heart, and could likewise work well with the "at the hands of the
mighty Jacob" reading of Gen. 49:24 seen above. If so, why did the
other motif, "Saw Father's Countenance," ever get started—and how?

One might be tempted to conclude that there simply is no textual
"home" for this motif. After all, midrashic motifs sometimes acquire
details that have no exegetical basis (such, for example, was the detail

of the "knives" held by the women of the court in the "Assembly of Ladies"). And in this case, it might also be that Joseph's "sudden attack of memory" was perceived by early exegetes to be insufficient from a psychological standpoint, and so they—someone—simply invented the "father's face" apparition, and the motif caught on. Moreover, exegetes might have been troubled by another detail with regard to the "Remembered Father's Teachings" motif: For if Joseph had said to Mrs. Potiphar from the very beginning of her advances that he could not "sin again God," then clearly he was already aware of his father's teachings; how then could he suddenly "remember" them afresh on that fateful day and change his mind *in extremis?* From this standpoint too, a sudden appearance of Jacob's face would be far more satisfying.

And yet, there are certain hints in the material seen that the "Saw Father's Countenance" motif is indeed rooted in the reading of a particular biblical text. One of these is the fact that various rabbinic sources which connect Joseph's change of heart with the vision of his father's face do indeed accompany this motif with a specific biblical citation, namely, "by the hands of the Mighty One of Jacob" (Gen. 49:24). Thus, for example, *Genesis Rabba ad loc.:* " 'By the hands of the Mighty One of Jacob': R. Huna in the name of R. Matna said: he saw the countenance of his father (*'iqonin shel 'abiv*) and his desire departed." Similarly, Talmud Yerushalmi *Horayot* 2: "R. Huna in the name of R. Matna: he stared intently and saw the countenance of our father (*'iqonin shel 'abinu*) and thereupon cooled his passion, 'at the hands of the mighty one, Jacob.' " Now it might be that this biblical text is simply being adduced to show that Jacob had *something to do* with Joseph's change of heart, that is, it all happened "at the hands of the mighty one, Jacob." Yet the fact that this verse so consistently accompanies specifically the "father's countenance" motif—indeed, the fact that, in *Genesis Rabba* and elsewhere, this verse is explained as *meaning* that Jacob's face appeared—certainly seems suggestive.

Yet what is there in this phrase that could have suggested that Jacob's *face* appeared to his son Joseph in Potiphar's house? Now of course it is possible that, in citing the first part of this verse, our rabbinic texts wished to allude as well to what follows it (a common enough practice), *viz.* "from there the Shepherd, the Rock of Israel." But this hardly clarifies things. For what is there in *any* of these words that might give rise to our motif? But here it is certainly relevant to note another interesting point in the tradition: our rabbinic sources do not speak literally of Jacob's "face" appearing—that is, the word *panim* ("face") is not used, nor yet *demut*, "likeness"—but two Greek loan-words in Mishnaic Hebrew which are ultimately of the same origin, 'iqonin shel 'abiv or dioqano shel 'abiv, the "countenance" or "portrait" of his father—both derived from the Greek εἰκών, "image" or "likeness" (often, specifically, an artist's rendering, a portrait or bust). This is the same word for "countenance" that was seen above in the "son of his old age" motif with regard to both Joseph and Isaac. But here there is no exegetical necessity to use this somewhat out-of-the-way term: here there is no word-play based on "splendor of countenance" (ziv 'iqonin = zequnim). And this fact too should ultimately help us to understand the origins of this tradition.

For in fact underlying this whole motif is a very primitive reading of "from there the Shepherd, the Rock of Israel"—one that, for good reason, is no longer remembered even by the exegetes cited. This reading takes the phrase "rock of Israel" just as it took the phrase "the mighty one of Jacob," not as an oblique reference to God, but as something having to do with Jacob himself, Jacob-who-is-called-Israel. But if so, then what might Jacob's "rock" or "stone" actually be? Apparently this word suggested a stone image or bust—an εἰκών—of the man Jacob/Israel who is Joseph's father. In other words, 'iqonin shel 'abiv is nothing more than a "translation" of the biblical phrase 'eben yisra'el, the "rock" or "stone" of Israel.[29] Likewise, it seems that ro'eh ("shepherd," written with the letter 'ayin) here is being purposely confused with its near-homonym ro'eh (written with an 'aleph), the latter meaning "he sees" or (repointing it) "he saw." (Again, there is ample evidence that the sounds of 'aleph and 'ayin were easily confused in late- and postbiblical Hebrew.)[30] It is interesting in this connection to observe that in one of the early manuscript families of the Samaritan targum,[31] the phrase "from there the Shepherd, the Rock of Israel" is rendered as "from there appeared ['ithazzei or mithazzei] the stone of Israel." In other words, ro'eh, "shepherd," is clearly being understood here as ra'ah, "he saw," hence, "there appeared."[32] Moreover, with regard to the connection of 'eben with 'iqonin, there is another piece of supporting evidence, namely, the anonymous explanation of Isaiah 31:9 that appears in Midrash Tehillim (ad Ps. 15:1). The Isaiah verse reads, "His rock (sal'o) will pass away in terror." These words are explained as follows: "His rock—this refers to his image ('iqonya)." It seems that here as well the presence of a rock/stone in the biblical text suggested the connection with a stone image, 'iqonin. And so it seems that the entire verse Gen. 49:24 was understood as meaning that Joseph's passions had cooled "at the hands of the mighty one, Jacob, because[33] he [Joseph] had **seen** the **'stone'** ['iqonin = "bust," "image"] of Israel."

It was noted in passing above that one rabbinic source still preserves the "Remembered Father's Teachings" motif found otherwise in
Jubilees, the *Testaments*, and other prerabbinic sources, and that is the
translation of Targum Pseudo-Jonathan, which renders "at the hands of
the Mighty One of Jacob" as "from the mighty *instruction* that he had
received from Jacob." If so, it now seems possible that the two motifs
that we have been tracing, "Remembered Father's Teachings" and
"Saw Father's Countenance," are not rival motifs that sprang up independently, but twin halves of a running exegesis of Gen. 49:24. For,
having established that this whole section of Jacob's blessing of his son
Joseph is a reference to his resistance to the temptations of Mrs.
Potiphar, the exegete proceeds to understand the end of v. 24 as setting
forth *how* it happened that Joseph was able to resist. His refusal was
brought about "at the hands of the Mighty One of Jacob"—that is,
thanks to Jacob's teachings, the "mighty instruction" referred to in Targum Pseudo-Jonathan—and these teachings suddenly came to mind at
the crucial moment "from there the Shepherd, the Rock of Israel," that
is, because Joseph, sorely tempted, suddenly "saw his father's face and
lost his desire."

This midrash, if I have correctly restored it, appears in its combined
form in only one place, the passing remark of *Joseph and Aseneth* that
Joseph had been able to resist temptation because he "always had the
face of his father Jacob before his eyes, and he remembered his father's
commandments." Elsewhere the two motifs are presented as alternative explanations, "Remembered Father's Teachings" surviving in *Jubilees*, etc., "Saw Father's Countenance" in the various rabbinic sources
seen. And in these latter, as we have likewise seen, the connection
between "stone" and 'iqonin was eventually lost, though the idea that
Gen. 49:24 was somehow connected to a vision of Jacob's face stayed
on. How natural, then, that this idea of Jacob's miraculous appearance
should come to be attached to the *name* of Jacob in the first half of the
verse (as it was in the Jerusalem Talmud, *Genesis Rabba*, and elsewhere)
freeing up the "stone of Israel" for a far more creative midrash, that of
the precious stones on the breastplate.

Jacob's Portrait on the Heavenly Throne

And yet, having come this far, we still have not traced all the elements
that went into this "Saw Father's Countenance" motif. One more tradition is relevant here, for it too speaks of Jacob's "countenance" or
"portrait." The tradition in question holds that Jacob's portrait is "en-

graved on the heavenly throne." This particular motif is widely distributed in rabbinic texts. Thus, for example, in *Numbers Rabba* (*Bemidbar*, 4:1) the verse from Isaiah 43:4, "Because you are precious in my eyes, you have been honored . . ." is explained: "God said to Jacob: Jacob, you are so precious in my eyes that I have, as it were, fixed your portrait (*'iqonin*) on the heavenly throne."[34] Similarly, one reads concerning the opening verse of chapter 2 of Lamentations: " 'How the Lord in his anger has beclouded . . .': Said God to Israel: Do you truly aggravate me? It is only the fact that the portrait (*'iqonin*) of Jacob is engraved on my throne. Here then, take it! And he threw it in their faces." And likewise in *Genesis Rabba* 78:3, on the verse "For you have wrestled with God and with men and have prevailed" (Gen. 32:28) we read: "You are the one whose portrait is engraved on high."

Any one of these might be adduced as *the* verse that gave rise to the motif in question. Thus, in the first case cited, the Isaiah verse reads in full: "Because you are precious in my eyes, you have been honored; and I have loved you, and I put men in your stead, and whole peoples in place of yourself." The phrase "I put men . . ." in Hebrew is really in the singular, "I put a man in your stead." Could this not have suggested that God had actually fashioned a "man," a figurine, of Jacob because he loved him so much, and placed that figurine on the heavenly throne, so that (citing the rest of the verse) "whole peoples [stand] underneath you[r image]"?[35] Similarly, the rest of the Lamentations verse reads: "He has cast down from heaven to earth the beauty of Israel." If the "beauty of Israel" is understood in concrete fashion, it might seem to refer to something of Jacob's, an actual object of beauty—hence, a beautiful portrait of Jacob. But if it was "cast down" from heaven, that must mean that it previously was there—and where might a portrait of Jacob have been but on the heavenly throne itself? Finally, the last example takes the Genesis verse "you have wrestled with God and men" as "you have exalted yourself with God and men."[36] But this might then imply that Jacob was in two places at once, both in Heaven with God and down on earth with men. But how could this be possible? It must have been that he was "exalted" in Heaven, as it were, by proxy, represented there by a statue or portrait of himself.

Yet the very fact that all of these work more or less well might suggest that none of them is at the origin of our tradition. And in fact a check of the rabbinic sources reveals that this particular motif, Jacob's portrait on the heavenly throne, is found most consistently associated not with any of the above texts, but with the description of Jacob's dream at Bethel. The biblical passage in question reads as follows:

> Jacob left Beer-sheba, and went toward Haran. And he came to a
> certain place, and stayed there for the night, because the sun had set.
> Taking one of the stones of the place, he put it under his head and lay
> down in that place to sleep. And he dreamed that there was a ladder
> set up on the earth, and its top reached to heaven; and behold, the
> angels of God were ascending and descending on it. And behold, the
> Lord stood above it [or "him"] and said: "I am the Lord. . . ." Then
> Jacob awoke from his sleep and said, "Surely the Lord is in this place,
> and I did not know it."
>
> (Gen. 28:12–16)

There are many interesting exegetical questions that were explored in
this passage, but the relevant one here is one that, at first glance, might
hardly have disturbed anyone: it is that the angels on the ladder are
said to be "ascending and descending on it." Now certainly in Hebrew,
as in English and many other languages, the order in which these two
verbs usually come is a matter of convention: things generally go "up
and down," not "down and up." So perhaps it was only in keeping
with this linguistic convention that our biblical text said "ascending and
descending" rather than the opposite. Yet angels are supposed generally to dwell in Heaven; should they not then have been more accu-
rately described as "descending and [then, afterwards] ascending"?

A number of midrashic answers to this question were developed.
One held that the angels who are said to visit Abraham (in Gen. 18:2–
15) were subsequently not allowed back into Heaven,[37] and wandered
about on earth until the time Jacob left his father's house to go to
Laban's. The angels escorted him to Bethel, and then were permitted to
ascend into Heaven on the ladder of Jacob's dream. So it was that these
angels could first *ascend* on the ladder and then some other angels could
descend, presumably for some further purpose (such as escorting Jacob
the rest of the way). But another approach saw "ascending" and "descending" not as two individual acts, a single going-up followed by a
single going-down, but as a series of repeated acts, that is, angels *kept*
going up and down between Heaven and earth. But why? The texts
says "ascending and descending *on it.*" But the Hebrew word *bo* here
can be translated not only as "on it," but also "on him" (that is, on
Jacob) or even "because of him" or "for his sake."[38] And so we find the
following:

> R. Ḥiyya the Great and R. Yannai [disagreed]: one said they went up
> and down [*bo*] on the ladder; the other said they went up and down
> [*bo*] for Jacob. . . . as it is said, "Israel, by you am I made glorious"
> (Isa. 49:3)—you are the one whose portrait is carved on high. They
> went up to see his portrait, then went down to see him sleeping.
>
> (*Genesis Rabba* 68:12)

According to this scenario, the angels are so taken with the righteous Jacob that they keep shuttling back and forth between Heaven and earth in order to see him, ascending *bo*, to see his heavenly portrait, and then descending *bo*, to see him in the flesh sleeping at the foot of the ladder. The text from Isaiah 49:3, "Israel, by you am I made glorious" is then adduced to further prove that Jacob's portrait is indeed located on high. For "to be made glorious" can also be understood as "to be made beautiful," hence, "to decorate." It is thus as if God were saying: Yes indeed, I have beautified my quarters up here *by you*, not of course literally by "you," but with your portrait.

It is interesting that there is even an echo of this midrash in the New Testament:

> Jesus answered him, "Because I said to you, I saw you under the fig tree, do you believe? You shall see greater things than these." And he said to him, "Truly, truly, I say to you, you will see heaven opened, and the angels of God ascending and descending upon the Son of man."
>
> (John: 1:50–51)

How can we know that this New Testament passage is part of the above midrashic tradition, and not simply an allusion to the mention of angels "ascending and descending" in Genesis? Because it says "angels of God ascending and descending *upon the Son of man*." Clearly this belongs to the exegetical school represented by R. Yannai above, that is, the one that takes *bo* in the Genesis text to mean not "on the ladder" but "for Jacob." So here too, *bo* is being taken as referring to a person, namely, "upon the Son of man." (It is also worth noting that, although the Gospel of John was presumably composed in Greek, this particular play on words could not work in Greek, since the word for ladder in the Greek Bible is feminine [κλίμαξ] and the only alternative to "on it" would thus be "for her.")[39]

These two explanations concerning "ascending and descending" are found harmonized in the version of Targum Pseudo-Jonathan:

> And he dreamt that there was a ladder fixed in the earth and its head reached the Heavens, and the two angels who had gone to Sodom and had then been exiled from Heaven for having revealed secrets of the Master of the world and had thus been wandering about until Jacob left his father's house, whereupon they lovingly accompanied him to Bethel—now they ascended to the upper heavens and called out: Come and see the faithful Jacob, who portrait is fixed on the Glorious Throne, since you have desired to see him. Then the other holy angels of the Lord went down to see him.

Here the angels that had been exiled on earth go up, but it is not just a single going-up followed by a single going-down: they call to their fellow angels to go and catch a glimpse of Jacob, and this feeds into the "ascending and descending for [i.e., in order to see] him" motif.

In any case, the origin of Jacob's heavenly portrait thus seems solved: "ascending and descending *on it*" gave rise to the reading "ascending and descending [repeatedly] for [that is, in order to see] *him*," and that in turn necessitated devising a reason for the angels to go *up* to see Jacob as well as *down* to see him. So a Jacob-in-Heaven, a heavenly portrait of him, was created to solve the problem; now there was a celestial counterpart to the earthly man[40] asleep on the ground.

And yet, despite this explanation, one might still entertain some doubts about the motif's ultimate origins. After all, the whole starting point of this exegetical line had been the problem of the order of the verbs that has the angels (first) ascending and (then) descending. One line of argument, as we saw, accounted for this by saying that there were already some angels on the ground, and that these went up and others came down. Now an alternate approach (one that, for some reason, either did not know of the first one—perhaps it was not yet invented—or did not approve of it) sought to read "ascending and descending" as repeated actions, something the angels *kept doing*. If so, then there was no real problem with the order "ascending and descending"—as rabbinic exegetes might observe, *lav davqa hu'*, the text did not mean specifically *first* ascending and *then* descending, it simply meant they kept going up and down. But if the problem of the order of the verbs is thereby solved, one still needs to explain *why* these angels kept going up and down. Now the "down" part was easy enough: they went down to see Jacob. *But if so, then the "up" part could have been solved in any number of other ways.* The angels could have been said to go down to see Jacob, and then go up to sing his praises before God on high, then go down again to catch another glimpse of him, and so forth. Or indeed, they might have been said to go down, see Jacob, and then ascend again to tell their fellow-angels, then escort the new ones down with them, and so on in greater and greater and greater throngs—indeed, this might be done in almost the same language as that seen above in Targum Pseudo-Jonathan: "Now they ascended to the upper heavens and called out: Come and see the faithful Jacob . . . since you have desired to see him. Then [they with] the other holy angels of the Lord went down to see him."

In other words, when one considers it, the whole idea of a heavenly portrait need not have been created in response to the "ascending and descending" problem—there were indeed far less taxing ways to solve it. And if it be objected—correctly—that midrash is not strictly and exclusively a matter of solving "problems" (even broadly conceived) in the biblical text, that it also frequently represents an attempt to connect ideological or historical or other concerns with the Bible, or simply, as perhaps in this case, to hang a pleasing idea on a biblical "peg," one must nevertheless ask: why *this* "peg"? We saw at the beginning of our exposition how well suited Isa. 43:4, "I put a man in your stead," or Lam. 2:1, "He has cast down . . . the beauty of Israel," or even Gen. 32:28, "You have exalted yourself with God and with men" were with respect to the motif of Jacob's heavenly portrait, or even how appropriately Isa. 49:3, "Israel, by you am I beautified," could be adduced for it in *Genesis Rabba.* If this idea needed a home, any of these verses would have provided a more comfortable one than "ascending and descending" does. (Equally appropriate might have been Ezekiel's mention of the "face of a man" in his description of the heavenly host, Ezek. 1:10, 26, a connection indeed suggested in later texts.) And yet, as noted, our rabbinic sources, especially the oldest ones, agree in connecting this motif specifically with Jacob's dream.

Such misgivings only become stronger when one turns to another ancient source in which something related to our motif, "Jacob's Portrait on the Heavenly Throne," seems to be present. The source in question is a somewhat out-of-the-way one, a brief pseudepigraphon known as "The Ladder" or "The Ladder of Jacob."[41] The period of this text's original composition is unknown: there is no reason to date it later than the first century C.E., but it might conceivably go back even before the common era. In style and in some of its details, it resembles some relatively early works. It survives only in various Slavonic versions,[42] but clearly these are based on an earlier Greek text; that text, in turn, might well have been translated from a Hebrew or Aramaic original, for the Jewish character of the underlying text is apparent. Elsewhere it might be of value to treat this text as a whole, but here we are interested only in its opening few sentences. These read as follows:

> Jacob then went to Laban his uncle. He found a place and, laying his head on a stone, he slept there, for the sun had gone down. He had a dream. And behold, a ladder was fixed on the earth, whose top reached to heaven. And the top of the ladder was the face of a man, carved out of fire. There were twelve steps leading to the top of the ladder, and on each step to the top there were human faces, on the right and on the left, twenty-four faces [or busts] including their chests. And the face in the middle was higher than all that I saw, the

one of fire, including the shoulders and arms, exceedingly terrifying, more than those twenty-four faces. And while I was still looking at it, behold, angels of God ascended and descended on it. And God was standing above its highest face, and he called to me from there, saying "Jacob, Jacob!" And I said, "Here I am, Lord."

I cannot claim to understand all of this strange text. The twenty-four faces are later on identified as the "kings of the ungodly nations of this age," the ladder itself thus representing "this age" and its "periods" (5:2–4). But the great, fiery "face of a man" at the top of the ladder is not identified in this text, and we are only left to speculate how it may be related to the heavenly portrait in our midrash. One brief remark above, however, is striking for our overall inquiry. For we read: "And behold, a ladder was fixed on the earth, whose top reached to heaven. *And the top of the ladder was the face of a man,* carved out of fire." Now anyone who knows the Hebrew text of Gen. 28:12 will immediately recognize the source of this image. For though the Bible says that in his dream Jacob saw a ladder whose *top* reached to the Heavens, the word for "top" in Hebrew, *rosh,* is the same word normally used for "head." And so our Slavonic text—or, rather, the Hebrew text that underlies it—apparently takes the biblical reference to the ladder's "head" as a suggestion that the ladder indeed *had* a head, a man's head, at its very top. The fact, then, of this biblical text's wording—"a ladder set up on the earth, *and its head* reached to heaven"—engendered the heavenly "head" in our pseudepigraphon.

But let us consider the entire sentence in the Bible: "And he dreamed that there was a ladder set up on the earth, and its 'head' reached to heaven; and behold, the angels of God were ascending and descending on it." We saw above that the inanimate *bo* of "ascending and descending *on it*" was midrashically transformed into an animate *him,* "ascending and descending *for him*" (or, in John 1, "upon him"). But what if the *its* of "its head" were similarly transformed from inanimate to animate? Why then we would have: "And he dreamed that there was a ladder set up on the earth. And *his* [Jacob's] head reached to heaven; and behold, the angels of God were ascending and descending upon him." Here, it seems, is the full origin of our midrash. For Jacob's "head" somehow reaches, via the ladder, to the Heavens—either, as in the pseudepigraphon, an image of his head stands at the top of the ladder, or perhaps such an image ascends via the ladder into Heaven—and the angels can thus go up and down between Jacob's heavenly head and his earthly one, presumably to admire both. In any case, one can easily see how this transformation of the ladder's "head" to a human head (already witnessed in the pseudepigraphon) could lead directly to the notion that some sort of bust, an 'iqonin, of Jacob existed on high.[43]

In this connection, one cannot but be struck by a remark in Horace Lunt's valuable introduction to his recent translation of the "Ladder."[44] For there, in speculating about the original language of this text, he notes that the word used here to designate the great "head" on the ladder is somewhat unusual: "no other Slavonic text has *lice,* 'face,' used to mean 'statue' or 'bust' (1:5, etc.), and there is no Semitic parallel." But there is! It is that Greek loan-word into Mishnaic Hebrew, 'iqonin. For as we have seen above, 'iqonin did come to mean "face," as in *ziv* 'iqonin, "splendor-of-countenance" or "features" — and yet its basic meaning of "portrait" or "bust" is preserved in a number of rabbinic usages, including, prominently, the 'iqonin shel 'abiv ("His Father's Countenance") motif studied above, where 'iqonin was generated, as we have seen, by the biblical phrase "the stone of Israel" (hence, stone figure, bust). And so there is little doubt that our pseudepigraphon, in seeking to "translate" the biblical phrase "his/its head reached to Heaven," reworded it in Mishnaic Hebrew as "his [Jacob's] 'iqonin reached Heaven," and this in turn gave rise to the presence of a Heavenly bust or portrait of Jacob on the divine throne.

And so we now have a fuller picture of the role of Jacob's 'iqonin in rabbinic exegesis: it occurs in connection with Joseph's change of heart in Potiphar's house, and it occurs in connection with Jacob's dream at Bethel. We might then logically inquire whether in fact Jacob's 'iqonin was imported from one of these motifs to the other, or whether it was generated spontaneously in both. While "spontaneous generation" is as unlikely a prospect in midrash as in biology, it seems at this point impossible to guess if the concept of Jacob's 'iqonin originally migrated from Potiphar's house to Jacob's dream, or vice versa. We have already seen the likelihood that the former motif goes back at least as far as the first century B.C.E., and this is certainly an impressive pedigree. Yet the existence of something very much like the motif of Jacob's 'iqonin in the "Ladder of Jacob" might suggest an equally ancient origin for it. And so this question must, for now, be left open.

One final point of a technical nature. We saw that, in the rabbinic versions of "Saw Father's Countenance," the biblical text cited to support it was "at the hands of the mighty one, Jacob," whereas the real source of this motif came a bit later in the same verse, "the stone of Israel." So similarly here, the biblical text cited to support the idea that Jacob's portrait was etched on the heavenly throne was the phrase "ascending and descending for him," whereas in reality the textual basis came a little earlier in the same verse "his/its head reached to Heaven." Now this is not an uncommon phenomenon in the way midrashic motifs develop, and, if we wished to give a name to the process by which it occurs, we might do no better than to borrow a term from psychology and call it **"transfer of affects,"** the process whereby a particular motif, generated to explain or elaborate text A, comes to be understood as an explanation for some other verse, B.[45] We have already seen above that this process can lead to the phenomenon of "midrashic doublets," whereby the same motif comes to be used to comment upon two different biblical texts. But sometimes, as in the above two examples, the process of "transfer of affects" does not result in "doublets" at all. Instead, the motif becomes utterly detached from its original home, so that no one is any longer aware of what that home was, and a certain amount of detective work is then required in order to track down the motif's origins. Thus it seems that, in the two cases just studied above, the "transfer of affects" was hardly conscious: what happened with both "Saw Father's Countenance" and "Jacob's Portrait on the Heavenly Throne" was that the motifs truly began to be connected with phrases (respectively: "from the hands of the mighty one, Jacob" and "ascending and descending for him") that were *not* the original homes of the motifs, and so their true relationship to the biblical text was lost. Now in these two cases, the transfer did not go very far—it led from one phrase to another within the same verse; but sometimes, as we will see, the jump can be much greater.

Notes

1. "The Testament of Joseph" 9:2–5, in J. Charlesworth, *Old Testament Pseudepigrapha*, 1:821.
2. See above, chapter 3, and J. Theodor and Ch. Albeck, *Genesis Rabba*, 1071–72, and notes.
3. Another answer to the problem of there being "no man in the house" is supplied in *Genesis Rabba*: "R. Samuel b. Naḥman said: Certainly Joseph went 'to do his work,' but: 'there was no man in the house.' He checked, and did not find himself to be a man" (87:7). This in turn is connected with the reading of Gen. 49:24 as a metaphor for loss of sexual appetite.
4. *Tanḥuma*, "*Vayyeshev*," 9. The passage continues with the "no man in the house" motif (above, n. 3). *Aggadot ha-Talmud* has: "the two of them went naked into bed." See E. Z. Melamed *Halakhic Midrashim* (Jerusalem: Magnes, 1988), 478.
5. I owe this observation to Prof. M. Kossovsky of the Hebrew University. He further points out that the absence of an expected *dagesh* in the "d" of

bebigdo in fact suggested to various commentators that this word is a by-form of *bebogdo* (unambiguously "in his betrayal"), in which the absence of the *dagesh* would be expected. See thus the discussion of *bebigdo* in Exod. 21:8 in b. *Qiddushin* 19 b, Rashi and Tosafot *ad loc.*, as well as the Pentateuch commentary of Ba'al ha-Ṭurim *ad* Exod. 21:8.

6. To rabbinic expositors one possible answer was that the prohibition of adultery was among the seven universal laws communicated to the sons of Noah ("The Noahide Laws"). The author of *Jubilees* knew of a tradition of Noahide commandments (see *Jubilees* 7:20–25), but apparently felt the necessity of nevertheless asserting that the prohibition of adultery had been specifically communicated to Joseph by his father, one of the divine statutes written on the "Heavenly Tablets" (though this may simply represent the manner in which these Noahide commandments were communicated).

7. Philo of Alexandria seems to have a similar tradition, but for him the "pre-Sinaitic revelation" is apparently not an issue—he assumes that Joseph knew the Torah, for such is his answer to Mrs. Potiphar: "We children of the Hebrews follow laws and customs which are especially our own. Other nations are permitted after the fourteenth year to deal without interference with harlots and strumpets and all those who make a traffic of their bodies, but with us a courtesan is not even permitted to live, and death is the penalty appointed for women who ply this trade [apparently based on Deut. 23:17]. Before the lawful union we know no mating with other women. . . . To this day I have remained pure, and I will not take the first step in transgression by committing adultery, the greatest of crimes" ("On Joseph," 43–44). All this, incidentally, is part of an expansive version of Gen.39:8–9, which Philo has tranferred to the very day of Mrs. Potiphar's seizing Joseph's garment.

8. See Ginzberg, *Legends of the Jews,* 5:187 n. 51; 192 n. 63; 225 n. 102. On Shem, see also below.

9. Cf. *Midrash ha-Gadol* (Margoliot, p. 897): " 'Tent' is not said here but 'tents': [this teaches] that he studied in many study-houses, the study-house of Shem and the study-house of Eber and the study-house of Abraham."

10. See Ginzberg, *Legends,* 5:92–93 n. 55; 235 n. 140; 259, n. 275.

11. Interpreted as meaning that Rebecca went to the study-house of Eber (or Shem): see Theodor-Albeck, *Genesis Rabba,* vol. 2, 684 and notes. Certainly the use of the verb "seek" (*darash*) suggested a connection with *midrash,* a nominal form of the same root; moreover, the fact that the text says that Rebecca *went* implies that this "seeking" of the Lord involved some human intermediary. It may also be that a woman was not to undertake such "seeking" directly: Josephus in his retelling of the biblical narrative states that it was *Isaac* who "consulted God" (*Jewish Antiquities* I 257).

12. This exhaustive catalogue of course implied that God had communicated a large number of divine laws to Abraham, a support for the basic motif "Patriarchs Kept the Commandments" (above, n. 7); moreover, the very profusion suggested that Abraham had to *study* these laws in order to master them. Beyond this, the plural "teachings" (*torotai*) suggested the rabbinic "two Torahs," the Oral and the Written. (Cf. Deut. 33:10 in rabbinic exegesis.)

13. Targum Pseudo-Jonathan: "May the Lord beautify the border of Japhet and let his sons convert [to Judaism] and dwell in the study-house of Shem."
14. This theme has been treated by M. Beer, "Issachar and Zebulun" (Hebrew) *Bar Ilan Annual* 6 (1968): 167–80.
15. *Beit ha-Midrash,* vol. 6, 82. Cf. Babylonian Talmud, *Ta'anit* 10 b, *Genesis Rabba* 94:2. Also, Ginzberg, *Legends,* 1:169 and 5:356.
16. Elsewhere: Yoḥanan b. Sha'ul, or b. She'ilah, or b. Shilah, a first-generation *'amora,* perhaps the brother of R. Yosi b. Sha'ul (see b. *Shabbat* 125 b).
17. An alternate approach would be to have the brothers explain to their father that the *'agalot* (wagons) outside are not only intended to carry Jacob and his belongings down to Egypt, but they are also an *allusion* to the last thing that Jacob and Joseph had studied together. This would better account for the wording "the wagons which Joseph had sent *to carry him*" and avoid having to interpret the last phrase as something like "to lift him up," that is, to revive his spirits. Yet another possibility was to read the *'agalot* here not as an allusion to the law of the heifer, but to the "wagons of the tabernacle" (Num. 7:6–8), or to the incident of the golden calf (*'egel;* Exod. 32). These were indeed proposed; see Theodor-Albeck, *Genesis Rabba,* 1173–74.
18. See above note.
19. See b. *Soṭa,* 38 b.
20. *Midrash Tanḥuma* ed. S. Buber (Vilna, 1899) "Introduction," 132. Oxford Ms. 183/187; number 156 on title page. See also Ginzberg, *Legends,* 5:357.
21. The text says literally that Jacob's "countenance (*'iqonin*) entered and appeared to him in the window." Clearly, then, this is a visionary Jacob whose face suddenly appears, framed, as it were, by the window. But it may even be that the word "window" here (*ḥalon*) should be emended to "dream" (*ḥalom*); this is the reading to be found in *Midrash Sekhel Ṭob, ad loc.* and in *Aggadot ha-Talmud.*
22. b. *Soṭa* 36 b. The first part of this midrash is truncated in the Munich manuscript of the Babylonian Talmud. All versions then add the connection with the "shepherd" of Ps. 80:2. See below, note 26.
23. See above, note 3. *Eitan* here is being understood as "normal [or "prior"] condition" (cf. b. Niddah 48b), based on Exod. 14:27.
24. Explained in our Talmudic passage (not cited above) as: "He stuck his hands in the ground so that his lust came out from between his fingernails."
25. *Talmud Yerushalmi, Horayot* 2; *Genesis Rabba* 87:7, *Midrash Tanḥuma, Vayyesheb* 9; *Pirqei R. Eli'ezer,* chap. 39.
26. In fact a further play on "shepherd" is provided at the very end of our Talmudic passage (not cited above): "And so Joseph was made a shepherd, as it says, 'Shepherd of Israel, hearken, who leadest Joseph as a flock' " (Ps. 80:2). This exegesis is dependent on reading "Joseph" in the Psalm 80 not as the object but the subject of the verb, i.e., as if it said: "Shepherd of Israel, hearken, O Joseph who leadest [Israel] as a flock." Thus, because of his exemplary conduct, Joseph merited being called the "shepherd of Israel." Cf. *Pirqei R. Eli'ezer,* chap. 39.
27. See above, note 25.

28. Sura 12:24. The Qur'anic phrase, *burhana rabbihi*, "the appearance of his master [= Jacob]," has an interesting history of interpretation, having been associated by commentators either with a divine appearance ("master" = Lord) or a vision of Potiphar ("master" = Potiphar). Its connection with our midrash has been discussed by numerous scholars since Geiger; see M. Grünbaum, "Zu 'Jussuf und Suleicha' "in his *Gesammelte Aufsätze zur Sprach- und Sagenkunde*, ed. F. Perles (Berlin: S. Calvary & Co., 1901), 515–51; I. Schapiro, *Die haggadischen Elemente im erzählende Teil des Korans* (Leipzig: Buchhandlung Gustav Fock, 1907), 40; D. Sidersky, *Les Origines des légendes musulmanes dans le Coran* (Paris: Librairie Orientaliste P. Geuthner, 1933), 61. cf. J. Macdonald, "Joseph in the Qur'an and Muslim Commentary: A Comparative Study," *The Muslim World* 46 (1956):113–31 and 207–24.

29. That an *'iqonin* is in fact a *carved* likeness made out of stone or some other material may further be supported by that other midrashic tradition (discussed below) to the effect that Jacob's *'iqonin* was *haquqah*, "engraved" or "carved," on the heavenly throne. See *Genesis Rabba* 78:3; *Lamentations Rabba ad* Lam. 2:1, etc. and below. Cf. Jerusalem Talmud *Abodah Zarah* 42 a-b.

30. The case of *'aleph* and *'ayin* is somewhat different from that of other gutterals, whose distinctiveness was, as Kutscher implies, better preserved. For *'aleph* and *'ayin*, the early confusion of these two sounds is frequently reflected in the ancient versions and early commentaries on such verses as Gen. 3:21 (cf. E. Tov, *Text Critical Use of the Septuagint* [Jerusalem: Simor, 1981], 201); for rabbinic sources see, e.g., the discussion of *'ed/'ed* in b. *'Abodah Zarah* 2a; cf. E. Y. Kutscher, *A History of the Hebrew Language* (Jerusalem: Magnes, 1982), 120–21.

31. Designated "M" by A. Tal in his recent critical edition, and dated by him to before the fourth century c.e.; see E. Tal, *The Samaritan Targum of the Pentateuch*, vol. 1 (Tel Aviv: University of Tel Aviv, 1980), 214.

32. A further proof comes from a motif sometimes appended to this one (it appears in *Genesis Rabba*, The Jerusalem Talmud, and some later texts): "He saw his mother's image and his passions cooled, [as it says] "from there he 'shepherded' the stone of Israel." This reading obviously takes the "stone of Israel" as a reference to Rachel; but if so it understands *ro'eh* not as "shepherded" but as "saw."

33. We saw above this causal reading of "from there, thence," and it might equally well apply here. But it may also be that the word *mi-sham* is being understood here as *mi-shum*, "because," "on account of."

34. The same motif had appeared in somewhat different form in *Midrash Tanḥuma* (*Bemidbar*, 19).

35. The preposition "in place of" in Hebrew (*taḥat*) also means "under."

36. Cf. Targum Onkelos *ad loc.* The verb "wrestle" here is being understood as derived from the word *sarar*, "be mighty" or "be exalted."

37. They were so punished for having revealed divine secrets—or, in another version attributed to R. Hama b. Hanina, because of their boastfulness, since they say (in Gen. 19:13) "*we* are going to destroy this place," whereas even Lot knows enough to correctly attribute the destruction to God ("for the *Lord* is about to destroy this city," Gen. 19:14). See *Genesis Rabba* 68:12.

As a result of their infraction, whatever it was, the angels were exiled and
not allowed back into Heaven until Jacob's dream.

38. This meaning is found in some biblical texts: see, e.g., Gen. 18:28, Lam.
2:19, Dan. 10:12.

39. Cf. R. Bultmann, *The Gospel of John: A Commentary*, trans. G. R. Beasley-
Murray (Philadelphia: Westminster, 1971), 105 n. 3; R. E. Brown, *The Gospel
According to John* (*The Anchor Bible*), vol. 1 (New York: Doubleday, 1966),
88–91.

40. See on this idea Y. F. Baer, *Israel Among the Nations* (Hebrew) (Jerusalem:
Mossad Bialik, 1955), 86–88; I have discussed it at greater length below,
chapter 9. Another possible New Testament echo of this motif is 1 Cor.
15:49.

41. For a translation of the text and useful introduction, see H. G. Lunt, "Ladder of Jacob," in Charlesworth, *Old Testament Pseudepigrapha*, 2:401–411.

42. Note in addition to those printed versions cited by Lunt the version found
in J. Franko, *Apokrifi i Legendi* (Lvov, 1891), 1:108.

43. It may even be that the word for "ladder" here, *sullam*, is being consciously
associated with the similar-sounding *ṣelem*, "image" or "statue." Since the
former is a *hapax legomenon* in the Hebrew Bible, occurring only here, commentators might have been encouraged to associate it with some other
Hebrew root. (My thanks to Prof. M. Kossovsky for this suggestion.)

44. See above, note 41.

45. In its psychological sense, "affects" here means "emotion" or "feeling"—so
applying it to the transfer of midrashic motifs is somewhat metaphorical.
Yet precisely because the process in midrash is so often, as in the psychological usage, an unconscious one, it strikes me as a happy phrase to use.

5.

Inaccessible Bones

We have seen above how different midrashic motifs, originally created in order to clarify or elaborate specific points in the biblical narrative, ultimately came together to create a Joseph somewhat different from that found in the Bible itself. He was, for early exegetes, a strikingly handsome young man—so much so that women became infatuated at the mere sight of him, casting their precious jewels at his feet, or cutting their hands with knives in contemplation of his beauty. Nor was his physical appearance entirely accidental: for Joseph had cultivated his good looks, and in this he displayed an adolescent vanity that was apparently not unrelated to the trials that subsequently overtook him. Indeed, as a youth Joseph had hardly been beyond reproach: his "evil reports" about his brothers had not only engendered their hatred for him, but had in and of themselves constituted a moral defect for which he was punished by being sold as a slave. And even on the day of his greatest trial, when Mrs. Potiphar seized him by his garment, Joseph's behavior was not, at least initially, beyond reproach: he had willingly gone to the deserted house, knowing full well what was waiting for him, and intending to cooperate. It was only thanks to the miraculous appearance of his father's countenance *in extremis* that Joseph was suddenly reminded of his duties and fled from the house— ultimately to suffer the vengeance of his scorned mistress, yet, it is clear from the rest of his story, also chastened and strengthened thereby, and thus able to rise not only over the mighty nation of Egypt, but over the past defects of his own character, in order to emerge as the virtuous and exemplary leader we encounter at the end of Genesis.

The Broader Context

The events in Potiphar's house thus constitute a turning point in Joseph's life for early exegetes, and there is something quite appropriate about the epithet "Joseph the Virtuous" being connected with his behavior in, as we have seen, specifically this incident. But having examined various motifs surrounding this incident and their development and connection with other motifs, we have still not quite set the story of Joseph and Potiphar's wife in its full exegetical context. For one might still legitimately ask why it was that these events, or indeed the story of Joseph as a whole, were approached by early exegetes in the way that they were: why exactly *was* Joseph "Joseph the Virtuous"? Why should he have been put forward as such a paragon of virtue at all? Could not the incident with Potiphar's wife have been read as merely one among many interesting interludes in the lives of the patriarchs, containing, it is true, some evidence of meritorious behavior on the part of its hero, but no more so than, say, many things in the lives of Abraham or Moses or other figures?

This may seem like a disingenuous question, for certainly we have already observed above (chapter 1) various factors that led early exegetes to focus on, specifically, the incident with Mrs. Potiphar as Joseph's most conspicuously virtuous act. And indeed, the text does say out-and-out "he refused" (Gen. 39:8): that a slave, even one in his relatively lofty position, should permit himself to refuse such a request from his master's wife, that he should refuse what amounted to repeated requests, "day after day," bespeaks both high moral standards and no small amount of courage. But the question here is not so much why the incident with Mrs. Potiphar was the one that exegetes turned to as *the* episode that most conspicuously illustrated Joseph's virtue, but why the idea of "Joseph the Virtuous" got started in the first place.

The answer (as likewise suggested above, chapter 1) begins with the somewhat "gratuitous" nature of the Mrs. Potiphar narrative within the overall history. For from a practical standpoint, the temptation by Mrs. Potiphar has no particular significance within the overall biblical story. It could be eliminated entirely—Joseph could be sold as a slave, then jailed for some entirely different reason, then meet up with Pharaoh's butler and baker in prison, etc., etc.—without any damage being done to the overall action. Likewise, in terms of the function that the entire Joseph story exercises within the larger chain of events in Genesis—Joseph is sold as a slave to Egypt and there rises to prominence, as a result of which Jacob and his children, the ancestors of the Israelites, all end up moving from Canaan down to Egypt, where their descendants are susbsequently enslaved and led out of captivity by Moses—the story of Joseph and Mrs. Potiphar has no particular role to play. And this "gratuitousness" in turn must have suggested to early exegetes that there was some *other* purpose for its inclusion: and what purpose could be more obvious than that it was there to teach something about Joseph's virtuous character and steadfastness in the face of temptation, a trait to be emulated by later generations?

But beyond this, there were a number of specific indications else-where in the Bible that Joseph was an extraordinarily virtuous individual. First, of course, was the obvious fact that Joseph was given a "double portion" in his father's inheritance: his sons Manasseh and Ephraim become coinheritors with their uncles, thus assuring Joseph's descendants twice as much as they should normally have inherited (Gen. 48:5). (This fact came later to be associated, as we saw briefly, with the [two] "daughter-vines" in Jacob's blessing, Gen. 49:22, and was of course connected as well with the bull's two horns in Moses' blessing, Deut. 33:17.) But why should Joseph merit this particular consideration? A double portion is in fact, according to Deut. 22:17, supposed to be given to the firstborn, and where there are multiple wives, to the firstborn of the first wife—so that Jacob's action in granting a double portion to Joseph might at first glance seem to contravene biblical law. This was evidently troubling to exegetes even before the Bible itself was complete: 1 Chronicles 5:1 begins its genealogy with the following:

> The sons of Reuben the firstborn of Israel (for he *was* the firstborn; but because he polluted his father's couch, his birthright was given to the sons of Joseph the son of Israel, so that he is not enrolled in the genealogy according to the birthright; though Judah became strong among his brothers and a prince was from him, yet the birthright belonged to Joseph).

The fact that Reuben did not get his due is explained in Chronicles by an allusion to the truncated narrative of Gen. 35:22: his action with Bilhah, his father's concubine, disqualified him from the double portion that would have been his. But why then was a double portion awarded at all, and why to Joseph? The text of Chronicles seems troubled by this problem—and specifically by the fact that the double portion was not then granted to the tribe of Judah, which would after all provide the nation with its legitimate hereditary monarchy, the Davidic line. No answer is even hinted at in the above passage, but no doubt exegetes were not hard pressed to come up with one.[1] For the fact is that it is Joseph who is the great hero of the latter part of the book of Genesis, and certainly the fact that he inherits the double portion must indicate that the events recounted in his long story contain within them the virtuous deeds that are apparently being rewarded in this inheritance. In other words, the fact of Joseph's receiving a double portion came to support the reading of his story as an account of meritorious behavior—and what, as we have seen above, seems more conspicuously meritorious than his behavior with Mrs. Potiphar?

Beyond the "gratuitous" existence of the Joseph story in its wider context in Genesis, and the fact of the double portion granted to Joseph, there were other elements that suggested that Joseph's virtuousness was exceptional. He was (again, as we have seen) mentioned in various psalms, in particular in Psalms 80, 81, and 105, in such a way as to suggest that there was something exceptional about him, that he stood out among the brothers in, perhaps, his virtuous conduct. This singling out of Joseph there would then quite naturally be brought back to any reading of the Genesis narrative, and the events of Joseph's life would, consciously or not, be analyzed in terms of the exemplary importance apparently being attributed to him in these Psalms. And of course the same might likewise be said of the existence of the "House of Joseph" in other biblical texts outside of the Pentateuch. This "House of Joseph" was of course the geopolitical entity described above (chapter 1); but the fact that the Northern tribes should ultimately be associated with Joseph in particular in these other biblical texts must again have suggested something extraordinary about this biblical figure.

Joseph's Bones

Beyond all these factors, however, is one final specific aspect of the Joseph narrative, the disposal of Joseph's bones after his death. For the biblical text seems to attach particular importance to this matter. Of course it is true that, before he dies, Joseph specifically instructs his brothers concerning his last remains:

> And Joseph said to his brothers: After I am dead, God will surely remember you and bring you out of this land to the land which he swore to Abraham, Isaac, and Jacob. And Joseph had the sons of Israel swear, saying, "When God remembers you, you will take my bones out from here." And Joseph died at one hundred and ten years of age, and they embalmed him and put him in a casket in Egypt.
>
> (Gen. 50:24–26)

But there the matter might have ended. Yet the book of Exodus goes on specifically to mention that Moses did in fact take Joseph's bones with him on the way out of Egypt, and in so doing alludes directly to the above passage: "And Moses took Joseph's bones with him; for he had had the sons of Israel swear, saying, 'When God remembers you, you shall bring up my bones from here with you'" (Exod. 13:19). What is more, the book of Joshua further goes on to recount the final disposal of Joseph's bones: "And the bones of Joseph which the people of Israel brought up from Egypt were buried at Shechem, in the portion of ground which Jacob had bought from the sons of Hamor the father of Shechem for a hundred pieces of money; it became an inheritance of the descendants of Joseph" (Josh. 24:32). In short, an extraordinary importance seems to be attached to the disposal of Joseph's last remains and their successful return to his homeland; why was so much attention lavished on this subject? Again, the answer for early interpreters was likely to have been that Joseph himself had been an extraordinarily virtuous individual, hence the text's insistence that his last wishes had in fact been carried out punctiliously. Had he been anything other than "Joseph the Virtuous," why the Israelites might surely have honored their vow and taken his remains with them—but there would scarcely have been any point in Scripture's mentioning this not once but twice more, in connection with Moses' removal of the bones and again with their final burial in the Holy Land, in the territory assigned to Joseph's descendants.

And so Scripture's emphasis on Joseph's bones was certainly another factor leading into the "Joseph the Virtuous" reading of his whole story. Indirect evidence of this may be found in the brief notice taken of Joseph in Ben Sira's catalogue of biblical heroes (Sir. 49:15), which says only: "There has not been born another man like Joseph, yea, his remains were taken care of." Clearly, the one element in the whole long Joseph narrative that Ben Sira has found worthy of comment is the fact that Joseph's bones are specifically mentioned in connection with Moses and again in the book of Joshua. If so, one can imagine that other early exegetes were similarly impressed by this detail, and read in it testimony of the extraordinary character of the one whose remains these were, "Joseph the Virtuous."

Beyond this, though, it is interesting to note that around the removal of Joseph's bones from Egypt there grew up yet another set of midrashic traditions, traditions that not only ultimately served to highlight the theme of "Joseph the Virtuous" but which, in their own way, are further instructive about some of the general traits we have seen above with regard to the development of exegetical motifs. Accordingly, it might be appropriate to conclude our survey of Joseph's virtuous behavior with this midrashic coda, the motif of the disposal of this righteous man's last remains.[2]

"Measure for Measure"

One starting point for this discussion is the text of the Mishnah, *Soṭa* 1:9. The section of the Mishnah just previous to this one had discussed the idea of reciprocity between crime and punishment, observing that "By the measure that a man measures out with, so is it measured out to him."[3] Having illustrated this principle with various biblical texts, the Mishnah then turns to the converse principle of the rewarding of virtue:

> And so is it for the good [as well]. Miriam waited but a short while for Moses, as it is said, "And his sister stood far off" (Exod. 2:4), therefore the Israelites were delayed on her behalf for seven days in the wilderness, as it is said, "And the people did not go forward until Miriam was gathered in" (Num. 12:15). [So similarly:] Joseph was the one who was found worthy to bury his father—and there was none among the brothers greater than him—as it is said, "And Joseph went up to bury his father, and there went up with him chariots and riders" (Gen. 49:7–9). Who then do you have greater than Joseph [who might in turn bury him]? Moses was the one who took care of him, it was Moses who was found worthy [to take care] of Joseph's bones, and there was no one in Israel greater than him, as it is said, "And Moses took Joseph's bones with him" (Exod. 13:19). Who then do you have greater than Moses [who might in turn bury him]? God himself was the one who took care of him, as it is said, "And he buried him in the valley [. . . but no man knows the place of his burial to this day]" (Deut. 34:5).

With regard to the rewarding of virtue, the principle does not seem to be "measure for measure" but rather that each virtuous act receives an even greater reward. Thus Miriam waited only a brief while to find out what would become of her infant brother Moses, cast into the Nile, and in reward for this seemingly insignificant act, the Mishnah asserts, the entire camp of Israelites waited seven days for her in the desert. A similar principle of ever-greater rewards is applied to the matter of burial. Joseph takes care of burying his father (for the biblical text says specifically that "*Joseph* went up to bury his father," and although it is clear that the others brothers joined him, apparently he is singled out because he was the one who saw to the fulfillment of this filial duty); since he, the greatest of the brothers, took this task upon himself, he is rewarded by himself being buried by a person of still higher rank, Moses, the greatest of the Israelites. But how then will Moses' virtue be rewarded in similarly disproportionate fashion? Here our exegete, observing both the fact that Moses' burial is described with the impersonal third-person active form of the verb (literally "he buried"; but in biblical Hebrew, such an an impersonal verb really has the force of our passive, that is, Moses "was buried"), plus the fact that the text asserts that "no *man* knows the place of his burial," concludes that in fact

Moses was not buried by a man at all, but by God himself, "*He* buried him in the valley." In this way, the crescendo of ever loftier buriers is maintained, and the principle that good deeds are rewarded with even better rewards is further illustrated. But more than that, the biblical attention given to the subject of Joseph's last remains is thereby explained: it was all part of a lesson concerning the rewarding of virtue.

The Bottom of the Nile

But now we come to a group of narrative expansions which, like those of the "Assembly of Ladies" motif, must appear somewhat astonishing at first glance. For various rabbinic works—the text in the *Tosefta* (*Soṭa* 4:7) corresponding to the above-cited Mishnah, as well as another *tannaitic* work, the *Mekhilta deR. Yishma'el*, and other early rabbinic sources—all recount something about Joseph's bones not mentioned in either the biblical narrative itself nor the Mishnah. According to these sources, not only did Moses take charge of removing Joseph's remains from Egypt, but in so doing found himself required to perform a miracle. Here is the form of the tradition as it appears in the *Mekhilta*:

> "And Moses took Joseph's bones with him" (Exod. 13:19)—[this is intended] to proclaim Moses' wisdom and piety, for all of Israel was occupied with the booty [taken from Egypt] but Moses busied himself with the commandment of [removing] Joseph's bones. It is about him that Scripture [speaks when it] says: "One wise of heart will take commandments . . ." (Prov. 10:8). But whence did Moses know where Joseph was buried? They said that Serah the daughter of Asher had survived from that time [that is, the time of Joseph's death] and she showed Moses Joseph's grave. She said to him: this is the place where they put him. The Egyptians had made for him a metal casket and dropped it in the middle of the Nile. He came and stood over the Nile. He took a pebble[4] and cast it in the midst [of the water] and cried out: Joseph! Joseph! [The time of] the oath has come which was sworn by God to our father Abraham, that he would redeem his sons. Give honor to the Lord, the God of Israel, and do not hold up your redemption, for on your account we are now held up, and if not, then we are hereby free from your oath [reported in Gen. 50:25]. Thereupon Joseph's coffin floated to the surface and Moses took it.
>
> (*Mekhilta Beshallaḥ*, 1)

This passage, as well as its parallels, present a compound of different motifs all wrapped together into a fairly harmonious package. It should not, however, be difficult to identify some of its constituents. Thus, for example, the connection of Moses with the words cited from

Prov. 10:18 has, it seems, been grafted onto an originally simpler story. In fact, the attempt to identify Moses with this verse's all-purpose "wise of heart" man should remind us of, for example, the attempt to identify Joseph with the all-purpose "wise son" of Prov. 29:3 that was seen above ("Joseph's Change of Heart") in our passage from the Babylonian Talmud: "A wisdom-loving man will please his father, but a shepherd of prostitutes loses [his] wealth." In both cases, a general maxim found in Proverbs is particularized by being **back-referenced** to a historical figure from the Pentateuch. In the case of Joseph, it will be recalled, the common term connecting the verse in Proverbs with the Joseph story was the word "shepherd." Here, with Moses, it is the verb "take." For after all, it is strange for Prov. 10:18 to say that the wise of heart will *take* commandments: should it not more properly say something like "will *perform* commandments," or "remember" or "keep" them, since these are the usual idioms used by the book of Proverbs?[5] Thus, the appearance of this strange expression, "take commandments," has drawn the attention of our midrashist, and has ultimately suggested to him a possible connection with Exod. 13:19, "And Moses *took* Joseph's bones." Perhaps then Moses' *taking* of Joseph's bones is what is being referred to in Prov. 10:18.

In order to convince his audience of this claim, our midrashist has somewhat stacked the deck. For notice that he begins his exposition by saying that Exod. 13:19, "And Moses took Joseph's bones," was intended "to proclaim Moses' wisdom and piety. . . ." Actually, the fact that Moses took the bones may have demonstrated his piety, but his "wisdom"?! It seems that the term "wisdom" has been deliberately stuck in next to "piety" in order to prepare us for the claim that this "wise of heart" person in Proverbs is indeed a reference to Moses in his taking of the bones.[6] In other words, "piety" is there because it is the appropriate term, the taking of Joseph's bones was indeed an act of *ḥasidut*; but "wisdom" is added on in order to justify the Proverbs connection. Note also that a little later on in the same sentence, our midrashist says that Moses "was busying himself with the *commandment* of [removing] Joseph's bones." Now technically speaking, the removal of Joseph's bones was a "*commandment*" (*miṣvah*) only in the sense that it constituted the fulfillment of an oath sworn by Joseph's brothers. Yet our midrashist specifically uses the word "commandment" in order once again to set his audience up for the verse from Proverbs. Thus, having described Moses as as having demonstrated *wisdom* in his *taking* of Joseph's bones and having said that this act was the fulfillment of a *commandment*, he has laid the groundwork for connecting each of the major terms in his Proverbs text, "wise-of-heart," "take," and "commandment" with Exod. 13:19, "And Moses took Joseph's bones."

Having said this, however, we can now turn to the rest of this narrative expansion to which this excursus on Moses and the Proverbs verse has been grafted. We might begin by noting in the opening sentence the statement contrasting Moses and the other Israelites: "all of Israel was occupied with the booty [taken from Egypt] but Moses busied himself with the commandment of [removing] Joseph's bones." This contrast seems to have an exegetical aim quite separate from the Proverbs connection just examined: it constitutes a separate motif, one apparently aimed at explaining why it is that the text singles out Moses as having been the one to take Joseph's bones in the first place. In other words, why does it say "And *Moses* took," when in fact all the Israelites were duty-bound to do so (and, as we have seen, the text of Josh. 24:32 in fact later says that the "people of Israel" had brought up Joseph's bones out of Egypt)? And the answer that this motif provides is that indeed at the precise time of the Israelites' departure, Moses was the only one to think about Joseph's bones—everyone else was occupied with booty taken from the Egyptians. So the text's singling out of Moses was hardly an accident or a shorthand reference: he alone did the good deed, while everyone else was thinking about other things.[7] We may call this motif "Busy with Booty."

But then our *Mekhilta* passage goes on to raise a question that would otherwise be totally unexpected: how did Moses know where Joseph was buried? There is no indication in the biblical text that Joseph's burial place was secret; on the contrary, one would suppose that such a distinguished figure would have been buried in some prominent location with full honors, and that his burial place would be well known to ordinary Egyptians, not to speak of his own kinsmen, the children of Israel. Yet our *Mekhilta* passage seems simply to assume that Moses himself would not have known. And so to the rescue comes a figure not otherwise of striking importance in the Bible, Serah, the daughter of Asher, one of Jacob's twelve sons;[8] she tells Moses where Joseph's bones are located. But why introduce Serah here? She is able to come to the rescue because of a curious detail in the biblical text. For she is in fact mentioned twice in the Pentateuch. The first mention comes in Gen. 46:17, in the list of the family members that accompanied Jacob and his sons down to Egypt: "The sons of Asher: Imnah, Ishvah, Ishvi, Beriah, and Serah their sister." The fact of this reference to her is in itself quite odd, since it is rarely the custom of biblical genealogies to mention female descendants. Why Serah? The answer for early exegetes seemed to come in that other mention of her, in Num. 26:46, for there, in a census list of the principal families descendant from Asher, is the statement "And the name of the daughter of Asher was Serah." Although it is hardly self-evident from the context, rabbinic exegetes read this statement as an assertion that Serah herself *was still alive* at the time of this census, just before the Israelites were about to enter the land of Canaan. But if so, then this woman had lived all the time from the Israelites' first entry into Egypt to their eventual exodus under the leadership of Moses, and had further survived the forty years of desert wanderings! No wonder her name had been singled out in Gen. 46:17, for she alone was going to survive the entire period of Egyptian captivity.

The motif of Serah's longevity existed quite independent of the story of Joseph's bones. But if we assume—as our text apparently does—that Moses would not know where Joseph was buried, then Serah is a convenient person to have around, since she alone has survived from the time of Joseph's death, and can thus be counted on to show Moses the precise location of his watery grave. Whereupon Moses summons up the metal casket, both by calling out to Joseph and by casting something in the water—a "pebble," or in other versions, a tablet inscribed with the divine name or other effective devices.[9] It seems, incidentally, that this doubling of means is another instance of **overkill:** it would be enough to have Moses call out to Joseph as he does without any need of physical props—indeed, the *Tosefta* and other versions of this midrash[10] simply have Moses call out to Joseph without casting anything into the Nile. But at a certain point the necessity of raising Joseph's coffin from the bottom of the Nile suggested a similar story found in the Bible, in which Elisha miraculously causes an iron axehead to float up from the bottom of the Jordan (2 Kings. 6:5); since Elisha there casts something into the water in order to perform the miracle, some exegetes apparently decided to have Moses do likewise, hence the "pebble," gold tablet, and so forth found in various sources. (Indeed, the *Mekhilta* and other texts go on specifically to mention Elisha's miracle in recounting this about Moses.)

That these two elements, the "miracle-working speech" and the "pebble," are quite independent of each other should in fact be apparent upon closer examination of the *Mekhilta* text cited above. For there we read:

> He [Moses] took a pebble and cast it in the midst [of the water] and cried out: Joseph! Joseph! [The time of] the oath has come which was sworn by God to our father Abraham, that he would redeem his sons.

Give honor to the Lord, the God of Israel, and do not hold up your redemption, for on your account we are now held up, and if not, then we are hereby free from your oath [i.e., Gen. 50:25]. Thereupon Joseph's coffin floated to the surface and Moses took it.

If Moses' action were truly to parallel Elisha's in 2 Kings 6:5, then he should simply cast something—the pebble—into the water and cause the coffin magically to rise. There is no speech at all in the case of Elisha, and should be none here if the analogy is to be perfect. But not only does Moses speak in this version, but it is most noteworthy that the speech that he utters makes no reference to the pebble that he has just cast into the water—the two acts are completely uncoordinated. That is, Moses does not say, as he surely would if these two elements had come from the same hand, "By this pebble I hereby summon you . . ." or something similar. Indeed, the speech he does make is essentially a threat, one which might be paraphrased: Joseph, come up *by your own power* or we will consider our oath to be null and void. But if so, the very existence of this threat, along with the demand that Joseph himself take charge of rising from the bottom of the Nile, implies that without this speech Moses would be powerless to raise Joseph. In other words, this speech in fact denies the whole analogy with Elisha and the act of casting the pebble which was apparently modeled upon it! Therefore we have no choice but to conclude that the miracle-working speech and the pebble were apparently quite separate elements. Indeed, it seems clear that the miracle-working speech came first into this motif, for it certainly would not have been added on *after* the analogy with 2 Kings 6:5 had been thought of and the gesture of throwing the pebble had been added in. But once the motif with the miracle-working speech was already established, the Elisha analogy suggested itself and the prooftext of 2 Kings 6:5 was adduced (this, it will be recalled, is the form of our motif as found in the *Tosefta*). Only after that was the pebble added on to make Moses' deed more clearly parallel to Elisha's.

The Tombs of the Egyptian Kings

This narrative expansion in the *Mekhilta* and *Tosefta* is followed immediately in both texts by another, contrary tradition concerning the location of Joseph's bones. The version of the *Tosefta* is somewhat fuller here, so I will cite it:

There are those who say that Joseph had been buried among the tombs of the [Egyptian] kings. So he [Moses] said, "Joseph, Joseph!

> The time has come for God to redeem Israel: The Divine Presence is held back because of you, and Israel is held back because of you, and the clouds of glory are held back because of you. If you now reveal yourself, all well and good; but if not, we will be free of the oath that you caused our ancestors to swear. Thereupon the casket of Joseph began to stir, and Moses came and took it.

Here, apparently, Joseph's burial place *per se* is not a secret, nor is there any need for Serah or anyone else to point out its location. But apparently Joseph's bones are somehow inaccessible—perhaps in a pyramid—or else the precise location of Joseph's casket among those of the Egyptian kings at this burial site is unknown,[11] for Moses has to resort to an exhortation similar[12] to his Nile-side speech in the previous motif in order to get Joseph's coffin to identify itself. But having thus managed to discover the precise location of Joseph's casket, Moses then is able to take it and go on his way.

Interestingly, the idea that Joseph's bones had been stored on royal property is found as well in a considerably earlier text, in the *Testaments of the Twelve Patriarchs:*

> And when Simeon had finished his instructions to his sons, he slept with his fathers at the age of one hundred and twenty years. They placed him in a wooden coffin in order to carry his bones up to Hebron; they took them up in secret during a war with Egypt. **The bones of Joseph the Egyptians kept in the treasure-houses of the palace** [another version: "in the tombs of the kings"][13] since their wizards told them that at the departure of Joseph's bones there would be darkness and gloom in the whole land and a great plague on the Egyptians, so that even with a lamp no one could recognize his brother.
>
> ("Testament of Simeon" 8:1–3)

Here too Joseph's bones are stored away under royal auspices. Although the reason was not stated in the *Tosefta* text, here Joseph's "royal treatment" does not apparently derive solely from the fact that he had been such an important personage in Egypt. It seems as well that Pharaoh's "wizards" and wise men foresee the disaster of the plague of darkness (Exod. 10:21–23) that is to befall Egypt at the time of the Exodus, and seek to forestall it.

A Common Structure

In any case, if one considers these two traditions—that Joseph's bones were dropped to the bottom of the Nile in a (waterproof) metal casket, and that they were hidden in the tombs of the Egyptian kings—it becomes clear that the two have one element in common: they both present Joseph's bones as having been hidden away in such a manner as to make it difficult for Moses to recover them. One might thus speak of a **basic motif** underlying the two, "Inaccessible Bones." But it is precisely this element which is most problematic for our relating either or both traditions to the biblical text. For the text of Exod. 13:19 says nothing of any *difficulty* that Moses encountered when he sought to remove Joseph's bones; it simply says, "And Moses took Joseph's bones with him." Where then did this idea come from? Of course one might make a virtue of a necessity and say that the fact that Moses is singled out in this verse (whereas in fact *all* the Israelites were supposed to take care of Joseph's bones) might have implied to early exegetes that there was indeed some difficulty associated with removing the bones, and that as a result *only Moses* could accomplish this difficult task. There is some merit to this explanation. But it still does not account for the full-scale invention of our stories' fantastic details, the coffin in the Nile or in the kings' tombs. Indeed, a far simpler and more reasonable explanation could have been obtained by following the same line of thought presented in our Mishnah passage: Moses was singled out because he was the most honored of all the Israelites, therefore the text tells us that it was specifically Moses who took Joseph's bones.

Some who have touched on this question in the past have sought its answer in parallels found elsewhere: in the Osiris myth,[14] or in other external sources.[15] And certainly it seems possible that the existence of at least the former has had a role in shaping the motif of Joseph's bones being place in a casket in the Nile. For according to this Egyptian legend, Osiris is placed in a box and cast into the Nile; his sister Isis desperately searches for him, finally finding him after three days. Yet one is left to wonder why our basic motif, "Inaccessible Bones," even if shaped somewhat by this myth, should ever have arisen in the first place. That is, why should exegetes have countenanced *any* tradition to the effect that some obstacle had come along and made it difficult for Joseph's bones to be removed, when in fact the biblical text gives no hint of it? It is true, of course, that Joseph's bones are said to be "brought up" from Egypt, and some scholars have suggested that the use of this verb might have engendered the motif of Joseph's bones being literally "brought up" from the bottom of the Nile.[16] But this is doubtful: first of all, the expressions to "go up" and "bring/take up" are generally used in biblical Hebrew for movement from Egypt to the land of Israel, just as "go down" and "bring/take down" are used of motion in the opposite direction—so there is nothing suspicious, or even suggestive, about their use here. Moreover, we have this usage precisely in the case of Jacob's last remains—they too are "brought up" (Gen. 50:5–9)—yet this did not lead to the creation of any such midrashic motif for Jacob's bones. Thirdly, the "bringing up" of Joseph's bones would hardly explain the origin of our parallel motif, that the bones were kept in the tombs of the Egyptian kings. So it seems the origins of this midrashic tradition are to be found elsewhere.

With characteristic sensitivity to the biblical text itself, Joseph Heinemann suggested another point of departure. For the wording of the very last verse of the book of Genesis (Gen. 50:26, cited above) is somewhat strange, or might have seemed so to early exegetes. It says, "And Joseph died at one hundred and ten years of age, and they embalmed him *and put him in a casket in Egypt.*" The last phrase is odd on two counts. It does not use the word "bury," which is what one would normally expect to be done with a dead body, but only says that the embalmed Joseph was "put in a casket." But if he was, therefore, *not* buried, then what was done with him? In addition to this, the verse adds that he was put in a casket "in Egypt." But surely one did not expect him to be put in a casket in Oklahoma—the whole narrative is situated in Egypt! For this reason, exegetes might have tended to regard this very vague reference to the place of the casket as indicating that, in fact, its exact location was, or came to be, unknown. Thus, because of these two factors within this verse, Heinemann argued, "the author of our aggadah came to two conclusions: the first, that the casket had not been buried in the ground; and the second, that indeed its precise location was unknown. And thus the door was opened to the various stories . . . concerning Moses' attempts to find Joseph's coffin."[17]

Tebat Marqa

Another text bearing on this tradition—and with it, another argument concerning its origins—is to be found in the collection of Samaritan exegetical writings known as *Memar Marqa* (but more correctly, *Tebat Marqa*).[18] A collection of writings of varied provenance (the oldest among which probably belong to the fourth century of the common era), this Aramaic source provides an important reservoir of ancient exegetical traditions. In the matter of Joseph's bones, *Tebat Marqa* relates that everything started when the Israelites found themselves unable to leave Sukkot:

> In Ra'amses they sacrificed, and then they moved on to Sukkot; but when they sought to leave it, they could not. The pillar of cloud and

of fire had stopped in front of them so that they could not leave the border of Sukkot. Moses and Aaron saw and were afraid, and the whole congregation was astonished. "What is this secret?" said Moses to Aaron. . . . The elders came to Moses and Aaron and [he said]: "Go about in peace, O elders of the congregation, and ask of every tribe what is this secret." . . . And the elders scattered among the tribes and began to inquire of each tribe. When they cried out amid the tribe of Asher, Serah the daughter of Asher went hurrying out to them. "There is nothing evil in your midst. Behold, I will reveal to you what this secret is." At once they surrounded her and brought her to the great prophet Moses and she stood stood before him. [She said: . . .] "Hear from me this thing that you seek: Praise to those who remembered my beloved [Joseph], though you have forgotten him. For had not the pillar of cloud and pillar of fire stood still, you would have departed and he would have been left in Egypt. I remember the day that he died and he caused the whole people to swear that they would bring his bones up from here with them." The great prophet Moses said to her, "Worthy are you, Serah, wisest of women. From this day on will your greatness be told." A rumor spread among the congregation and it was said to them: "Indeed, Joseph will go up from this place with us." Serah went with all the tribe of Ephraim around her, and Moses and Aaron went after them, until she came to the place where he was hidden. And they uncovered the coffin and brought it quickly. Then Serah departed from Moses and Aaron.[19]

The similarity of this passage to our rabbinic sources is evident: not only does Serah play a similar role, but more generally the basic idea that Joseph's bones were hidden or inaccessible is likewise maintained. (Indeed, the mention of the "pillar of cloud and fire" as being the cause of the delay is also somewhat reminiscent of the language of Moses' miracle-working speech, "Behold, the Divine Presence is held back because of you, Israel is held back because of you, the *clouds of glory* are held back because of you.") The difference is that here Moses does not simply set out to remove Joseph's bones and then encounters difficulties. He seems to have forgotten utterly that there was any need to remove the bones until Serah tells him. For this reason, Serah's great age serves a double function in the story: as someone who was around at the time when Joseph had had his brothers swear that they would remove his bones, she alone is capable of understanding what the problem is with the pillars of cloud and fire, for she alone is aware of the oath. And what is more, she alone knows where Joseph "is hidden"—since here too he is apparently hidden away, though we are not told where.

Can this story illuminate the origin of our midrash? Its focus on the timing and geography of the events in question—that is, the fact that the Bible does not mention the removal of Joseph's bones (Exod. 13:19) until after it says that the Israelites had left Raʿamses and gone to Sukkot (Exod. 12:37)—may indeed be an important clue. For could not Moses and the Israelites have recovered Joseph's bones before they began their journey out of Egypt? Why did they wait? What is more, immediately following the mention of Joseph's bones in Exod. 13:19, the text continues, "And they moved on from Sukkot, and encamped at Etham . . . and the Lord went before them by day in a pillar of cloud to lead them along the way, and at night in a pillar of fire. . . ." Here again one has cause for puzzlement: why are the pillars of cloud and fire being mentioned now—were they not with the Israelites from the beginning of their journey?

Considering this arrangement of things, the Talmudist Saul Lieberman suggested that it was the strange order of events in the biblical text that stands behind the entire midrashic tradition—including *Tebat Marqa*—that we have been examining. "The question is: why did not Moses get Joseph's bones at the first stage, in Raʿamses, and why did he wait until the second stage, Sukkot? . . . And likewise, why were the clouds of glory not mentioned in Raʿamses," that is, at the beginning of the exodus from Egypt?[20] According to Lieberman, the *Tebat Marqa* version demonstrates one early answer to these questions: the Israelites had in fact forgotten about Joseph's bones, but there was no need for them to be reminded of them until after they had arrived in Sukkot, the region in which the bones had actually been hidden. There the pillar of cloud and fire suddenly stopped and refused to move. And for the same reason, the pillar had not been specifically mentioned before in the biblical text: no doubt it had accompanied the Israelites from the very beginning, but it is first mentioned in connection with Sukkot as a "hint" to the fact that at Sukkot it suddenly stopped, holding up the Israelites until Moses could take up Joseph's bones (v. 19). Immediately thereafter (v. 21), the text says "And the Lord went before them by day in a pillar of cloud [etc.]," that is, as a result of Moses' action, the pillar once again moved forward. In other words, this whole passage in *Tebat Marqa* springs from a curiosity about the timing and location of the mention of Joseph's bones (and the "pillar of cloud") within the narrative. Indeed, the very fact that the bones were, according to this view, buried in some out-of-the-way place near Sukkot, might easily have led to the notion that they had been "hidden"—and this in turn may have led to the other forms of "hiding" that we have seen above, Joseph's bones being stored in the "treasure-houses of the palace," the "bottom of the Nile," or the "tombs of the kings."

Starting Point of the Tradition

All of these explanations—the connection of this midrashic motif with the Osiris legend, or with the strange wording of Gen. 50:26, "they put him in a casket in Egypt," or with the fact that the bones are only mentioned when the Israelites get to Sukkot—no doubt contributed to the development of our basic motif. Indeed, were it not for one piece of evidence, I would certainly be convinced that any one of them, or some combination of the three, could have been responsible for the creation in the first place of the idea—not at all present in the biblical text—that Joseph's bones were somehow inaccessible and required extraordinary measures in order to be removed. Yet the piece of evidence in question is such as to suggest that these other factors came into play only after there already was a well established motif of Joseph's "Inaccessible Bones." And that piece of evidence is none other than the brief excerpt from the "Testament of Simeon" 8:1–3 seen above. Let us look at it again, seeking to read it without preconception:

> And when Simeon had finished his instructions to his sons, he slept with his fathers at the age of one hundred and twenty years. They placed him in a wooden coffin in order to carry his bones up to Hebron; they took them up in secret during a war with Egypt. The bones of Joseph the Egyptians kept in the treasure-houses of the palace, since their wizards told them that at the departure of Joseph's bones there would be darkness and gloom in the whole land and a great plague on the Egyptians, so that even with a lamp no one could recognize his brother.
>
> ("Testament of Simeon" 8:1–3)

This is the oldest datable reference to the motif of the hiding-away of Joseph's bones, and so presumably it might give us a clue as to the motif's ultimate origins. But we must try to understand this passage on its own terms. For when we do so it becomes clear that the passage is not the slightest bit interested in explaining why Moses *alone* took out Joseph's bones, nor in how Moses might have known where they were, nor why the biblical text says that Joseph's bones were put "in a casket in Egypt," nor yet why their removal was put off until the Israelites had gotten to Sukkot. In fact, this passage has no concern whatsoever for Exod. 13:19, "And Moses took Joseph's bones"! It makes no mention at all of that verse, nor does it appear to be the slightest bit interested in Moses, nor, for that matter, even in what will become of Joseph's bones *at the time of the exodus*. Rather, its focus is on Joseph at the time of his death, because the exegetical question it is seeking to answer does indeed concern the things narrated at that moment. Its question is:

Why were not Joseph's bones removed for burial in the land of Israel *immediately after his death*, just as Jacob's were? Let us look again at the last sentences of Genesis:

> And Joseph said to his brothers: After I am dead, God will surely remember you and bring you out of this land to the land which He swore to Abraham, Isaac, and Jacob. And Joseph had the sons of Israel swear, saying, "When God remembers you, you will take my bones out from here." And Joseph died at one hundred and ten years of age, and they embalmed him and put him in a casket in Egypt.
>
> (Gen. 50:24–26)

Apparently, Joseph knows even as he is preparing himself for death that his brothers will not be allowed to remove his bones immediately afterwards—this can be the only explanation for why he has them swear that they will do so "when God remembers you" rather than right away. But it remained for exegetes to come up with an answer as to *why* Joseph knew this. And so the "Testament of Simeon" proposed an answer: the "wizards" of Egypt foresaw that "at the departure of Joseph's bones there would be darkness and gloom in the whole land and a great plague on the Egyptians," that is, they foresaw the ninth of the Ten Plagues of Egypt (Exod. 10:21–23). And foreseeing this, they sought to forestall the disaster by resolving to place Joseph's body in the "treasure-houses of the palace."[21] In this way, the bones could be kept indefinitely under lock and key. Nor, apparently, did they hide their intentions from Joseph—for he quite obviously does know before his death that his body cannot be *immediately* transported to his homeland. But he likewise knows that, as he says to his brothers at the end of Genesis, eventually "God will surely remember you and bring you out of this land to the land which he swore to Abraham, Isaac, and Jacob." And knowing this, he insists on an oath to the effect that at the time of that exodus his bones will not be left behind.[22]

The same problem of why Joseph's bones were not removed at once had bothered other ancient exegetes as well. The following explanation is found in the *Book of Jubilees:*

> And before he [Joseph] died he gave instructions to the Israelites to take his bones with them when they went out of the land of Egypt. And he put them on oath regarding his bones, for he knew that the Egyptians would not take him and bury him in the land of Canaan. For Makamaron, king of Canaan, while living in the land of Assyria, fought in the valley with the king of Egypt and killed him there, and pursued the Egyptians to the gates of Ermon. But he was not able to get inside, because another king, a new one, had become king of

Egypt, and he was stronger than he was, and so he returned to the land of Canaan. And the gate of Egypt was shut, and no one went out of Egypt and no one went in. And Joseph died . . . and they buried him in the land of Egypt. And all his brothers died after him. And the king of Egypt went out to war with the king of Canaan . . . and the Israelites brought out all the bones of Jacob's children except Joseph's, and they buried them in the country, in the double cave in the mountain. And most of them returned to Egypt.

(Jubilees 46:5–10)

According to this explanation, Joseph has his brothers swear that they will remove his bones at the time of the exodus because the Egyptian-Canaanite border was shut tight at the time of his death, preventing anyone from leaving. When the border is reopened, however, the Israelites for some reason remove the bones of all the brothers *except* Joseph.[23] The text of *Jubilees* does not tell us why, but perhaps the reason is that the wording of Joseph's deathbed oath now worked against him: he had demanded that his bones be removed "when God shall surely remember you," that is, at the exodus itself, which had yet to take place.[24]

In any case, here is another attempt to explain why it is that Joseph does not request that his bones be removed to Canaan right away. The answer—that the border had been closed by war—explains both the fact that Joseph requested the oath that he did, and the fact that the other brothers' bones were not said to be removed with Joseph's at the time of the exodus (they already had been, as soon as it became possible to do so). And indeed, both these same problems stand behind our passage in the "Testament of Simeon." Only here, a different solution was found. Joseph requests the oath because he knows that the "wizards" are planning to keep Joseph's remains inaccessible, but at the same time, Simeon's body is brought "in secret during a war with Egypt"—for that will explain why his body, and those of the other brothers,[25] were not taken out with Joseph's at the final exodus.

If so, then the whole motif of "Inaccessible Bones" is really just another case of **transfer of affects.** This motif was originally devised to answer a problem at the end of Genesis: why does not Joseph have his brothers swear that they will remove his bones right away, as was the case with Jacob? But once created, the answer found in the "Testament of Simeon"—that Joseph knew that his bones were going to be stored away by the "wizards" to forestall the exodus—moved from one time frame, Joseph's death, to another, the exodus itself. For if Joseph's bones had been hidden away at the time of his death, why then they must still have been hidden away when it came time for Moses to retrieve them. And so, as the motif's original *raison d'être* disappeared from view, the idea that Joseph's bones were somehow inaccessible came to be understood as elucidating Exod. 13:19, "And *Moses* took Joseph's bones." Why Moses and not all the Israelites? Well, if the bones were somehow inaccessible, then perhaps only Moses was capable of retrieving them.[26]

Historical Development

With this orientation, all the exegetical passages seen above can be understood and put into some historical order. The oldest of them all, quite probably, is that of *Jubilees*, to the effect that the Egyptian-Canaanite border had been sealed.[27] As explanations go, however, this one was fairly weak, since it also required the bodies of the other brothers to be secretly brought by their descendants for burial in Canaan— but if so, then why not Joseph's bones as well?—and then have the descendants not stay in Canaan but go back to Egypt, get enslaved, and so on and so forth. The very awkwardness of such a scenario called out for an alternative solution; and in fact we have seen two. One was the passage from the Mishnah with which we began. *For the whole idea that Joseph could only be buried by someone greater than himself, Moses, and that Moses in turn could only be buried by God—all this was, at its origin, an elegant attempt to solve the very same problem of why Joseph did not request that his reburial in Canaan take place immediately after his death.* If Joseph was to be buried by someone greater than himself, then he could not very well ask his brothers to do so, for, as the Mishnah observes (somewhat gratuitously, unless one understands the exegetical motive), "there was none among the brothers greater than him."[28] He therefore has them swear (apparently on behalf of their descendants) that his bones will be brought up at the time of the exodus, when (he may reason, or even prophetically foresee) the one who will lead them out of Egypt will be sufficiently worthy to perform such a task.

But the other solution was to have Joseph's bones purposely kept and prevented from leaving by the Egyptians. For what reason? The "Testament of Simeon" suggested that Pharaoh's wise men foresaw the disaster accompanying the exodus and sought to forestall it. (This parallels another midrashic motif, whereby the same wise men, foreseeing the same disaster, have Pharaoh order that every baby boy be cast into the Nile, to prevent a "Moses" from being born).[29] For that reason Joseph's bones were made inaccessible, put away in the "treasure-houses of the palace." And this "Inaccessible Bones" basic motif was then transferred from the time frame of Joseph's death to that of the exodus, and in turn engendered the various versions seen above—that of *Tebat Marqa*, and the two presented side-by-side in both the *Mekhilta* and *Tosefta*, "Bottom of the Nile" and "Tombs of the [Egyptian] Kings."

Of these, the "Tombs of the [Egyptian] Kings" seems to be the closest and most obvious descendant of the "Treasure-houses of the Palace." Yet elements of the *Tebat Marqa* passage also bespeak its antiquity, and may now serve to focus our understanding of all three explanations. The starting point of *Tebat Marqa*, it will be recalled, was the fact that Joseph's bones are only retrieved after the Israelites have traveled from Ra῾amses to Sukkot (cf. Num. 33:5). How could an exegete explain this fact? Certainly one hypothesis, perhaps the simplest, is that the bones were in fact located in or around Sukkot, so that it only made sense for the Israelites to retrieve them after they had traveled there. Now this idea does seem to be present in the account in *Tebat Marqa*, for as soon as Serah tells Moses about the bones, they all go off and get them at once: there is no talk of returning to Ra῾amses or some other city—apparently, Sukkot is where the bones are located. At the same time, it is clear that the bones are not simply *at* Sukkot— they are *hidden*, for Serah leads Moses "until she came to the place where he [Joseph] was *hidden*." Thereupon "they *uncovered* [or "discovered"] the coffin and brought it quickly." So it seems that here *Tebat Marqa* has in fact combined the idea that the bones simply always had been in Sukkot (which would explain why Moses does not get around to taking them until Exod. 13:19) with the idea, imported from the "Testament of Simeon" tradition, that Joseph's bones had been *hidden* by the Egyptians: the bones are now *hidden in Sukkot*, and need to be revealed by Serah.

But in *Tebat Marqa*, this new "Hidden in Sukkot" motif has been further combined with another one, logically independent of it and even contradictory to it, namely, that the reason why the bones were not retrieved before was not because Sukkot was where they happened to be, nor because they had been "hidden," but simply because they had been forgotten by the Israelites until the pillar of cloud and fire refused to move and so prevented them from continuing their journey.[30] Indeed, this element of *forgetting* is stressed in our *Tebat Marqa* text: when the pillar stops Serah says to Moses, "you have forgotten him"; were it not for the pillar stopping, "you would have departed and he would have been left in Egypt."

Now of course this motif, "Forgotten by Everyone," works at cross-purposes with "Hidden in Sukkot," and their combination in *Tebat*

Marqa is therefore quite awkward, particularly with regard to the role of Serah. For if the Israelites had simply forgotten about Joseph's bones, and if the pillar of cloud and fire stopped them at Sukkot in order to remind them, then what need was there of Serah? Let them be reminded of their error by this stopped pillar, retrieve the bones, and continue—that would perfectly well account for all the things in the text which this motif seeks to explain, and there would be no need to mention Serah, whose "reminding" function merely duplicates that of the pillar itself. Moreover, there is another difficulty besides Serah's redundancy: for if indeed Serah, as the lone survivor from those days, was the only one capable of knowing about the bones, why did she wait until after the attempted departure from Sukkot and the delay caused by the pillar of cloud and fire in order to speak up? She should have spoken up long before they came near the place of Joseph's bones to remind everyone—if reminding were necessary—of Joseph's death-bed oath. Thus, Serah only needs to have a part in the story if that story relates that Joseph's bones had been *hidden away* (but not *forgotten*) and cannot now be found. The narrative in *Tebat Marqa*, containing as it does both Serah and the stopped pillar thus constitutes yet another case of **overkill,** and this fact clearly indicates that the two motifs in question were originally quite separate. Indeed, considering things schematically, we can now see that the passage in *Tebat Marqa* actually combines four logically separate elements: the received tradition about Joseph's bones having been hidden ("Inaccessible Bones"); the idea that the bones were located at or near Sukkot, and hence were not retrieved until after the Israelites traveled there ("In Sukkot"; combined with the former, this creates the motif "Hidden in Sukkot"); the contrary idea that Joseph's bones had simply been forgotten and left behind, until the pillars of cloud and fire stopped the Israelites at Sukkot in order to remind them ("Forgotten by Everyone"); and finally the tradition of Serah's great age ("Serah Knows"), which allowed her first to be the one to show Moses where the bones were hidden, and which was then harmonized with the "Forgotten by Everyone" motif in *Tebat Marqa*.

A Later Motif

Let us turn next to the "Bottom of the Nile" motif. Just because it is not attested in as ancient a source as the "Testament of Simeon" does not mean that it is not as old. For it certainly could have been designed to solve the same problem as the "Treasure-houses of the Palace" motif there, that is, to explain why Joseph does not request immediate reburial in Canaan—he knows that the Egyptians are planning to make his remains inaccessible and hence forestall disaster. Only here the inaccessibility is achieved by borrowing a motif from the story of Isis and Osiris and having Joseph placed in a waterproof casket and dropped to the bottom of the Nile. Logically, this borrowing could have taken place independently of (and even earlier than) the solution presented in the "Testament of Simeon," or, just as possibly, it may have been an embellishment designed to replace the "Treasure-houses of the Palace" motif in the latter, finding the bottom of the Nile to be a more dramatic and wholly satisfactory hiding place.[31] What is more, the "Bottom of the Nile" motif could take advantage of that other feature seen in Exod. 13:19, namely, its singling out of Moses as the one who took the bones. For if the bottom of the Nile was the hiding place, then surely extraordinary means would be required to recover the bones. From this developed Moses' miracle-working speech and the other (alternate) means seen for bringing up Joseph's bones, the pebble, the magical inscription, etc.

Nevertheless, there are certain signs of the relative "youth" of "Bottom of the Nile" vis-à-vis the others, at least in the form in which it has been passed down. One suspicious element (though it hardly *proves* our point) is the fact that, in the versions found in both the *Mekhilta* and *Tosefta*, this motif is preceded by the "Busy with Booty" motif, that is, by the sentence "[this is intended] to proclaim Moses' wisdom and piety, for all of Israel was occupied with the booty [taken from Egypt] but Moses busied himself with the commandment of [removing] Joseph's bones." This contrast of Moses with the rest of the Israelites is, as we have seen, meant to explain the fact that the Bible says "And *Moses* took Joseph's bones. . . ." But if the "Bottom of the Nile" motif were already in existence, there would hardly be any reason to suggest that the reason why Moses is singled out here is that the other Israelites had all neglected their duty (and still less reason to tie this neglect to the presence of "booty" from the Egyptians—what were they doing with it that they could not attend to Joseph's bones?). The text could, as noted, just as easily have said what the rest of "Bottom of the Nile" makes clear—that Moses is singled out precisely because the task of removing his bones required a miracle-working speech, that is, that only Moses *could* perform the task. That this is not the case, but that the Israelites are specifically said to be unmindful of Joseph's bones, seems to suggest that "Bottom of the Nile" only came into existence after "Busy with Booty." Indeed, the element of forgetfulness in "Busy with Booty" suggests yet another deep connection, one between this motif and "Forgotten by Everyone" motif of *Tebat Marqa,* whereby all the Israelites are *forgetful* concerning Joseph's bones until the pillar of cloud and fire stops to remind them.

A somewhat clearer sign of relative lateness in the "Bottom of the Nile" motif in the *Mekhilta* and *Tosefta* versions is the fact that Moses' miracle-working speech also alludes to an element in the "Forgotten by Everyone" motif (seen in *Tebat Marqa*), that of the pillar of cloud and fire stopping in order to remind the Israelites of Joseph's bones. For there is no need to have Moses speak of the pillar in this speech or invoke the idea of "delay" at all: he, the virtuous Moses, has not had to be reminded of Joseph's bones in this version, he alone has always had the bones in mind. Yet in calling out to Joseph's bones, he nonetheless says: "Joseph! Joseph! the time has come for God to redeem Israel—behold, the Divine Presence is held back because of you, the Israelites are held back because of you, the *clouds of glory* are held back because of you. . . ." This clearly is an evocation of the setting in Sukkot, and thus seems to be dependent on an already-existing motif that has the pillar of cloud *delayed* until the bones are retrieved. If so, at least the versions of the "Bottom of the Nile" motif that we possess already assume an earlier motif similar to "Forgotten by Everyone" in *Tebat Marqa.*

Now the sentence from the miracle-working speech just cited is as it appears in the *Tosefta* version of the "Bottom of the Nile" motif. But in the parallel *Mekhilta* version, this list of people and things being delayed is lacking. One might then conclude that the *Mekhilta* version is ultimately older than *Tosefta*'s. But note: in the *Mekhilta* Moses shouts, "Joseph! Joseph! [The time of] the oath has come which was sworn by God to our father Abraham, that he would redeem his sons. Give honor to the Lord, the God of Israel, and *do not hold up* your redemption, for on your account *we are now held up.* . . ." These very last words thus indicate that underlying even this version is the notion that the people were somehow *delayed.* One can thus conclude that the element seen in *Tebat Marqa* of the Israelites being stopped by the uncooperative pillar at Sukkot has been internalized by both the *Mekhilta* and *Tosefta* versions of the "Bottom of the Nile" motif.

Summary

And so now something of the evolution of the midrash of Joseph's bones can be established. Because the tracing of these different motifs has been somewhat involved, we may do well to conclude by summarizing their development in outline form:

I.   Starting point of the tradition: why does not Joseph request
     immediate reburial in Canaan, as Jacob had? To this question
     three answers were proposed:

  A.   The Egyptian-Canaanite border had been closed and
       Joseph knew that his body could not be transported
       immediately (*Jubilees*).

  B.   Since Joseph was the greatest of the brothers, his good
       deed in burying his father could not properly be rewarded
       until someone even greater than himself, Moses, could
       come along to bury him (Mishnah).

  C.   Pharaoh's "wizards" foresaw that disaster would
       accompany the removal of Joseph's bones, and so resolved
       to hide them away in the "treasure-houses of the palace."
       Knowing this, Joseph has his brothers swear that his
       bones will be removed at the time of the exodus
       ("Testament of Simeon").

II. An originally separate problem: why is the removal of Joseph's
     bones not mentioned until Exod. 13:19, after the Israelites have
     already set out from Ra'amses and reached Sukkot?

  A.   The bones were in fact located in Sukkot ("In Sukkot," an
       ancestor of *Tebat Marqa*).

  B.   The Israelites forgot about the bones until after they
       reached Sukkot. They only remembered there because the
       pillar of cloud and fire refused to allow them to move
       forward ("Forgotten by Everyone," incorporated into *Tebat
       Marqa*).

    i. A further refinement of this element of "forgetfulness":
       The fact that Moses is singled out in Exod. 13:19 as the
       one who took Joseph's bones is used to argue that *Moses
       alone* remembered at this point, while all the other
       Israelites continued in their forgetfulness. (This tradition
       is still reflected in the opening sentence of the "Busy
       with Booty" motif in the *Mekhilta* and *Tosefta* versions:
       "[this is intended] to proclaim Moses' wisdom and piety,
       for all of Israel was occupied with the booty [taken from
       Egypt] but Moses busied himself with the commandment
       of [removing] Joseph's bones.")

III. The motif of Joseph's bones being hidden away ("Treasure-
     houses of the Palace," I.C. above), which originally belonged to
     one time frame, that of the oath before Joseph's death, is now

transferred to another time frame, that of the retrieval of the bones (Exod. 13:19): for if Joseph's bones were hidden away at the time of his death, were they not still in the same place at the time of the exodus? This transfer, along with the singling out of Moses in the words "And Moses took Joseph's bones . . . ," etc., implied that there might therefore have been some *difficulty* associated with removing Joseph's inaccessible bones, a difficulty only Moses could overcome:

A. Joseph's bones had been placed in the "tombs of the [Egyptian] kings" and now needed to be retrieved by Moses. He makes his miracle-working speech, "Joseph, Joseph! . . ." etc., whereupon Joseph's bones at once begin to stir (the "Tombs of the [Egyptian] Kings" motif in *Mekhilta* and *Tosefta*).

   i. (Note that the "miracle-working speech" in "Tombs of the [Egyptian] Kings" contains a reminiscence of II.B. above, the refusal of the pillar to move, in the words "the clouds of glory are delayed because of you.")

B. A variant version of this: Joseph's bones have been dropped to the bottom of the Nile in a metal casket. How to get them up again? Moses goes and makes his miracle-working speech, "Joseph, Joseph! . . ." etc., and Joseph's casket at once rises to the surface.[32] (This is an early stage of the "Bottom of the Nile" motif in *Mekhilta* and *Tosefta*).

C. The bones are in or near Sukkot (as per II.A.), but now no one knows exactly where (this version thus incorporates the "inaccessibility" element suggested by III). Moses struggles to find them. Here the tradition of Serah's great age (derived from Gen. 46:17 and Num. 26:46) is enlisted to involve her in Moses' recovery of Joseph's bones. This motif, "Serah Knows," is unattested in this form; we only know it (in *Tebat Marqa*) in combination with the "stopped pillar" element that was part of the "Forgotten by Everyone" motif (II.B.):

   i. Arrived in Sukkot and *reminded by the pillar* that Joseph's bones need to be retrieved (II.B.), the Israelites are still unable to find them until Serah shows Moses where they are hidden. (Almost the final version found in *Tebat Marqa*. This is further modified to):

   a. Arrived in Sukkot, the Israelites cannot proceed because

of the pillar, but no one knows why. Serah tells Moses
why, but must further show him where the bones are
hidden (*Tebat Marqa*).

IV.   At some point, the element of Serah's longevity ("Serah
      Knows," III.C.) is combined with "Bottom of the Nile" (III.B.).
      The story thus becomes: Joseph's bones have been dropped to
      the bottom of the Nile in a metal casket, but Moses does not
      know where they are.[33] Serah tells him. Moses goes and makes
      his miracle-working speech, "Joseph, Joseph! . . ." (This is
      almost the complete "Bottom of the Nile motif" in *Mekhilta* and
      Tosefta).

      A.   Various refinements: The prooftext from 2 Kings 6:5 is
           inserted (*Tosefta*). Then, in order to make Moses' conduct
           more like that of Elisha, he is said not only to make a
           miracle-working speech, but to drop a pebble (*Mekhilta*) or
           inscription of the divine Name or various other things
           (later midrashic collections) into the Nile and so cause the
           casket to rise.

      B.   Moses is singled out ("And Moses took Joseph's bones
           . . .") not just because he alone can make the miracle-
           working speech and cast the pebble, etc., but because all
           the other Israelites have forgotten about the duty to
           recover Joseph's bones. (This represents an infiltration of
           II.B.i).

      C.   Introduction of the connection of Moses' "taking" of bones
           with "wise-of-heart will *take* commandments" (Prov. 10:18).

Conclusion

The midrash of Joseph's bones thus became a rather complicated combination of exegetical motifs, originally created independently for the
purpose of elucidating different difficulties within the biblical text. In
this sense it is not unlike some of the other material we have examined
above. It is perhaps most reminiscent of the "Assembly of Ladies" midrash, for both well illustrate the manner in which one motif can be
heaped upon another and so successfully harmonized and/or transformed that the original starting point becomes completely obscured.
But this was true in other motifs seen as well: the starting points of
"Sees Father's Countenance" and "Jacob's Face on the Heavenly
Throne" in the previous chapter had likewise completely disappeared

from view. Moreover, in examining the manner in which such developments take place, we have encountered certain recurrent phenomena, some of which have been discussed specifically ("doublets," "transfer of affects"), and others of which we shall come to consider below.

Of course, there is much more to the midrashic elaboration of the story of Joseph than the story of Joseph and Mrs. Potiphar; and even in regard to our treatment of this theme in early exegesis, it should be said that there are items that have been mentioned only in passing or not at all. But the above discussion, as noted, has been framed with one overall purpose in mind: to explore the relationship between various midrashic motifs as we find them and the underlying biblical text(s) that they were originally conceived to illuminate. Before, then, finally standing back and seeking to draw some conclusions about this subject, we shall now turn in part II to a discussion of some other midrashic motifs from outside of the Joseph story—the story of the blind giant Lamech in Genesis 4, the early exegesis of Psalm 137, and the early interpretation of a passage of biblical law, Lev. 19:17–18—in order to see how these might further illustrate some of the same principles and processes seen above.

Notes

1. Certainly relevant in this search was the verse Gen. 48:22, which was interpreted, *inter alia*, in connection with Joseph's double portion. See Theodor-Albeck, *Genesis Rabba*, vol. 3, 1249.
2. On the subject of this midrashic tradition there is already a considerable secondary literature, most recently, and penetratingly, represented by Joseph Heinemann's treatment in his book, *Aggadah and its Development* (Jerusalem: Keter, 1974). I would not have ventured to add to what Heinemann says there were it not the case that I find myself in disagreement with his analysis of, specifically, this midrashic motif's origins in the biblical text; since this matter of biblical origins is the overriding theme of the present book, I thought it appropriate nonetheless to examine this motif yet again.
3. See above, chapter 3, n. 27.
4. See the *Mekhilta* edition of H. S. Horovitz and I. A. Rabin ((Jerusalem, 1970), 78; the Munich National Library ms. has Moses cast a "golden tablet engraved with the name of God" into the Nile, but this appears to be a later development. (On this matter I must disagree with J. Goldin, "The Magic of Magic and Superstition," in E. S. Fiorenza, *Aspects of Religious Propaganda in Judaism and Early Christianity* [Notre, Dame, IN: Univ. of Notre Dame Press, 1976], 127–28.) See below.

5. See on this M. Weinfeld, *Deuteronomy and the Deuteronomic School* (Oxford: Oxford University Press, 1971).

6. The version of this motif presented in *Pesiqta deR. Kahana* has "[this is intended] to proclaim Moses' *praise*, for all of Israel was occupied with the booty. . . ." (See B. Mandelbaum, ed., *Pesiqta deR. Kahana* [New York: Jewish Theological Seminary, 1962], 187). This wording, more idiomatic, only highlights the fact that our version's "wisdom and piety" was specifically coined in order to create another connection to Prov. 10:18.

7. This motif, unconnected to the "wise of heart" or any of the other motifs in the above passage, is found in Ephraem's Commentary on Exodus, *ad loc.*: "While the people were taking the booty of the Egyptians Moses took Joseph's bones, and they went out armed." See *Sancti Ephraem Syri in Genesim et in Exodum*, ed. R.-M. Tonneau (Louvain: L. Durbecq, 1955), 122.

8. The midrash of Serah has been fully treated by Heinemann in the above study (note 2); the curious reader is referred to it for a more complete survey of the rabbinic material.

9. For variant versions see Goldin, "Magic of Magic," as well as S. Lieberman, *Tosefta Kifshuto* (New York: Jewish Theological Seminary, 1955–), b. *Soṭa*, p. 649.

10. See *Mekhilta deR. Shim'on b. Yoḥai*, p. 46; b. *Soṭa* 13a, *Pesiqta deR. Kahana*, "Beshallaḥ" (Mandelbaum, ed., p. 187).

11. See Lieberman, *Tosefta Kifshuto*, p. 650.

12. In fact, the language of Moses' speech here and the one he recites in the *Tosefta* version of the previous midrash is virtually identical.

13. The manuscript tradition that has the "treasure-houses of the palace" [or: "of the kings"] is that preferred on textual grounds by H. Hollander and M. De Jonge in their recent commentary, *The Testaments of the Twelve Patriarchs: A Commentary* (Leiden: Brill, 1985), 128. Apart from the textual argument, we shall see below (note 21) that it is to be preferred on grounds of simplicity.

14. The connection between this motif and our midrash was first explored by M. Güdemann, *Religionsgeschichtliche Studien* (Leipzig, 1876), 26–40. Cf. B. Heller, "Egyptian Elements in the Haggadah," in *I. Goldziher Memorial Volume*, vol. 1 (Budapest: Globus, 1948), 414–15; J. Guttmann, *Judeo-Hellenistic Literature* (in Hebrew) (Tel Aviv, 1957–63), 111.

15. See Ginzberg, *Legends*, 5:376 n. 438.

16. J. Horovitz, *Die Josephserzählung* (Frankfurt a. M.: Kaufmann, 1921), 120–46.

17. J. Heinemann, *Aggadah and Its Development*, 52.

18. See Z. ben Hayyim, *Tebat Marqa* (in Hebrew), (Jerusalem: Academy of Sciences, 1988), 14–15.

19. Ben Hayyim, *Tebat Marqa*, 98–101.

20. Lieberman, *Tosefta Kifshuto*, 648.

21. As noted above (note 13), the version that Joseph's bones were put "in the treasure-house of the palace" is to be preferred to "tombs of the kings," since it clearly states the intention to make Joseph's bones inaccessible to the Israelites, whereas this is only implied by the "tombs of the kings." What the latter is intended to do, on the other hand, is to reflect the fact that Gen. 50:26 mentions that Joseph was "embalmed" and so to suggest that his body was in fact disposed of in the manner of the Egyptian kings,

embalmed (and so not buried, as this verse indeed implies) but then hidden somewhere in the Egyptian desert.

22. Alternately, one might argue that Joseph, like Jacob, had prophetic powers at the time of his death, and foresaw both the fact that his body would be hidden away by the Egyptians and that there nevertheless would come a time when the Israelites would be allowed to leave Egypt. He therefore had his brothers swear that at the time of the exodus his bones would be taken along.

23. The same idea is found in Josephus, *Jewish Antiquities* 2. 198: "[Joseph's] brethren also died after sojourning happily in Egypt. Their bodies were carried some time afterwards by their descendants to Hebron and buried there. But as for Joseph's bones, it was only later, when the Hebrews migrated from Egypt, that they conveyed them to Canaan, in accordance with the oath which Joseph had laid upon them." This idea may likewise be hinted at in the New Testament (Acts 7:16).

24. This is evidently Josephus' understanding (above note): "But as for Joseph's bones, it was only later, when the Hebrews migrated from Egypt, that they conveyed them to Canaan, *in accordance with the oath which Joseph had laid upon them.*" It is of course also possible that the *Jubilees* version presumes some sort of story such as that in the "Testament of Simeon," to the effect that Joseph's bones had been put under lock and key and could not be removed. But there is no hint of this in *Jubilees* itself.

25. This is said specifically in "Testament of Benjamin" 12:3. Cf. "Testament of Gad" 8:5.

26. Some rabbinic versions of the "Bottom of the Nile" motif supply a reason for the bones having been made inaccessible: the version in b. *Soṭa* 13a, for example, suggests that the Egyptians deposited Joseph in the Nile "so that its waters might be blessed." *Deuteronomy Rabba* 13 suggests on the contrary that the Egyptians had originally done so because Pharaoh's wise men "had said to Pharaoh: Is it your wish that this people [the Israelites] never depart from this place? If [it is arranged so that] they are forever unable to find Joseph's bones, then they can never depart." Now this is basically the same rationale as that of the "Testament of Simeon." If so, it seems that the original motif in the "Testament of Simeon," a motif that served there to explain an item in the biblical text (Joseph's deathbed oath), survived (or was reinvented) in *Deuteronomy Rabba* in order to elucidate not a biblical problem but the basic premise of our midrashic motif, which stipulated that, for some reason or another, Joseph's bones were at the bottom of the Nile at the time of the exodus.

27. Note that some tradition of a war with Egypt is known to our "Testament of Simeon" passage, which reports that Simeon's bones were taken up "in secret during a war with Egypt." This too may indicate that something like *Jubilees'* explanation is the oldest of all.

28. That is, there would have been no point in the Mishnah's mentioning that Joseph was the greatest of the brothers if its sole purpose were to prove the principle of ever-greater rewards for a virtuous deed. For such a purpose the Mishnah need simply have noted that Joseph, who was second to the king (Gen. 41:40), took charge of burying his father, for which he was rewarded by being buried by none other than Moses, himself not only a

king (Deut. 33:5 in traditional interpretation) but the greatest of the prophets; Moses, in turn, was buried by God. If, however, the Mishnah nonetheless adds that "there was none among the brothers greater than him," is not this observation merely the fossilized remainder of an earlier version, a version that had presented this motif *specifically as an answer to the question:* why did not Joseph request that his own brothers carry his remains back to Canaan? Only then would it have been necessary to observe that, since Joseph was greater than any of his brothers, they could not take charge of burying his remains in Canaan, for to do so would fail to uphold the principle of ever-greater rewards. Joseph's bones thus had to wait around until the arrival of Moses in order to be buried by someone of still greater standing.

29. See b. *Soṭa* 11a–12a, *Midrash Tanḥuma, Vayyaqhel* 4; *Exodus Rabba* 1:9, 18.
30. The very idea in this motif that the pillar's nonmovement prevented the Israelites from continuing was no doubt generated, perhaps unconsciously, by Exod. 40:37, which mentions that when the cloud did not move from above the tabernacle, the Israelites could not move forward.
31. This in turn seems to have generated that other motif, found in b. *Soṭa*, to the effect that Joseph's bones were dropped to the bottom of the Nile "so that its waters might be blessed."
32. Although there is no definite proof, it seems likely that the miracle-working speech, found in both "Tombs of the [Egyptian] Kings" and "Bottom of the Nile," was initially designed for the former. For note that Moses, addressing Joseph, says "If you *reveal* [*megalleh*] yourself, well and good . . ." This verb would be quite appropriate for bones that were hidden inside a tomb or indistinguishable from other bones, but somewhat less than appropriate for bones at the bottom of the Nile, which should on the contrary have been urged to "raise yourselves up," "cause your coffin to float," etc.
33. This element, treated somewhat off-handedly in the versions of "Bottom of the Nile" mentioned above, is stressed in another version found in *Deuteronomy Rabba* (11, *Zot habberakhah*), which recounts that Moses "went all around the city and tried for three days and three nights to find Joseph's coffin."

Part II

6.

Why Was Lamech Blind?

The biblical story of Cain and Abel was one that was retold and elaborated with great relish by the Bible's earliest interpreters. This was so not only because of the tale's intrinsic interest—it concerned, after all, the children of the very first human beings, Adam and Eve, and recounted a brutal crime, indeed, the world's first murder—but as well because, like so many of the early narratives in Genesis, the biblical account itself seemed here and there to cry out for further explanation and detail. One such detail, missing in the Genesis account itself, is the manner in which Cain himself ultimately died. This lacuna was obviously of some concern, if only because early readers of the Bible were curious to know the circumstances under which the archetypal murderer had met his own demise, and specifically whether his death bore some relationship to the crime he had earlier committed. A narrative expansion eventually came to fill in this blank, according to which Cain was accidentally killed by his own descendant Lamech in a hunting accident.

The details of various versions of this expansion will be examined below; but it is worth noting initially that this story is one that has not suffered from inattention among modern students of the history of biblical exegesis. Lamech's killing of Cain was, for example, a favorite subject of Louis Ginzberg, who treated it at the beginning of his scholarly career, discussed its sources in detail in his *Legends of the Jews*, and turned to it again in a later essay on Jewish folklore.[1] It was also treated at length by Victor Aptowitzer in his book-length study on the Cain and Abel tradition;[2] nor has the story been neglected in more recent times.[3] Indeed, some of this interest among modern scholars was no doubt stirred up by the many depictions of the death of Cain that survive from the Middle Ages, for the legend in question was prized by sculptors and illustrators.[4] No other such tale, observed one recent writer on the subject, "seems to have had such persistent appeal in the literature and art of West and East."[5]

As noted, the story in question relates how Lamech, Cain's great-great-great-grandson, ends up killing his ancestor quite by accident. Lamech is in fact blind in both eyes, but despite this handicap, he has become a very proficient hunter, by which means he succeeds in supporting himself and his family. He manages this by having himself led through the woods by a guide—his son Tubal-Cain, or an unnamed boy, or a shepherd, according to various sources—who both helps him along and points his hands in the direction of any potential prey. Lamech is an excellent shot, and, thus guided, is able to dispatch animals with arrow, stone, or other instrument. But on the day in question, Lamech's guide mistakes Cain (in some versions: by seeing Cain's horns, the "sign" that God granted him in Gen. 4:16, protruding from behind a bush or tree) for a wild animal. Lamech's aim is true, and the "animal" falls, only to be discovered to be Lamech's own ancestor, Cain. In his grief Lamech then blindly claps both hands together and inadvertently kills his guide as well. Although he is thus the author of two deaths, Lamech nonetheless protests that both killings were accidental and begs forgiveness, exclaiming, "Have I killed a man for my hurt—so that I be hurt on his account? Or a boy for a bruise—that I be bruised on his account?"[6]

Origins

"Cain Killed by Lamech" was, as noted, a very popular story, and one that followed its own career in diverse Jewish and Christian writings of late antiquity and the Middle Ages.[7] Nor are its exegetical origins particularly difficult to uncover: it clearly has been specially crafted in order to explain the brief and somewhat puzzling utterance spoken by Lamech in Genesis:

> . . . And Methushael engendered Lamech. And Lamech took two wives: the name of the first was Adah, and the name of the second was Zillah. . . . And Lamech said to his wives: "Adah and Zillah hear my voice, oh wives of Lamech listen to my words: **For I have killed a man for my wound, and a boy for my bruise.** If Cain is avenged sevenfold, then Lamech seventy-seven."

Who were the unnamed "man" and "boy" that Lamech confesses to killing here—and why is he saying these things in the first place? Today a biblicist would of course approach this text, and these questions, with the assumptions and methods of modern historical criticism. Lamech's "war-boast," as it is known to biblical scholars nowadays, is simply that: a ferocious bit of chest thumping, presumably promulgated by the Lamech clan or tribe, to the effect that any would-be attacker ought to beware, for Lamechite retribution will be even fiercer than the (apparently already proverbially fierce) retribution of the Kenites, descendents of Cain. Indeed, the verbs in this saying of Lamech's are, even in many Bible translations commonly used today, still slightly mistranslated; for their perfective form ought really not to be rendered (as above) as if past tense, "I have killed a man," but rather in the present, or even conditionally, "I *would* kill a man for [that is, to avenge] a wound, indeed, I would kill a[n innocent] boy for [to avenge] a bruise; if Cain [whose unequal retribution is already proverbial] is avenged sevenfold, then Lamech seventy-seven!"[8] In other words, the "man" and "boy" referred to are purely hypothetical, part of Lamech's (that is, the Lamech-clan's) threatened retribution. Presumably, these words at some point constituted a well-known tribal saying, not unlike the tribal sayings that presently appear as the "Blessings of Jacob" in Genesis 49 or the "Blessings of Moses" in Deuteronomy 33.

But of course such an approach to understanding this text, even if it had occurred, would have been quite incompatible with the assumptions and methods of those Jews and Christians who sought to expound biblical texts in the closing centuries before and just after the start of the common era. For them, to begin with, this text was part of a great and harmonious sacred history, one which, therefore, could hardly be read in isolation or analyzed atomistically. If Scripture had Lamech refer to his killing of a "man" and a "boy" (that is, as if to actual past *events*, for so the verbs were now understood), were not these references, however cryptic, nonetheless significant bits of information, *facts* to be fitted into an overall understanding of this primeval period and its various inhabitants? And indeed, Lamech's very mention of Cain in the next line of this saying certainly suggested that there was some relationship between the whole story of Cain and Abel and the "man" and/or "boy" being referred to here. And so this saying of Lamech's was doubtless scrutinized from an early period by exegetes bent on discovering what information it might contain about the later fate of Cain.

It certainly would be convenient for the "man" in Lamech's saying to be identified as Cain—that is, to interpret Lamech's saying as a confession that he killed his ancestor—for the very absence in the Bible of an account of Cain's demise was, as we observed initially, something of an exegetical problem. True, there are many early figures whose death is not mentioned in the Bible, but in Cain's case, the scriptural silence might be taken to imply that Cain died a natural death, which in turn might suggest that the intentional murder of Abel went unpunished, or underpunished, by God, with exile as Cain's final sentence. Now this is in fact virtually stated in the biblical account, but was obviously unsatisfactory to exegetes: it was necessary for Cain to die for his crime—indeed, if possible, to die by the hand of a man, in keeping with the principle of Gen. 9:6 "Who sheds man's blood, by man shall his blood be shed."

All this might make of Lamech, via his reference to having killed a man, a welcome possible instrument of divine justice. There is a further factor in the connection of this saying of Lamech's with Cain: it lies in the actual wording of Lamech's apparently innocent formulation, "For I have killed a man." Now 'ish, "man," was hardly as pale a word to early exegetes as its translation might suggest. For although it generally means "man," it sometimes appeared to early exegetes to refer specifically to angelic or quasidivine men as well: Jacob wrestled with a divine creature, an angel, who is identified in Gen. 32:25 as an 'ish; Abraham is visited in Gen. 18:2 by three "men," 'anashim, who were commonly reckoned by Jewish exegetes to be angels;[9] Daniel similarly is addressed by a quasidivine 'ish in Daniel 12:7. Now, thus far in the book of Genesis, there is one person in the world who has been specifically called by this (therefore evocative) title 'ish, and that is Cain: for upon his birth his mother had exclaimed, "I have acquired an 'ish with the Lord" (Gen. 4:1). So if Lamech somewhat later on says: "I have killed an 'ish"—placing the word, in fact, before the verb, in what might appear to exegetes to be emphatic position—he is virtually identifying the victim as Cain. And the mention of Cain in the next line could only have been seen as confirmation that this was indeed the case.

From this basic set of assumptions most of the other details of the motif follow. Thus we can easily understand why Tubal-Cain or "the boy" is present in so many versions of this story. Lamech will kill both a man, Cain, and a boy, his guide, and so his words in Gen. 4:23 will become more comprehensible: "I have killed a *man* . . . and a *boy*. . . ." (The identification of the "boy" in this saying as Tubal-Cain seems to have been encouraged by the fact that Tubal-Cain's birth is in fact mentioned in the verse just preceding the saying). The exegetical origins of this motif are thus quite indisputable.

Lamech's Blindness

But there is still one question which to my knowledge has never been answered with regard to this widely diffused motif, a question that is, the more one considers it, rather striking, namely: Why is Lamech blind? Or, to state things a bit more pointedly: Why should an exegete have gone to all the trouble of dreaming up the improbable circumstances whereby Lamech is both blind and yet also a hunter, so that he can end up killing Cain in a blind hunting accident? Surely there is no mention in the Genesis text of Lamech being blind, and no necessity for him to be blind in order to kill off Cain and Tubal-Cain. And so it seems as if here too (as it might have at first appeared in the case of the "Assembly of Ladies" motif, or "Sees Father's Countenance," or "Jacob's Face on Heavenly Throne") we have a motif, or a good part of one, that has no exegetical connection to the biblical text it purports to explain.

In seeking to discover its purpose, we must say an additional word about the overall exegetical framework in which Lamech's saying was viewed. To modern biblicists, as noted, his words appear essentially as a tribal boast, but to early exegetes they would have seemed quite the opposite: a Jewish or Christian exegete living in late antiquity surely would wish to find Lamech's "confession" of murder to be just that, a confession, and one tinged with some contrition and regret. For if not, why should Scripture have recorded his saying these terrible things, "I have killed a man . . . ," etc., and in an apparently pointless and inconsequential fashion? And why, if he were really boasting, was he not immediately struck down for his violence and arrogance? It might therefore seem only natural to early exegetes that, far from boasting, Lamech was in fact seeking to exculpate himself in this saying, indeed, seeking to distinguish himself from his ancestor Cain, the world's first murderer. And so, via various strategies, Lamech's words were turned by early exegetes into a kind of *a fortiori* argument for divine forgiveness: if Cain, who deliberately murdered his own brother in cold blood, nevertheless found some measure of divine mercy and had his just execution put off (for so Gen. 4:15 was understood),[10] then I, blind Lamech, who have killed quite by accident, should be all the more entitled to forgiveness. Thus, as we have seen in the words cited above, Lamech's "boast" in Gen. 4:23 is turned into a question: "Have I killed a man for my hurt—so that I be hurt on his account? Or [have I killed] a boy for a bruise—that I be bruised [on his account]?"[11]

But then, do we not have here the explanation for Lamech's blindness? That is, did not exegetes make Lamech out to be blind in order to make him into an *inadvertent* murderer, thus supporting his apparent plea for forgiveness in Gen. 4:23? No doubt this may appear to be the case after the fact,[12] but if one puts oneself for a moment in the original exegete's position, there seems to be no compelling necessity for creating the unlikely figure of a blind Lamech in order to have his words here be understood as a plea for mercy. For, to repeat: if the whole point of this legend is to explain Lamech's words "I have killed a man" as a reference to Cain, and so have Abel's murder punished by Cain's own progeny—then why not have him just kill Cain plain and simple? Now if, in order for the troubling verse 4:23 ("I have killed a man," etc.) to make sense in Lamech's mouth, it is necessary to believe that he killed Cain by accident and is now begging to have that fact taken into account on his behalf, well then have him kill Cain by accident—a hunting accident, by all means! But what need is there to make the hunter *blind?* Certainly hunting accidents have frequently occurred in the past (and are no doubt still occurring) without the hunters in question being blind: and if Cain's "sign" is interpreted (as it was in various traditions) as a set of horns or some other animal-like mark of fierceness, one capable of warding off potential attackers, why then the chances of Cain's being mistaken for a beast certainly increase, and the likelihood of just such an accident occurring seems all the greater. Indeed, as we have seen above, many versions of this legend do indeed have Tubal-Cain catch sight of Cain and mistake him for a animal. So why not have the mistake be entirely Lamech's, that is, have a seeing Lamech catch sight of the animal-like Cain, kill him by accident (along with, perhaps, a boy conveniently accompanying him), and then exclaim, "For I have killed a man . . ."?

Indeed, there is such a variant of our motif. An Armenian account, published by J. Issaverdens at the turn of the century, says simply this:

> "And Lamech, having mounted a horse and gone hunting, Cain came in sight from afar with his horns and skin; Lamech, on seeing him thought it was a stag, and letting an arrow fly from his bow, he killed Cain."[13]

Is it possible that this Armenian variant is actually the oldest form of our basic motif, and that the element of a blind Lamech was only created later on? I do not think so. Not only is Lamech's blindness an integral part of so many other attested versions of this story (including versions undoubtedly older than the above-cited Armenian text), but there is little possibility of explaining how an originally simple and workable story, one in which a seeing Lamech kills Cain by mistake, might then be turned into a complicated and unlikely one involving a blind hunter who is nonetheless a good shot and so on and so forth. On the other hand, precisely because the blind hunter is so improbable, the reverse process—whereby the original element of Lamech's blindness was dropped, because apparently unnecessary, from the Armenian version—is all too understandable.[14] And let no one argue that Lamech was made blind in order to account for his killing of Tubal-Cain by clapping him between his hands! If a seeing Lamech could accidentally kill Cain, he might just as easily do away with Tubal-Cain without having to be blind: the same arrow shot by Lamech might kill Cain, pass through him, and pierce the innocent passerby, Tubal-Cain; a sword drawn back to dispatch the wounded Cain might accidentally lop off Tubal-Cain's head; and so forth. But what this Armenian text does show is that a Lamech story that has Lamech kill Cain by accident was certainly possible without Lamech being blind; and this only further highlights our question—why *was* Lamech blind?

In considering this question, it is interesting to observe that, while virtually all of our other extant variants of this motif are unanimous in making Lamech blind, *how* he came to be blind is almost never stated— and this also seems, on reflection, somewhat odd. The exceptions of which I am aware are two. The first comes in a somewhat neglected source of early exegetical traditions, the so-called *Palaea Historica*;[15] it begins its version of the Lamech legend by stating that "Lamech was born blind from the belly of his mother." Quite the opposite is the account contained in the medieval aggadic collection *Sefer ha-Yashar:* in typical fashion it assimilates Lamech's case to that of Isaac in the Bible, stating, "And Lamech, advanced in years, became faint of sight."[16]

The latter surely is a literary flourish, one of those bits of rebiblicizing that *Sefer ha-Yashar* loves to perform on midrashic motifs. But it is perhaps worthy of our attention that both explanations, blindness from birth and blindness in old age, are eminently sensible—for these are indeed two of the commonest causes of blindness. Why then, one might ask, were they not part of our legend from the beginning? Yet it is a fact that one finds these explanations not only in two relatively late sources, but sources which—it is true of both of them—are usually highly expansive and enjoy adding new details and explanatory matter to traditions received in far sparser form. Is there some reason for the earlier sources not telling us how Lamech came to be blind?

"For My Hurt . . ."

The answer to all of these questions, it seems, is to be found—as with so much in this tale—in the very words of Gen. 4:23, "For I have killed a man for my hurt, a boy for my bruise." Now the meaning of most of this sentence, in the context of the legend that we have been tracing, is fairly clear: the "man" in question is the only *'ish* specifically so designated thus far, Cain, and Lamech, far from boasting, is here seeking to exculpate himself, claiming that, unlike Cain, he is an accidental murderer and thus deserving of forgiveness. Now in turning Lamech's boast into an apology, the makers of our legend found themselves obligated to alter somewhat the significance of the words *lefiṣ'i,* "for my hurt," and *leḥabburati,* "for my bruise," as well. For if the original sense of the boast hinged on the idea of revenge—"I would kill a man *for* [that is, to avenge] a hurt [literally, a "wound"] to me, and a boy *for* my bruise"—it was now necessary to account in some other fashion for these same words. And so we saw above that various sources turned the whole into a question, "Have I killed a man for my hurt—so that I be hurt on his account? Or a boy for my bruise—that I be bruised on his account?" This manner of glossing Lamech's words turns them from an apparent reference to a *past* hurt into an allusion to a future punishment: Lamech argues that he ought not to be "hurt," punished, for these two deaths, since they were both unintentional.

It is interesting to observe that while this is the tactic adopted in most of the rabbinic texts cited, it was far from the only one available. Another variant of the motif, also found in *Yalquṭ Shim'oni* and, in slightly different form, the version attributed by Rashi to *Midrash Tanḥuma,*[17] reads as follows:

> [Lamech protested:] "The man whom I killed, did I hurt him inten-
> tionally, so that the hurt might be called by name [that is, attributed
> to me]? And the boy whom I killed, by *my* bruise was he killed, and
> was I not an accidental killer?

In this reading, the words "my hurt" and "my bruise" are being turned from what classical grammarians used to call "objective" to "subjective" genitives, that is, "my hurt" is no longer being understood as "a hurt inflicted upon me" but as "a hurt I have inflicted." What is more, the preposition *le-* (rendered above as "for") is here being understand more as "by." Lamech's argument thus becomes: True, the man was hurt, but was it really by *my* hurt[ing], i.e., did I do it "intentionally, so that the hurt [literally, "wound"] might be called by my name"?[18]

The collection *Midrash Aggadah,* edited by S. Buber, adopts a some-what similar, yet still distinct, tactic:

> [Adah and Zillah, Lamech's wives] said to him: You have killed Cain
> our forebear, and you have likewise killed Tubal-Cain our son; so we
> will not heed you. Whereupon he said: Have I killed a man for my
> hurt, and a boy for my bruise? This refers to Cain, whom I did not kill
> intentionally as Cain himself had done, who killed his brother Abel
> with wounds and bruises (*bifṣa'im ubaḥabburot*) intentionally.

According to this understanding of the text, Lamech's rhetorical ques-tion is really: did I, like Cain, kill a man with wounds and bruises? In this reading, similar to the one just seen, the phrase "for my hurt" is understood as "by my hurting [lit. "wounding"] him"—but it is understood to mean: did I kill him in such a manner, with wounds and bruises, so that my intention to kill was unmistakable—as was the case with Cain's killing of Abel?[19] The expected answer is "Of course not"; Lamech thus hopes to gain exoneration by the absence of signs of beating on Cain's body.[20]

These quite divergent explanations should, if nothing else, return us to the two mysterious words they seek to gloss, *lefiṣ'i* and *leḥabburati,* "for my hurt [= wound]" and "for my bruise"; for the very variety of explanations suggests that, at least with regard to the significance of these two words, there was no single, clear tradition in the hands of our exegetes.[21] Is it possible that the various readings seen, which in one way or another all seek to turn Lamech's sentence into a rhetorical question—"And should my [accidental] killing of a man turn to my detriment, my wound?" "Did he die by *my* wounding?" etc.—conceal a still older reading, one which saw in this no rhetorical question at all, but the simple assertion that Lamech had indeed killed both a man and boy by accident, an accident due to his blindness? In this case, *lefiṣ'i* and *leḥabburati* would both be references to one and the same circumstance, Lamech's blindness, and the ambiguous preposition *le-* would thus be understood as meaning "because of," "on account of."[22] "I have killed a man because of my wound," says Lamech, "indeed, a boy because of my bruise," in other words, it is not my fault, these things happened because I am blind. If so, then behind this understanding of *peṣa'* and *ḥabburah* as references to the fact of Lamech's blindness might lie an original tale that had Lamech blind not—as the *Sefer ha-Yashar* has it—in his old age, nor yet—as the *Palaea* has it—from birth, but as the result of some wound inflicted upon him.

"Knocked Out Both His Eyes . . ."

There is no direct evidence of such a story. But there is one variant of our motif which, it seems to me, might support such an interpretation. It appears in a version of *Combat of Adam and Eve with Satan* and published by Dillmann as *Das Christliche Adambuch:*

> Lamech drew his bow and let fly an arrow and prepared . . . [*sic*] and the slingshot. And now, as Cain was coming out of the field, the shepherd said to Lamech: Shoot, here he comes! And he shot him with an arrow that struck him in the side, and then he shot at him from the slingshot, and struck him in the face and **knocked out both his eyes,** and he fell straight down and died. Then Lamech went off toward

him, and the youth said to him, "O my lord, it is indeed Cain whom you have slain."[23]

What this account seems to be at pains to tell us is that Lamech, in killing Cain, also *blinded him* in the process. In fact such an intention could not be more obviously, or awkwardly, stated: for in this version Lamech first shoots Cain with an arrow, then takes a stone—apparently this text wishes Cain to be finished off with the same murder weapon with which he killed Abel—and strikes him with it, knocking out both Cain's eyes and so killing him. But why have Lamech kill Cain by knocking out his *eyes?* Apparently the reason for this otherwise gratuitous detail is to provide some justification for the (as we have seen) difficult words that Lamech speaks just after the deed is done, *ki 'ish haragti lefiṣ'i*. For according to this scenario, what Lamech appears to be saying is "I have killed a man *by means of* my wound," that is, I knocked out his eyes and so inflicted upon him the same wound from which I myself suffer, save that he has died from it. But if so, then this story presupposes that Lamech himself had indeed suffered a *peṣa'*, a wound, which deprived him of his sight. For this story has been devised to explain *haragti lefiṣ'i* as "I killed *by* my wound," that is, I killed him in exactly the same manner that I myself had been wounded, in the eyes.[24]

Let us retrace our steps. The whole motif of Lamech's killing of Cain was generated by the mysterious words, "For I have killed a man . . . ," etc. in Gen. 4:23. Early exegetes identified the "man" in question as Cain—thereby arranging for Cain to be "executed" and duly punished by divine justice—and identified the boy as Lamech's own son Tubal-Cain. Lamech would kill the two "for my hurt and . . . for my bruise." But these words, if understood in terms of revenge, might in themselves still pose a problem, implying an intentional murder and presumably thus requiring that Lamech, too, be punished. Could not the words be understood in some other fashion? And so it was that the particle *le-* came to be read at some point as "on account of," "because of"; Lamech's boast was turned into an apology—"I killed a man on account of my wound." If the wound in question were such as to prevent Lamech from functioning properly—from, in fact, *seeing*— why then Lamech could both finish off Cain and yet be free of any charge of revenge; and what is more, the words "for my wound," etc. in Gen. 4:23 would have been turned from an exegetical liability into an exegetical asset.

Here then is one more instance of an exegetical motif, or part of one, whose original *raison d'être* has been lost—and not lost, as had been the case with other motifs seen, through **transfer of affects,** but simply lost track of, forgotten—so that while the **element** of Lamech's blindness remained in almost all the variants of this motif, sometime relatively early in the history of its transmission, the exegetical purpose of that element was forgotten. But such forgetting of course then left the words "for my wound" and "for my bruise" unexplained—for people no longer understood these words as references to Lamech's blindness. And so, as we have seen, new solutions were proposed: "as a wound to me" (that is, that I should be wounded, punished, because of my action), "because of my wound[ing]," and so forth. As noted, the very disagreement among rabbinic and other sources concerning the significance of *lefiṣ'i* and *leḥabburati* should have indicated by itself that there was no clear ancient tradition to explain these words, or, rather, that some ancient explanation or way of accounting for these words had been lost. And, as we have seen, that ancient explanation was not so much "lost" as hiding in an apparently incidental detail, the fact of Lamech's blindness.

Notes

1. L. Ginzberg, "Die Haggada bei den Kirchenvättern und in der apokryphischen Literatur," *Monatsschrift für Geschichte und Wissenschaft des Judenthums* 43 (1899):293–99; *The Legends of the Jews* (Philadelphia: Jewish Publication Society, 1913), 1:116–17 and 5:145–47; idem., "Jewish Folklore East and West" reprinted in his *On Jewish Law and Lore* (New York: Atheneum, 1977), 61–73.

2. V. Aptowitzer, *Kain und Abel in der Agada* (Vienna: R. Löwit Verlag, 1922).

3. For some recent references see E. Reiss, "The Story of Lamech and Its Place in Medieval Drama," *Journal of Medieval and Renaissance Studies* 2 (1972):35–48; cf. below.

4. See on this R. Mellinkoff, *The Sign of Cain* (Berkeley: University of California Press, 1981).

5. Sh. Spiegel, "Introduction," in L. Ginzberg, *Legends of the Bible* (New York: Simon and Schuster, 1956), xx.

6. א''ל כי איש הרגתי לפצעי שיבואו עלי פצעים, וילר לחבורתי שיבואו עלי חבורות בשבילו? This particular wording of Lamech's exclamation, cited in *Yalquṭ Shim'oni* (ed. D. Heiman, I. N. Lehrer, and I. Shiloni [Jerusalem: Mosad ha-Rav Kook, 1973], 1:135) is somewhat similar to a version cited by Rashi in his biblical commentary *ad loc.* and attributed there to "R. Tanḥuma" (see below); note, however, that that particular text is in fact not to be found in either the standard *Tanḥuma* or in Buber's edition. See also J. Theodor and Ch. Albeck, *Genesis Rabba* (Jerusalem: Wahrmann, 1965), 224–25 and notes for other (minor) variations on this exclamation of Lamech's.

7. Among Jewish sources, this story is to be found in *Midrash Tanḥuma* (*Bereshit* 11) (on a similar *yelammedenu* fragment cf. Aptowitzer, *Kain und Abel*, 159 n. 243, and on the other version attributed to Tanḥuma, see Rashi *ad loc.* and above, note 6); Targum Pseudo-Jonathan (*ad loc.*); *Midrash Aggadah*, ed. S. Buber (Vienna, 1895), 13–14; *Midrash ha-Gadol*, ed. M. Margoliouth (Jerusalem: Mosad ha-Rav Kook, 1975), I:127; *Sefer ha-Yashar*, ed. L. Goldschmidt (Berlin: Benjamin Harz, 1923), 7–8; *Leqaḥ Ṭob*, ed. S. Buber (Vilna: Romm, 1880), I:31. Among early Christian sources see: Jerome, Epistle 36 (to Damasus) in I. Hilberg, *S. Eusebii Hieronymi Opera Sect. I Pars I* (*Corpus Scriptorum Ecclesiasticorum Latinorum*, vol. 54) (Leipzig: G. Freytag, 1910), 269–75; Ephraem Syrus, *Sancti Ephraem Syri in Genesim et Exodum Commentarii*, ed. R. M. Tonneau (*Corpus Scriptorum Christianorum Orientalium*, vol. 152) (Louvain, 1955), 53 (Latin translation, pp. 41–42); C. Bezold, *Die Schatzhöhle* (Leipzig: J. C. Hinrichs'sche Buchhandlung, 1883), Syriac and Arabic 48–50, German 11–12; S. C. Malan, *The Book of Adam and Eve, also called the Conflict of Adam and Eve with Satan* (London: Williams and Norgate, 1882), 121–123 — cf. A. Dillmann, *Das Christliche Adambuch des Morgenlandes* (Göttingen: Dieterichsche Buchhandlung, 1853), 85 and 140; and further sources mentioned below. There are other Christian historians and chroniclers who apparently were aware of a tradition linking Lamech with Cain's death, but they do not present the story in detail: see thus J. A. Fabricius, *Codex Pseudepigraphicus Veteris Testamenti* (Hamburg: Felsiner, n.d.), I:119–22. Cf. Aptowitzer, *Kain und Abel*, 59–68 and notes.

8. See the discussion in my *Idea of Biblical Poetry* (New Haven: Yale University Press, 1981), 31–32 and n. 83.

9. See thus Targum Pseudo-Jonathan and *Genesis Rabba ad loc.*, also b. *Baba Meṣiʿa* 86b. Later Christian interpreters sometimes understood this passage in terms of the doctrine of the Trinity; see Augustine, *On the Trinity* II 10–12.

10. See Targum Onkelos *ad loc.*, and the sources cited above, note 7; note also the discussion in Aptowitzer, *Kain und Abel*, 82–93.

11. Perhaps this transition was abetted by reading the sentence's initial word, *ki* ("for," "indeed," etc. in biblical Hebrew), as if it were Mishnaic Hebrew's interrogative particle *vekhi*. Note that Targum Onkelos does not even translate Lamech's words as a question, but a negation: "I have not killed a man, that I should suffer punishment for his sake; nor have I even injured a child, so that my offspring should be destroyed for his sake." Such a reading, as Aptowitzer pointed out (*Kain und Abel*, 69), appears to carry the rhetorical question one step further: the expected "No" answer turns the question into a negative assertion. It is also to be noted that Onkelos apparently takes no account of our legend in his translation: Lamech has nothing to do with the death of Cain. Indeed, underlying his words may be only the midrashic motif (see thus Theodor-Albeck, *Genesis Rabba*, I:224–25) of Lamech's wives' refusal to bear more children since they will in any case only be swept away in the coming Flood. Lamech's protest, à la Onkelos, is thus that since he is innocent of even so much as injuring a child, his own children ("seed") should not be swept away. (The only problem that exegetes might find with this understanding is that, if Lamech has indeed killed no one, even by accident, then why is he urging that his

"punishment" be put off for seventy-seven generations? What punishment?) *Genesis Rabba* still more explicitly eschews the Lamech legend in explaining Gen. 4:23 ("Cain killed and had [his punishment] suspended seven generations; I, *who have not killed*—does it not follow that mine be suspended seventy and seven?"), but it is to be observed nevertheless that its rewording of Gen. 4:23 itself is almost identical with that of *Yalquṭ Shim'oni*, etc. cited above, and would be entirely compatible with our legend. It seems possible, then, that the *Genesis Rabba* version has taken what was already a traditional rewording of Gen. 4:23—one originally connected to the Lamech legend—and fitted it to an interpretation which, in keeping with Onkelos, no longer makes use of it. Somewhat conversely, later Jewish sources, while intent on incorporating the Lamech legend into their understanding of Gen. 4:23, had then to struggle in order to accommodate the Onkelos translation to fit the legend. See, most awkwardly, Rashi *ad loc.*, and cf. *Midrash Tanḥuma* (above, note 7) and sources cited below.

12. I suspect that this is why Ginzberg et al. never turned to consider the cause of Lamech's blindness specifically.

13. J. Issaverdens, *The Uncanonical Writings of the Old Testament* (Venice: Armenian Monastery of St. Lazarus, 1901), 39. Cf. the Armenian version published by E. Preuschen, "Die Apokryphen Gnostischen Adamschriften," in W. Diehl et al., *Festgruss Bernhard Stade* (Giessen: J. Ricker, 1900), 197–98, where Lamech sees Cain but fails to recognize him. Nor was this the only way to have Cain killed by accident: the account of Eutychius says that Lamech, "shooting an arrow in play, hit his ancestor Cain through the heart and killed him" (Aptowitzer, *Kain und Abel*, 65; cf. Malan, *Book of Adam and Eve*, 228 n. 18).

14. Indeed this is quite clearly what happened in the *Book of the Bee* (above, note 7), which dropped the detail of Lamech's blindness although its source, *The Cave of Treasures*, had included it.

15. On this source see D. Flusser, "Palaea Historica: An Unknown Source of Biblical Legends," in *Scripta Hierosolymitana* 22 (1971):48–79; S. Lieberman, "Zenihin" (in Hebrew), *Tarbiz* 42 (1972–73):42–54; and E. Turdéanu, *Apocryphes slaves et roumains de l'Ancien Testament* (Leiden: E. J. Brill, 1981), 392–403.

16. Goldschmidt, *Sefer ha-Yashar*, 8. A similar assumption may underly Malan's *Book of Adam and Eve* (above, note 7), which has Lamech on the fateful day take up "a bow he had kept ever since he was a youth, ere he became blind."

17. See *Yalquṭ Shim'oni*, 136 and n. 44.

18. The same understanding seems to underly the version found in the aforementioned *Sefer ha-Yashar*, which restates Lamech's words thus: "Now you may have thought that I killed a man *lefiṣ'i* and a boy *leḥabburati* as a violent act. But do you not know that I have grown old and grey and my eyes have become heavy with age, so that I did this deed unwittingly?"

19. Note in this connection the explanation of the anomalous plural "bloods" in the Gen. 4:10 that is found in Mishna *Sanhedrin* 4:5.

20. This version is in turn somewhat reminiscent of one cited in the Genesis commentary of Ephraem Syrus. There, Lamech's wives, descendents of the (good) Seth, urge their husband to right conduct, whereupon he exclaims,

"And do you see anything hateful in me, similar to that which my father Cain did? Indeed, have I killed a man for my wounds, as Cain did? Or, have I—in the same way that he rained down blows upon Abel, as upon a boy, and then killed him—have I so killed a boy with my blows? If I had done as Cain, and Cain received retribution sevenfold, I truly pass sentence upon myself that I shall receive seventy and seven" (Tonneau, *Ephraem Syri in Genesim* . . ., 53).

21. The Septuagint translation renders *lefiṣ'i* as εἰς τραῦμα ἐμοί. Apart from rendering the particle *le-* with what is its frequent Greek equivalent, this translation may incorporate the understanding seen above, "for the purpose of my being wounded," i.e., שיבואו עלי פצעים (for this use of εἰς see W. Bauer, *A Greek-English Lexicon*[2] revised by F. W. Gingrich and F. W. Danker [Chicago: University of Chicago, 1979], 229, 4 d and e); or possibly in the instrumental sense, "by my wound" or "by my wound[ing]" (Bauer, p. 230, 9 b). The Vulgate's *in vulnus meum* may reflect the same sense of purpose, although Jerome's letter to Damasus (above, note 7) has *in vulnere meo* which, while far from unequivocal, would seem to favor the instrumental approach.

22. Cf. Onkelos' translation of it here as *bedil*.

23. Dillmann, *Das Christliche Adambuch*, 85. Cf. Malan, *Book of Adam and Eve*, 122–23. Cf. two recent joint studies by A. Battista and B. Bagatti, *La Caverna dei Tesori* (*Studium Biblicum Franciscanum Collectio Minor* 26) (Jerusalem: Franciscan Printing Press, 1979), and idem., *Il Combattimento di Adamo* (*SBF, Col. Min.* 29) (Jerusalem: Franciscan Printing Press, 1982).

24. As noted, this version of the story is found in Dillmann's *Christliche Adambuch*. The text shows signs of its author having harmonized two separate versions (perhaps one of them similar to that found in the Syriac *Cave of Treasures*)—for this would explain the somewhat awkward fact that, in his retelling, Lamech uses two separate weapons, bow and slingshot, to kill Cain. It is interesting that in the Syriac version of the *Cave*, Lamech's arrow is said to strike Cain *byt 'yny'*. The phrase can mean "between the eyes" (so it is translated by Bezold, *Der Schatzhöhle*, 50; Budge, *The Book of the Cave of Treasures* [London: Religious Tract Society, 1927], 78; cf. Battista-Bagatti, *Caverna*, 53 "tra gli occhi") or else "forehead" (= "place of the eyes"). This is an odd place for a fatal arrow to strike! Perhaps behind it stands the same sort of attempt to understand *lefiṣ'i* as "by means of my wound." (That it is also connected with the place of Cain's "sign"—which, according to one midrashic tradition, was a letter of the divine name placed on Cain's forehead—certainly seems possible, but such would run quite counter to the "sign's" purpose, namely, to ward off would-be murderers; what is more, in many of the versions cited Cain's sign is explicitly *not* a letter or mark on the forehead, but a set of horns.)

7.

Psalm 137

Heretofore we have been concentrating on exegetical motifs from the Torah (Pentateuch). In this respect our study reflects the general state of affairs within early biblical interpretation, for the fact is that the great bulk of exegesis that we have from the earliest periods is indeed devoted to elucidating verses or passages from these first five books of the Bible. (This is only to be expected, given the overriding importance attached to these books by Jews at the time when our earliest exegetical texts originated.) Yet this interest in the Pentateuch hardly meant that the rest of the Hebrew Bible was left untouched. We have already seen how, in the course of explaining a verse dealing with Joseph or Moses, rabbinic exegetes were fond of bringing in a verse from Proverbs or Psalms in order to assert that both referred to the same subject. And if such **back-referencing** appears to be a specifically rabbinic mode, it is nonetheless true that some prerabbinic sources do in fact touch extensively on biblical verses or passages from outside of the Pentateuch: this is characteristic not only of a number of pseudepigraphic texts, but of the biblical exegesis practiced at Qumran (as witnessed in the "Dead Sea Scrolls" and allied writings), as well as that of early Christian exegesis, which sought to find in verses from the Psalms, Isaiah, and other books predictions or commentaries on the events of the Gospels.

It might be appropriate, then, to examine closely a biblical text from outside of the Pentateuch in order to study the development of its exegesis. The text to which I should like to turn is Psalm 137 ("By the rivers of Babylon . . ."). This psalm is one that was of special interest to Jews at a particular moment in their history, the late first and early second centuries of the common era. For while this psalm is set against the background of the Babylonian destruction of the Temple in Jerusalem in the sixth century B.C.E., the analogy between that event and the destruction of the Second Temple by the Romans in 70 C.E. must have seemed only obvious to Jews during or shortly after the latter catastrophe. How natural, then, for them to look back to Psalm 137 and the events to which it alludes in order to seek consolation and hope amid the difficult conditions of their own time. Indeed, its stirring declaration, "If I forget you, O Jerusalem, let my right hand wither; let my tongue cleave to the roof of my mouth if I do not remember you, if I do not set Jerusalem above my chief joy," has served even in subsequent ages to keep Jews mindful of Zion during the long centuries of their exile, and its picture of steadfastness in the face of suffering has helped to keep Jewish hopes alive in some of history's darkest hours.

If this psalm was one that was particularly prized in the aftermath of the Roman destruction of the Temple, it was no doubt also one that was especially *interpreted*, looked into deeply, during that same period. For as we shall see presently, its opening verses in particular posed problems for early interpreters, and resulted in the creation of a number of well-known (and well-travelled) exegetical motifs. Eventually we shall consider some of these exegetical motifs. But it might be well to begin not with exegesis itself (at least not as it is narrowly conceived), but with a question of a more general character: Who, in the opinion of early biblical interpreters, was the author of Psalm 137?

Davidic Authorship

This might seem a simple question. For, as is well known, numerous Jewish sources attribute the authorship of all the biblical psalms to King David, and this view, well attested in rabbinic and contemporaneous writings (it is, incidentally, perhaps witnessed as well within the sect of the Dead Sea Scrolls),[1] eventually acquired authoritative status and was passed on as fact to generations of readers and scholars. Thus, David wrote Psalm 137 along with all the other psalms. Yet this idea of the Davidic authorship of the psalms had hardly been a *unanimous* Jewish view in late antiquity, and even after it had become generally accepted among both Jews and Christians, the questions surrounding it did not entirely cease. It was in fact one of the first bits of traditional dogma to be challenged with the rise of modern biblical scholarship in the eighteenth and nineteenth centuries—and, interestingly, it was our psalm, Psalm 137, that was often marshalled as proof of the falsity of the traditional view. For how could David, living in the tenth century B.C.E., have written a psalm that describes the woes of the Babylonian exile four hundred years in the future, and indeed, why should he have written of that exile apparently in the past tense ("By the rivers of Babylon, *there we sat down* . . . ," and so forth), as of an event that had already taken place? So successful was the modern critical assault on the tradition of David's authorship, in regard to this psalm and to the psalms in general, that by the turn of the present century many biblical scholars claimed that only a small portion of the Psalter could even be dated to the *preexilic* period, that is, before the Babylonian conquest of Judah in 587 B.C.E. This was the opinion of the biblical critic Julius Wellhausen; his contemporary B. Duhm went so far as to deny the existence of *any* preexilic psalms, and held that our psalm, Psalm 137, was in fact the oldest one in the Psalter! (It may be of some limited comfort to observe that current critical opinion is less extreme, holding not only quite a few psalms to be preexilic, but one or two to be pre-Davidic as well.)

The difficulty with the idea of Davidic authorship was not, of course, lost on ancient exegetes, but those who nonetheless subscribed to it found some support for their position in a curious detail in the greatest potential offender, Psalm 137 itself. For while the opening and closing lines of our psalm clearly invoke the Babylonian exile and *bat babel ha-shedudah*, the Babylonian oppressor, v. 7 asks God to remember the role of another people, the Edomites, in the destruction of Jerusalem: "Call to account, O Lord, the Edomites for the day of Jerusalem, how they said, 'Rase it, rase it, down to its very foundations!' " Who were these Edomites and why are they mentioned? For those who saw the psalm as a prophetic composition of David's, the reference was not to cooperation by Israel's near neighbor Edom in the Babylonians' destruction of Jerusalem. No, the name "Edom" here is to be understood in accordance with the usage common in later Jewish texts, that is, as a reference to Rome:

> Said R. Yehuda: Rab said: [this psalm] proves that God showed to David the destruction of the First Temple and the destruction of the Second. The First Temple as it is said, "by the rivers of Babylon" [where the Jews were exiled after the First Temple was destroyed], the Second Temple as it is said, "Call to account, O Lord, the Edomites for the day of Jerusalem" [that is, the Romans who conquered Jerusalem in 70 C.E.].[2]

According to this view, the reference to "Edom"/Rome is thus an allusion to the Roman destruction of Jerusalem in 70 C.E. If so, then there is no denying that this psalm is in fact a prophecy—for by any estimate it was written centuries before 70 C.E.! Given this "proof" of the psalm's prophetic quality in its referring to the Romans' destruction of Jerusalem, might not its reference to Babylon have been equally prophetic—in which case, might not the whole psalm have indeed been written by David?

Jeremiah's Authorship

This notwithstanding, it is to be observed that a number of early Jewish texts seem to reject the Davidic authorship of this psalm and to suggest that it was actually composed by another biblical figure, Jeremiah. This is evidenced, *inter alia*, by a tradition, attested in some manuscripts of the Old Greek ("Septuagint") translation of the Bible, of attaching a particular heading to Psalm 137: for while some Septuagint manuscripts have the heading "to David," others contain the notation "to [or "of"] Jeremiah." It actually appears that the oldest tradition of the Greek Psalter was to have no heading at all for this psalm, as indeed the Masoretic Text has none; but that two traditions of late antiquity, the one connecting the psalm with David and the other with Jeremiah, eventually found expression in the various Greek headings, the two sometimes subsequently being harmonized in the clumsy "To David, of [or "through," διά] Jeremiah" found in yet other mss.[3] It is to be noted that even within rabbinic writings one sometimes finds our psalm specifically connected to Jeremiah. Thus, for example, the collection *Eikhah Zuṭa* reports that the psalm was spoken by Jeremiah "when the Israelites left Jerusalem," while others locate its singing at the Euphrates at the time when Jeremiah took his leave of the exiles.[4]

There are a number of good reasons to connect the psalm specifically with Jeremiah. It is not just that he is the prophet of the Fall of Jerusalem, and thus chronologically appropriate; nor yet that he is the traditional author of the book of Lamentations, *Eikhah*, and thus might conceivably have written this brief lament as well, with its mournful *'eikh nashir . . .* , "How can we sing a song of the Lord?"[5] But he also prophesied the return from exile, and as such might well have been the one to have prayed in Psalm 137 that the Edomites (not the Romans, but the real Edomites) pay for their crimes against Israel after the exile's end, "Call to account, O Lord, the Edomites for the day of Jerusalem . . ." (v. 7), or similarly to have envisaged the vengeance to be visited upon Babylon, "Happy the one who repays you in kind for what you have done to us" (v. 8). In fact, Jeremiah *did* foretell the punishment of the Edomites in our canonical book of Jeremiah (Jer. 49:8–22), and our psalm's mention of "repaying" Babylon (*'ashrei sheyyishallem lakh*) is reminiscent of the precise wording of Jer. 51:24: *veshillamti lebabel . . .* , "And I will repay Babylon and all the inhabitants of Chaldea all the evil which they did in Zion. . . ." Our psalm's concluding verse, "Happy the one who takes your children and dashes them (*venippeṣ*) on the rock," is likewise strongly reminiscent of this same passage in Jeremiah, which begins with God speaking repeatedly of "dashing" the guilty ones, *venippaṣti bakh goyim*, "I will dash nations through you," *venippaṣti bakh sus verokhebo,* "And I will dash through you horse and rider," and so forth for a total of nine times, all leading up to "I will repay Babylon" in v. 24.[6]

There is one apparent difficulty with the idea of Jeremianic authorship, however. The psalm speaks as if from personal experience of the woes of Babylonian captivity, "there *we* sat down and wept." Yet our biblical account says specifically that Jeremiah did not go with the exiles to Babylon but chose to remain in Jerusalem, until he was forcibly removed to Egypt (Jer. 43:1–8). How then could *he* say, "there we sat down and wept"?[7] One solution, well attested in rabbinic texts, has Jeremiah accompany the exiles just to the Babylonian border, or specifically up to the "rivers of Babylon" mentioned in Psalm 137:1, whereupon he takes leave of them and returns to Judah in accordance with the biblical account, and then ultimately is removed to Egypt. This does no real violence to the biblical narrative, and can accord fairly well with words of the psalm: he first sat down and wept with the exiles, and then left.

But another possibility exists: that the words of our psalm were indeed spoken by Jeremiah, not at the beginning of the exile, but at its very end, the wording "there we sat down and wept" implying in fact that such sitting and weeping was now a thing of the past. Could such a hypothesis coexist with the plain facts of our biblical history? It seems that, to one equipped with a midrashic imagination, the biblical narrative (and particularly its silences) might indeed suggest just such a scenario. True enough, as the book of Jeremiah informs us (Jer. 43:7), Jeremiah did go to Egypt, to the border city of Taḥpanḥes (modern Tel Defenneh). But there is no account of his death in Egypt—in spite of the fact that so much of the latter part of the book of Jeremiah is devoted to biographical, third-person narrative. In fact, in that chapter of Jeremiah and the next, the prophet warns that Nebuchadnezzar will conquer Egypt, and that some people (whether Jews or Egyptians is not clear) will be "taken prisoner" (Jer. 43:11).

Apparently basing himself on this—and perhaps also Jer. 44:12–14, which likewise implies that at least some of the Jews who sought refuge in Egypt would escape destruction—the first-century Jewish historian Josephus reports that the Jews of Egypt were in fact deported to Babylon after Nebuchadnezzar's conquest of Egypt, where presumably they joined the other exiles:

> But when they came there [to Egypt], the Deity revealed to the prophet [Jeremiah] that the king of Babylon was about to march against the Egyptians, and he bade the prophet foretell to the people

that Egypt would be taken and that the Babylonian king would kill some of them and would take the rest captive and carry them off to Babylon. And so it happened; for in the fifth year after his sacking of Jerusalem, which was the twenty-third year of the reign of Nebuchadnezzar, Nebuchadnezzar marched against Coele-Syria and, after occupying it, made war on both the Moabites and the Ammonites. Then, after making these nations subject to him, he invaded Egypt in order to subdue it, and having killed the king who was then reigning and appointing another, **he again took captive the Jews who were in the country and carried them to Babylon.**[8]

Presumably the prophet Jeremiah himself might have been in such a group of deportees, and would thus have rejoined his brethren in Babylon, where he ultimately might have composed the words of Psalm 137 while waiting out with them the predicted seventy years of exile. That Jeremiah not only did so, but even survived beyond the end of the exile, might seem to be supported by another detail, the mention of a certain "Jeremiah" listed among the leaders in the time of Nehemiah, that is, after the return from exile (Neh. 10:2, 21:1, 12, 34). Who was *this* Jeremiah? The fact that he was not only a person of some importance but, like our prophet Jeremiah, is described as a priest, could only imply that the two were one and the same. If so, early biblical interpreters might well conclude that Jeremiah had indeed not only gone back to Babylon, but had survived long enough to return from there with the other exiles.

Whether or not such a hypothesis is in the end plausible is irrelevant. The fact is that the removal of Jeremiah from Egypt to Babylon with the other exiles—countenanced, if not specifically stated, in the above-cited passages from Josephus—was indeed specifically stated by other early Jewish exegetes. Thus, *Seder 'Olam Rabba* recounts that Jeremiah and Baruch were both taken prisoner by Nebuchadnezzar in Egypt and brought back to Babylon:

> In the twenty-seventh year of Nebuchadnezzar, Egypt fell into his hands. "He took its multitude and its booty and spoils, and this was the pay for his army" [Ezek. 29:19]. And he exiled Jeremiah and Baruch to Babylon in the twenty-fifth year of our Exile.[9]

A similar tradition underlies the account found in the collection known as *'Aqtan deMar Ya'aqob,* and the account in the *Chronicles of Yerahme'el,* which may depend on the former text or its *Vorlage,* which would appear to be quite old.[10] Here we read:

> Then Nebuchadnezzar rose up against Egypt and besieged it and captured it and laid it to waste, fulfilling what had been said, "Egypt shall

be laid waste and Edom a desert waste" [Joel 4:19], and he killed all the Jews he found in Ammon and Moab and in the surrounding parts of Egypt. And he found Jeremiah and Baruch in Egypt and brought them up with him to Babylon."[11]

Other rabbinic texts, perhaps heir to the same tradition, place Baruch in Babylon until the return of Ezra—in fact, Ezra was a student in Baruch's study-house.[12] Moreover, a number of pseudepigrapha apparently originating in the Second Temple Period or just after place Jeremiah in Babylon with the exiles, although Baruch is sometimes said to have remained behind in Jerusalem.[13]

Such an idea, it should be noted, must have seemed even more probable given the well-established tradition that Jeremiah was the author of the biblical book of Lamentations. For that book, and particularly its last chapter, suggests that its author saw not only the destruction of Jerusalem, but the subsequent Babylonian exile as well, the Jews "hard-driven on our necks" by their captors (Lam. 5:5) and brought to a place where "slaves ruled over us." Deported, according to the popular imagination, en masse and almost to a man,[14] the Jews must thus have been on their way to, or *already in*, Babylon when these lines of chapter 5 of Lamentations were spoken; indeed, there they suffered the indiginities of forced servitude, "Young men are compelled to grind at the mill and boys stagger under loads of wood" (Lam. 5:13). Therefore, if Jeremiah wrote these and similar verses, it could only have been that he had witnessed the sufferings of his people in exile firsthand, and not just at the exile's beginning, but (so this last-cited verse might suggest) when the people had already been settled into the dreary routine of servitude. If so, the same Jeremiah might well have written Psalm 137, and written it still later on, at a time when weeping and sighing over Zion could be spoken of in the past tense, when a vow not to "forget" Jerusalem would carry more significance, indeed, when hope was quickening for revenge on those had brought about Israel's suffering.

In short, rabbinic and prerabbinic sources sometimes connect the prophet Jeremiah with the authorship of Psalm 137, placing him at "the rivers of Babylon" either at the very beginning of the exile, or, with some imaginative dexterity, through to the very end of it, perhaps transplanted there (as we have just seen) by Nebuchadnezzar after the latter attacked Egypt. Surely Jeremiah, the author of Lamentations, was a fit candidate for authorship of this brief lament as well, all the more so because, as a prophet, he had announced in his oracles the same vengeance on Babylon and Edom that our psalm speaks of—and in strikingly similar language. And if we locate the time of its composition toward the *end* of the exile, it will further accord with the curious mixture found in the psalm of retrospective contemplation of suffering (". . . we sat down and wept") with the prospective (because apparently still unfulfilled) contemplation of a return to Jerusalem ("If I forget you, O Jerusalem . . .") and the vengeance still to be wreaked on Israel's enemies (vv. 7 and 8).

Exegetical Motifs

Attributing the composition of this psalm to Jeremiah does not, however, solve all of an exegete's difficulties. A number of problems, great and small, have attracted the attention of commentators since late antiquity and generated a number of memorable exegetical motifs. In the following I should like to present a brief, and somewhat pointed, sampling thereof. For an example of—quite literally—small problems within the psalm, one might turn first to the psalm's use of two short and apparently unnecessary words in its very first line, "By the rivers of Babylon, *there* we sat down, *yea* we wept. . . ." Both the words "there" (*sham*) and "yea" (*gam*) seemed to early exegetes to require some special explanation, and many of the rabbinic texts that touch on this psalm or part of it begin precisely with these problems.

The first word mentioned, *sham*, seemed to imply some sort of distinction, "By the rivers of Babylon, *there* was where we sat down . . .", there and nowhere else. Picking up on this clue, many of the sources seen above[15] present a form of the following:

> "There we sat down, yea we wept . . ." Why does it say *"there* we sat down?" This teaches that they had no rest-stop from the time they left the Land of Israel until they reached the Euphrates. They had no rest to sit down because they [the Babylonians] had taken counsel concerning them. They had said: the God of these people is merciful and when they turn to him he relents and has mercy upon them. [Let us arrange it so] that they do not repent and all gather together and call upon their God and they return, and we will have accomplished nothing. Therefore they pressed them and harried them against their will, as it is said, "On our necks we were pursued . . ." [Lam. 5:5] "Swift were our pursuers" [Lam. 4:19].[16]

In this version of the events, the apparently emphatic quality of "there" is explained: *there* we sat down and wept but not before, because we had no opportunity before to do so: the Babylonians out of fear kept us marching until we reached the "rivers of Babylon."

This explanation reads very smoothly, and at first, or even second, glance, one might hardly even consider the possibility that it was not specifically created to explain Ps. 137:1. Yet the starting point for this motif is not, as it might seem to be, simply the fact that *"there* we sat" can be taken to imply that *elsewhere* we did not, or could not, sit down. In fact, it seems more likely that the original point of departure for this motif was the verse Lam. 5:5, only partially cited by the midrashist above. For the full verse reads: "On our necks we were pursued, *exhausted, we were given no rest."* Now this verse as a whole is somewhat ambiguous in context. Like other verses in this section of Lamentations, it might conceivably be understood to describe conditions *within Babylon* at the start of the exile, and "we were pursued" could then simply · mean "we were persecuted" by Babylonians once we arrived there. But if one understands the word not as "persecuted" but as "pursued" in the more usual sense of "chased" or "harried," then "On our necks we were pursued" would appear to be a reference to the journey itself from the land of Israel to Babylon. And if so, of course, "we were given no rest" is likewise a reference to that journey. From this observation (and probably this alone) sprang an original motif, "No Rest-stop in Israel," a straightforward expansion of the biblical verse Lam. 5:5: the phrase "we were given no rest" gave rise to additional narrative to the effect that the Babylonians did not allow the Jews a single rest-stop all the way to Babylon, but forced them to march nonstop.

Having so interpreted "we were given no rest," our midrashist then further seeks to present some rationale for the Babylonians' apparent cruelty. And so he adds the part about the Babylonians fearing that the Jews might "repent and all gather together and call upon their God" and in such a way bring about their successful escape from captivity. To give repentence (a favorite rabbinic theme) such a role in this explanation of the Babylonians' action in Lam. 5:5 was no doubt pleasing from a theological standpoint. Indeed, our motif is found in slightly different form in *Lamentations Rabba,* and there the theme of repentance is even more prominent. For in that version Nebuchadnezzar warns his general: "The God of these people accepts the *penitent,* and his hand is outstretched to receive those who *repent;* when you conquer them, *do not allow them to pray,* lest they effect *repentance* and their God have mercy on them, and I be sorely embarrassed."[17]

Now it is to be noted that neither of these versions fits particularly well with Psalm 137. For if the author of our passage had really wished to make a solid connection between his narrative expansion and the opening words of the psalm, he would probably have said that the

Babylonians were afraid that the Jews might *sit down* and reflect on the cause of their downfall and so come to repent—and not that they were afraid that the Jews might "repent and all gather together and call upon their God," such an act of prayer being accomplished, it goes without saying, *standing up.*[18] The fact that there is no verbal cue here to the opening verse of Psalm 137 and that, in fact, the precise wording seems to work at cross-purposes with that verse, might further indicate that, despite the opening rubric's mention of Ps. 137:1, this motif itself had originally been conceived solely with Lam. 5:5 in mind. What is more, there is in any case something of a theoretical difficulty in joining this motif and its theme of prayer and repentance with the opening words of Psalm 137. For if the whole point of pushing the Jews nonstop was to prevent them from praying and repenting, then why should things be suddenly different once they entered Babylon proper? If the Jews were indeed allowed to rest, and to pray, in Babylon—if *"there* we sat down" thus meant that the Jews did have the time in Babylon to gather together and effect repentence—then would not their prayers be equally efficacious from the other side of the Babylonian border? In other words, the distinction implied by Ps. 137:1 (*there* in Babylon but not earlier, in the Land of Israel) could not easily coexist with the idea that it was Jewish *repentance* that the Babylonians were afraid of.

This uneasiness is in fact represented in another version of our basic motif. It appears elsewhere in *Pesiqta Rabbati* and parallels. Here is the text:

> When Nebuchadnezzar came and burned the Temple and exiled Israel and took them prisoner, he did not make a rest-stop in all of the Land of Israel, but they [the Babylonians] pursued them as it is said, "On our necks we were pursued . . ." [Lam. 5:5]. And why did they pursue them, save that they were **worried for their own lives,** saying: This nation's God is waiting for them to repent, and if indeed they should repent **while they are still within their own land, then he will do to us as he did to Sennacherib.** Therefore there was no rest-stop **in the Land of Israel.** But when they came upon **the rivers of Babylon** and saw that they [the Israelites] were now held in their hands and in their land, they immediately made a rest-stop.[19]

What the Babylonians fear now is not simply that the Jews might repent and be saved, but rather more specifically that God might—on the analogy with what he did to Sennacherib and the Assyrians during the last siege of Jerusalem[20]—suddenly turn against the invaders while they are within the land of Israel and massacre them, forcing a retreat. This analogy is a clever device, for it seems to justify the Babylonian concern with the Jews' repenting "while they are still within their own land": the Assyrian soldiers were stricken within the Land of Israel, and so might the Babylonians be. But, as noted, this new concern with getting across the border because of the Sennacherib analogy is only the result of the incompatibility of the repentance element in "No Rest-stop in Israel" (at least in the versions seen previously) being combined with the geographical distinction implied in the apparent emphasis in "*there* we sat down."

Killer Euphrates

Such, in any case, is one common motif that came to explain the distinction implied by "*there* we sat down." But there were others. In many of the above-cited sources, this explanation coexists with another one of simpler construction:

> Why did Israel see fit to weep along the rivers of Babylon? R. Yohanan said: The river Euphrates killed more people among the Israelites than the wicked Nebuchadnezzar had killed. For when Israel had been dwelling in the Land of Israel, they drank only rain water, running water and spring water; when they were exiled to Babylon they drank the water of the Euphrates, and many of them died.[21]

This explanation, perhaps rooted in realia as well as biblical texts (for the latter see especially Jer. 3:18, "And what do you gain by going to Assyria, to drink the waters of the Euphrates?"),[22] connects the weeping in Babylon with that weeping's cause: *there* was where we sat down and wept because it was there, at the rivers of Babylon, that more of us died than had died even at the hands of Nebuchadnezzar. It is to be noted that such a reading not only justifies the emphatic "there," but gives new meaning to the psalm's opening words, *'al naharot babel*—not so much "by" or "beside" Babylon's rivers as *because of* Babylon's rivers we sat down and wept, for they were the cause of our greatest suffering.

"We Also Wept . . ."

As for the word *gam*—"yea" or "also"—this term (much as is specified in the well-known rabbinic exegetical principle of *ribbui*) appeared to imply an inclusion or extension of the act of weeping beyond what is actually said in the text. So it is that one commonly cited midrash explains:[23] "Why does it say '*yea* [or 'also'] we wept'? To show that they caused the Holy One, Blessed Be He, to weep along with them."[24] Here the word *gam* is construed to imply that our weeping "also" came in addition to other weeping, that of God Himself. Somewhat similar is the explanation found in *Seder Eliyahu Rabba*: " '*And* we wept' is not written here, but '*yea* we wept.' This teaches that they wept and grew silent and then began to weep again" (*bakhu veshatequ vehazeru ubakhu*).[25] Yet another explanation seems to solve the problems of *sham* and *gam* together: for as was mentioned earlier, some rabbinic sources situate the recitation of this psalm in Babylon at the time when Jeremiah takes leave of the exiles (Jer. 40:1 ff). Seeing their prophet departing, the forlorn Jews begin to weep,[26] whereupon Jeremiah says, "I call Heaven and Earth as my witnesses, if you had but wept one time while you were yet in Zion, you would not have been exiled," and he departs weeping.[27] This motif, "Had You Wept But Once," accounts for *sham*, "There we sat down" in mourning, that is, *there* in Babylon but not in the Land of Israel, where it might have done us some good (in bringing about repentance); and *gam* now apparently means "in addition to Jeremiah," who himself weeps.[28]

Hanging Harps

This hardly exhausts the explanations offered up for these or other, rather limited, problems in the psalm's wording, but we might now pass to what is really the major difficulty of these opening lines and the subject of much exegetical speculation: the somewhat strange gesture of the Israelites in hanging their harps on willow trees, and the subsequent exchange reported between the Babylonians and their captives, culminating in the question, "How shall we sing a song of the Lord in a foreign land?"

About the gesture itself it is to be noted that most modern commentators (as indeed ancient ones) see in it an act of defiance, a refusal of the captives to comply with the request for song.[29] But if what our psalm records is such a gesture of defiance, it is indeed a strange one! One might expect the Jews simply to refuse verbally to comply, indeed, in view of their later question, "How can we sing a song of the Lord . . . ?", to break forth instead into dirges and wailing.[30] And granting for the moment that the singers were already standing with their instruments in hand (though even this item, as we shall see, occasioned some questions), if we should try on our own to imagine some gesture of defiance on their part in refusing, would it not be to cast their instruments onto the ground, nay, to smash them to bits? Against such a background of speculation, the act of hanging these harps in the trees seems passing strange.

The question is treated somewhat obliquely in a widely disseminated rabbinic expansion based on our psalm's words:

> [When he saw the Jews lamenting], Nebuchadnezzar said to them "Why are you sitting and weeping?" and he called to the tribe of Levi and said to them, "Prepare yourselves: before we eat and drink I demand of you that you go and play your harps before me just as you used to play in your Temple before your God." They looked at one another and said, "Is it not enough that we have destroyed His sanctuary by the multitude of our sins, but now must we go and play our harps before this dwarf?[31] Whereupon they all conferred and hung up their harps on the willows that were there and mastered themselves and put their thumbs in their mouths and crushed them and mutilated them. And David sets it forth specifically: ". . . On willow trees in its midst we hung up our harps . . ." For the tribe of Levi hung their harps there on the edge of the river, since "Our captors there asked of us words of song, and our tormentors entertainment: 'Sing us a song from the songs of Zion . . .' [The words] "We *shall not* sing" are not written here, but "*How* shall we sing?"—and they showed them their fingers.[32]

This narrative expanison is, not surprisingly, also a conflation of different exegetical motifs; but the main problem to which it is addressed is the curious wording, "*How* shall we sing a song of the Lord in a foreign land?" If an actual refusal were intended, "How shall we sing . . . ?" ought, to a certain way of thinking, have been better expressed as "We *will not* sing!" And so this vignette presents the Levites in an act of great physical courage, the mutilation of their own thumbs, which then allows them to pose the question squarely to their tormentors: how indeed can we sing if we are no longer able to play our instruments?[33] With this has been integrated another motif, aimed at the psalm's precise wording of the Babylonians' request: "Sing *to us* a song from the songs of Zion." Now in the context of the psalm, this may have been a simple request for entertainment, "Sing us one of your local songs, a song of Zion [= Jerusalem]." But in our text this request is "translated" and somewhat transformed as: "I demand of you that you go and play your harps *before me* just as you used to do in your Temple *before your God*." We should note that "song of Zion" is being interpreted here as, specifically, a sacred song associated with the Temple in Jerusalem. This interpretation seems only reasonable in the light of the Jews' response to the Babylonians' request within the psalm itself—"How shall we sing a *song of the Lord* in a foreign land?"—but, as we shall see presently, other interpretations were also possible. Moreover, the request for this sacred song now comes not from "our captors" in general, but from Nebuchadnezzar himself. Both these elements combine to turn the Babylonians' "sing *to us*" in the psalm—in itself a request calculated to bring pain to the Jewish exiles—into the blasphemous and grotesque demand of Nebuchadnezzar that the Jews sing "before me just as you used to do in your Temple before your God." And this request has been made to appear even more grotesque by having it come specifically at mealtime, with the sacred song demanded as some sort of entertainment before the meal.

It is to be noted that, in this particular version of the events, the Jews' hanging of their harps seems to be a casual sort of expedient, a way of freeing their hands so as to allow them to mutilate their fingers. But the gesture produced another explanation as well:

> R. Isaac expounded "On willows in its midst we hung our harps . . ."
> While they were still in the land of Israel, Jeremiah would say to them,
> "Repent before a decree is sealed against you." But they did not accept
> his words. However, when they were exiled they began to treat divine
> commandments with sanctity, they took their harps and hung them
> on the willows.[34]

Apparently this act of hanging the harps is here understood as one of extraordinary care and delicacy, the penitant gesture of those who once trod on the most important of divine decrees and so brought about the Temple's downfall but who now, in exile, take care to treat their useless harps, sacred instruments of that same Temple, with special respect, even going to the trouble of hanging them in the trees and so not placing them "on foreign ground."[35] Not all subsequent commentators were content to choose among such alternatives, however. Although it hardly falls under the rubric of "early exegesis," we might turn for a moment to the Psalms commentary of the medieval Provençal scholar R. Menaḥem b. Solomon Meiri, who reads these same words of Psalm 137 in a startlingly different fashion:

> All the commentators have explained that we abandoned our harps
> and hung them upon the trees, but I am astonished at this explanation
> of theirs. For how could they [the Jews] be carrying the harps, and as
> for the [Babylonian] enemies, how could they permit them *not* to sing
> according to their request? But the proper explanation is that the en-
> emies, once they were in their own territory, began to rejoice and
> make merry, and they had in their own possession all the instruments
> of the Temple, and they ordered that they [the Jews] sing from the
> songs of Zion, and they were forced to do so, and they took out their
> harps and put them in their hands to tune their strings and pegs and
> pull them, and this tuning [the text] calls "hanging" (*teliyyah*), for any
> stretching of a thing and extending it to establish it in its proper po-

sition is described by the word (*teliyyah*), as "hanging the earth over the void" (Job 26:7) and in the rabbinic usage, "One may suspend [*tolin*] a strainer over a vessel on a festival day" [m. *Shabbat* 20:1], which means he extends it over the vessel and stretches its mouth on either side in a circle and it is made like a tent over the open part of the vessel, and similarly "on the fourth day the stars were put into place" [*nitlu* in *Genesis Rabba*, 3]. . . . And the lament [that is, the "weeping"] was because they forced them to sing a song of Zion. As for "*on* willow trees," it means *near* willow trees and in between them. . . . All this is the exculpation for the singing, for not willingly did we sing, but only forced by those whose power ruled over us.[36]

Thus Meiri sees in our psalm not a refusal to sing but reluctant acquience: '*eikh nashir* really means not so much "How *can* we sing . . ." as "How *will* we sing . . . ," or perhaps even "How are we singing . . . ?"

An incidental problem sometimes associated with this gesture of our "hanging our harps" (*talinu*) is the somewhat similar sounding word in the next verse, *tolalenu*. The latter is an extremely rare word (in fact, in this form it occurs only once in the Bible, here in our psalm), and commentators have exercised much ingenuity in trying to explain it. Modern translators usually render it as "captors" or the like—"For there those who had taken us prisoner asked of us words of song, and our captors [demanded] celebration"—but this translation is based only on the analogy with the first part of the verse and its better known term, *shobenu* ("those who had taken us prisoner"). The Aramaic targum of the Psalms renders the word as "despoilers," reading the apparent Hebrew root *talal* as related to Hebrew *shalal*, "spoils." Medieval Jewish exegetes (including the just-cited Meiri) have also associated it with *yalal*, "moan," or indeed *talah* or *talal* in the sense of to "hang" or "make high." This last is the position of, among others, Abraham ibn Ezra, who thus reads *tolalenu simḥah* as "our hanging up [instruments] of celebration."[37] The midrashic tradition traced above, according to which the Jews mutilate their fingers in order to be unable to play and sing, concludes with yet another exegetical motif related to *tolalenu*. For, enraged at this turn of events, the Babylonians (or Nebuchadnezzar) thereupon slay "heaps and heaps," *tillei tillim*, of their captives, "and though they killed many of them, it was for them [the Jews] a source of joy that they did not sing before the idolators, as it is said, *vetolalenu simḥah*, 'and their heaping us up was a joy.' "

As for the question "How shall we sing a song of the Lord in a foreign land?", we have already seen that its very form—the "How . . . ?"—aroused the curiosity of exegetes. But beyond this formal difficulty is the matter of the question itself. For taken at face value, it seems to imply that a "song of the Lord" is *not* to be sung in a foreign land. But can this indeed be the case? Would that not imply too close a bond between Israel's religion and Israel's territory, such that the former cannot ultimately survive elsewhere but in the latter? One can well imagine how such a question might prove problematic to Jews in a later period when, with the Jerusalem Temple once again in ruins and the Jewish people again dispersed, not only to Babylon but to Rome and points still more distant, singing a song of the Lord in a foreign land was an act not of desecration but the opposite, indeed, one of the few remaining acts of communal piety and national cohesion.

The struggle with this particular issue is long and varied. The targum's translation of "in a foreign land," *'al 'ar'a ḥilonita'*, might also be rendered "in an unholy land"; this nuance might in turn open the way to implying that a "song of the Lord" is to be ruled out not in *any* foreign land, but particularly in the unholy Babylon of Nebuchadnezzar, destroyer of the Temple. One might note in this connection the restatement of this verse found in *Midrash ha-Gadol*, which renders "in a foreign land" as *be'ereṣ ṭeme'ah*, "in an impure land," perhaps, a land made impure by its idolatry.[38] Meanwhile, we have already seen above another tactic for confronting this problem, the narrative expansion of our psalm which has Nebuchadnezzar request that the Jews sing a song "before me" (or, in other versions, "before an idol").[39] Here it is not particularly the fact of being in a foreign land that makes a "song of the Lord" impossible, but the use to which the foreign captors wish to put that song. Yet another midrashic motif (often harmonized with this one, but logically distinct) understands the question "How shall we sing . . . ?" as a kind of *a fortiori* moral argument: If we did not sing as we should have in Jerusalem, how can we sing *now* in a foreign land? Here "singing in Jerusalem" is something of a metaphor for carrying out all the commandments properly.[40] But since we did not do so under the best of circumstances, how can we be expected to do so now, under the worst? And of course the contrast is only heightened by having Nebuchadnezzar request specifically that the Levites "play your harps before me just as you used to do in your Temple before your God,"[41] or by requiring the Levites to sing a "song of the Lord" in front of an idol.[42]

It is interesting that the tenth century Jewish scholar R. Se'adya Ga'on wrestled with the same question in his Psalms commentary and came to a very different conclusion. He used this verse to argue, in his longer "Introduction," that it was the *musical recitation* of the psalms that was forbidden outside of the Temple. Psalm headings that refer to musical performance, such as *lamnaṣṣeaḥ* ("For the choirmaster"), *bingi-*

not ("with stringed instruments"), or *shir* ("song") thus exist in the Psalter in part as a warning that such performance is restricted.[43] Having alluded to the first two types of headings, Se'adya continues:

> And likewise the *shir* ["song," that is, a class of musical psalms] is entirely special to the Holy Land, as you may know [from the fact] that the people of Babylon asked our forefathers to perform a hymn in its regular [musical] fashion in the Exile, and they refused, and so they explained when they said, "For there those who had taken us prisoner asked of us words of song and our captors celebration, Sing for us from the song [*shir*] of Zion." And they said, "How can we *sing* a song of the Lord in a foreign land?" But by way of [public] reading, it may be read in a simple reading, since it is maintained that it is a book for the perfection of mankind.[44]

In keeping with this position,[45] Se'adya translates the verse in his Psalms translation "How can we sing the *special* song of God in a foreign land," and explains: "Since a hymn to God is not in itself forbidden outside of the Holy Land, I have therefore added the word 'special' in my translation and said 'How shall we sing the special song of God . . . ?'" (that is, the one designated *shir*).

Se'adya does not remark on it specifically, but there is an asymmetry in our psalm between the demand of the Babylonians and the Jews' response, one noted in passing above. The former say "Sing to us from the songs *of Zion*," while the latter respond "How can we sing a song *of the Lord* . . . ?" Now the key element for Se'adya is the common term *shir*, with its (for him) specialized meaning. The medieval commentator Abraham ibn Ezra, somewhat differently, saw in the response of the Jews a statement about the sacred character of the psalms as a whole, for "they are sacred songs and songs of the Lord, as the Levites said to the Babylonians, 'How shall we sing a song of the Lord in a foreign land?'"[47] Thus, by answering a request for a "song of Zion" with a statement about the "songs of the Lord," the Jews were, in essence, supplying the grounds for their refusal: the songs of Zion *are* songs of the Lord and as such unfit for these circumstances.

The Oldest Datable Commentary

There remains much to be said about the exegetical history of this psalm, and if the foregoing survey has been limited to a handful of brief excerpts, it is because my aim has been simply to identify what appear to be the major issues for ancient commentators grappling with this psalm's opening words, and so to set the stage for what I believe is in fact the oldest datable "commentary" on Psalm 137. The sources we have been examining are by and large from the amoraic period or later, indeed, medieval exegesis, whereas the text I wish to present is generally dated to the late first or early second century c.e., to the period between the destruction of the Jerusalem Temple by the Romans and the Bar Kokhba Revolt. What is more, although a citation of Psalm 137 has long been recognized in this text, its specifically *exegetical* character has not, in my opinion, been sufficiently appreciated heretofore.

I am referring to the document known variously as 4 Baruch or the *Paraleipomena Ieremiou*, the "Chronicles of Jeremiah," or the "Rest of the Words of Jeremiah." This text survives in Greek and various other translations of an apparently Hebrew original. The book's connection with other documents and themes of this period in Jewish history has been remarked upon, and in particular its somewhat "proto-rabbinic" character,[48] although some of its specifically rabbinic connections remain to be explored in detail.[49] Because of its decidedly Christian ending, the book was at one time thought to be the work of an early Jewish Christian; however many scholars have since concluded that its Christian elements are merely interpolations introduced by a later, Christian editor. Behind our present text there would thus seem to stand an earlier Jewish document, one that had been written or redacted in the first part of the second century and which aimed specifically at rallying Jewish hopes after the destruction of the Temple in 70 c.e. (It is also to be noted that it belongs to a larger complex of Second Temple writings centering on the persons of Jeremiah and Baruch, and much remains to be done in unraveling their complex interrelationship.)[50]

In general, the *Paraleipomena* presents a narrative of the destruction of Jerusalem by the Babylonians and of the subsequent removal of the Jewish captives to Babylon; then the narrative jumps to the period just before the end of the exile. In this particular version of things, in common with some other pseudepigrapha and a few of the rabbinic texts that we have mentioned, Jeremiah is brought with the exiles to Babylon; Baruch, however, remains behind in Jerusalem. This allows for (among other things) the literary device of having Baruch send to Jeremiah a letter of instructions dictated to him by an angel, in which the manner of the return from exile is specified. Jeremiah, in turn, sends a letter back to Baruch in which he speaks of the travails of the Jews during their long captivity.[51]

It is precisely this letter of Jeremiah that is of interest to us here. The text of the letter varies somewhat among the different manuscript traditions; the following is based upon the eclectic text recently produced by R. A. Kraft and A.-E. Purintun,[52] although, in an additional note, I should like to add a word about the various recensions:

And Jeremiah wrote a letter to Baruch, saying thus: My beloved son, do not be negligent in your prayers, beseeching God on our behalf, that he might direct our way until we come out of the jurisdiction of this lawless king. For you have been found righteous before God, and he did not let you come here, lest you see the affliction which has come upon the people at the hands of the Babylonians. . . . For since we came here, grief has not left us for sixty-six years today. For many times when I went out I found some of the people hanged by King Nebuchadnezzar, crying and saying: "Have mercy on us, God Zar!"

When I heard this, I grieved and cried with twofold mourning, not only because they were hanged but because they were calling on a foreign god, saying "Have mercy on us." But I remembered days of festivity which we celebrated in Jerusalem before our captivity, and when I remembered, I groaned, and returned to my house wailing and weeping. Now, then, pray in the place where you are, you and Abim-elech, for this people, that they may listen to my voice and to the decrees of my mouth, so that we may depart from here. For I tell you that the entire time that we have spent here they have kept us in subjection, saying: Recite for us a song from the songs of Zion, the song of your God. And we reply to them: How shall we sing for you, being in a foreign land?

And after this Jeremiah tied the letter to the eagle's neck.

(*Paraleipomena Ieremiou* 7:24–35)

The last two sentences of Jeremiah's "letter" clearly evoke vv. 2 and 3 of Psalm 137. But we should note that, in this version, the Babylonians say "Recite for us a song from the songs of Zion, the song of your God," which is actually a paraphrase of their words in the psalm, "Sing to us from the *song(s) of Zion,*" combined with the response of the Jews, "How can we sing a *song of the Lord* . . . ?" Now if our author's purpose were simply to cite a well-known verse from Scripture, he will be seen to have botched the job somewhat, for exact quotation, rather than paraphrase, is what is called for—especially if the putative speaker of both the psalm and our text is the prophet Jeremiah! But in the light of what we have seen above, the act of paraphrasing here makes perfectly good sense: for we saw how the apparent conflict between "song of Zion" and "song of the Lord" required, on through the Middle Ages, some exegetical exertions on the part of commentators like Abraham ibn Ezra. By paraphrasing the Babylonians' demand in such a way as to include, and indeed equate, "songs of Zion" and "song of the Lord," our author has thus defused a danger: he puts both (now equated) terms on one side, in the mouths of the Babylonians, and has the Israelites merely refer to "singing" so that the full thrust of their answer is communicated without any distracting conflict between the type of song specified by the one group and that specified by the other.

But if so, then we must consider the posture of our author. For apparently, he is not merely seeking to *evoke* Psalm 137, which he could have done more effectively by exact quotation, but to *explain* a difficulty in the wording. He is, in other words, something of a bare-faced exegete here. And this might lead one to examine other elements in the surrounding sentences to see if they too have some *exegetical* relationship to Psalm 137, or indeed to some other biblical text.

Suggestive in this connection is the sentence in our text where Jeremiah is represented as saying: "But I remembered days of festivity which we celebrated in Jerusalem before our captivity; and when I remembered, I groaned and returned to my house wailing and weeping." To begin with, one might wonder why, amid the gruesome spectacle of his fellow Jews being hanged, it is the thought of festivities celebrated in Jerusalem that sets Jeremiah to "wailing and weeping"; surely these are odd circumstances in which to remember happy holidays and celebration! But our text is apparently quite insistent: "But I *remembered* days of festivity which we celebrated in Jerusalem . . . and when I *remembered* I groaned. . . ." This curious sentiment and insistent wording makes better sense, however, when one realizes that the sentence in question is nothing but a paraphrase of Psalm 137's words, "there we sat down and *wept as we remembered Zion*." Our text not only echoes these words, but again seeks to flesh out the meaning: what Jeremiah remembered was not simply the physical place from which the Jews had been removed, but Zion more particularly as the place in which feast days were "celebrated in Jerusalem before our captivity."[53] It is this in particular that moves Jeremiah to tears, and it ties in well with the exiles' later response to their captors' demand, "Recite for us a song from the *songs of Zion*, the song of your God." For *remembering* the "days of festivity which we celebrated in Jerusalem before our captivity," and being thus keenly aware of the proper use to which these songs were put in Zion, the answer given by Jeremiah and his countrymen to the Babylonian demand can only be "How can we sing for you" songs that were made for celebrating the holy festivals we kept in Jerusalem now that we are no longer there, "being in a foreign land." Thus our text's insistence on remembering is in effect a verbal cue to the psalm's own *bezokhrenu 'et ṣiyyon* ("when we remembered Zion"), and its further definition of "Zion" not as a physical locale so much as the site of Temple rejoicing is an attempt to flesh out the reason for the mournful "How shall we sing?" in v. 3 of our psalm.

Another detail in our text that cries out for explanation is its specification of the sufferings of the Jewish people in Babylon. Now certainly to the historical imagination many sorts of suffering might suggest themselves—slavery, oppression, hunger, pillage—but our text mentions only one thing: "For often enough when I have come out of doors I have found some of the people hanged by King Nebuchadnezzar." This is in marked contrast to some of the other Jeremiah/Baruch apocrypha mentioned, which say nothing of "hanging" but do detail physical ailments, cold, hunger, thirst, hard labor, and so forth.[54] That is to say: not only is it somewhat strange here that death, as opposed to all these other forms of suffering, should be mentioned, but stranger still that the form of death, "hanging" (= crucifixion)[55] should be specified. But the reason is that this detail too is generated by the words of Psalm 137. It seeks to understand that exegetical difficulty we have seen in the psalm, the rare and difficult word *tolalenu.* For underlying our text's description can be discerned an early explanation of this word's significance, not (as we saw in the ingenious rabbinic reading) "those who killed heaps and heaps of us," nor yet "our despoilers" or "our captors," but, quite simply, *tolalenu,* "those who hung us."

Hearing the cries of the hanged men, Jeremiah says he "grieved and cried with a *twofold mourning,* not only because they were hanged, but because they were calling on a foreign god." This double lamentation (δισσὸς κλαυθμὸς) is curious as well. The two reasons offered of course support it, but that is just the point—it is as if they are being offered as explanation for some *given,* some "double lamentation" already known. Our psalm does not speak of a double lamentation; but it does contain the curious, and apparently unnecessary, *gam* in the phrase "yea [or "also"], we wept." We saw above that this was explained in *Seder Eliyahu Rabba* as "they wept and were silent and then wept again." It seems entirely probable here that our exegete understands *gam bakhinu* in a similar fashion, as more than simple *bakhinu* — that is, not just "we wept," but "we wept and wept," *bekhi 'al bekhi* in Hebrew (or, more in keeping with the Hebrew of the rabbinic period, *bekhi kaful umkuppal,* which would become in Greek δισσὸς κλαυθμὸς). And so our text has Jeremiah explain: yes, I did weep a double weeping, not only because of their hanging us, *tolalenu,* but because those who were hanged cried out to a foreign god.

Lastly we ought to note the precise wording of the Jews' reply. We have already seen that our author exegetically rephrases the Babylonians' demand to read: "Recite for us a song from the songs of Zion, the song of your God." But just as this is not an exact citation of our psalm's words, so does the Jews' reply contain a slight swerve, "How shall we sing *for you,* being upon a foreign land." The words "for you" do not appear in the psalm, though they are clearly generated by the Babylonian's request in the psalm, "Sing *for us* from the songs of Zion." But why has our author now repeated this idea in the Jews' reply? Certainly he would have done less violence to his act of alluding to Psalm 137 if he had omitted them (as the psalm does); indeed, even having rewritten the Babylonians' request, he still would have done well here to have the Israelites reply with the text's exact words, "How shall we sing a song of the Lord upon a foreign land?" And so again we must see in this act of nonquotation an exegetical purpose. For it is not the singing of a song of the Lord in a foreign land that is the problem, but singing a song "for you"—for you Babylonians instead of for our God. We saw above how some of our rabbinic restatements of the Babylonians' request seemed likewise framed with such a purpose in mind, having Nebuchadnezzar or the Babylonians say, "Play *before me* on your harps the same way that you used to play in your Temple before your God." So once again, the rewording of the psalm's own language serves to clarify something in the psalm, in this case the reason for the Jews' objection.

Here then are five elements in our narrative—the harmonistic misquotation "Recite for us a song from the songs of Zion, a song of your God'; the stress on Jeremiah's *remembering* the Jerusalem festivals as the cause of his lamenting; the curious detail of the Jews being *hanged (tolalenu)* by Nebuchadnezzar; the attempt to explain why Jeremiah wept a "twofold" weeping; and finally the explicative misquotation "How shall we sing *for you* . . . ?"—that together suggest that these details in our narrative do not represent the free play of the author's imagination but a systematic attempt to explain certain textual difficulties in Psalm 137. Or, to put it more pointedly, one might say that the "letter" of Jeremiah in the *Paraleipomena Ieremiou* is essentially the beginning of Psalm 137 itself, but Psalm 137 paraphrased and explained in accordance with an already-known understanding of its words.

Why so? Why did not the author of the *Paraleipomena* simply make up a whole new letter for Jeremiah to send to Baruch, rather than seek to rework the material of Psalm 137? Surely this author does not elsewhere stint at putting words in Jeremiah's mouth. But to raise this question is to address the very understanding of the authorship and time of composition of this psalm with which we began. For the author of the *Paraleipomena* shares the view that not only is Jeremiah the author of Psalm 137, but that he wrote it toward the end of the exile.[56] His act of inserting a paraphrase of part of it as a "letter" sent back to Baruch is essentially an attempt to define this psalm and say what it was, a kind of report by Jeremiah, well into the exile, both looking back on Jewish sufferings and looking forward to the coming redemption. That is, by placing some of Psalm 137's words, along with their proper exegesis, here in his narrative, our author seeks both to *corroborate* its Jeremianic authorship and *situate* it historically, providing a plausible scenario for its composition: Jeremiah did write it, not long before the end of the Babylonian exile, as his thoughts were turned to the Jerusalem he vowed never to forget.

"Have Mercy On Us, God Zar"

There remains only one detail to be accounted for in this letter, but it is the most tantalizing one of all: those who have been hung by Nebuchadnezzar cry out, "Have mercy on us, god Zar." The name "Zar" means nothing in Greek—patently it is the Hebrew *zar*, "foreign," indeed, the Hebrew underlying our Greek text must have had the people crying out *raḥem 'alenu, 'el zar* "Have mercy on us, foreign god!" (This is clearly demonstrated in the very next sentence, where Jeremiah explains that he was grieved to hear the people "calling on a foreign god, saying 'Have mercy on us.' ") But there is nary a hint of "calling on a foreign god" in Psalm 137; whence did this element come? And why should the people call out to any deity (to whom, presumably, they are appealing for help) with the somewhat unflattering appelation, "foreign god"? Finally, why does our Greek translator leave the word *zar* untranslated, treating it as a proper name, when clearly (as the very next line indicates) he knows that it is the adjective "foreign"?

The phrase *'el zar* occurs exactly twice in the Hebrew Bible, in Pss. 44:21 and 81:10. The latter is a general usage and need not detain us here, but the former occurs in the midst of a psalm that seemingly refers to the Babylonian exile and its woes.[57] The Psalmist laments:

> You have cast us off and abased us, and have not gone out with our armies; you have made us turn back from the foe, and our enemies have gotten spoils. You have made us like sheep for slaughter, and have scattered us among the nations. You have sold your people for a trifle, demanding no high price for them.
>
> (Psalm 44:11–13)

This might well refer to the Jews in Babylon, as even some modern commentators suggest. Now amidst all this suffering, the psalm goes on to assert, Israel has not deserted its God: "All this has overtaken us, but we have not forgotten you, nor have we been false to your covenant" (v. 18). But then, as it were, the Psalmist leaves open the slightest bit the question of Israel's faithfulness to God during the exile, for he continues:

> If we *have* forgotten the name of our God, and held up our hands to *a foreign god*, will not God probe this, for he knows the secrets of the heart?

It is this verse, I believe, that is responsible for Jeremiah's description of the Jews' crying to the god Zar in his letter.[58] For the terrible truth, he says, is that in the rigors of exile we did *not* remain faithful to our God, but just as the psalm foretold, we (or some of us) have cried out to a foreign god. Indeed, it is not only Psalm 44 that foretold this, but even the Torah itself. For there, in the celebrated "admonition" section of Deuteronomy 28, in which the Israelites are told of the exile that they will suffer if they fail to keep God's covenant, it is said:

> The Lord will bring you, and your king whom you set over you, to a nation that neither you nor your fathers have known; and there you shall serve other gods, of wood and stone.
>
> (Deut. 28:36; cf. v. 64)

This indeed is precisely what has happened, Jeremiah says in his letter, showing once again that all that was foretold of Israel's sufferings in exile has been carried out.[59]

But an exegete, contemplating the precise wording of Ps. 44:21, might be pressed to explain one detail. For it does not say (as might have been expected) "If we have forgotten our God, and stretched forth our hands to a foreign god . . ." but "If we have forgotten the *name* of our God. . . ."[60] Mention of Israel's forgetting, specifically, its own God's *name* surely seems to imply that the *name* of some other god was cried out in its place.[61] But what name was that? The rest of the verse simply says that they prayed (that is, stretched forth their hands) to an unnamed foreign deity. Unless . . . unless the word *zar* itself is taken as that other god's name, that is, we forget the name of *our* God and called upon the god Zar (*la'el zar*) instead. Such a reading, with the name Zar in the second half of the verse, would successfully account for the otherwise unnecessary reference to forgetting (specifically) our God's *name* in the first half.

I have found no explanation of this verse along such lines in rabbinic writings or elsewhere, but I nonetheless am inclined to believe some such reading underlies our author's reference to the "god Zar" in Jeremiah's letter. The Greek translator, aware of this exegesis, by which *'el zar* is put into proper alignment with "the *name* of our God," simply freezes it in translation, "I found some of the people hanged by King

Nebuchadnezzar, crying and saying, 'Have mercy on us, god Zar.' "
No other interpretation will explain why he has rendered *zar* as a
proper name, when its meaning was (as the next sentence testifies)
certainly clear to him.

We began by observing that scholars are generally agreed in dating
the *Paraleipomena Ieremiou* sometime between 70 and 135 C.E. Jeremiah's
"letter" in the *Paraleipomena*, both in its insistence on interpreting "remembering Zion" as remembering not the physical place but the festivals that had been celebrated there, and in its interpretation of the
question "How shall we sing . . . ?" so as to downplay the "foreign
land" element and stress a "for you" not in the psalm itself, seems to
reflect an exegesis of this psalm belonging to this period of 70–135 C.E.
(and not later, when the physical place of Zion was to become inaccessible). It may be that our author, or a later editor, simply adapted for
his purposes a set of expositions of the opening words of Psalm 137,
perhaps a homily thereon. But whatever the precise scenario, the letter
that we have been examining seems to embody an old—arguably, the
oldest datable—commentary on Psalm 137, and a fascinating bit of evidence about the processes of biblical interpretation in the opening centuries of the common era.

Another Interpretation

It will finally be of interest to note that the "Jeremiah apocryphon"
literature contains another reference to Psalm 137, and one which likewise reflects, I believe, an early form of biblical interpretation. It appears in both the Karshuni Jeremiah apocryphon published by Mingana
in 1927 and in the Coptic one published by K. H. Kuhn in 1970. These
texts in fact contain two separate allusions to our psalm. The first is
simply a version of the same approach seen in the *Paraleipomena* and
elsewhere:

> The children of Israel were hanging their harps on the willow trees,
> resting themselves until the time when they were to work. The Chald-
> eans said to them: Sing us one of the songs that you sang in the house
> of God in Jerusalem. But they sighed, saying: How can we sing the
> song of our God in a strange land? (And) the Chaldeans afflicted
> them.[62]

Here is basically what we have seen above; the only new element (but
it is reminiscent of the midrash in *Pesiqta Rabbati*) is the mention that the
Israelites were "resting themselves"—presumably an explanation of
"there we sat down" (that is, to rest) and perhaps even an echo of the

motif seen earlier to the effect that the Babylonians did not allow the
Jews to rest on the way to Babylon.

But there is a second allusion to Psalm 137 somewhat later in the
story. For after Nebuchadnezzar dies, he is immediately replaced by
"Cyrus the Persian," who here is a bad king who maintains the Jews in
captivity. After some preliminaries, the narrative continues:

> Now after a long time the king commanded that they should gather
> together the people of the Hebrews, and the masters in charge of their
> labors gathered [them] together. King Cyrus said to them: Bring to me
> your harps and your lyres with which you sing praises to your God in
> Jerusalem and play here. They said to him: We are afraid to pluck our
> harps here, for we are in a strange land, surely it is not the will of the
> Lord. The king said to them: I say to you: Sing praises to your own
> God. They said: the Lord hath set apart the sons of Levi to be his
> priests, and it is they who sing praises, they who stand and bring their
> harps and their lyres with which we sing praises to God. Then the
> king made them set apart the tribe of Levi, (and) they stood before the
> people. They took up their harps [and] began to pluck them, even as
> they used to play in the house of God. They struck up in unison.
> Immediately the land on which they were singing praises rose up, so
> that they said: He has wanted to take the children of Israel to Jeru-
> salem. The walls of the palace sounded forth and sang praises with
> them. The saints heard the sound of their hymns, the glory of God
> enveloped them. The inhabitants of Jerusalem knew that the time had
> come for Him to have mercy on his people. Then Cyrus the Syrian
> [read: "Persian"] was afraid and adjured the Hebrews: Do not pluck
> your harps until you return to your land, Judea.[63]

What is one to make of this passage? It is true that it too bears
certain similarities to some of the rabbinic traditions sampled above.
Thus, for example, its specific mention of the Levites should recall the
passage cited above from *Pesiqta Rabbati* and elsewhere, according to
which the singers were not (as one might think from the words of the
psalm itself) merely ordinary Israelites, but Levites. And other details,
as we shall see, similarly suggest a connection between it and rabbinic
sources. Yet despite such resemblances, the passage presents a rather
different reading of Psalm 137, one unattested in our rabbinic sources
and which may therefore represent a relatively ancient grappling with
this psalm's wording. Of course—as was the case with Jeremiah's letter
in the *Paraleipomena*—this text is hardly presented as an *interpretation* of
Psalm 137, nor does it even contain anything so commentary-like as the
explanation of the apparently pleonastic *gam* in "we *also* wept," or the
other problems that we have seen addressed in the *Paraleipomena*. Yet

this levitical ascent into heaven must have been created for some purpose. Let us see if it is not an exegetical one.

The beginning of this narrative is reminiscent of the rabbinic material surveyed above in one regard in particular—for here too is the blasphemous proposal that the Jews' sacred songs designed for the Temple service now be performed for the entertainment of the foreign king: "Bring to me your harps and your lyres with which you sing praises to your God in Jerusalem and play here." But then this text suddenly adopts a very different course. The blasphemous comparison does not then become the basis for the Jews' rejection in the psalm, "How can we sing . . . ?" On the contrary, King Cyrus goes on to reassure them that he only wants them to "sing praises to your own God." Thus put at ease, the Levites do indeed start to play, only to find that when they do so they immediately begin to ascend into heaven, a miraculous ascent that leads the onlookers to think that the return from exile has begun, as the palace walls and the very heavens resound with God's praise. Finally Cyrus orders them to cease until they have actually been returned to their homeland.

On reflection, this miraculous ascent seems nothing more than an attempt to explain the Psalmist's words, "How shall we sing a song of the Lord in a foreign land?" For the problem raised by those words—why should the singing of hymns outside of the land of Israel, perhaps even outside of the Temple precincts, be forbidden?—is not being answered here, as it was in other instances, by means of the king's blasphemous request. On the contrary, Cyrus becomes, as we have just seen, strangely reassuring on that score, and the fact that the Levites do indeed proceed to sing divine praises vouchsafes the fact that so doing outside of Israel's land is perfectly permitted. But if so, then what could have been the meaning of the Psalmist's words, "How shall we sing . . ."? In the light of what happens next, it appears that this question might best be rephrased as: "How can we sing a song of the Lord *and still remain* in a foreign land?" Will not God at once seek to remove us from there? For what follows is a dramatic enactment of just this understanding: the very ground on which the Levites have been standing lifts off that "foreign land" and carries them up to heaven, *"so that they said: He has wanted to take the children of Israel to Jerusalem"*! In the most literal and striking fashion, their singing causes them to be removed from the land of Babylon. Moreover, there may be another exegetical motive behind this strange detail of the ascent to heaven. For v. 2 of our psalm says: "On willow trees in its midst, we hung up our harps"—an action which, as we have seen, fired the curiosity of many ancient and medieval exegetes. Here there is no direct mention of that verse. But if indeed the Israelites are made to rise high into the air, is it not that this verse's "on" (*'al*) is being understood in its other meaning of "above," and "hung up" is being explained in the (equally acceptable) sense of "lifted up, put on high"? And so this levitical ascent to heaven appears to answer two separate exegetical problems; and in proposing a striking new scenario in order to address these concerns, the originator of this motif demonstrates a midrashic creativity not very different from that of "No Rest-Stop in Israel" or some of the other rabbinic motifs that we have surveyed. Indeed, the particularly midrashic character of this passage might be made clearer if it were reworded more in keeping with the conventions of a rabbinic-style comment on these verses. Such a comment might read as follows:

> "On willow trees in its midst . . . [etc.]"—This teaches that when the king requested the Levites to sing, they took up their harps and began to play in unison. At once the ground on which they stood rose into the air, as it says, "On [that is, "above"] willow trees in its midst we lifted up our harps." The people thought that the end of the exile had come. The walls of the palace sounded forth and sang praises with them. The ministering angels heard the sound of their hymns, the glory of God enveloped them. Then the king called and said to them: What have you done? They said (Ps. 137:4): "How can we sing a song of the Lord [and remain] on foreign ground?" He said: I command you, do not pluck your harps until you return to your land, the land of Israel. They said: We will cease, if such is the word of the king. Nonetheless, (ibid., v. 5) "If I forget you, O Jerusalem . . ."

Now this narrative expansion conflicts with the other understanding of Psalm 137 presented earlier in the same text (and cited above), a clear sign of this text's composite nature. That other understanding was, as noted, reminiscent of the one presented in the letter of Jeremiah contained in the *Paraleipomena* as well as in the rabbinic explanations collected in *Pesiqta Rabbati* and other sources. It is impossible to say which of these two rival motifs—which we might call, respectively, "Levites Ascend to Heaven" and "Babylonians Blasphemously Demand Songs" ("blasphemously" because, as we have seen, the question "How shall we sing . . . ?" is explained in it by rewording the Babylonians request as "Sing before us [or: "our gods," etc.] *as you used to sing before your God*")—is earlier. It is nonetheless of interest that, in the form in which it has been transmitted, the former motif is in any case prefaced with words "Bring to me your harps and lyres with which you sing praises to your God in Jerusalem and play here"—an element apparently drawn from the other motif. So much does this sentence thus seem to be part of the tradition received by our author that he then has to go out of his way and have Cyrus "clarify" the fact that what he is really requesting is that they simply sing divine hymns to *their* God (and hence not, as it apparently must have first appeared, to him or his gods). This too only reinforces the impression that the wording of his initial request was in keeping with the "Babylonians Blasphemously Demand Song" motif. All this implies that the form of the motif "Levites Ascend to Heaven" known to our author was one that had itself been influenced by the prior existence of "Babylonians Blasphemously Demand Song"—though of course this does not rule out a still earlier form of the motif in which no hint of the blasphemous demand was present. Lastly, it should be pointed out that, despite their divergences, the "Levites Ascend to Heaven" motif in its present form agrees with the letter of Jeremiah in the *Paraleipomena* on one important matter: it also seems to assume that the words of Psalm 137 were spoken at some time just before the end of the exile. This is clear not only from the fact that Cyrus has now become king and it is he who requests that the Levites sing, but from the sentence that follows immediately after this incident in the apocryphon: "And it came to pass after this that the seventy years of the captivity were nearly completed." Thus, according to both texts, our psalm was uttered at a time when the sufferings of exile had already begun to fade and hope was quickening for a speedy return.

Additional Note

A complete text-critical edition of *Paraleipomena Ieremiou* has yet to be produced. The "provisional" edition by Robert A. Kraft and Ann-Elizabeth Purintun, cited above, provides not only a history of this text's career in modern scholarship, but also a useful overview of the textual problem and some preliminary conclusions about the meaning of various textual witnesses. Until a full text-critical edition is available, it would obviously be premature to speculate about the history and development of this text in general or, more particularly, those of the brief "letter" from Jeremiah to Baruch which has been our focus. Nevertheless it may be useful here to make a few very tentative observations.

Jeremiah's letter appears, even within the "long form" tradition of the *Paraleipomena*, in various formats, a lengthier version of it appearing in some witnesses (Kraft-Purintun's group Ceth), an abbreviated version in others (ABarm), and at least one intermediate version (P). In their edition, Kraft-Purintun chose to follow the lengthy version (Ceth), from which we have cited above. Nevertheless, it may be useful here to present together the full texts of both the lengthy and abbreviated versions as described by Kraft-Purintun in order to compare them:

Ceth

^{7:24} And Jeremiah wrote a letter to Baruch, saying thus:

My beloved son, do not be negligent in your prayers, beseeching God on our behalf, that he might direct our way until we come out of the jurisdiction of this lawless king. ²⁵ For you have been found righteous before God, and he did not let you come here, lest you see the affliction which has come upon the people at the hands of the Babylonians. ²⁶ For it is like a father with only one son, who is given over for punishment; and those who see his father and console him cover his face, lest he see how his son is being punished, and be even more ravaged by grief. ²⁷ For thus God took pity on you and did not let you enter Babylon lest you see the affliction of the people. ²⁸ For since we came here, grief has not left us for sixty-six years today. ²⁹ For many times when I went out I found some of the people hanged by king Nebuchadnezzar, crying and saying:

"Have mercy on us, God Zar!"

³⁰ When I heard this, I grieved and cried with two-fold mourning, not only because they were hanged but because they were calling on a foreign god, saying "Have mercy on us." ³¹ But I remembered days of festivity which we celebrated in Jerusalem before our captivity; and when I remembered, I groaned, and returned to my house wailing and weeping. ³² Now, then, pray in the place where you are, you and Abimelech, for this people, that they may listen to my voice and to the decrees of my mouth, so that we may depart from here. ³³ For I tell you that the entire time that we have spent here they have kept us in subjection, saying:

Recite for us a song from the songs of Zion, the song of your God.
³⁴ And we reply to them:

How shall we sing for you, being in a foreign land?
³⁵ And after this Jeremiah tied the letter to the eagle's neck . . .

ABarm

And Jeremiah wrote a letter to Jerusalem to Baruch and Abimelech before the whole people [concerning] the tribulations which had come upon them—how they had been taken away by the king of the Chaldeans, and how each man beheld his father bound, and each father his child subjected to punishment. But those who wanted to console the father covered his face lest he see his son being punished. And God covered you and Abimelech, lest you see us being punished; and when I remembered, I groaned, and returned to my house wailing and weeping. Now, then, pray in the place where you are, you and Abimelech, for this people, that they may listen to my voice and to the decrees of my mouth, so that we may depart from here. For I tell you that the entire time that we have spent here they have kept us in subjection, saying:

Recite for us a song from the songs of Zion, the song of your God.

And we reply to them: How shall we sing for you, being in a foreign land?

And after this Jeremiah tied the letter to the eagle's neck.

One conclusion that suggests itself upon preliminary examination is that neither of these texts can represent the original form of Jeremiah's letter.

The composite character of the ABarm version emerges most clearly from the fact that it switches in midstream from being an account of *what* Jeremiah's letter contained to being the letter itself. This change becomes obvious with the second-person address to Baruch, "And God covered you and Abimelech." It seems possible that a text-form similar to that of Ceth, which actually presented the text of the letter, became combined with a text-form that merely summarized its contents, commenting briefly on the Jews' sufferings.[64] Indeed, in ABarm, the parable of the father whose son is to be punished seems to have emerged out of the preceding description of actual suffering: for first each "father" in Babylon is said actually to have seen "his child subjected to punishment," then this description becomes the basis for the parable explaining why Baruch and Abimelech, figurative "fathers," had their faces "covered" by God, that is, were allowed to remain outside of Babylon, lest they behold the sufferings of their people.

Now the parable itself is of some interest. The topos of covering the face to prevent one from seeing is known to the Hebrew Bible, thus Ezek. 12:6 "You shall cover your face and not see," cf. Ezek. 12:12, "He shall cover his face in order that he not see." Beyond this, it is to be noted that numerous rabbinic parables (*meshalim*) speak specifically of a father or king whose son is to be punished, much to the father's discomfort. Indeed, a parable in some ways comparable to ours is to be found in the collection *Sifrei Bemidbar*, a tannaitic midrash on Numbers. Commenting on the verse "And the cloud departed from atop the tent" (Num. 12:10), the text observes: "This is comparable to a king of flesh and blood who said to [his son's] tutor, 'Punish my son, but punish him only after I have gone away [that is, so that I not witness it], for a father's mercy is upon his son.' "[65] So here the father's face is covered by his consolers "lest he see how his son is being punished and be even more ravaged by grief."

But is this parable appropriate to the circumstances? It hardly seems so. If God wished to spare the "father" the grief of seeing the "son's" suffering, would not that "father" be first and foremost Jeremiah, and not Baruch and Abimelech? And would this not be all the more likely since, in the *Paraleipomena*, Baruch addresses Jeremiah as "Father," "Father Jeremiah," and Jeremiah reciprocates with "my beloved son"? To have "Father Jeremiah" explain to his "beloved son" Baruch that the latter has been spared the sight of Israel's sufferings (while Jeremiah himself has not) because of the principle of a "father's" face being hidden from his child's sufferings—well this is little short of ludicrous! And so it seems all the more likely that this parable was generated out of what was originally no parable at all but an actual description of the Jews' sufferings in Babylon.

Two further observations follow from this one. The first is that such a description of fathers-beholding-sons'-sufferings may well have been generated by the great admonition of Deuteronomy 28 (just as we saw above that some of the details of that admonition were reflected in the descriptions of suffering found in some of the related Jeremiah apocrypha).[66] For there we read: "Your sons and your daughters shall be given to another people, *while your eyes look on and fail with longing* for them all the day; and it shall not be in the power of your hand to prevent it. . . . so that you shall be driven mad by the sight which your eyes shall see" (Deut. 28:32–34). This may well be what led to the version in ABarm that described "how each man beheld his father bound, and each father his child subjected to punishment," such description then becoming the basis for the subsequent parable.

The second point is that behind the parable lies a genuine concern with explaining why it is that Baruch and Abimelech have been spared the pains of exile while Jeremiah has not. A similar concern—but without the father-son parable—appears in the other Jeremiah apocryphon:

> When Jeremiah saw [Abimelech] he dismounted from his horse, embraced him, cried aloud to him and said: "Be welcome, be welcome, O my beloved Abimelech! Look at the honor that God bestowed on you. He does this to anyone who is merciful and charitable to his fellow-creatures. You had pity on me in the day of my tribulations, and the Lord has overshadowed you with His holy arm and placed

you in a refreshing sleep till you saw Jerusalem reconstructed and glorified for the second time.[67]

To sum up, then: the father-son parable seems to represent a combination of two originally independent elements: (1) the description of fathers seeing their sons being delivered over to punishment (itself possibly generated, as we have seen, by Deut. 28:32–34); and (2) the attempt, seen just above, to have Jeremiah explain why someone (in this case, Abimelech) was spared the pain of exile to Babylon.

If we now turn to the text of the Jeremiah's letter as it appears in the Ceth text tradition, we may see that the father-son parable interrupts somewhat the letter's flow there, and might well be dispensed with:

> [7:24] And Jeremiah wrote a letter to Baruch, saying thus:
>
> My beloved son, do not be negligent in your prayers, beseeching God on our behalf, that he might direct our way until we come out of the jurisdiction of this lawless king. [25] For you have been found righteous before God, and he did not let your come here, lest you see the affliction which has come upon the people at the hands of the Babylonians. [26] **For it is like a father with only one son, who is given over for punishment; and those who see his father and console him cover his face, lest he see how his son is being punished, and be even more ravaged by grief. [27] For thus God took pity on you and did not let you enter Babylon lest you see the affliction of the people.** [28] For since we came here, grief has not left us for sixty-six years today. [29] For many times . . . [etc.]

Not only is it the case that the passage indicated could be omitted without damage to the flow of ideas, but it is to be noted that v. 27 is actually a **narrative resumption** of part of v. 25, that is, an attempt to repeat the same idea in different words and so "get back" to where the text was before. As we have seen, such resumptions are frequently an indication of an editorial insertion. Thus, it appears to me that the Ceth text-tradition represents a conflation of two distinct earlier versions, one with its longish description of Jewish sufferings in Babylon but without the father-son parable, the other (similar to ABarm) a shorter description but with the father-son parable.

Finally, it is to be noted that the Ceth text minus the parable need not necessarily represent the earliest stage of this particular form of Jeremiah's letter—quite the contrary. For, as was suggested above, this entire letter of Jeremiah comes in the *Paraleipomena* narrative as something of an afterthought. Its creation was probably suggested by Baruch's letter to Jeremiah, a letter which does play a somewhat more important role in this text. But Baruch's letter might well have gone unanswered. If our author did decide to have Jeremiah reply, was it not for the reason seen above, in order to insert part of Psalm 137, that classic and concise evocation of Jewish suffering during the exile, into the narrative, indeed to put it, as it were, specifically in the mouth of Jeremiah? But this might have been accomplished in far simpler fashion: our Ceth text could indeed originally have jumped from the present v. 24 all the way to v. 33. (And note that v. 32 is also a **narrative resumption,** returning the text to where it was in v. 24.) If such a form did once exist, one can then well imagine how a later editor might come along and decide to expand this brief picture of Jewish suffering, and expand it precisely on the basis of the preceding verses of Psalm 137, or, rather, those verses as they had been (commonly?) understood—the "double" lamentation implied in *gam,* "remembering Zion" as remembering the Temple festivals, *tolalenu* as "those who hung us" (that is, the cruel practice of crucifixion), and so forth—an exegetical reading which, as we have seen, explains many of the otherwise puzzling elements in this description. When such a "later editor" might have accomplished this expansion is unclear, but I believe it was certainly anterior to the final (Christian) editing of the *Paraleipomena,* for such an expansion would hardly suit a Christian editor's purposes; moreover, as indicated, the equation of "remembering Zion" with remembering the Temple festivals may point to the period between 70 and 135 c.e.

Notes

1. I have discussed this question in "David the Prophet," in J. Kugel, *Poetry and Prophecy* (Ithaca, NY: Cornell University Press, 1990), 62–75.
2. Babylonian Talmud, *Giṭṭin* 57b.
3. This is the conclusion of A. Pietersma, "David in the Greek Psalms," *Vetus Testamentum* 30 (1980): 225.
4. For the former, see S. Buber, *Midrash Zuṭa* (Vilna, 1895), 59 (Arabic numerals); the latter tradition, based on Jer. 40:1 ff, is found for example in S. Buber, *Midrash Tehillim* (Jerusalem, 1977), 522 (Arabic numerals); also M. Ish-Shalom (Friedmann), *Pesiqta Rabbati* (Vienna, 1880), chapter 26, p. 130b; also the *Targum Sheni* to Esther *ad* Esther 1:3.
5. This connection between the words 'eikh and 'eikhah—both traditional lament introductions—is perhaps being played upon in *Pesiqta Rabbati* 144a and in S. Buber, *Eikhah Rabba* (Vilna: Romm, 1899), Pet. 19 (= p. 15). In presenting parallel motifs in this chapter, I will cite principally from the Friedmann edition of *Pesiqta Rabbati;* I have, however, checked the relevant passages against various manuscript and printed versions of this text, principally those of Ms. Parma 1240 (3122) and *Yalquṭ Shim'oni.* See Leo Prijs,

Die Jeremiah-Homilie—Pesikta Rabbati Kapitel 26 (Stuttgart: Kohlhammer Verlag, 1966), 11–20.

6. I owe this point to E. Slomovic, "The Formation of Historical Titles in the Book of Psalms," *ZAW* 91 (1979): 361–62.

7. Of course, it could be argued that Jeremiah, being a prophet, wrote this psalm even before the exile was to take place. The same argument was advanced with regard to the book of Lamentations; see *Eikhah Rabba* 1:25, p. 43.

8. Flavius Josephus, *Jewish Antiquities*, 10:180–82 (translation taken from Ralph Marcus, Josephus' *Works* [Loeb Classical Library], vol. 6 [Cambridge, 1937] 256–59). Note that Josephus' mention of the twenty-third regnal year of Nebuchadnezzar as the time of the deportation of the Jews from Egypt may be intended to explain Jer. 52:30, which reports a deportation—from where is not specified—of Jews in Nebuchadnezzar's twenty-third year.

9. D. B. Rattner, *Seder 'Olam Rabba* (New York: Talmudical Research Institute, 1966), 120 (Arabic numerals).

10. See the discussion of H. Schwarzbaum in M. Gaster, *The Chronicles of Jerahmeel* (New York: KTAV, 1971), "Prolegomenon," pp. 68–69, as well as Gaster's "Introduction," pp. c–ci.

11. J. D. Eisenstein, *Oṣar ha-Midrashim*, vol. 2 (New York: E. Grossman, 1956), 438; cf. Gaster, *Jerahmeel*, 185–86. *Midrash 'Eser Galuyyot* as printed in A. Jellinek, *Beit ha-Midrash*, 4:135, puts the date as the twenty-ninth year of Nebuchadnezzar's reign at the time he attacked Egypt and "took Jeremiah and Baruch and exiled them to Babylon."

12. See b. *Megillah* 16b; *Shir ha-shirim Rabba* 5:4

13. 2 Baruch (Syriac) 10:2–3; 33:2–3 (cf. 2 Macc. 2:1–8), on 4 Baruch see below; also A. Mingana, "A Jeremiah Apocryphon," in *Woodbrooke Studies*, vol. 1 (Cambridge, 1927); K. H. Kuhn, "A Coptic Jeremiah Apocryphon," *Le Muséon* 83 (1970): 95–135 and 291–350; and the two Armenian Baruch tales in J. Issaverdens, *The Uncanonical Writings of the Old Testament Found in the Armenian Manuscripts of the Library of St. Lazarus* (Venice: Armenian Monastery of St. Lazarus, 1907), 173–89.

14. See 2 Chron. 36:20 (and contrast somewhat 2 Kings 25:11–12, 21–22); cf. Jer. 52:27. 2 Baruch 80:6.

15. Above, note 4.

16. *Pesiqta Rabbati* 28 (p. 135a), cf. Ms. Parma 1240 *loc. cit.*; also, Buber, *Midrash Tehillim*, p. 522, and in somewhat different wording, *Pesiqta Rabbati*, chapter 31 (p. 144a), cf. Ms. Parma 1240, p. 186.

17. Buber, *Eikhah Rabba*, 156. The version in *Midrash Tehillim* is rather close to this. Here the Babylonians say: "The God of these [people] is merciful, and if they should return again to Him, He will have mercy upon them again; *lest they return and all unite themselves and call to their God and He come to their aid, and we will fail utterly.*" The italicized portion seems redundant, since the "returning" had already been countenanced in this first part of the sentence. But the additional words present a good rationale for continuously driving them (that is, preventing them from "uniting" and *together* calling on their God—for apparently only *that* will be effective). In any case, here too is a motif created strictly for Lam. 5:5 (it is indeed cited a few words later) which could not really countenance the distinction implied in

"*there* we sat down . . ."—for if the Jews "returned" and "united themselves" and "called to their God" at their first rest-stop in Babylon, would He not answer them then?

18. Indeed, he might have had them "sit down in fasting" (something that is always done sitting in the rabbinic idiom).

19. *Pesiqta Rabbati* 31 (p. 144a), cf. Ms. Parma 1240, p. 186. This text appears to be related to a (more primitive?) version in *Eikhah Rabba* 5:5 (p. 156).

20. The seige of Jerusalem by the Assyrians under Sennacherib is described in 2 Kings 18 and 19. In that episode, disaster was staved by repentance and, specifically, the prayer of Hezekiah, whereby the fortunes of the Assyrians were suddenly reversed: "And that night the angel of the Lord went forth, and killed a hundred and eighty-five thousand in the camp of the Assyrians; and when the men arose early in the morning, behold, these were all dead bodies. Then Sennacherib the king of Assyria departed and went home, and dwelt in Nineveh" (2 Kings 19:35–36). Note that some traditions relate that Nebuchadnezzar had been a soldier in Sennacherib's army and miraculously survived this disaster. See P. Churgin, "The Great Event of the Exile . . ." in his *Studies in the Times of the Second Temple* (in Hebrew) (New York: Horeb, 1949), 154.

21. *Midrash Tehillim*, p. 522; *Pesiqta Rabbati* 135a (chapter 28).

22. See Buber, *Eikhah Rabba*, Pet. 19 (= p. 15).

23. *Pesiqta Rabbati* 136a and parallels.

24. For a similar idea, cf. 2 Baruch 67:2–4, where the angels mourn before God.

25. M. Ish-Shalom, *Seder Eliyahu Rabba veSeder Eliyahu Zuṭa* (Jerusalem: Wahrmann, 1969), 149.

26. Cf. 2 Baruch 32:8–9, where it is Baruch who departs, causing the people to weep.

27. *Pesiqta Rabbati* 131 b; cf. *Midrash Tehillim*, 522.

28. It may also be that underlying this reading, as that of *Seder Eliyahu Rabba* above, was the notion of two distinct "cryings." That is, we wept for all our sufferings when we first sat down by the rivers of Babylon, and then, at Jeremiah's mention of "Zion" in his reproach, "We wept again when we thought of Zion."

29. Indeed, various modern exegetes, following (by and large unwittingly) the lead of both rabbinic and medieval Jewish commentators (see below), have suggested that the putative speakers of this psalm are not run-of-the-mill Israelites, but Temple singers who might have been separated off from their countrymen and brought as prize booty to the Babylonian king. Ancient Near Eastern records of booty taken in conquest sometimes specifically mentioned singers and musicians, and indeed Sennacherib in his account of the siege of Jerusalem recounts that Hezekiah sent him, *inter alia*, "his [own] daughters, concubines, male and female musicians" (J. B. Pritchard, *Ancient Near Eastern Texts Relating to the Old Testament* [Princeton, NJ: Princeton University Press, 1955] 287). "Male and female singers" are a sign of royal splendor as well in Eccles. 2:8.

30. It ought perhaps to be noted here that the Hebrew *shir* is not precisely the equivalent of English "song," being both somewhat broader and yet narrower in scope. Thus, on the one hand, it is not restricted to vocal music, but may refer as well to the playing on instruments to accompany the voice

(for this sense, see below). On the other hand, there is no indication that *all* forms of vocal music can be called *shir*—lamentations are a notable exception; in both biblical and rabbinic Hebrew, *shir* seems to mean more precisely "song of praise or celebration." See my "Is There but One Song?" *Biblica* 63 (1982): 329–49, esp. note 28.

31. The tradition of Nebuchadnezzar the dwarf seems to be connected with Dan. 4:14 (in some Bibles, Dan. 4:17): "the lowliest of men he sets over it." Note the discussion and further references in J. Theodor and Ch. Albeck, *Genesis Rabba* (Jerusalem: Wahrmann Books, 1965), 147. Ms. Parma 1240, p. 186, reads here: "before this people."

32. *Pesiqta Rabbati* 144a and parallels.

33. Indeed, while singing and playing musical instruments are easily identified with one another (see above, note 30), it is to be noted that our text goes out of its way to prepare us for the Jews' inability to *play* as a reason not to *sing*, for in this version Nebuchadnezzar's request is not, as in the psalm "sing to us," but, "I demand of you that you go and *play your harps* before me."

34. *Pesiqta Rabbati* 136a.

35. The same gesture has inspired all manner of other intrepretations, from the Christian reading of it as a prefiguring of the crucifixion (the "harp" of David hung upon a tree) to that which connected the suspended instruments with the Æolian harp, hung in the air where it was played upon by the winds (that is, divine inspiration) rather than by human fingers. Indeed, this sort of harp is known not only in rabbinic literature (see b. Ber. 3b, where David is aroused at midnight by the play of the wind upon the harp suspended at his bedside), but perhaps in earlier Jewish writings as well. Ode 6 of the Odes of Solomon begins: "As the wind glides through the harp and the strings speak, so the Spirit of the Lord speaks through my members." ("Wind" is, unfortunately, a conjectural reading of the defective Syriac text; see J. H. Charlesworth, *The Odes of Solomon* [Oxford: Clarendon Press, 1973], 30–31.) How this particular motif was explored in the English Renaissance may be glimpsed in John Hollander's brief but illuminating discussion of translations of our psalm in F. Kermode and J. Hollander, *The Oxford Anthology of English Literature,* vol. 1 (London: Oxford University, 1973), 534–42. Something of the complexity and interrelationship of the various motifs mentioned may be observed in the explanation found in the medieval Yemenite collection, *Midrash ha-Gadol,* which observes: "And when the Temple was destroyed for our sins, divine inspiration ceased and the manner of singing was taken away. So it is that when the Chaldeans [= Babylonians] exiled the Jews they said to them, "Play for us from your own [manner of] singing," as it is written, "For there our captors asked of us words of song [(saying) 'Sing to us from the *song* of Zion]" (Ps. 137:2) [i.e., the singular *shir* in this verse is apparently being understood as "manner of singing"]. They replied, "We cannot sing in an unclean land, and what is more, we have already forgotten the [manner of] singing and our singing has been turned to lamenting. (Z. M. Rabinowitz, *Midrash ha-Gadol,* vol. 4 [Jerusalem: Mossad ha-Rav Kook, 1978], 39–40). This explanation is really a harmonization of no less than four different themes. First, there is the theme of the cessation of prophecy brought about by exile (note, in this

connection, E. E. Urbach, "When Did Prophecy Cease?" *Tarbiz* 17 [1946]: 1–11); second is the somewhat associated matter of the loss of the secrets of Temple singing (see M. Yoma 3:11; cf. M. Soṭah 9:11); then, there is the theme of the unfitness of any land other than Israel's for prophecy (on which see H. S. Horovitz and Y. A. Rabin, *Mekhilta deR. Yishma'el* [Jerusalem: Wahrmann, 1970], 2–3) which may be linked to the idea of the "impurity" of Babylon (suggested already in Targ. Ps. 137, on which see below), perhaps also associated with its idolatrous practices; and finally the motif already seen (*Eikhah Rabba* Pet. 19) that the songs of joy of the Temple (a "song of the Lord") were replaced in Babylon by lamentations (i.e., "*How can we sing . . .*"). Because of the much elaborated biblical and midrashic connection between harp and prophecy, the mention of the cessation of prophecy in this passage may be connected in particular to the gesture of hanging up the harps, but *Midrash ha-Gadol* is not explicit on this point.

36. Meiri, *Perush leSefer Tehillim*, ed. Yosef b. Ḥayyim ha-Kohen (Jerusalem, 1936), 271.

37. See his discussion *ad loc.* as well as that of J. ibn Jannah in *Sefer ha-Sharashim*, ed. W. Bacher (Berlin, 1896), 534.

38. See above, note 34.

39. *Pesiqta Rabbati* 144a and parallels.

40. One might say, midrashically, it stands for "serving the Lord your God with rejoicing and merriment," Deut. 28:47.

41. *Pesiqta Rabbati* 144b; cf. Targum Sheni of Esther: "The songs which you used to sing before your great Master who is in Jerusalem, let them come and sing before me."

42. Sometimes the parable of R. Isaac b. Tablai is also adduced: "To what may the matter be compared? To a king of flesh and blood who married a princess. He said to her: Come and give me a cup to drink, but she was unwilling to give him to drink. He became angry with her and sent her from his house. She went off and married a man afflicted with boils [i.e., the lowliest sort of spouse]. He said to her: Come and give me a cup to drink. She said to him: Fool! I was a princess and married a king. But because he told me, 'Give me a cup to drink' and I did not want to, he grew angry with me and sent me from his house. And if I had given him to drink I would only have been adding my glory to his own and I would still be in my place. And now you tell me, 'Come, give me to drink'?! Just so did Israel say to the nations of the world: Had only we sang before God in our place for all the miracles that He did for us, we would be sitting in our place and not have been exiled—and now shall we sing before idols?!" (*Pesiqta Rabbati* 136a and parallels).

43. Here I find myself somewhat in disagreement with a minor point in the translation of this text and accompanying notes provided by M. Sokolow, *Proceedings of the American Academy for Jewish Research* 51 (1984): 133–73, and especially p. 166. It seems that Se'adya here is addressing specifically the headings mentioned, and his reference to *al-shir* should thus not be understood as "singing [the Psalms (*shir*)]," but as a reference to "the *shir*," that is, that class of compositions called *shir* in the psalm headings.

44. R. Se'adya Gaon, *Tehillim*, ed. Y. Qafih (Jerusalem, 1966), 33. Se'adya's explanation ought perhaps to be connected to the extraordinary role of

psalm singing and the "prayer of song" (*tefillat ha-shir*) in the prayer rite of Palestinian Jewry. See E. Fleischer, *Eretz-Israel Prayer and Prayer Rituals as Portrayed in the Geniza Documents* (Jerusalem: Magnes Press, 1988), 215–58.

45. And not, I think, in contrast to it; cf. Sokolow, 166 n. 161.

46. Se'adya, *Tehillim*, 272.

47. From ibn Ezra's first commentary on Psalms, reprinted in U. Simon, *Four Approaches*, 238.

48. Note *inter alia*: K. Kohler, "The Pre-Talmudic Haggadah," *Jewish Quarterly Review*, old series 5 (1893), 407–19; J. Licht, "Paralipomena Jeremiae," *Annual of Bar Ilan University* (Ramat Gan: 1963), 66–80; G. Delling, *Jüdische Lehre und Frömmigkeit in den* Paralipomena Jeremiae (Berlin: Walter de Gruyter, 1967).

49. To mention but one instance, otherwise irrelevant to our subject : When Jeremiah learns that Jerusalem is to be delivered over to the "Chaldeans" (= Babylonians), he puts dust on his head and rends his garments (2:1–2), traditional gestures of mourning. When Baruch asks him, "Father, what is this?" Jeremiah replies, "Refrain from rending your garments—rather, let us rend our hearts" (2:4–5). In none of the editions of this text that I have consulted is it pointed out that Jeremiah's response is actually a biblical paraphrase (Joel 2:13); but it is further to be remarked that Jeremiah's words seem strangely inappropriate—after all, he just *had* rent his garments! This use of the Joel verse might, however, seem more appropriate if it could be shown from elsewhere that the verse functioned as something of a *locus classicus* with regard to sincere repentance. While it is no proof, the Mishnah's mention of the use of just this verse in a standard homily for fast days suggests that this may well have been the case: "What is the procedure for fast days? The ark is taken out to the town square, ashes are placed on the ark and on the heads of [those present . . .], and the eldest among them speaks to them words of admonition: "Brothers, Scripture does not say of the people of Nineveh 'And God saw their sackcloth and their fasting . . .' but 'And God saw their works, that they turned from their evil ways'; And in the prophet it is said, 'And rend your heart and not your garments" (M. Ta'anit 2:1).

50. Cf. the works mentioned above, note 13.

51. The idea of Jeremiah sending a letter back to Baruch may have been influenced by the apocryphal composition called the "Letter of Jeremiah," which is certainly of a far earlier period.

52. R. A. Kraft and A.-E. Purintun, *Paraleipomena Ieremiou Texts and Translations*, Pseudepigrapha Series 1 (Missoula, MT: Society of Biblical Literature, 1972).

53. Cf. 2 Baruch 84:8 "And remember Zion and the Law and the holy land and your brothers and the covenant of your fathers, and do not forget the festivals and the sabbaths."

54. See e.g., Mingana, "Jeremiah Apocryphon," 174–77. It is to be noted that the list of hardships on the way to and inside Babylon is created specifically to contrast with elements of the Israelites successful forty years in the desert (thus, "their dresses were spoiled" [Mingana 174] contrasts with "your clothing [*simlatekha*] did not wear out" Deut. 8:4) as well as to echo parts of the divine admonitions listed in Leviticus 26 and Deuteronomy 28. So sim-

ilarly the catalogue of Jewish sufferings in 1 Baruch is intended to "fulfill" the admonitions of Deuteronomy, e.g., 1 Baruch 4:15, "For he brought upon them a nation from far away, a ruthless nation speaking a strange language, who had neither respect for old men nor pity for children," which is meant to echo Deut. 28:47, "The Lord will bring a nation against you from afar, from the end of the earth, as swift as the eagle flies, a nation whose language you do not understand, a nation of stern countenance, who shall not regard the person of the old nor show favor to the young."

55. This term is regularly used for crucifixion, and the fact that that is what is intended here is supported by the fact that those who have been "hanged" are nonetheless able to speak and cry out to a "foreign god" (see below). Of course crucifixion was the hated form of execution favored by the Romans. See D. J. Halperin, "Crucifixion, the Nahum Pesher, and the Rabbinic Penalty of Strangulation," *Journal of Jewish Studies* 32 (1981): 32–46. Note also, however, that it accords well with another depiction of Jewish suffering also attributed to Jeremiah, namely, the book of Lamentations, for there (Lam. 5:2) we read that "princes were hung by their hands."

56. Again, this is the explicit view of the other Jeremiah apocrypha to which our text bears the closest relationship, the Karshuni and Coptic apocrypha published by Mingana and Kuhn. See below.

57. The psalm is ascribed in its heading to the sons of Korah—to midrashic sensibilities, Korah's actual sons and not "descendents"—but these were endowed with prophetic gifts and so could foresee future events and tell of them in the psalms ascribed to them. See L. Ginzberg, *The Legends of the Jews* (Philadelphia: Jewish Publication Society, 1928), 3:302 and 6:104–5; 215.

58. That this verse lies in the background of the *Paraleipomena* here is supported by the fact that the related Jeremiah apocryphon, published in its Karshuni and Coptic forms (above, note 13) also make reference to Israel forgetting, specifically, God's *name*. Thus in the Karshuni God says: "After all these things which I did for you, you have forgotten my name and said, 'There is no God but Ba'al and Zeus' " (Mingana, "Jeremiah Apocryphon," 150). (In the Coptic version of the same speech, this remark comes out as "There is no God but Ba'al and Astarte"; see Kuhn, "Coptic Jeremiah," 109.) The mention of Ba'al here may further be a reflex of Jer. 23:27, where the prophet denounces those "who think to make my people forget my name by their dreams which they tell to one another, even as their fathers forgot my name for Ba'al."

59. Cf. 1 Baruch, in the so-called "Letter of Jeremiah," 6:4–6—"Now in Babylon you will see gods made of silver and gold and wood, which are carried on men's shoulders and inspire fear in the heathen. So take care not to become at all like the *foreigners* or let fear for these gods possess you, when you see the multitude before and behind them worshiping them. But say in your heart, 'It is thou, O Lord, whom we must worship.' "

60. Indeed, v. 18 (cited above) said specifically that "All this has overtaken us but we have not forgotten *you*." Perhaps this verse must be taken in the most literal sense—it is not You, but only Your name, that is involved—if it is not to contradict v. 18.

61. It is to be noted that in the Karshuni and Coptic Jeremiah apocrypha (above, note 13), the Jews are said to have forgotten God's name even in

their own homeland and to have substituted for it the name of Ba'al and other gods.

62. Kuhn, "Coptic Jeremiah," 306–7. Cf. Mingana, 175–76.

63. Kuhn, "Coptic Jeremiah," 311–13.

64. See for the latter the summary version exemplified in, e.g., Issaverdens, *The Uncanonical Writings*, 183–85. "And Jeremiah wrote to Baruch an answer, and told him of the sufferings they had endured in Babylon from ungodly men; and he fastened it upon the neck of an eagle."

65. H. S. Horovitz, *Sifrei Bemidbar* (Jerusalem: Wahrmann Books, 1966), 103; cf. *Midrash Tanḥuma Ṣav* 13 (in the commonly reprinted *Tanḥuma* with H. Zundel's commentaries, this section is found in Part II, p. 10).

66. See above, note 54.

67. Mingana, "Jeremiah Apocryphon," 187. The parallel in the Coptic apocryphon has: "Because of this God has protected thee (and) [= so that?] thou didst not see the destruction of Jerusalem, nor did they take thee into captivity" (Kuhn, "Coptic Jeremiah," 323).

8.

Hatred and Revenge

The biblical texts examined so far in this study have all been of a nonlegal character—the story of Joseph, the brief tale of Lamech, and Psalm 137. Yet legal exegesis was in fact a major concern of early interpreters of the Bible, for reasons that are readily apparent. After all, the laws contained in the Bible had been given by God in order to be applied in daily life, and it was therefore necessary to make sure that each and every Jew knew what precisely was demanded by biblical statutes. This implied a considerable body of learning, for biblical laws touch on a broad spectrum of subjects: from the procedures to be followed in the Temple and the laws of ritual purity to relations between neighbors, certain sorts of business dealings, torts and damages—in short (as the rabbinic idiom has it) both matters "between man and God" and matters "between man and his fellow."

This is not to say, however, that the Bible presents in itself a complete and self-sufficient religious, civil, and criminal code—far from it! All manner of subjects basic to any such code are mentioned only in passing in the Bible, if at all. The procedure for divorce, for example, is nowhere specified, though the necessity for a written "bill of divorcement" is hinted at in Deut. 24:1; other civil matters are similarly only alluded to, or their existence merely implied in some narrative text. Still other laws are clear enough in their general outline, but no doubt required much filling-in of details before they could be workably applied in society. What, for example, did the Bible mean to require when it enjoined Israel to "keep the Sabbath" and to avoid doing "any work, you or your son or your daughter or your manservant or your maidservant or your cattle or the sojourner who is within your gates" (Exod. 20:10)? That is, what did "any work" include—small-scale gardening, cooking, setting the table, studying? Answers to these questions had to be fixed and definite, not only because individuals needed to know precisely how to carry out the divine statutes, but as well because the Bible requires that those who violate the Sabbath law be brought to justice (Exod. 35:2). And so there developed a considerable body of legal interpretation for this and similar statutes, part of an ongoing attempt to understand what the Torah required and how to put it into practice.

"You Shall Not Hate Your Brother . . ."

In order to see how such legal exegesis worked, as well as how its development can be traced through a variety of ancient documents, we shall begin by considering one particular law in the Bible, the injunction of Lev. 19:17 that reads, "You shall not hate your brother in your heart; you shall surely reproach your neighbor, and you shall bear no sin because of him." Now this is just the sort of law that might challenge early biblical exegetes. For if it is viewed as more than merely good advice, but as an actual legal requirement, then a whole host of questions emerges: What does the Torah mean by *forbidding* hatred? How am I to observe such a law, and how far do I have to go before I can be deemed to have violated it? Moreover, why should I "reproach" my neighbor—for what purpose? And what connection, if any, does this reproaching have with not hating my brother? Finally, what is meant by "you shall bear no sin"—is this a further commandment (in which case, what is the "sin" involved?), or is it a result promised for observing the previous commandment, or yet something else? These are, in fact, some of the questions that early interpreters of this law asked themselves. But before turning to their answers, we might begin (as no doubt they themselves did) by considering this law in its broader context in the book of Leviticus. It comes in the midst of a section of Leviticus known to modern scholars as the Holiness Code, in a chapter containing a miscellany of civil and cultic prescriptions. Here are the verses that immediately precede and follow it:

> [15] You shall do no injustice in judgment; you shall not be partial to the poor, nor defer to the rich, but in righteousness shall you judge your neighbor. [16] You shall not go as a tale-bearer among your people; you shall not stand idly by the blood of your neighbor; I am the Lord. **[17] You shall not hate your brother in your heart; you shall surely reproach your neighbor, and you shall bear no sin because of him.** [18] You shall not take revenge or bear a grudge against your countrymen, and you shall love your neighbor as yourself; I am the Lord.
>
> (Lev. 19:15–18)

One thing does become clear in the light of this broader context: the difficulty associated with trying to forbid "hatred" of one's brother is not the only such difficulty in this passage. Indeed, if its various injunctions have a common thread, it is apparently that *all* the things that they seek to govern are very difficult, or even impossible, to determine judicially. For how can one peer into the heart of a judge in order to be sure that he does no "injustice in judgment" but eliminates any internalized preference, either deference to the high and mighty (do not "defer to the rich") or, on the contrary, a tendency to give an edge to the down-and-out ("you shall not be partial to the poor")? Similarly, how can one outlaw so common (and subtle) a practice as gossip or slander ("you shall not go as a tale-bearer . . .")? How can one legislate against mere passivity, separating an inability to act on a neighbor's behalf (or simply ignoring his plight) from willful inaction, "standing idly by" his blood, in the language of our passage? Perhaps most of all, how can one legislate human emotions, outlawing not only (in our verse) hatred of one's brethren, but the desire for revenge, or grudge bearing, and enjoining no less than love toward one's fellow? And so it seems that this particular paragraph of laws is a kind of summons to go beyond merely externally lawful conduct in order to purify utterly one's thoughts and deeds—the purification that is a touchstone of "holiness" in Leviticus.

Within this group, our particular focus, v. 17, might, as suggested above, conceivably be construed in various ways. For example, the first part of the verse might be understood quite separately from the rest: "You shall not hate your brother in your heart" could simply be taken as a blanket injunction to avoid hatred of one's "brother"—either, rather literally, to avoid family squabbles, or, more freely, to to avoid hatred in the greater "family" of Israel. "You shall surely reproach your fellow and you shall bear no sin because of him" might then be taken to refer to an entirely different matter—perhaps the case of someone who sees his fellow about to commit a sin, or in the midst of one: he must "reproach" him at once or share in the responsibility for the infraction.[1] And none of this need necessarily be connected to the next verse, with its prohibitions of vengeance and grudge bearing, and its exhortation to love one's neighbor. Indeed, the profusion of different objects in these various exhortations—"your brother," "your fellow," "your countrymen," "your neighbor"—virtually invites the reader to see them as separate matters.

Against this approach, however, stands the fact that "brother," "fellow," "neighbor," "countryman," and "people" are all used throughout the Holiness Code of Leviticus in what appears to be deliberate alternation, one that argues their interchangeability.[2] This, along with the general interrelatedness of the ideas, has led both an-

cient and modern commentators to connect one thing with another and
to suggest that the verse should be understood: "You shall not hate
your brother in your heart, *but instead* you shall surely reproach your
neighbor, and you shall *thus* bear no sin because of him." In other
words: Do not let hatred simmer inside of you—if your fellow has done
something to incite your hatred, reproach him, tell him openly what he
has done wrong, and avoid thereby being led to sin. (The "sin" being
referred to could thus be any sin that one might be tempted to commit
as a result of not having openly reproached him—plotting against him,
striking him, and so forth.)

Hatred in the Heart

If these various clauses are indeed to be related in such fashion, one
might still inquire more deeply into the first of them: what precisely is
meant by not hating your brother *in your heart?* The answer to this
question is to be found in a rather unlikely and far-distant biblical
source, the book of Proverbs. For not only is the concept of "reproach"
a favorite one of Proverbs and other "wisdom" texts,[3] but indeed the
concept of hating one's fellow "in the heart" is likewise well known
there.

> He who hates dissembles with his lips, harboring treachery within him
> (*beqirbo*); though he makes his voice kindly, do not trust him, for there
> are seven abhorrences in his heart (*belibbo*).
>
> (Prov. 26:24–25)

Hatred *in the heart* seems to be, specifically, hatred that is immediately internalized, kept "in the heart" while the hater's external attitude shows nothing of what is inside. For so it is in these Proverbs
verses: hatred leads to deceit and hypocrisy ("He who hates dissembles
with his lips") and "abhorrences" in the heart are masked by gracious
speaking. Similarly:

> He who conceals hatred has lying lips, and he who utters slander is a
> fool.
>
> (Prov. 10:18)

Here again is the association of hatred with deceit. Indeed, this proverb
apparently seeks to connect hatred "in the heart" with another evil,
slander (*dibbah*). For the *not telling* that is involved in hating another
person yet dissembling one's hatred in front of him is pointedly contrasted here to the act of slander, that is, *telling others* about the object
of one's hatred behind his back. In other words, the two parts of this

proverb are, as with all two-part Hebrew proverbs, thematically related: he who covers up his hatred from his enemy not only acquires the "lying lips" of the first part of the proverb, but will likely also end up in front of his friends as the second part's slandering "fool."

What is the alternative to "hatred in the heart" and the hypocrisy and slander that it engenders?

> Argue your case with your neighbor himself, and do not disclose a secret to another;[4] lest anyone who hears you expose you to shame, and your own slander (*dibbatekha*) not return.
>
> (Prov. 25:9–10)

Rather than cover over one's grievance against one's neighbor by both hiding one's hatred from him and slandering him behind his back (here: "disclose a secret to another"), one ought to confront him directly and try to settle the matter in person. That is, "argue your case with your neighbor himself" rather than reveal its content to a third party; this will not only save one from the potential embarrassment involved in an actual public grievance procedure,[5] but will also avoid the slandering of one's neighbor which, because slander travels fast and far, can ultimately lead to retaliatory slandering of oneself by others.

Now all this seems to resonate very well with our Leviticus passage, which itself prohibits slander ("You shall not go as a tale-bearer among your people," v. 16), then goes on to forbid "hatred in the heart" (v. 17) along with vengeance and grudge bearing (v. 18), and meanwhile enjoins open reproach (v. 17) and, finally, love toward one's neighbor (v. 18). Especially in the light of our Proverbs citations, it seems that our passage in Leviticus is thus an exhortation of the broadest moral character, urging Israelites at all times to deal frankly and lovingly with one another and so avoid hatred, slander, vengeance, and so forth. Yet it is extremely characteristic of *all* early Jewish biblical exegesis to specify and particularize, to turn general or vague pronouncements into something more focused and precise. And so it was with this verse.

Ben Sira's Interpretation

The earliest datable "interpretation" of the Leviticus injunction to reproach one's fellow and so forth is to be found in the book of Ben Sira (early second century B.C.E.). Unfortunately, the passage presents several difficulties. It is known to us only through the Greek, Syriac, and other translations of the lost Hebrew original, and these disagree among themselves on a number of significant details. Yet while certain questions about the passage must thus remain unresolved, one or two general points about its understanding of Lev. 19:17 may nonetheless emerge:

> Reproach a friend lest he do;[6] and if he did, lest he continue.
> Reproach a neighbor, lest he say; and if he said, lest he repeat.
> Reproach a friend, for often it is false gossip, and do not believe every word.
> A person may have stumbled, but not intentionally; and who has not sinned with his speech?
> Reproach a friend before getting angry,[7] and give place to the Law of the Most High.

Although Ben Sira presents these words without direct reference to our verse, the fact that he is in reality thinking of the Law of Reproach in Lev. 19:17 is announced both by his insistent use of the word "reproach" at the beginning of successive lines, along with the coupling of this verb with "neighbor" (as in Lev. 19:17) and the equivalent terms "friend" and "fellow,"[8] as well as by his final invocation of the "Law of the Most High," that is, the Pentateuch in which this law appears. No doubt Ben Sira could count on his readers to recognize immediately this allusion to Lev. 19:17. His purpose in invoking it here is to elaborate on the biblical verse by examining, specifically, the benefits of reproach in daily life. Chief among these, in his opinion, is reproach's ability to *limit the damage*—to prevent an offense from being committed,[9] or, if committed, from being repeated. For the act of warning can head off an offense, or at least see to it that no new offense is committed. Moreover, open reproach will serve to bring the facts of the case to light, often avoiding unjustified anger, since the report of the offense may be untrue ("often it is false gossip"), or because the offense itself may have been unintentional. This is especially the case with verbal offenses ("who has not sinned with his speech?"). Reproach, in other words, has a preventive function—as Ben Sira observes only shortly afterward (20:2), "It is better to reproach than to be angry." Such would also appear to be the specific sense of the last line of our cited passage, "Reproach a fellow before getting angry." Though the sense of the underlying Hebrew is hardly undisputed,[10] reproach here again seems to be depicted as heading off some action better avoided by the offended party, "growing angry," "threatening," "wronging," and the like.

What does this tell us about Ben Sira's reading of Lev. 19:17? It suggests (and this is hardly surprising) that he read the latter part of it in integrative fashion, as seen above: "You shall surely reproach your neighbor and *thus* you shall bear no sin because of him." The "sin" is here specificed somewhat by Ben Sira's verb—"grow angry," "threaten," or whatever the Hebrew original was; *it* is what will be headed off by the act of reproaching. Now all this may seem a perfectly obvious and self-evident understanding of Lev. 19:17—and one not terribly different from our own preliminary attempt to make sense of this verse—but its interest lies precisely in the contrast that will become apparent between it and other early approaches.

Testament of Gad

The *Testaments of the Twelve Patriarchs*, as we have seen in connection with the story of Joseph, is a composition which may have originated as early as the first or second century B.C.E., and which takes the form of a series of spiritual "last wills" of Jacob's twelve sons, each of whom reflects on his own life and, not infrequently, faults and misdeeds. It is Jacob's son Gad who speaks most directly about the sin of hatred and its avoidance—he deeply regrets his own ill will toward Joseph—and so it is not surprising that his words contain the most direct reference to our Leviticus verse. Thus, the author of the "Testament of Gad" must have been thinking of Lev. 19:17, with its prohibition of "hatred in the heart" juxatposed to the injunction to love one's neighbor in the next verse, when he wrote:

> So beware of hatred, my children, because it leads to lawlessness against the Lord himself. For it does not wish to hear his commandments concerning love of neighbor, and it thus sins against God. For if a brother stumbles, it wants to report it forthwith to everyone, and is eager for him to be brought to trial for it and punished and put to death.

> (4:1–3)

The reference to Lev. 19:18 ("his commandments concerning love of neighbor") is clear enough; but the connection of it to personified "hatred's" action against, specifically, a "brother" suggests that the preceding verse, "You shall not hate your brother in your heart," is likewise relevant. (Who better than Gad could elaborate on the theme of not hating, literally, one's *brother*?) Indeed, instead of reproaching the "brother" face-to-face (the other part of Lev. 19:17), personified "hatred" here spreads the report of the offense to others, thus substituting slander for open reproach in the manner condemned above by Prov. 10:18.

A fuller presentation of this theme appears somewhat later on:

> And now, my children, each of you love his brother and remove hatred from your hearts, and love one another in deed and word and thought. For in my father's presence I would speak peaceably to Joseph, but when I went out from him, the spirit of hatred darkened my mind and aroused my soul to kill him. Love one another from the heart, and if anyone sins against you, speak to him peacefully, having banished the poison of hatred; and do not maintain treachery in your soul. And if he confesses and repents, forgive him. But if he denies, do not dispute with him, lest he swear and you thereby sin doubly.
>
> ("Testament of Gad" 6:1–4)

At first glance, the connection between this passage and our section of Leviticus might seem strained—and indeed, this is hardly "exegesis" in any explicit sense. But one thing should emerge on closer inspection: the theme of this passage and the various things being urged in it is not simply the result of the writer's own insights into human nature. He is thinking specifically of Lev. 19:17–18, nearly all of whose provisions are restated in his own words. To the injunction of v. 18, "And you shall love your neighbor like yourself," corresponds his opening sentence, "And now, my children, love each of you his brother," as well as the later remark, "Love one another from the heart." Our verse's "You shall not hate your brother in your heart" comes out here as "Remove hatred from your hearts . . ." and "do not maintain treachery in your soul" (for the author understands "hatred *in the heart*" as we have explained it above, *hidden* hatred that is treacherously dissembled). "You shall surely reproach your neighbor" appears here as: "If anyone sins against you, speak to him peacefully," for what follows ("If he *confesses* . . .") indicates that this speaking "peacefully" is not simple conversation, but a broaching the subject of the offense committed. (That is, "speak to him peacefully . . ." means "*reproach* him peacefully.")

But what about the last clause of Lev. 19:17, "and you shall bear no sin because of him"? We saw that this is a potentially ambiguous phrase: Ben Sira had connected it to "growing angry"—anger was the "sin" that was avoided by reproaching one's neighbor. But this passage in the "Testament of Gad" interprets the phrase slightly differently. It takes "and you shall bear no sin because of him" as referring to *how* one should go about the business of confronting him. For if the offenders denies his guilt, the "Testament" says, "do not dispute with him, lest he swear, *and you thereby sin doubly*." What is this "double sin"? Apparently, it consists both of "disputing" with the offender (instead of merely "reproaching" him and leaving it at that) and, if this dispute leads the offender to "swearing,"[11] why then the guilt for that offense is likewise to be borne by the reproacher, for he did not perform his task correctly. In other words, the "Testament of Gad" interprets the Leviticus verse's words "you shall surely reproach your neighbor, and you shall bear no sin because of him" as meaning: "you shall surely reproach your neighbor *in such a way that* you shall bear no sin because of him"—the latter including responsibility for some sin that he might commit if you reproach him improperly and end up in an argument. (In that case, bearing a sin "because of him" would, somewhat punningly, be understood as bearing a sin "against him," bearing a sin that *he* committed and that would normally have been counted against him instead of you.)[12]

We might point out (though it hardly seems remarkable) that in this interpretation, the "Testament of Gad" sees a close relationship between avoiding "hatred in the heart" and reproaching one's neighbor—the latter is the means to the former. But it was theoretically possible to interpret "You shall not hate your brother in your heart" as an entirely separate matter from "you shall surely reproach your neighbor"—indeed, some other Jewish interpreters did read the verse in just this fashion.[13] Not the "Testament of Gad," however, which says, "If anyone sins against you, speak to him peacefully, *having banished the poison of hatred*." Thus its overall reading of our verse might be expressed as: "You shall not hate your brother in your heart, *but instead* you shall surely reproach your neighbor, *yet only in such a way that* you shall bear no sin because of him."

Lastly, we might note some connections in this author's mind between Lev. 19:17 and some of the Proverbs verses cited earlier. Not only do we find here the idea that "hatred in the heart" entails hypocrisy, "treachery in your soul" (just as it did in Prov. 10:18 and 26:24), but moreover in this connection Gad specifically admits to having hated his brother Joseph while *dissembling* his hatred from his father Jacob: "For in my father's presence I would speak peaceably to Joseph, but when I went out from him, the spirit of hatred darkened my mind and aroused my soul to kill him." Furthermore, just after the passage cited, Gad continues, "In a dispute, do not let an outsider hear your secrets, lest he hate you and be an enemy, and commit a great sin against you"—and this bit of advice is strongly reminiscent of another Proverbs passage, Prov. 25:9–10 cited above: "Argue your case with your neighbor, and do not disclose a secret to another, lest one who hears you expose you to shame, and your own slander not return."

Reproach at Qumran

Additional material bearing on the early understanding of our verse comes from the ascetic Jewish community whose writings were discovered at Qumran on the shores of the Dead Sea, starting in the 1940s (the "Dead Sea Scrolls"). The writings of the Qumran sect, which go back to the closing centuries before the common era, include, in addition to biblical texts and commentaries, regulations for the community itself, and it is here in particular that one finds allusion to our law in Leviticus.[14] One such allusion comes in the sect's "Manual of Discipline" (1QS) 5:24–6:1, which enjoins community members

> to reproach each other in tru[th] and humility and in loving consideration to a man. Let one not speak to hi[m][15] in anger or in contentiousness or stub[bornly or in a] mean spirit,[16] and let him not hate him in [. . .][17] his heart, but on that very day let him reproach him and not bear sin because of him. Moreover, let a man not bring against his fellow a matter before the assembly [literally, the "Many"] which had no reproach before witnesses.

Here we encounter some of the same themes seen above: reproach is to be carried out with great care, "in loving consideration" and without anger or contentiousness or in a mean spirit. Moreover, reproach seems here to be an antidote to simmering hatred, for rather than allowing hatred to remain hidden in their hearts, members of the sect are told to reproach each other "on that very day" (presumably, on the day an offense is committed) and so bear no sin because of the offender—presumably, the sin of "hatred in the heart." All this is in keeping with what we have seen above. But what is one to make of the last sentence? It seems to introduce a new note, whereby reproach must take place "before witnesses" prior to someone formally charging his fellow "before the assembly."

This sentence refers specifically to the *judicial role* that reproaching played in the life of the Qumran community: for it seems that court procedure at Qumran required issuance of some sort of preliminary, official "warning" before a person could actually be charged with a willful violation. This idea, which has ancient Jewish roots and which was paralleled in rabbinic Judaism,[18] was apparently attached at Qumran to the Law of Reproach in Lev. 19:17—that is, "reproach your neighbor" was taken as the biblical source of the practice of giving fair warning to offenders before they could be officially charged. We know this from other writings of the Qumran sect, and in particular from the "Damascus Document," a text connected with this sect[19] that deals with certain matters governing the behavior of community members. Here we read:

> As for that which it says, "You shall not take revenge or bear a grudge against your countrymen" (Lev. 19:18): Any man from the members of the covenant who brings against his fellow a charge **which has had no [prior] reproach before witnesses,** but brings it out of anger, or tells of it to his Elders in order to shame him [i.e., his fellow], he is [guilty of] taking revenge and holding a grudge; but it is written specifically that He [God] takes revenge on his enemies and holds a grudge against his foes (as per Nahum 1:2). If he was silent toward him from day to day and [then] when he was angry at him spoke against him for some capital crime,[20] his sin is upon him **insofar as he did not carry out the commandment of God who said to him, "You shall surely reproach your fellow and shall bear no sin because of him."**
>
> ("Damascus Document" 9:2–8)

Here too, apparently, reproach is to serve as some sort of judicial preliminary, for anyone who brings a charge against his fellow without first reproaching him is deemed guilty of violating the law that immediately follows our Law of Reproach in Leviticus, namely, "You shall not take revenge or bear a grudge against your countrymen" (Lev. 19:18). For it seems that at Qumran, charging someone formally in public—before the "Elders" in this passage, or before the "Many" in the previous one—would at the least result in great shame and injury, and was in any case unfair because the offender had received no warning. This being so, anyone who did in fact bring a charge against his fellow in this fashion was, on the face of things, guilty of bearing a grudge against the accused and motivated by some sort of desire for revenge: to avoid this charge, it was necessary for the accuser to precede any public accusation with "reproach." Yet note that even reproach here is not entirely private: in both passages it takes place "before witnesses," and was thus apparently an official, legal preliminary. Moreover, it is striking that neither of these texts specifically states that the reproacher has suffered injury at the hands of the reproached, and this omission is particularly striking in the case of "Damascus Document." The "fellow" in question now need not have offended anyone—he may be guilty, for example, of having violated the law forbidding work on the Sabbath. Yet according to the "Damascus Document," someone who witnesses such a violation cannot simply bypass the offender and report the Sabbath infraction to others: he must first reproach him directly, in fact, in the presence of witnesses. And it would be particularly grievous, apparently, for someone who witnesses such an infraction to "store it up" for the right moment, or, in the words of our passage, to be "silent toward him from day to day," and only at the opportune moment, or when his anger flares up, suddenly bring out the charge. For it seems that this "being silent" is none other than hating his fellow "in the heart": instead, he ought to reproach him at once, and so avoid sinning.

How then does the "Damascus Document" understand Lev. 19:17? Preliminarily we might reword its interpretation might as follows: You shall not hate your brother in your heart, *but instead* you shall surely reproach your fellow, *for by doing so* you shall bear no sin because of him, *namely* [the sin that would result from violating the law of the next verse:] "You shall not take revenge or bear a grudge against your countrymen."

Interestingly, a similar understanding of reproach is found in the New Testament, Matt. 18:15:

> If your brother sins against you, go and tell him his fault, between you and him alone. If he listens to you, you have gained a brother. But if he does not listen, take one or two others along with you, that every word may be confirmed by the evidence of two or three witnesses. If he refuses to listen to them, tell it to the church; and if he refuses to listen even to the church, let him be to you as a Gentile and a tax collector.

Here indeed is a scenario reminiscent of Qumran's, although there are important differences. In this case, the reproacher *is* the offended party ("If your brother sins against you . . ."): gratuitous denunciation is apparently not the problem here. Then, the first act of reproach is to take place between the principals alone: only if that act fails are the witnesses to be brought along, and that (as at Qumran) is only a preliminary to the lodging of a formal complaint before the authorities.

Sifra

Some of these same concerns surface in the last text that we shall survey in this connection, the tannaitic commentary *Sifra* on Leviticus, which may have achieved its final form in the third century c.e. Here is part of its comment on our verse:

> "You shall not hate your brother in your heart"—. . . And whence [do we know that] if you have reproached him even four or five times [and it has not worked], go back and reproach him further? From the ["doubling" of the verb] "reproach." Might you understand this to mean that you should reproach him even to the point of embarrassment? Scripture says, "and you shall bear no sin because of him."

The point of departure of *Sifra*'s remark is the fact, not mentioned heretofore, that Lev. 19:17 contains a grammatical peculiarity, the combination of the finite verb "reproach" with its infinitive absolute, resulting in what rabbinic exegetes called a "repetition" or "doubling" of the verb (thus here: *hokheah tokhiah*). This is a familar form of emphasis in biblical Hebrew, but it is one that rabbinic, and possibly earlier,[21] exegetes were anxious to explain: why was a "doubled" verb necessary when a single verb would have been sufficient? *Sifra*'s answer is that the "doubled" verb indicates that the act of reproaching is to be repeated as often as necessary: "If you have reproached him even four or five times, go back and reproach him further."[22] But having advanced this reading, *Sifra* then sees the words "you shall bear no sin because of him" as stating a limitation on the act of reproaching: the doubled verb, however much it exhorts the reproacher to be persistent, does not provide a warrant for shaming the offender. "You shall bear no sin because of him" is taken to refer specifically to the sin of putting one's fellow to shame in public.[23]

Thus *Sifra* devises yet another solution for the ambiguous "sin" of Lev. 19:17, different from those of Ben Sira (who identified it as "growing angry" or the like), the "Testament of Gad" (which saw it as at least potentially, responsibility for a further sin, "swearing," committed by the offender in response to overzealous reproaching), and the "Damascus Document" (which connected it with the prohibitions of vengeance and grudge bearing in the next verse). Nor does that exhaust the possibilities. For the very position argued against in *Sifra* is preserved in Targum Pseudo-Jonathan's translation of Lev. 19:17:

> Do not speak hypocritically with your mouth while hating your brother in your heart; you shall surely reproach your fellow, but if he is embarrassed, you shall bear no sin because of him.

Apparently, the "doubling" of the verb is here taken as license to reproach insistently no matter what the consequences, and the last clause, "you shall bear no sin because of him," is now taken as an assurance that such insistence will not be deemed a counter-offense, even if leads to (public) shaming.

Two Different Approaches

It is time to put some order into the various interpretations seen. For in fact underlying the different texts surveyed above are two fundamentally opposed understandings of the commandment to "reproach your neighbor." These two understandings would be clear enough, were it not for the fact that—in this bit of legal exegesis no less than in the previous examples of exegesis of the Joseph story and other biblical narratives—one generation of interpreters has tended to pass on the previous generation's views in somewhat garbled form, not infrequently seeking to harmonize one opinion with another in the process.

The first approach to our law might be described as the "externalizing" understanding of reproach. For this reading sees reproach as an antidote to anger or "hatred in the heart," a means of externalizing the resentment caused by some slight inflicted by one's fellow. Therefore, if X does something to offend Y, Y must openly reproach X and get the matter off his chest, lest he himself become a sinner by reason of X's offense. This is the function of reproach presented in the sayings cited from Proverbs and Sir. 20:2, as well as in Sir. 19:13–17 examined above in detail. In this first sort of interpretation of the Law of Reproach, the *manner* in which the reproach is administered is all-important: it must serve to externalize the offended party's hurt (for this is how hidden hatred is overcome), yet not in so forthright or aggressive a fashion as to constitute an offense in itself, or so as to cause the reproached party only to become obdurate. So it is that the "Testament of Gad" asserted that "if anyone sins against you, speak to him peacefully. . . . If he denies his guilt, do not dispute with him. . . ." So similarly, the brief passage cited from the Qumran "Manual of Discipline" stressed that reproach be administered "in truth and humility, and in loving consideration." The reproacher is not to speak "in anger or contentiousness or stubbornly," nor, on the other hand, is he free to keep silent if any hatred remains in his heart, "but on that very day let him reproach and not bear sin because of him." As all of these texts suggest, the Law of Reproach follows on the heels of the prohibition of "hatred in the heart" because the former helps to prevent the latter.

The other understanding of the Law of Reproach is the "judicial" one, the one that sees reproaching as an official warning or reprimand that must be made before the offender can be formally charged with a crime. Here, the person required to do the reproaching need not be a victim—indeed, the offense involved may be a victimless crime. But the reproacher is enjoined to inform the offender at once of his violation before making it a matter of full public accusation: he may not "save" the knowledge of this offense and use it later in order to shame the offender in public, for such activity constitutes vengeance seeking and grudge bearing. In this second kind of reproach, the presence of witnesses is vital (whereas for the first kind no witnesses are mentioned), because the accuser must be able to document in any subsequent public proceedings that he himself is no mere vengeance seeker, having used the offender's misstep to settle some old score. Thus, these two approaches differ not only as regards the identity of the reproacher (in the first he is the offended party, in the second, not necessarily), and in the requirement of witnesses (no in the first, yes in the second), but indeed in the whole framework and purpose of reproach.

The judicial reading is of course most clearly set forth in the "Damascus Document," but hints of it occur in two other places as well. The first is the passage from the "Testament of Gad" 4:3, cited in passing above, which observed:

> So beware of hatred, my children, because it leads to lawlessness against the Lord himself. For it does not wish to hear his commandments concerning love of neighbor, and it thus sins against God. **For if a brother stumbles, it wants to report it forthwith to everyone, and is eager for him to be brought to trial for it and punished and put to death.**
>
> ("Testament of Gad" 4:1–3)

Here, strikingly, personified "hatred" acts just like the vengeful accuser in the "Damascus Document," who sought to shame his errant fellow and bring him to swift justice without any prior reproach. Moreover, it is to be noted that in this passage there is no implication that "hatred" has been the victim of the "brother's" misstep, or that there has been any victim at all.

The "Manual of Discipline" passage likewise presented the judicial understanding of our verse—but only in one sentence at the end of the passage. Let us look at it again: members of the sect are enjoined

> to reproach each other in tru[th] and humility and in loving consideration to a man. Let one not speak to hi[m] in anger or in contentiousness or stub[bornly or in a] mean spirit, and let him not hate him in [. . .] his heart, but on that very day let him reproach him and not bear sin because of him. **Moreover, let a man not bring against his fellow a matter before the assembly [literally, the "Many"] which had no reproach before witnesses.**

This passage, clearly, is a conflation of the two approaches. The first or "externalizing" approach is evident in the first two sentences, with their emphasis on the care to be taken in the act of reproach which, while it is designed to prevent "hatred in the heart," must not externalize the hurt to the point of offending and leading to a dispute. The last sentence, however, is a capsule summary of the "judicial" reading. That the two are, to this text's author or editor, still quite separate matters is clear: he not only indicates their separation by the word "moreover" (*vegam*)—as if to say, "Now here is a separate aspect of the Law of Reproach"—but he has also clearly distributed the various requirements of the two kinds of reproach in their proper places (that is, the first sort of reproach must be administered "in truth and humility," etc.; only the second requires the presence of witnesses).

The separation is not quite so clear in another conflation, the New Testament passage cited above, Matt. 18:15:

> If your brother sins against you, go and tell him his fault, between you and him alone. If he listens to you, you have gained a brother. But if he does not listen, take one or two others along with you, that every word may be confirmed by the evidence of two or three witnesses. If he refuses to listen to them, tell it to the church; and if he refuses to listen even to the church, let him be to you as a Gentile and a tax collector.

Here the two approaches have been fully harmonized with one another. In accordance with the first, "externalizing" approach, the reproacher is here defined to be an offended party ("If your brother sins against *you* . . ."). The act of reproach is to take place—again, according to the first view—"between you and him alone," and if successful, will bring about a reconciliation ("you have gained a brother") and presumably, along with it, the avoidance of "hatred in the heart." But then, if this first kind of reproach fails, we move to the second, "judicial" sort—reproach before witnesses, prior to a formal complaint (that is, "tell it to the church"). It would be difficult to tell from this passage—if we did not have our other texts—that two different interpretations have been merged here, for the "externalizing" sort of reproach has now become a preliminary to the "judicial" sort, itself a preliminary to formal accusation.

Origin of the Readings

But where might these two very different understandings of our verse have come from? Was it merely a matter of one set of interpreters understanding reproach in the "externalizing" fashion and the other set, perhaps of a more formal bent, reading the verse in the "judicial" manner? I do not think so. Instead, the answer lies in the overall context of our verse as seen above:

> [15] You shall do no injustice in judgment; you shall not be partial to the poor, nor defer to the rich, but in righteousness shall you judge your neighbor. [16] You shall not go as a tale-bearer among your people; you shall not stand idly by the blood of your neighbor; I am the Lord.

¹⁷ You shall not hate your brother in your heart; you shall surely reproach your neighbor, and you shall bear no sin because of him. ¹⁸ You shall not take revenge or bear a grudge against your countrymen, and you shall love your neighbor as yourself; I am the Lord.

(Lev. 19:15–18)

For the "externalizing" approach, v. 17 is a self-contained unit: it sees reproach as a means to avoiding hatred in the heart, and however much the avoidance of such hatred may be similar to the other matters mentioned in this passage, the law itself has no formal connection to them. The judicial approach, on the contrary, sees all the verses as related, and this for one simple reason: it takes the opening sentence, "You shall do no injustice in judgment," as establishing a *judicial setting* for everything that follows. In other words, the prohibition of tale bearing or "standing idly by" in v. 16, the Law of Reproach in v. 17, and the prohibition of revenge and grudge bearing in v. 18—all of these have to do with how one should behave in court!

Evidence of such a reading comes from *Sifra*, the tannaitic commentary on Leviticus cited briefly above. For while the passage already quoted from it does not interpret the Law of Reproach in a specifically judicial manner, other injunctions preceding this verse are read there in a surprisingly narrow, and *judicial*, fashion. Thus v. 16, "You shall not go as a tale-bearer among your people," is understood by *Sifra* not only in the general sense of tale bearing, but also specifically as applied to courtroom conduct—to the judge who, upon leaving the courtroom, declares: "I have found innocent but my fellow judges found guilty, so what can I do since they outnumber me?"²⁴ Tale bearing here is thus understood narrowly as tale bearing in a court of law. Strikingly, Philo, when he seeks to comment on the same law (Lev. 19:16) in his *Special Laws* (4:183), says it applies specifically to "anyone who has undertaken to superintend and preside over public affairs"—again, apparently limiting what otherwise might be understood as a general prohibition of tale bearing and applying it only to community leaders (including, of course, judges). In a similar vein, *Sifra* applies "You shall not stand idly by the blood of your neighbor" to one who might otherwise keep silent and not testify *in a judicial proceeding.*

Sifra, as noted, does not apply this judicial reading to v. 17, "You shall not hate your brother in your heart. . . ."²⁵ But apparently other exegetes did. For the interpretation presented in the "Damascus Document" is, as we have seen, wholly judicial. "You shall not hate your brother in your heart" meant, in what we might hypothesize was an early phase of this reading: Stay out of court! Reproach your fellow when you see him misstep, and do not "save it up" for use against him in court, since this constitutes (again, in the judicial sense) vengeance and grudge bearing. Finally, at Qumran (as we have seen) this understanding of reproach was transmuted into an actual requirement of the judicial process, so that reproach "before witnesses" preceded formal accusation.

Thus, the two ways of interpreting Lev. 19:17 that we have been tracing are ultimately rooted in the biblical text itself. The first takes the verse in isolation and understands reproach very much in the same spirit as Proverbs had, as a means to avoiding hatred and deception. The second reads this verse in the light of v. 15, and hence seeks to apply it specifically to the judicial process. This being the case, it is not possible to identify one or the other as the earlier form of exegesis: both seem to have sprung up independently, surfacing side-by-side but in still distinguishable forms in both the "Testament of Gad" (i.e., the two passages cited) and in the "Manual of Discipline" from Qumran, then more fully harmonized in Matt. 18:15.

"You Shall Not Take Revenge . . ."

We have not yet, however, finished exploring the ramifications of this minor bit of early biblical exegesis. For the different ways of understanding this passage in Leviticus turn out to have made for major consequences not only within (in particular) the little sect at Qumran, but as well within a sect of considerably larger historical impact, the early Christian church. It was not the Law of Reproach alone that was significant in this regard, but its neighbor v. 18, "You shall not take revenge or hold a grudge. . . ." Let us take another look at our passage above from the "Damascus Document":

> As for that which it says, "You shall not take revenge or bear a grudge against your countrymen" (Lev. 19:18): any man from the members of the covenant who brings against his fellow a charge which has had no [prior] reproach before witnesses, but brings it out of anger, or tells of it to his Elders in order to shame him [i.e., his fellow], he is [guilty of] taking revenge and holding a grudge; but it is written specifically that He [God] takes revenge on his enemies and holds a grudge against his foes (as per Nahum 1:2). If he was silent toward him from day to day and [then] when he was angry at him spoke against him for some capital crime, his sin is upon him insofar as he did not carry out the commandment of God who said to him, "You shall surely reproach your fellow and shall bear no sin because of him."
>
> ("Damascus Document" 9:2–8)

We might, were it relevant here, look more closely into the overall structure of this passage, for it too bears signs of a certain harmonizing activity on the part of its author.[26] But let us instead consider an apparently minor matter, and ask what the precise significance might be of the verse from the prophet Nahum that is paraphrased at the end of the first long sentence. (The whole verse in Nahum reads: "The Lord is a jealous God and avenging, the Lord is avenging and wrathful; the Lord takes revenge on his enemies and holds a grudge against his foes.") Why is it being adduced here?

This question has actually proven to be a minor source of disagreement among scholars. Without ever quite sparking a full debate, the verse's use here has been interpreted in two broadly opposed fashions, reflecting two somewhat different understandings of the overall context. Solomon Schechter, who first published the "Damascus Document," may have tipped the scales somewhat in his translation of the Nahum verse. His translation read: "He *will* take vengeance on his adversaries, and He is bearing a grudge against His enemies." Schechter's use of a future verb "He will take vengeance"—when in fact the Nahum passage is essentially tenseless, a description of God's (eternal) attributes—seems to indicate that he understood the passage's overall significance to be that vengeance is an entirely divine prerogative, and that since God *will* take revenge in the future, there is no purpose in humans taking revenge now.

If this "divine prerogative of vengeance" reading was implicit in Schechter's rendering, it has been made explicit by subsequent translators. Thus, for example, Chaim Rabin's version of the same passage reads: "HE taketh vengeance on HIS adversaries, and HE reserveth wrath to HIS enemies." Rabin's use of capital letters seems designed to stress what is all too ambiguous in the Nahum citation, that only God is the proper agent of vengeance (and, collaterally, that only God is a fit judge of the objects of that vengeance).[27] "HE taketh vengeance on HIS enemies," but humans ought not to take vengeance on theirs. In a note Rabin attributed the source of the citation to Nah. 1:2 and added: "cf. the exegesis of Deut. 32.35 ["Vengeance is mine . . ."] in Rom. 12.19," the *locus classicus* of the "divine prerogative of vengeance" theme. The same line of interpretation has been followed explicitly by other translators, notably A. Dupont-Sommer, G. Vermes, and E. Cothenet.[28] More recently, the question of this Nahum verse was taken up again by J. A. Fitzmyer, who translated it, "He is the one who takes vengeance on his enemies and he bears a grudge against his adversaries," and added: "Nahum was describing God's vengeance and insisted that it was reserved to God and did not belong to man. The words of the prophet are now cited in the same sense."[29]

None of these renderings is correct, in my opinion. For the point of this citation in the "Damascus Document" is not that vengeance is strictly God's prerogative, nor yet that vengeance *per se* is bad, but that God takes revenge specifically on his *enemies* and bears a grudge against his *foes*, and that Jews ought indeed to do likewise and not subject their *countrymen* to vengeance and grudges, but that they should reproach them openly as required in Lev. 19:17.[30]

This interpretation of the significance of the Nahum verse is far from novel: it has been around almost from the time that the "Damascus Document" was first published. Thus R. P. Lagrange, after correctly translating the Nahum verse, observed in a footnote: "The injunction to charity is thus obligatory only within the sect. The example of God [in Nahum 1:2] removes the obligation with regard to enemies."[31] The same year, R. H. Charles added a similar note to his rendering of the passage: "The implications here is that no consideration is due to an enemy."[32] Since those early years, however, this interpretation has lost ground.[33] The fact that so many other renderings, especially the highly visible translations of Schechter, Rabin, and Dupont-Sommer, had adopted the "divine prerogative of vengeance" reading—without, so it seems, even considering the other possibility—has served to eclipse the true function of the Nahum citation in the "Damascus Document."

This misunderstanding is all the more remarkable in view of the existence of a use of the same verse from Nahum in exactly parallel fashion in rabbinic sources. *Genesis Rabba* 55:3, for example, contains the following:

R. Abin cited the verse, "Since the king's word is law, and none can say to him 'Do not do so!' " (Eccles. 8:4). Said R. Abin: [This is comparable] to a teacher who orders his student and says to him, "Do not loan out at interest," and it turns out that he himself had loaned out at interest. He [the student] said to him: "My teacher, you told me, 'Do not lend out at interest,' and yet you loan out at interest." He said to him: "I told you, 'Do not loan out at interest to Israel' [that is, to fellow Jews, as per Deut. 23:20], but to the nations you may lend, as it is said, 'To the foreigner you may lend' [Deut. 23:21]." So similarly did Israel say to God: "Master of the world, you wrote in the Torah, 'You shall not take revenge . . .' [Lev. 19:18], yet you yourself are 'avenging and wrathful, the Lord takes revenge on his enemies and holds a grudge against his foes' [Nahum 1:2]." God said to them: "I wrote in the Torah, 'You shall not take revenge and you shall not hold a grudge [against your countrymen, that is] 'against *Israel*. But as regards the nations, 'Avenge the children of Israel' [Num. 31:2]."

Similarly in the Babylonian Talmud (*Abodah Zarah* 4a):

R. Ḥama b. R. Ḥanina found a contradiction between the verse "I have no anger" (Isa. 27:4) and "the Lord is avenging and wrathful [the Lord takes revenge against his enemies and hold a grudge against his foes]" (Nah. 1:2). This is not difficult: the former applies to Israel, the latter to idolators.

Both these texts, in other words, understand the words "enemies" and "foes" to be the crucial part of the Nahum text: it is against *them* that God takes vengeance and holds a grudge, for, when dealing with enemies, such actions are quite proper.

A World Full of Enemies

There is more at stake in this question than might first appear. For if Nahum is indeed being made out to say, "God certainly does take revenge and holds grudges, but only against enemies," then this divine example will in turn color the whole significance of the verse from Leviticus with which the passage begins, "You shall not take revenge or bear a grudge *against your countrymen*." For, in the light of the Nahum citation, this verse may now be understood as suggesting that while revenge and grudge bearing are indeed forbidden against one's "countrymen," against actual *enemies* these things may not be forbidden at all, they may in fact quite conceivably constitute proper behavior.

But who are one's "countrymen" (literally, "the sons of your people")? It might seem to us that the meaning is only obvious: one's countrymen, the sons of one's people, are one's fellow Israelites. So, apparently, did it seem obvious to *Sifra*, which offers the same sort of restrictive reading of this verse without, however, even bothering to define who "countrymen/ sons of your people" are: " 'You shall not take revenge or bear a grudge against the sons of your own people'— but you shall take revenge and bear a grudge against others." Not so, however, for the drafters of the "Damascus Document." It seems likely that for them the "sons of your people" was a far narrower concept. For throughout their writings it is clear that they viewed the border between themselves and other Jews as absolute, and practices enjoined within the community did not apply to those outside. The world outside the sect was indeed full of "enemies."[34]

And so it is significant that our "Damascus Document" passage started by defining the applicability of Lev. 19:17–18 specifically to "the members of the covenant," a phrase that at Qumran designated the members of the community alone:

> . . . any man **from the members of the covenant** who brings against **his fellow** a charge which has had no [prior] reproach before witnesses, but brings it out of anger, or tells of it to his Elders in order to shame him [i.e., his fellow], he is [guilty of] taking revenge and holding a grudge.

The restriction of this application of Lev. 19:17–18 to "members of the covenant" might well indicate that a community member would not be guilty if he failed to reproach some "enemy" outside the sect. But then what is to be his attitude toward such an enemy if he is not to go off and reproach him? Reproach, as we have seen, is what protects society from "hatred in the heart." Thus, in the "Damascus Document," it was reproach that was supposed to prevent a person from secretly hating his fellow and being "silent toward him from day to day." So if the Law of Reproach does not apply to "enemies," then perhaps the prohibition of "hatred in the heart" in the same verse does not apply either. That is, if you shall surely reproach your neighbor, your fellow community member, *and thus* avoid "hidden hatred," then if you are *not* to reproach your non-neighbor, there is no apparent safety valve to head off "hidden hatred." Hating your non-neighbor in your heart seems virtually prescribed by this interpretation.[35] (As Lagrange correctly explained it above, "The injunction to charity is thus obligatory only within the sect.")

If so, then the boundaries between the little community at Qumran and those Jews outside the group were, in the case of these laws as in others, crucial: strictures from the Torah that applied within the community were, as a matter of fact, here turned into their opposite with regard to Jews outside. And so an ironic reversal seems to have taken place. For while the verse "You shall not take revenge . . ." in the Pentateuch appears to have been specifically intended to rule out, among other things, vengeance and internecine strife between one group of Jews and another, the mention of the "countrymen" in this verse was apparently used at Qumran as an important restriction, one that could now be construed in such a way as to limit the applicability of this law to members of the sect alone. Thus a law that, at first glance, might have seemed absolutely to forbid vengeance and strife between one group and another was now being interpreted as doing just the opposite, permitting or perhaps even *requiring* members of the Qumran sect to hold grudges and hate *in their hearts* those other "enemy" groups with whom they disagreed.

We in fact see such a requirement elsewhere in the "Manual of Discipline." There community members are urged

> not to reproach or enter into disputes with the Men of the Pit, and to keep hidden the [secret] counsel of the Torah from among the men of perversion; but to reproach those who choose the Way with true knowledge and right judgment, each according to his spirit and to what is proper for the time, to guide them in knowledge and so to introduce them to wonderful and true secrets within the members of the community (9:16–18).

Here the commandment to reproach one's neighbor is explicitly not to be extended to the Men of the Pit (that is, to people outside the sect);[36] reproach is to be reserved for community members, and moreover seems to form the basis of their introduction into the sect's hidden doctrines. But does this not then imply that such outsiders, denied the benefits of open reproach, are fair game for "hatred in the heart"? The "Manual" goes on to say:

> These are the indications of the path for the wise one in these times, both as to his loving and his hating: eternal hatred for the Men of the Pit, **in the spirit of hiding;** to abandon their property and the work of their hands, as a slave to one who rules over him, and humility before him who has power over him, but to be yet a man [i.e., a freeman?] waiting for the Law and its time at the day of vengeance (9:21–22).

Unprotected by the restriction imposed in Lev. 19:17, the "Men of the Pit" are indeed to be the object of "eternal hatred . . . in the spirit of hiding"—here surely is no chance formulation! For what is this phrase but a simple rewording of "hatred in the heart"? In other words, Lev. 19:17, in the Qumran reading of it, had not only defined the limit within which the "reproach" rule was applicable, but by its juxtaposition of this clause to the prohibition of hating one's brother in one's heart, the Bible had in effect also *prescribed hatred* as the proper attitude toward "enemies" outside the community. Once "your brother," "your neighbor," and "your countrymen" had been reduced, through interpretation, to a small circle of like-minded believers, then these exhortations in Leviticus, by the very limitations implied in their wording, became a scriptural injunction to hold grudges and seek revenge, indeed, to hate in one's heart all those who were not one's "brother."

"Hate Your Enemy . . ."

All this may clarify somewhat a long-standing difficulty in part of the "Sermon on the Mount," Matt. 5:43–44. The text reads:

> You have heard that it was said, "You shall love your neighbor and hate your enemy." But I say to you, love your enemies and pray for those who persecute you.

These verses pose a problem, for while the words "You have heard it said, 'You shall love your neighbor . . .' " seem to mean "You all know the biblical injunction 'You shall love your neighbor' found at the end of Lev. 19:18 . . .," the apparent quotation "hate your enemy" has no biblical source. Where did anyone hear *that* said? Some scholars have suggested that "hate your enemy" is not being made out to be an actual biblical commandment, but may simply reflect some common teaching or practice of the time—and they have sought its source in the "Manual of Discipline," which elsewhere enjoins members to "love all the children of light, each man according to his lot, in the counsel of God, and to *hate all the children of darkness*, each man according to his guilt, in the vengeance of God."[37] Was this not the source of the teaching being specifically rejected in the "Sermon on the Mount"? This solution has sometimes been coupled with the mention of an Essene oath in Josephus' *Jewish War* (2:139), "to hate the wicked always, and to fight together with the good," to suggest that Matt. 5:43–44 is inveighing against a sectarian statute.

But it would appear from the preceding that a more straightforward and symmetrical solution is available. Matt. 5:43–44 may simply represent the restrictive exegesis of Lev. 19:17–18, interpreting these verses conjointly as they are interpreted in the "Damascus Document." That is, "You shall love your neighbor . . ." in the Sermon represents the end of Lev. 19:18, "you shall love your neighbor as yourself"; ". . . and hate your enemy" derives from the similarly restrictive interpretation of Lev. 19:17, "You shall not hate your brother in your heart," i.e., but your enemy you *shall* hate. For we have not only just seen how "hatred in the heart" was prescribed as the proper attitude toward the "Men of the Pit," but we have seen as well that vengeance and grudge bearing against enemies is not only not forbidden by Lev. 19:17, "You shall not take revenge or hold a grudge *against your countrymen*," but is in fact, via the proper understanding of Nah. 1:2, nothing less than *imitatio Dei*.

Thus "hate your enemy" in Matthew is not merely a floating sectarian doctrine, nor even quite, as Morton Smith suggested, a corollary generated by "Love your neighbor" (that is, love your neighbor but hate your enemy).[38] Instead, it is the result of a restrictive reading of "You shall not hate your brother . . ." in Lev. 19:17. For just as the "Damascus Document" saw in the biblical prohibition of vengeance against "your countrymen" no obstacle to vengeance against all who were not "your countrymen," so was the biblical prohibition of hating "your brother" interpreted (as we have just seen in the "Manual of Discipline") as in fact a positive injunction to hate your enemies, indeed, to dissemble that hatred in hypocrisy and the "spirit of hiding" until the "day of vengeance" when the long-restrained loathing will at last find full expression. "You shall love your neighbor and hate your enemy" is thus a restatement of how Lev. 19:17–18 was interpreted, at least in some quarters.

A Legal Boundary

Early Christianity rejected such notions of obligatory hatred and vengeance. Yet the underlying idea—that there was a significant, *legal* boundary between members of the community and those outside it—does appear to survive in a number of texts. One of these occurs in 2 Thess. 3:14–15:

> If anyone refuses to obey what we say in this letter, note that man and have nothing to do with him, so that he be put to shame. [Yet] do not consider him an enemy, but warn him as a brother.

Here again is a hint to the stark opposition of insiders and outsiders as reflected in the Qumran exegesis of Lev. 19:17–18: An errant "brother" is to be warned, shunned, and even brought to public embarrassment,[39] yet "do not consider him an enemy"! If, as a "brother," he is thus reproached, shunned, and shamed, what then (one might wonder) can this further admonition mean? But in the light of the foregoing, its meaning ought perhaps to be understood as: Do not treat him as the enemy (= nonbrother) alluded to in the interpretation of Lev. 19:17–18, that is, do not hate him in your heart as if you had been relieved of the obligations of open reproach and love, and do not seek revenge or even hold a grudge against him. For, according to that interpretation of our verses, to do so would necessarily imply that the person had somehow crossed the community boundary and become an actual outsider, truly an "enemy" in the sense we have seen.[40]

In this connection, the last line of the "reproach" instructions in Matt. 18:15–17 are significant. For there, it will be recalled, the text required first a personal act of reproach, "between you and him alone," then a public reproach before "two or three witnesses," then a report on his behavior "to the church," and finally, if even this step fails to produce results, "let him be to you as a Gentile and a tax-collector." Again, this phrase should not be understood merely as an act of mental disapproval ("You worthless lout, you are nothing but a Gentile and a tax-collector!"), but rather more precisely as representing a *crossing of the community boundary* so central to the understanding of Lev. 19:17–18. For having failed to listen even to the church, the offender has in effect taken himself out of the circle of insiders for whom the institution of reproach is to play its crucial role in the emotional hygiene of the community. "Let him be *to you* as a Gentile and a tax-collector" means: let him henceforth be considered an outsider (for there could be no more extreme expression of outsider status than Gentile and tax-collector— that is, he is not only no longer a member of the community, but, as far as you are concerned, he might as well be a non-Jew, indeed, an agent of the enemy oppressors of the Jews). In other words, the very last stage in the steps envisaged in Matt. 18:15 is the crossing of the crucial insider-outsider boundary with regard to Lev. 19:17–18.

The Good Samaritan

It is interesting that this same issue of community boundaries is the subject of the famous parable of the Good Samaritan in Luke 10:29–37. The parable itself is well known: A man fallen upon by robbers and left half-dead on the road is neglected by a priest and a Levite, two fellow Jews, and only helped by the "good Samaritan"—a foreigner—who comes along and immediately attends to him. But it is interesting for us to observe the question that this parable serves to answer. For the introduction to the story reads as follows:

> And behold, a lawyer stood up to put him to the test, saying, "Teacher, what shall I do to inherit eternal life?" He said to him, "What is written in the Torah? Have you read it?" And he answered, "You shall love the Lord your God with all your heart, and with all your soul, and with all your mind; and your neighbor as yourself." And he said to him, "You have answered right; do this, and you will live." But he, desiring to justify himself, said to Jesus, "And who is my neighbor?"
>
> (Luke, 10:25–28)

The last question really means: how restrictively should Lev. 19:17–18 be interpreted? Does "and you shall love your neighbor as yourself" apply only to community members or to all Jews? This is hardly an idle question (nor necessarily, as the text suggests, one posed by the questioner in order "to justify himself"): it was a *crux interpretum*, answered, as we have seen, quite differently in different quarters. And so the answer suggested by the parable presents the broadest sort of applicability of our law: just as the Samaritan, an outsider, offered aid to the victim, so is the questioner urged to "go and do likewise" (Luke 10:37), that is, to apply Lev. 19:18 even to Samaritans.

In sum, the early exegesis of our brief passage from Leviticus had far-reaching implications for the behavior of different Jewish communities in late antiquity. This exegesis, no less than the other instances of early interpretation surveyed herein, depended on a very close sifting of the Bible's words: "You shall not hate *your brother* in *your heart;* you shall *surely* reproach *your neighbor,* and you shall bear no *sin because of him.* You shall not take revenge or bear a grudge *against your countrymen,* but you shall love your *neighbor* like yourself. . . ." Each of the italicized words, as we have seen, was the subject of speculation. The restrictions that were imposed on the basis of such expressions as "your brother," "your neighbor," and "your countrymen"; the hypocrisy and hiding that were understood to be meant by hatred "in the heart"; the multiple acts of reproach suggested by the emphatic, "doubled" verb (translated above as "*surely* reproach"); and the various identifications proposed for the unspecified "sin" avoided by open reproach—all of these interpretations came out of the most minute examination of the divine text and its implications.

This is of course nothing new: we have seen a similar care that went into the reading of the story of Joseph and other instances treated above. And as in these examples, so with the legal exegesis studied now we have seen how interpretive traditions can become harmonized and even confused with one another, until a new generation of interpreters no longer understands fully the thinking underlying the traditions that have come down to it from the past. There is, however, one striking difference between the exegesis of biblical laws and biblical narrative. For the latter was largely without practical consequence: that Joseph was strikingly handsome, or that he was truly tempted by Mrs. Potiphar, or that Jacob appeared to him in a vision—these readings likely produced no tangible results in the behavior of those who transmitted them or espoused them. Not so, of course, for the interpretation of biblical law; here, how a verse was understood had immediate consequences in daily life. And so we have seen with regard to our passage from Leviticus: whether one went about gingerly reproaching one's fellow, or on the contrary blasted away without regard for his public shame, or yet considered him no "fellow" at all, and hence fair game for dissembled hatred and hypocrisy—all depended on how one read the verse. In the extreme, matters no less weighty than love and hate, perhaps even life and death, depended on biblical interpretation.

Notes

1. This is precisely how this text was understood by some medieval Jewish commentators: see the discussion *ad loc.* in the Pentateuchal commentaries of Naḥmanides and Baḥya b. Asher, as well as Maimonides' *Book of the Commandments*, ed. J. Qafih (Jerusalem: Mossad ha-Rav Kook, 1971), 162, 222.

2. Note the discussion of this question, with references to secondary literature, in K. Berger, *Die Gesetzauslegung Jesu* (Neukirchen-Vluyn: Neukirchener Verlag, 1972), 81–97.

3. See, in addition to the texts discussed below, Prov. 3:12, 27:5–6, 28:23; Sir. 20:2.

4. Reading conjecturally *vesod le'aḥer 'al tegal* (the Masoretic text has: *vesod 'aḥer 'al tegal*, "and do not disclose another's secret"). I prefer the former reading, despite the fact that the latter might better support our theme of the connection between open reproach and the avoidance of slandering someone (i.e., as if the verse said: Argue it out with your neighbor and do not reveal *his* secret to some third party). But on the grounds of sense as well as context, it seems obvious that the "secret" (= confidential matter) in question belongs jointly to the disputants, and they are being urged to settle things privately and so not involve "another" in their quarrel. Note that "Testament of Gad" 6:5 (discussed below) presumes something like the text of Prov. 25:9 as I have emended it, for its restatement reads, "In a dispute do not let another hear *your* secret."

5. Cf. the preceding vss. Prov. 25:7–8.

6. The Syriac text has "lest he do wrong," while the Greek has "perhaps he did not do." It seems reasonable to suppose that the common antecedent of these two is, as conjectured by M. H. Segal (*The Complete Book of Ben Sira* [in Hebrew] [Jerusalem: Bialik, 1972], 115), *'asher lo' ya'aseh* ("that he not do," "lest he do"). Such pithiness is quite characteristic of Ben Sira's Hebrew, but its ambiguity may have pushed the (frequently loose and periphrastic) Syriac to add the word *bish* ("evil," "wrong"). The Greek tradition, meanwhile, may have read *'asher lo' 'asah* ("that he did not do"), forcing "lest" to be revised into "perhaps"; and/or the confusion may have entered, via the Greek μήποτε (both "lest" and "perhaps"), in the transmission of the Greek text itself.

7. The underlying Hebrew verb is probably *za'am* (Segal: *za'ap*); the Greek ἀπειλέω implies this, or possibly *ga'ar*, but the latter would hardly be used without a following *bo* not represented in the Greek. The Syriac *ṭelam* ("oppress," "wrong") appears interpretive, translating in the light of the previous two lines.

8. Above, note 2.

9. The Greek tradition, "Reproach [lit., "Question"] a friend, perhaps he did not do," represents, I believe, a faulty transmission of the original (above, note 6). It nevertheless highlights another preventive function of "reproach," namely, allowing the reproach to ascertain what really happened and, in some cases, to prevent him from being angry on false premises. Attractive as this reading is, it makes for redundancy in vss. 15 and 16, so on those grounds as well, the Syriac is to be preferred. Ultimately, the

original Hebrew and possibly the Greek were based on a homiletical explanation of the Hebrew use of the infinitive absolute in Lev. 19:17, *hokheah tokhiah* on which see below, note 21.

10. See note 12.

11. The nature of this "sin" requires some clarification. It appears that the offender, having been pressed by the reproacher, might be tempted to swear a false or unnecessary oath as to his innocence. There is ample evidence to suggest that both were considered sinful by Jews in late antiquity. See thus: on reserve with regard to invoking the divine name in general, the Septuagint and Onkelos' rendering of Lev. 24:16, and cf. Philo, "Life of Moses," 2.206 and 1QS 6:27–7:2; and on the use of divine names in oaths, Philo, "On the Decalogue," 84–86, and "Of the Special Laws" 2:2–5; cf. "Damascus Document" 15:1–5, and Matt. 5:33–37. It is possible that the "swearing" mentioned in the "Testament of Gad" is actually a cursing of the reproacher with the divine name—a practice amply condemned in Jewish sources (see thus Mishna *Shebu.* 4:13, also b. *Sanh.* 66a and b. *Shebu.* 36a; b. *Tem.* 3a, b. *Mak.* 16a, and y. *Sheb.* 3:10)—but in this case our text's use of the word ὀμνύω is problematic.

12. Note that Targum Onkelos renders עלוי not as "because of him" but "because of his own [sin]" על דיליה. This deviation requires some explanation, and the simplest may be that Onkelos wished thereby to reject other possible explanations and imply more specifically that the phrase refers to a transfer of responsibility for the infraction from the transgressor to the one who failed to carry out the commandment to reproach properly. Such is Nahmanides' explanation of Onkelos: " 'And you shall bear no sin because of him . . .' for *you* will be guilty if he sins and you have not reproached him. And the wording of Onkelos implies this [understanding] when it translates ולא תקביל על דיליה חובא that you yourself should not receive punishment for his sin."

13. See the interpretation of *Sifra,* discussed below; also Maimonides, *Book of the Commandments,* 162, 222, and Nahmanides, *Commentary, ad loc.*

14. The Law of Reproach at Qumran has been discussed most recently by L. Schiffman in his *Sectarian Law in the Dead Sea Scrolls: Courts, Testimony, and the Penal Code,* Brown Judaica Series 33 (Chico, CA: Scholars Press, 1983), 89–109. I am indebted to him for his many insights.

15. The text reads here אליהוהו, apparently by dittography of the final הו.

16. For this restoration see Schiffman, *Sectarian Law,* 106 n. 61.

17. Schiffman (ibid., 107 n. 64) proposes reading בערלת לבבו, "in the stubbornness of his heart," citing with approval Brownlee's rejection of S. Iwry's suggestion of בכתלי לבבו ("in the walls of his heart") on the grounds that "the context requires an adversative reference to the heart." On the contrary, the whole point is that this clause is an elaboration of Lev. 19:17, "You shall not hate your brother in your heart," and a tying together of that stricture with the Law of Reproach. An "adversative reference" would not only obscure that relation but would eliminate the true sense of "hatred in the heart" that is plainly being invoked here. This said, I have left the space blank since any emendation appears highly conjectural and, for the reason just stated, "in . . . his heart" conveys the essential meaning. Cf. A. R. C.

Leany, *The Rule of Qumran and Its Meaning* (Philadelphia: Westminster, 1966), 176.

18. See on this S. Japhet, *The Ideology of the Book of Chronicles* (in Hebrew) (Jerusalem: Mossad Bialik, 1978), 158–63.

19. The "Damascus Document" was first found in a medieval copy in the *genizah* of a Cairo synagogue and published by Solomon Schechter in 1910. See S. Schechter, *Documents of Jewish Sectaries* with "Prolegomenon" by J. A. Fitzmyer (New York: KTAV, 1970).

20. Hebrew בדבר מות and cf. "Damascus Document" 9:17. The sense may be that *even* in the case of a capital charge, the transgressor's guilt is to be transferred to the one who failed to reproach him, but this could have been stated more explicitly. Instead, the sense seems to be that the transferral of guilt takes place *specifically* in the case described, when someone fails to reproach his fellow for a capital offense and stores it up "from day to day," only to accuse him publicly later on. See below.

21. That this was a concern of early exegetes may be attested, *inter alia*, in the attempts of the Septuagint translators to imitate this construction in Greek by juxtaposing a finite verb with its participle or (as here) with the dative of a cognate noun. Obviously these translators believe this feature of the Hebrew text to be important enough to merit this (at times awkward) form of imitation, and this may bear witness to attempts, as early as the third century B.C.E., to attribute some addition significance to the Hebrew use of the infinitive absolute. The passage from Ben Sira cited above might be another indication of such a reading. For it urges that one reproach one's friend "lest he do, and if he has done, lest he continue," and then urges a similar twofold reproaching with regard to speech. Why this particular before-and-after scenario? Indeed, how is one to know that one's friend is going to commit an offense in word or deed before he does it?! (This difficulty, incidentally, may have contributed to what was seen above, note 6, as the Greek's deviation from the hypothetical Hebrew original.) But the twofold act of reproaching makes perfect sense if one understands that Ben Sira is trying to explain the "doubled" verbal form *hokheah tokhiah*—the first verb refers to reproaching that takes place before the offense is done, the second after the fact.

22. "Four or five times" is apparently to be taken as "repeatedly." Cf. b. *Baba Meṣiʿa*, 31a, where the doubling is alleged to give warrant for reproaching "even a hundred times."

23. On which see m. *Abot* 3:11.

24. *Sifra, ad loc.* Note that the first explanation offered by *Sifra* for this law, namely, that one ought not to be a tale-bearer (*rakhil*) in the sense of being "soft (*rakh*) of speech to one and hard to the other" surely also is aimed not at the ordinary citizen (for who then would the "one" and the "other" be?) but the judge in his treatment of the two litigants.

25. *Sifra*'s brief treatment of reproach does not give many clues as to whether it is related to one or both of the approaches discussed above. Yet, on close inspection, it does seem to be a distant cousin of, specifically, the "judicial" approach. Of course the "warning" function of reproach at Qumran was carried out in rabbinic Judaism by the institution of "admonition" (*hatraʾah*) and so "reproach," considered a separate matter, had no specifically judi-

cial function. Yet it is clear from our *Sifra* text and elsewhere that reproach is a similar kind of (potentially victimless) moral instruction, delivered from one person to another not for the purpose of externalizing hatred but as a way of making each community member responsible for correcting flaws in each other's behavior. For note that in *Sifra* and later rabbinic texts, the reproacher is not necessarily the victim: he is one who "sees some fault in his fellow" (b. 'Arak. 16b) and seeks to correct it with four, five, or a "hundred" reproaches if necessary. Such multiple correction would, if the complaint were of a personal nature—a property dispute, for example—likely only lead to an argument. And in any case, if the matter could not be settled out of court after the first "reproach," why then let it be settled in court. But if, instead, the rabbinic notion of reproach was essentially that of a moral exhortation or a remonstrance for less than exemplary practice, then the requirement to reproach one's fellow repeatedly acquires more plausibility. Pertinent in this light is the continuation of *Sifra*'s treatment of our verse, which makes it clear that the sort of reproach in question is not that of an offended party to the offender, but an attempt by one person to prevent another from sinning. In a similar vein, b. Baba Meṣ. 31a understands the "doubled" verb in our verse as implying that reproach can go not only from "master to disciple" but "disciple to master"—here again, the clear sense is that the reproach is an attempt at moral correction rather than personal redress.

26. This passage too is an exegetical conflation. The first, long sentence is aimed at explaining "You shall not take revenge . . ." and connecting it to a failure to carry out the Law of Reproach. But the second sentence, "If he was silent . . . ," was originally an independent analysis of v. 17: the reference to being "silent" is an allusion, a restatement really, of "You shall not hate your brother in your heart"—being "silent" is an indication that the person in question is secretly hating his fellow and thus violating the Law of Reproach. The rest of the sentence explained how, under such circumstances of "silent" hatred, the crime of which the silent hater ultimately accuses his enemy is now to be charged against him, that is, he himself will bear the penalty for it, even if it is a capital offense. Now all this was intended to explain the wording of the end of v. 17, "and you shall bear no sin because of him"—that is, if you fail to reproach as required, you shall indeed be judged guilty of a sin, the very sin of which you accuse him. Only proper reproach, in other words, guarantees that you will not bear a sin "because of him," that is, in his place! That this exegesis is independent of the first part of our "Damascus Document" passage should be clear. Not only does each part stand on its own without the other, but in the first, the unspecified "sin" is the revenge spoken of in v. 18, whereas in the second the "sin" is whatever sin the silent hater has accused his fellow of committing.

27. In both these matters Rabin may have been influenced by L. Ginzberg, *Eine Unbekannte Jüdische Sekte,* vol. 1 (New York, 1922), 57.

28. Dupont-Sommer, in his translation, rendered the citation literally, ". . . or il est écrit seulement: Lui [Dieu] se venge de Ses adversaires, et Lui garde rancune à Ses ennemis," but he added in a footnote: "The text of Nahum is adduced in the sense that one must leave to God alone the task of

revenge and must therefore not seek to venge oneself on one's own" (A. Dupont-Sommer, [Paris: Payot, 1959], 164). G. Vermes, in his English translation of Dupont-Sommer's book, made the author's understanding more explicit through the (somewhat misleading) insertion of a parenthetical "that": "whereas it is written (that) only he (God) takes vengeance on his adversaries and bears malice against his enemies" (A. Dupont-Sommer, *The Essene Writings from Qumran*, trans. G. Vermes [London: Blackwell, 1961] 148). Actually, the "that" belongs *after* the "only"; Rabin had in any case more correctly rendered this expression in his version as "it is expressly written." Note that Vermes' own later translation is far better— "although it is expressly written, 'He takes vengeance . . . [etc.]' "—see G. Vermes, *The Dead Sea Scrolls in English* (Hammondsworth, England: Penguin, 1968), 110. E. Cothenet's translation was as follows: "Il se venge, Lui (Seul), de Ses adversaires, Il garde rancune à Ses ennemis." He observed in a note, "This prophetic text is interpreted in the same manner as Deut. 32:35 in Romans 12:19; vengeance is a divine 'privilege' " (J. Carmignac, E. Cothenet, and H. Lignée, *Les textes de Qumran*, vol. 2 [Paris: Letouzey et Ane, 1963], 186–87.) L. Ginzberg adopted a somewhat intermediate position: while he asserts that the meaning of the citation is that God alone has the prerogative of vengeance, he was clearly aware of the restrictive understanding of Lev. 19:17 (see below) and its implications for the citation, as well as of the rabbinic exegesis of Nah. 1:2. See *Eine Unbekannte Sekte*, 57, 269, 291.

29. J. A. Fitzmyer, "The Use of Explicit Old Testament Quotations in the Qumran Literature and in the New Testament," *New Testament Studies* 7 (1961): 307.

30. This is of course not to say that the "divine prerogative of vengeance" idea is not found elsewhere in ancient texts. It exists in Ben Sira (28:1), "He who takes vengeance will find himself avenged by the Lord . . .," and is even present in the "Testament of Gad," shortly after the passage cited above: "But if he is shameless and persists in his wrongdoing, even so forgive him from the heart, and leave vengeance to God." Nonetheless, such is not the sense of the Nahum citation as it is being used in context in the "Damascus Document."

31. R. P. Lagrange, "La Secte juive de la Nouvelle Alliance au pays de Damas," *Revue Biblique* 9 (1912): 229. I. Levi's handling of the verse in his translation (in *Revue des Études Juives* 61 [1911]: 161–205 and 63 [1912]: 1–19) had been ambiguous.

32. This observation received wide exposure in Charles' edition of the Pseudepigrapha, published the following year; see R. H. Charles, *Apocrypha and Pseudepigrapha of the Old Testament* (Oxford: Blackwell, 1913), 2: 823.

33. One well-known translation in English, T. H. Gaster's *The Dead Sea Scriptures* (Garden City NY: Doubleday, 1976), did get the right sense, even deviating somewhat from literal translation to stress its interpretation: "Scripture says of God Himself that it is only upon His adversaries that He takes vengeance . . ." (p. 80).

34. That the Qumran community saw itself as a people apart is of course nothing new; this view has been explored in numerous works of scholarship including some of those cited above. But the views expressed on this ques-

tion in the Qumran texts must themselves be examined in the broader context of the pressures and problems of self-definition within the period in question. See on this in particular the collection of essays by E. P. Sanders et al., *Jewish and Christian Self-Definition* (Philadelphia: Fortress Press, 1981).

35. See below. Note that the end of Lev. 19:18, "And you shall love your neighbor as yourself," is alluded to elsewhere in the "Damascus Document" (6:20), where, however, it is transmuted into אהוב איש את אחיהו כמוהו, "Let each of you love his *brother* like himself." The substitution of "brother" for "neighbor" may not be significant; on the other hand, the point of the change in wording may be specifically to deny other interpretations that construed "neighbor" more broadly in order to extend the applicability of this commandment beyond the members of the sect. Moreover, here (as elsewhere in early Jewish exegesis) the biblical injunction to "love your neighbor as [or "like"] yourself" may be made more restrictive by limiting its applicability only to the neighbor/brother who is indeed "like yourself," that is, a member of one's group or sect. See further Ginzberg, *Unbekannte Sekte*, 291.

36. See Schiffman, *Sectarian Law*, 108 n. 82.

37. The connection between this passage and Matt. 5:43 was first suggested by Morton Smith, "Mt. 5:43: 'Hate Thine Enemy,' " *Harvard Theological Review* 45 (1952): 71–73. Smith went on to suggest that a "a targum used in Galilee in Jesus' day glossed the words 'thou shalt love thy neighbor' with the words 'and hate thine enemy.' " See also: O. J. F. Seitz, "Love Your Enemies," *New Testament Studies* 16 (1969): 39–54, especially pp. 42–43.

38. Above, previous note.

39. Cf. the translation of Lev. 19:17 in Targum Pseudo-Jonathan cited above.

40. Cf. Krister Stendahl's observation: "Apart from the general use in Gal. 4:16 and Phil. 3:18, neither Paul nor the New Testament at large ever uses 'enemy' for a fellow Christian." ("Hate, Non-Retaliation, and Love," *Harvard Theological Review* 55 [1962]: 345).

9.

Nine Theses

Having examined in the previous chapters various specific examples of the ways in which exegetical motifs are created and develop, I should like now to try to formulate some more general conclusions about the workings of early biblical exegesis as a whole. I must stress at the outset that not all of what follows derives solely, or even principally, from the foregoing chapters; there are many aspects of early biblical exegesis which I have not been able to touch upon above. Nevertheless, to the extent that it is possible, I will try to illustrate the broad characterizations that follow with examples taken from the exegetical motifs studied, and so to anchor them in specific and by now familiar instances. Nor, should I add, is my purpose here quite so provocative as the propounding of general "theses" about this subject might imply: what follows is not in the nature of a manifesto. Rather, my intention is simply to reflect on some aspects of early biblical exegesis as they have presented themselves to me, both in the above studies and in others, and to try to crystallize these reflections in the form of broad statements about the subject. The following, then, are nine "theses" about early biblical exegesis.

1. **Most of the narrative expansions found in rabbinic midrash and other early texts have as their point of departure some peculiarity in the biblical text itself. That is to say, these expansions, whatever other motives and concerns may be evidenced in them, are formally a kind of biblical exegesis.** In the light of the foregoing, this may seem a mere truism; after all, what we have been examining is precisely the way in which peculiarities in the Bible's language—"See! He has brought to us a Hebrew man," "The daughters climbed upon a wall," "From there the stone of Israel," and so forth—led early exegetes to dream up whole incidents not reported in the Bible itself. Yet it seems nonetheless important to assert that the exegetical motive witnessed in these examples is altogether characteristic of the material as a whole. For there is a tendency in readers—perhaps encouraged by the very form of these narrative expansions—to regard them as mere "poetic flights," or as expressions of some political/theological program that came to be associated, more or less at random, with one part or another of the bib-

lical text, or again, as leftover bits of popular folklore that eventually became fused with this or that biblical figure or incident. Nor has the modern scholarly study of midrash always appeared anxious to dispel this impression. As noted earlier, Louis Ginzberg's masterful *Legends of the Jews* announced its approach even in its title: these expansions were "legends," bits of Jewish folklore, and their exegetical function was discussed, if anywhere, only in that study's wonderful footnotes. Other scholars of early exegesis have chosen to focus on what narrative expansions may reveal about the historical and political circumstances in which they were created, or how they embody something of the ideology or religious views of their creators. In addition to this, more recent scholars have sought to see in them sophisticated literary compositions whose artistry ought therefore to constitute a worthy object of criticism in its own right.[1] And so it seems worthwhile here to assert once again, without seeking to denigrate any of these other interests and fields, that the *exegetical* side of these texts deserves our primary attention: anyone seeking to come to grips with such texts must first reckon with the exegetical motives of their authors before turning to these other concerns.

But let us go a step further: are we therefore to conclude that such narrative expansions constitute "pure" exegesis, that they derive solely from the efforts of early exegetes to explain the meaning of biblical passages? Hardly. *The early exegete is an expositor with an axe to grind.* At the very least, he wants to show us that the text means much more than it seems to mean, that there are hidden implications which, without him, we would likely pass over. But quite often his "axe" is polemical indeed: he is out to prove that, despite appearances, Jacob was a man of exemplary character, and that Esau was no mere bumbling fall guy, but a wicked schemer; or that any number of beliefs and practices dear to his group (rabbinic Judaism, or the Qumran covenanters, or various Christian sects, or yet other groups) are not later inventions or deviations from ancient ways, but in fact derive from Sacred Scripture; or that one or another prophetic passage in the Bible actually finds its application in the events or situations of his own day.

In fact, the material presented in the foregoing chapters offers something of a representative sampling of the ways in which exegetical and other elements mingle in the creation of midrashic motifs. Thus, I have little doubt that the "Assembly of Ladies" motif got started because the anomalous plurals "to us" and "to 'sport' with us" were in fact troubling in the biblical narrative: the "royal we" is extremely uncommon in biblical Hebrew, and its use here therefore seemed to call out for some sort of commentary or explanation. So behind this motif (or, rather, its first two stages) stands a fairly obvious exegetical problem. But the next complication that came to join that motif—the one that saw in the imperative "See!" an allusion to Joseph's actual presence at the time of the assembly—is of a slightly different order. I doubt that any reader was seriously *troubled* by that "See!" (whose true direct object, if one were absolutely necessary, might be found in the "garment" mentioned in the preceding and following verses). Instead, this is a more playful expansion-of-an-expansion; one might possibly read the "See!" in such fashion, and so one did. As for the later additions, the knives, the forgotten wine, and other props that came to inhabit this expansion, we have seen above that they have no *exegetical* connection to the text; they simply made for a better story, and so came to be included in it.

Let us consider another instance. With regard to Psalm 137, we saw that much exegetical attention was turned to explaining the word *sham* in *"there* we sat down. . . ." Now no doubt the apparently emphatic nature of this word did call out for some comment; still, it would be foolish to characterize the rabbinic expansions that we saw merely as attempts to grapple with the sense of the verse. The motif "No Reststop in Israel," for example, accomplished much more: it heightened the pathos and sufferings of the exiles, and the cruelty of their Babylonian captors; it came to suggest (at least in one form) a close connection between Psalm 137 and Lam. 5:5 (and possibly 4:19); and it also allowed the Babylonians to demonstrate by their conduct the belief that repentance, even *in extremis,* can cause a divinely-sent punishment to be overturned. Similarly, the motif " 'Had You Wept But Once . . .' " not only supplied a rationale for *sham* in this verse, but connected it to the problematic *gam* in the same verse, and attached the whole to an ever-relevant exhortation about repentance that was put in the mouth of Jeremiah, thus further suggesting the precise circumstances under which this psalm was first uttered. And this is wholly characteristic of the sorts of considerations that regularly shape narrative expansions.

Another, somewhat different instance: the motif "Jacob's Portrait on the Heavenly Throne" formally *explains* the phrase in Gen. 28:12, "and his/its head reached to the Heavens." But is it fair to call this *exegesis* at all?[2] Could not the phrase have been left unambiguously as "its head . . ." and its sense be perfectly obvious? Of course. Nor is it likely that this motif merely reflects the chance encounter of an unfettered imagination with an exegetical opportunity. For there is no doubt that, in late antiquity, neo-Platonists believed in the existence of a heavenly plan or image or prototype of the earthly man—gnostic texts bear witness to this belief, as do, for that matter, some passages in the New Testament. It thus seems probable that our Ur-exegete was aware of such an idea and, for one reason or another, chose to read the phrase "its head" in the text as "his head" in keeping with it. In other words, here is one vivid instance of a common phenomenon, whereby a particular line of interpretation "explains" a biblical verse by going out of its way to connect up the verse with some preexisting doctrine or idea or practice or even historical event quite external to the text. This is far indeed from what one might call "pure" exegesis.

But then there is a further question one might ask, indeed, it is a question that poses itself in myriad other cases: did the exegete start with an idea (in this case, that of a heavenly image of a human being) and then go looking for an appropriate biblical verse to hang it on, or did he, to the contrary, start with the verse, and find its "solution" amid the cultural or historical baggage of his age? Sometimes, indeed often, this question cannot be answered definitively. In the case at hand, we nonetheless have some clues. For as suggested above, the most obvious biblical locus for such an idea would probably have been the opening chapter of Ezekiel, especially Ezek. 1:10 or 1:26, both of which speak of "human faces" in connection with the Heavenly Throne. Certainly an exegete seeking to "park" this human-image-in-Heaven idea somewhere in the Bible might first have gone there. Indeed, of the various specific human beings whom one might expect *a priori* to have been chosen by God for the honor of having a heavenly image, Jacob seems a somewhat less likely candidate than, say, Moses, or Abraham—and certainly exegetical opportunities for either of these were not lacking.[3] Indeed, the biblical account of Adam, who was fashioned according to God's "image" (Gen. 1:27) and who himself fathered Seth "in his [Adam's] likeness *and in keeping with his image*"—certainly this account and these particular phrases might have been used to suggest that the preexisting image mentioned was in fact an image of the first man, one that God consulted in creating him and that was subsequently kept in Heaven.[4] Thus, the fact that according to our motif it is Jacob, and only Jacob, whose face is etched on the Heavenly Throne, and that this motif is firmly anchored to one biblical verse, Gen. 28:12, suggests that, in this instance at least, the exegete started off with the verse: the possibility of reading *"his* head" was what suggested the connection with the heavenly image idea.

But even when we can be less sure about the answer to this type of question, our uncertainty is in any case of little consequence for the "thesis" propounded above. For I was careful to say that narrative expansions, whatever other motives and concerns may be evidenced in them, are *formally* a kind of biblical exegesis. That is, however they may come into existence—and often this sort of second-guessing is utterly speculative—they do not come into existence as mere stories, floating around the biblical text, or only subsequently come to be attached, more or less at random, to this or that biblical verse. From the start they are presented as illuminating, bringing out the hidden implications of, something that *is* in the biblical text; that is to say, they are presented as a form of exegesis (even though, as we have also seen repeatedly, their precise exegetical point of departure can subsequently become quite obscured in later versions of the expansion). And just for that reason, it is necessary for us first of all to try to understand these expansions *as exegesis,* as something related—usually in quite precise and detailed fashion, as we have seen—to a peculiarity in the Bible's manner of expression, and not treat them merely as free fancy or polemics.

From this follows a programmatic statement about the study of this material, and it may be formulated thus:

2. **The study of midrashic motifs is thus first an exercise in "reverse-engineering," in which, therefore, certain standard questions ought repeatedly to be asked.** "Reverse-engineering" is a concept drawn from the world of modern technology (and patent infringement!). It is the process by which engineers examine a finished product, some complex piece of equipment or machinery, and then try to recreate the thinking and procedures that led up to its having the form and components that it has—in a sense to "reinvent" the machine by proceeding backwards. Now the whole process of understanding the development of midrashic motifs works in just this fashion: we examine a finished product, a text somewhere, and try to recreate the thinking that stands behind each and every one of its components.

But the machines of early exegesis sometimes embody, as we have seen, extraordinary inefficiencies: there are two components that accomplish essentially the same job, and either one of them would be sufficient; or there is a component that apparently serves no useful purpose whatsoever, and turns out to be a leftover from some previously designed machine. And so the job of the reverse-engineers of early exegesis consists of asking certain standard, oft-repeated questions about the texts before them: Is this expansion based on a single exegetical motif, or some combination? Are all the elements of the motif(s) integral to the exegesis? If not, are some borrowed from else-where? Apart from these obvious and quite direct questions, these is another, somewhat more general one, a difficult and seemingly sub-jective question which, to my mind, is nonetheless worth posing in each instance. It is the **reverse-engineering question** *par excellence:* Would an exegete, faced with problem X in the biblical text, be likely to create *ex nihilo* solution Y? If not, then solution Y probably already existed as the answer to some entirely different problem, or in some other way came to be "borrowed" by the exegete and recycled as an answer, or part of an answer, to problem X.

Now as noted, this question is often difficult to answer with any certainty, at least at first; but it is nonetheless worth asking straight-away, if for no other reason than that it helps to focus our thinking by putting us in the shoes of the original exegete. And indeed, we have seen above, for example, that in the case of **midrashic doublets,** one occurrence of the motif sometimes suits perfectly the exegetical ques-tion it purports to answer, whereas the second is flat and lame. Thus, for example, we saw that the motif "Bedaubed his Eyes" worked beau-tifully as an explanation for the problem of "And it came to pass *after these things*" in Gen. 39:7—it explained what the "things" were, men-tioned three of them so as to fit the plural "things," and, best of all, it established a clear causal connection between these "things" and what follows immediately in the same sentence, the mention of Mrs. Potiphar taking an interest in Joseph. On the other hand, this same motif was both forced and irrelevant with regard to the problem of Joseph's being a seventeen-year-old "boy" (*na'ar*) in Gen. 37:2; many better and more direct solutions were available for that particular prob-lem. Therefore, the answer to our primary **reverse-engineering ques-tion** (which is, to repeat: Would an exegete, faced with problem X in the biblical text, be likely to create *ex nihilo* solution Y?) must be, with regard to this second instance, no: the motif has evidently been bor-rowed from Gen. 39:7.

Other instances are not so easy to be categorical about. Still it has appeared, in the foregoing, that the motif explaining "old age" (*ze-qunim*) as "splendor-of-countenance" (*ziv 'iqonin*), found with regard to both Joseph and Isaac, probably was created for the former and the problem raised by Joseph's being described as the "child of [Jacob's] old age"—that is, Joseph and not the obvious candidate, Benjamin. Next to this, the problem of Isaac's potentially disputable paternity seems less problematic: surely this "solution" only tends to call attention to the problem, and, as we have seen, other, more direct assertions in the text could in any case have functioned to answer the same problem. So here again, the **reverse-engineering question** leads us to favor one of the doublets and so identify it as the original.

Nor is this question posed only with regard to such **doublets.** We asked it in another form with regard to "Jacob's Portrait on the Heavenly Throne." There, it will be recalled, the question took this form: would an exegete, faced with the problem of the angels "ascending and descending" in Gen. 28:12, be likely to create the celestial portrait as a solution? And again, we saw that other, simpler solutions were certainly available, and this in turn led to the examination of the phrase "his/its head" and its role in the creation of this motif. "Why Was Lamech Blind?" was essentially the same sort of exercise: putting ourselves in the exegete's shoes, we asked why he had to include in his finished product the unlikely figure of a blind hunter—was this *blindness* necessary in order for Gen. 4:23 to be read as a protestation of innocence? And again the answer was no: something else must thus have been responsible for the element of blindness having been introduced. With regard to "Inaccessible Bones," we asked the reverse-engineering question repeatedly: Why should Serah be mentioned at all in "Bottom of the Nile"? Why, in *Tebat Marqa,* should the Israelites be reminded by both the stubborn pillar of cloud and Serah? Why explain the singling out of Moses in Exod. 13:19 by accusing the Israelites of neglecting their duty ("Busy with Booty") and then go on to suggest that only the miracle-working speech of Moses could in any case have gotten the job done? All such questions address the efficiency, the economy, of the midrashic machine: the reverse-engineer's job is to rethink the original problem and to try to account for what lies before him in the finished product. Certainly the comparison of different versions of a motif, and an attempt to relate these to outside historical and ideological considerations and the like, are all valuable ways to a solution. But somewhere early on in the process it is wise to step into the exegete's own shoes and ask what the exegetical problem really is, and how the exegete might have gone about solving it in the simplest and most efficient fashion.

Out of this inquiry into the exegete's own thinking have emerged a few broad observations about the ways of exegetical motifs. These observations might now bear explicit formulation:

3. **Exegetical motifs generally arise out of only one focus or site, usually a troubling or suggestive word or phrase within a specific verse. Only later, in a given narrative expansion, will the motif be made out to be addressing two or more verses simultaneously, often verses at**

some remove from one another. We have seen above some of the ways in which new exegetical foci come to be added to the original one—how, for example, Prov.29:3, "A shepherd of prostitutes loses his wealth," came to be **back-referenced** to Joseph and then combined with an already existing motif that had explained the phrase "stone of Israel" in Gen. 49:24 as a reference to the priestly breastplate. In general, the incorporation of such additional biblical texts into an originally simple motif, so that the motif then seems simultaneously to address multiple problems from different places in the Bible, is a very common phenomenon. It will be discussed further presently.

But for now it is important to make more explicit, albeit in somewhat guarded terms, the full claim of the first sentence of this "thesis." For it is my impression that there are relatively few exegetical motifs that may have come into existence by an exegete actually contemplating two separate verses simultaneously and saying to himself, "I will take care of them both with a single story." Theoretically, of course, there is no reason why this should not have taken place; but it does not seem to have happened often. Even in the case of Psalm 137, where "No Rest-stop in Israel" seemed to account beautifully both for the pleonastic "there" in "*there* we sat down" and, at the same time, to explain the full significance of Lam. 5:5, "On our necks we were pursued; exhausted we were given no rest," upon closer examination we found it probable that only the latter verse was the original focus of this motif, and that, in fact, the attempt to join Ps. 137:1 to it required, in one of the versions examined, some radical restructuring of the Babylonians' motive in pressing the Jews on.

As noted, there is no reason why this "single point of origin" theory ought to hold true in every case—and indeed, exceptions do turn up here or there. But this observation, it seems to me, can be stipulated to be *generally* true. And this in turn should sharpen our very definition of an **exegetical motif:** an exegetical motif, it appears, is concerned—at least at it origins—with one verse and one verse alone. Now if we make this an operating assumption whenever we come to deal with early exegetical material, then a particular narrative expansion that makes reference, explicit or otherwise, to more than one verse will of necessity be, on the face of it, either a combination of different motifs or, at the least, a later form of an originally simpler motif, one that has been elaborated through the inclusion of an additional biblical reference and, sometimes, other new elements.

Incidentally, it is not difficult to imagine why this single-verse focus in our motifs came about. It is because early biblical exegesis is relentlessly verse-centered. Quite apart from the whole phenomenon of narrative expansions, it is generally true that the basic unit for the midrashist is the biblical verse, or the troublesome or suggestive word or phrase within it. That is, our midrashists did not as a general rule seek to explicate larger units—a whole pericope or chapter—at one blow, and even when they wished to comment on some larger theme, those comments took the form of narrow observations about a single stimulus in the text, a word or phrase. In this respect, our present midrashic collections are somewhat deceiving, since they seem to constitute running commentaries on entire biblical books, whereas in fact most are anthologies of individual, verse-centered comments strung together by the editor. This verse-centeredness of classical midrash, in turn, may reflect the way in which the biblical text itself was learned and carried about by ancient midrashists. But since I have discussed this whole matter at length elsewhere, it will be useful here to move on to other aspects of the way motifs develop and change.[5]

4. **Exegetical motifs travel.** In fact, they travel in various ways. The phenomenon of **midrashic doublets** discussed above represents one form of travel: a motif originally created to explain one verse is adopted by an exegete to explain another verse as well. Such doublets are sometimes (as was the case of with "Bedaubed His Eyes" or "Face Resembled Father's") an act of simple repetition, whose overall effect is therefore not particularly creative or enlightening: in fact, the redundancy is likely only to confuse or disappoint the person acquainted with both parts of the doublet. But sometimes the second instance is in fact more like an allusion to the first instance, or a development thereof. Thus, when an exegete wittily suggests (as we saw briefly above) that Lam. 2:1, "He has cast down from heaven to earth the *beauty of Israel,*" is actually a reference to God's casting Jacob's (= Israel's) portrait down from the Heavenly Throne, he is not merely reusing an old motif, but developing it in the light of a new verse—and this is in fact a fairly common phenomenon in rabbinic texts.

Quite unlike this, however, is another form of travel that we have investigated, **transfer of affects,** whereby the original connection between a motif and the verse it was designed to explain becomes lost, and the motif then can become attached to something else—for example the motif "Saw Father's Countenance," which was transferred from the phrase "from there the stone of Israel" in Gen. 49:24 to the preceding phrase in the same verse "at the hands of the Mighty One of Jacob." With regard to "Inaccessible Bones," we saw that that motif apparently originated in an attempt to answer the problem of Joseph's deathbed request in Gen. 50:24–25, but that the connection between the motif and those verses does not appear after the "Testament of Simeon": instead, the motif came to be transferred to another verse, Exod. 13:19, and was applied to solve the very different exegetical problems there. This then is another form of travel. Sometimes the "traveling" really amounts to garbling: we saw, for example, that the motif "Cast Their Jewelry"—originally designed to explain the word ṣaʿadah in Gen. 49:22—appears in the first-century Greek romance *Joseph and Aseneth* as unspecified "gifts of silver and gold" that are "sent" (not thrown!) to Joseph by the women of Egypt. Here the motif has not really moved or become attached to another verse, but it has become so altered that it could no longer serve the exegetical purpose for which it was originally designed, and this is, in another sense, a form of "traveling." But perhaps the most common form deserves separate treatment:

5. **Motifs, and individual elements belonging to them, often become combined or harmonized with other motifs.** Combination is indeed the commonest form of "travel"; behind it usually stands an attempt by the exegete to reconcile two traditions, both of which he considers authoritative, or which he feels at least ought to be given their due in his exposition. Thus we saw that the development of "Inaccessible Bones" was an unremitting story of such combinations and harmonizations: The version of this story found in *Tebat Marqa*, for example, was shown to be a combination of the motif "Hidden in Sukkot" (itself based on the earlier motif recounting that Joseph's bones had been *hidden* by the Egyptians to prevent their departure, a motif represented in "Treasure-houses of the Palace" in the "Testament of Simeon") with a rival-motif according to which the bones are not hidden but "Forgotten by Everyone." Now both these motifs had originally been designed to answer the same question—why is not the retrieval of Joseph's bones mentioned until Exod. 13:19? In combining them, then, the *Tebat Marqa* expansion inevitably ended up with a certain amount of **overkill:** the role of the pillar of cloud in reminding the Israelites of the cause of the delay (a clever means, incidentally, of connecting this motif with another problem, the fact that the first mention of that pillar does not occur until Exod. 13:21) was duplicated by the role of Serah in "Hidden in Sukkot." But no matter: the new story managed thereby to harmonize two different attempts to explain the same problem in a now all-inclusive explanation. Meanwhile, Serah's role as presented in "Hidden in Sukkot" had come to be incorporated into another motif, "Bottom of the Nile," where it really served no purpose—its presence there only

indicates that, in quite similar fashion, this story of Serah's role in the retrieval of the bones had acquired enough popularity or authority so that room for it had to be made within the framework of an expansion in which it was basically irrelevant. Moreover, that same "Bottom of the Nile" expansion contains, as we saw, another reminiscence of the delay-at-Sukkot scenario in the words spoken by Moses, "Behold, the Divine Presence is waiting for you, Israel is waiting for you, *the clouds of glory are waiting for you.*" Here then are multiple examples of motifs and elements traveling via combination.

The same phenomenon of combination and harmonization is evidenced with regard to the "Assembly of Ladies": once the element "knives" in that motif had become sufficiently well known, perhaps via the *Tanhuma* text, more than one editor/copyist of the Aramaic poem then felt constrained to insert the element "knives" alongside the element "wine" contained in the original poem. Once again this act of combination or harmonization made for **overkill** in the expansion, yet even here the combination was achieved in such away that only an alert reader might notice the awkwardness.

Nor is this practice of combination and harmonization found only in narrative expansions. We saw, for example, that the two readings of Lev. 19:17, the "externalizing/moralistic" and the "judicial" approaches, were quite different in the way they understood the nature, form, and purpose of the "reproach" spoken of in that verse. These differences might have struck us as quite irreconcilable; it is thus remarkable to see how the two readings interact with one another. They are both presented in a single text, "The Testament of Gad"; what is more, they even appear side-by-side in the 1QS 5:24–6:1; and in fact the two came later to be fully harmonized into a single reading in Matt. 18:15!

But even when motifs or elements do not travel from one place to another or become combined and harmonized, they nonetheless can exert some influence beyond their immediate borders. Specifically:

6. **One exegetical motif can influence the creation or development of another.** The most telling example of this phenomenon seen above was the case of the motif "Daughters Climbed the Wall." For we saw that this motif, evidenced in the first century, doubtless had some role in shaping the "Assembly of Ladies" as it came to be elaborated from its terse beginnings in *Genesis Rabba* to the later versions studied, in which the Egyptian ladies in Potiphar's house, just like the "daughters" who climb atop the walls and towers of Egypt, stand awestruck at Joseph's beauty. Of course the two stories have no *exegetical* connection to one

another: they are addressed to two entirely different sets of problems. Nor is one simply a version or reworking of the other; indeed, the creators of the "Assembly of Ladies" may have been quite unaware of the influence of "Daughters Climbed the Wall" on their creation. Nevertheless, from our standpoint that influence is obvious enough: the whole later development of the "Assembly" followed the lines of the earlier motif.

In similar fashion, the idea underlying "Remembered Father's Teachings"—that Jacob had "studied Torah" with his son Joseph—is clearly connected to a whole complex of traditions which speak in one form or another of rabbinic-style academies and study-houses that existed in the time of the patriarchs. We saw that this theme surfaces, for example, in motifs explaining such different verses as Gen. 9:27, 25:22 and 27, 26:5, as well as Deut. 33:18. It is quite impossible to determine which of these motifs emerged first, and in any case that is probably irrelevant to our point here. For that point is simply that whichever of these various motifs came first, once launched on its career it could not but have aided in the creation of the others, until the idea of rabbinical-style study of Torah existing in the time of the patriarchs[6] became something of a midrashic commonplace. Moreover, we have seen how the specific motif "Remembered Father's Teachings," which represented Joseph as having once studied "Torah" (or the "words of Abraham" according to *Jubilees*) with his father, doubtless contributed to the development of that later motif "Jacob Saw the Wagons," for its whole premise is that father and son had indeed been "studying Torah" at the time of their last separation. So once again we see how, without actually traveling, a midrashic motif can bring about or influence the creation of another motif.

This matter of influence raises a very difficult question, one that in truth is far too broad for treatment in the present context, but which ought nonetheless to be mentioned. The question is this: Can we, in examining the very earliest exegetical texts that we possess, determine that only certain sorts of questions tended to be asked at those first stages of biblical exegesis, and that only certain sorts of answers tended to be put forward? Can we, in other words, write a history of the development of exegetical methodology?

The monumental study of Isaac Heinemann, *The Methods of Aggadah*,[7] is notably uninterested in this developmental question, save for its last chapter, where some of the methods of prerabbinic and rabbinic exegetes are briefly contrasted. In another context it might be interesting to explore Heinemann's conclusions (with which, I should perhaps say at the outset, I find myself in some disagreement). For the present, I should like only to state in tentative form a conclusion suggested by the previous chapters, a conclusion that may seem obvious enough, but which may nonetheless be worth elaborating briefly here:

7. **Our earlier exegetical sources tend to be concerned with relatively simple or obvious exegetical problems, whereas later texts tend to raise less obvious questions and/or to answer them in a more sophisticated and involved fashion.** This observation has a corollary, namely: **the more obvious the problem raised by a biblical text, the likelier it is that there exists a very ancient motif to answer it.** With regard to the kinds of questions posed by our earliest texts, we have seen that they generally are not the highly sophisticated or extremely playful sorts of questions that we have seen to underlie, especially, rabbinic texts. Instead, their questions (which may, *contra* Heinemann, involve the exegete in close philological questions and other forms of commentary proper) seem to be distinguished by the obviousness and *urgency* of their object. Thus they ask: What can this incomprehensible verse possibly mean? Why does such-and-such happen in the story when no explanation is given for it? How can we reconcile what is said here with what is said there, which seems to contradict it?

Indeed, a number of the foregoing chapters tell the story of how an essentially simple question was at first answered by an equally simple motif, but how subsequently that motif came to be developed or modified in order to accommodate increasingly detailed or sophisticated questions. Thus, the motif "Saw Father's Countenance" began as an attempt to explain the words *ro῾eh ῾eben yisra῾el* in Gen. 49:24, and it did so in straightforward fashion: the "stone" of Israel (= Jacob) was a stone bust, and *ro῾eh* is to be read as *ra῾ah*, "saw." But eventually, in the version cited from b. *Soṭa,* a far more complex motif developed on the scaffolding of the first: *῾eben yisra῾el* now came to be reinterpreted as a reference to the stones of the priestly breastplate, *ro῾eh* then reverted to the meaning of "shepherd" in order to be connected to a verse in Proverbs, and from this in turn was built an entire imaginary speech delivered at the critical moment by Jacob's "image" to his son Joseph. Despite the common scaffolding, then, the old question—what does *ro῾eh ῾eben yisra῾el* mean?—is now being answered in radically different (and far more involved) fashion, and in such a way as to connect the answer with other biblical texts and questions: the description of the priestly breastplate in Exod. 28:15–21 and 39:8–14 and the meaning and relevance of the proverb found in Prov. 29:3 (to this subject we shall return presently).

Another example: the questions to which "Inaccessible Bones" became an answer present a clear crescendo of sophistication and complication. The first question was quite straightforward: why does Joseph make his strange deathbed request (Gen. 50:15)? Now it is interesting that we saw this question, and this question alone, being addressed by the expansions in *Jubilees* and *The Testaments of the Twelve Patriarchs*. Later rabbinic sources have not entirely forgotten this "plot question," but they have other things to ask about this same verse—specifically, and characteristically, about the slight difference in wording between Gen. 50:25 and Exod. 13:19.[8] The big "plot" question eventually takes something of a backseat to these more local issues.[9] In the meantime, the career of "Inaccessible Bones" moved forward. The next question to which it came to be applied (if my reconstruction is correct) was a less obvious or pressing issue, but one that nonetheless stood out somewhat: why are Joseph's bones mentioned in connection with the march to Sukkot? Compared to these two, the "question" to which our rabbinic sources attach the same motif—why the stress on Moses in Exod. 13:19?—seems hardly a question at all: once again, the rabbinic query really only takes the form of a question so as to highlight in sophisticated fashion the text's precise wording. And this whole line of inquiry certainly seems in any case less urgent than the other two; it has to do with a relatively minor choice of words rather than something so basic as "plot."

Indeed, we have seen this pattern repeated again and again. The "Assembly of Ladies" starts with the disturbing "royal we," then moves to the far less disturbing "See!" (This is, incidentally, a rabbinic tradition from start to finish; still, the complications and sophistication seem to build with the passage of time.) The *Testaments*, Josephus, and other early sources see the phrase "comely of form and comely of appearance" in Gen. 39:6 as significantly emphatic, and seek to account for it as such; but rabbinic sources see it as an allusion the description of Rachel's beauty in Gen. 29:17. The "bad reports" that Joseph brings against his brothers involved, according to the "Testament of Gad," their slaughtering the animals that they were supposed to be guarding; according to the rabbinic sources examined, slaughtering (or rather, eating a limb from a live animal) was only one of three possible bad reports, and each of these was in any case tied to a rather more complex "make the punishment fit the crime" scenario that linked up with various later events in the same story. And so forth. Of course these data need to be nuanced (for they will not hold true in every case—nor, it should be added, need they do so) and need not be explained solely with reference to a process of increasing sophistication in the development of biblical exegesis. For one thing, the nature of the written sources in which our exegesis appears may have had some role: books written for patently polemical purposes, or intended for audiences of various degrees of education and sophistication, may concentrate on questions and answers by nature different from those found in books written for very different purposes and audiences. Still, the *observation* stated above certainly appears valid, and tentatively at least, we may say that the matters of historical development and increasing sophistication appear to constitute at least one plausible factor that might account for it.

But in the above observations lies the seed of a rather more specific one concerning rabbinic exegesis:

8. **As compared to other early exegetical sources, rabbinic texts have a striking interest in connecting one biblical text or problem to another at some remove from the first. This interest might be said to reflect the overall "canonizing" concern of rabbinic exegesis.** One of the most obvious manifestations of this tendency is the common rabbinic practice (witnessed above) of **back-referencing** verses, especially verses taken from the Psalms, Proverbs, Job, the Song of Songs, and Ecclesiastes. In this sort of reading, the rabbinic exegete radically alters the meaning of the verse by making it seem to refer back to some specific person or incident known from, usually, the Pentateuch. Consider for example the two verses from Proverbs that we saw back-referenced with regard to aspects of the Joseph tradition: "One wise of heart will take commandments, but he who is wicked of speech will falter" (Prov. 10:8), and "A wisdom-loving man will please his father, but a shepherd of prostitutes loses [his] wealth" (Prov. 29:3). Taken at face value, these verses seem to be little "truths" about human conduct and the proper path in life, sentiments of general import and eternal validity. And yet that is precisely how rabbinic exegetes do *not* like to treat such verses. For as we have seen in these two cases, the subject of the general proposition—the "wisdom-loving man" or the "wise of heart"—is instead explained as referring to someone in particular, here Moses and Joseph respectively. Thus these verses from Proverbs, and hundreds of others from that and the other books mentioned, are **back-referenced** to something in (especially) the Pentateuch.

It is interesting—striking, really—that one almost never finds such gratuitous integration of distant texts in prerabbinic sources.[10] Nor is at least one reason for this phenomenon difficult to discover. For as far as many ancient Jewish writers were concerned, the Pentateuch was Scripture *par excellence*, and if there was anything more to their "canon"—and in many cases even to speak of a canon is quite anachronistic—the Pentateuch was in any case the focus of their interest. Consequently, potential connections between non-Pentateuchal material and the Pentateuch were, as far as they were concerned, largely irrelevant. But this fact should hardly obscure the significance of our "thesis." For surely it is of more than passing interest to observe that, within rabbinic circles, this "integrative" interest did develop in such striking and consistent fashion, so that one of the most characteristic traits of rabbinic exegesis as a whole is its endless establishing of connections between Pentateuchal verses and other, quite "distant" biblical texts—not just texts at some physical remove from them, but in particular texts taken from the books cited.

Why should this practice have developed? It seems to me that it was fundamentally aimed at nothing less than the canonization of those books. This is not to say "canonization" in the technical sense: that these books were part of holy Scripture went largely without saying.[11] And yet, what is one to make of saying like "A wisdom-loving man will please his father, but a shepherd of prostitutes loses [his] wealth"? From a rabbinic standpoint, if this verse were seriously intended to tell us how we *must* behave, that we must in some specific sense love wisdom, avoid sinfulness, and so forth, then it really ought to have been a divine commandment: indeed, it ought to have been part of the divine revelation granted to Moses on Mount Sinai. Its status as an independent "proverb," then, without legal force and apparently quite oblivious to those Pentateuchal commandments, must therefore have been problematical. One could not say of it, as one could of the verses of other books outside of the Pentateuch, that it set forth the later history of Israel, in which the great divine plan was carrried forward in time; nor could one say that it contained prophecies of the future. But to read such a verse not as a general truth but as a specific allusion to Joseph, part of a speech pronounced by his father's "image" that day in Potiphar's house, is to reintegrate it into the rabbinic understanding of Scripture and the special status of the Pentateuch therein. For the verse now becomes, via such a reading, an *adjunct* to the Pentateuchal narrative—no independent proverb at all, but an elaboration of the story of Joseph and Potiphar's wife. And the same is true of similar wise sayings in Job and Ecclesiastes, or of individual verses in the Psalms—all of these were interpreted here and there as allusions to biblical history (or occasionally, even as expressions of principles bearing on *halakhah*)—or of the Song of Songs, which came to be read from beginning to end as a series of allusions to the history of Israel from the patriarchs to the exodus and the revelation at Sinai on to the construction of the tabernacle and still later events. All of these non-historical texts were thus *turned into history via interpretation*, so that their apparently independent status could be subsumed into the history of Israel narrated in the Pentateuch and other books.

Certainly the most dramatic enactment of this "canonizing" interest has not been evidenced in any of the above chapters, but it is still worth mentioning in this context. I mean the well-known rabbinic institution of the *petiḥta*, a brief sermon apparently designed to introduce the regular Pentateuchal reading on Sabbaths in the synagogue. For the very essence of the *petiḥta* is that it begins with some out-of-the-way verse—usually one from one of the books mentioned—and then only slowly, by unfolding an argument about the full significance of that verse, makes it way (usually via other verses) to the verse in the Pentateuch that begins that Sabbath's reading. Scholars have put forward various explanations for this meandering form—it was so designed to heighten tension in the audience, or to arouse their curiosity about the connection with the weekly reading, and so forth. But certainly when juxtaposed to the phenomenon of **back-referencing** just discussed, the *petiḥta* appears to have the form it has for yet another purpose: is it not primarily a demonstration, nay celebration, of the unity and interrelatedness of the canon, in which verses that at first seem quite unrelated are shown to have a profound hidden connection? Indeed, the same claim of unity and interconnectedness is extended to include elements of the Oral Law via another midrashic phenomenon, the *yelammedenu*-style sermon found in *Midrash Tanḥuma* and other texts. For here the starting-point is not some far-flung verse in Proverbs or Ecclesiastes, but an even more far-flung halakhic (or pseudohalakhic) question that then leads to a reflection on, eventually, a Pentateuchal verse. Once again, the aim seems to be *inclusion*, a claim that material apparently quite distant and independent of the Pentateuchal text in fact bears some hidden relevance to it.

And of course even in some of the lesser examples cited above, this proprietary interest of rabbinic exegetes in interrelating *all* of Scripture shines through. So, to repeat, the fact that the Rabbis read the emphatic "comely of form and comely of appearance" in Gen. 39:6 as no independent statement about Joseph but as an allusion to the description of Rachel's beauty in Gen. 29:17, or that they interpreted the "bad reports" that Joseph brings against his brothers in the light of subsequent mishaps that befall Joseph later in Genesis, likewise bespeaks a striking sensitivity and concern for intrabiblical connections. To be sure, it is not that such things are *never* to be found in prerabbinic texts; but once one is aware of this "canonizing" interest as a category, one cannot but be struck by its prevalence, its virtual omnipresence, in rabbinic texts from earliest times. Here truly is one of the most characteristic features of rabbinic exegesis vis-à-vis earlier forms of biblical commentary.

I have reserved for last an observation that touches on the matter of narrative expansions and what they may indicate about the overall picture of early biblical exegesis. For it is a striking fact that texts as different *Jubilees, The Testaments of the Twelve Patriarchs, Joseph and Aseneth,* Josephus' *Jewish Antiquities,* the *Paraleipomena Ieremiou,* and so on and so forth (and there are in fact dozens and dozens of similar texts that have not been mentioned above) all have one thing in common: they present a great deal of biblical interpretation, and yet they do not present it as such. Instead, they simply retell biblical stories with the "interpretations" included in the retelling—this is, indeed, the essence of the narrative expansion as we know it in these texts, interpretation that is presented as additional narrative. Now one might ask: why is this? After all, everything we know about this period indicates that the Pentateuch in particular was a *studied* book: in all manner of contexts, its meaning was pondered and its application to daily life set forth. What one would expect, therefore, would not be the "Retold Bible," in which interpretations are simply incorporated in an expanded rewording of the original, but a running commentary, some sort of *Glossa Ordinaria* that explicitly sets forth, verse by verse, the interpretation of the text.

Indeed this lack could not be more striking than in the context of the foregoing studies. For what we have been at pains to illustrate above is that various apparently fanciful elaborations of biblical texts are in fact rooted in precise details of those texts' wording. But if so, then why were our ancient authors apparently so reluctant to say so, explicitly—that is, to sit down and write such a *Glossa Ordinaria*? Why present all this interpretation in such backhanded fashion, by inference and indirection, instead of setting it out in straightforward, commentary-style fashion? Yet the fact is that, with the exception of Philo's Greek exposition of the Pentateuch and the *pesher* sort of running commentaries of the Qumran sect, we have no instances of such sustained, straightforward commentaries until we get to the tannaitic midrashim (put together, presumably, in the third century of the common era).

There is another observation, perhaps not unrelated to this one, that derives as well from the above studies. For we have seen many instances in which a common interpretive line is adopted by the most diverse sources. Both the *Testaments of the Twelve Patriarchs* and the *amora* R. Samuel b. Naḥman know the midrash of "Joseph resembled Jacob in all things." That Joseph's being a "child of his [Jacob's] old age" referred specifically to Joseph's *wisdom* is a bit of interpretation apparently shared by *Genesis Rabba,* the targum of Onkelos, Philo of Alexandria, and even possibly the third–second century B.C.E. historian Artapanus. The practice of interpreting the "doubled verb" of Lev. 19:17 as implying two or more acts of reproaching is known not only to various rabbinic sources but, as we have seen, to Ben Sira in the early second century B.C.E., and possibly even to the authors of the Septuagint in the previous century. The *Testaments* and R. Meir both know that Joseph's bad reports concerned, specifically, his brothers' eating from the flocks for which they were supposedly caring. The *Paraleipomena Ieremiou* and *Seder Eliahu Rabba* both know that the *gam* in Ps. 137:1 indicates some additional weeping, a "double lament" or two sequential weepings. Josephus and "the school of R. Ishmaʿel" both know that the reason why Potiphar's house was empty was that there was a festival of the Nile that day. *Sifra,* the *Testaments,* and the Qumran sect all know that the apparently general injunctions to good conduct in Lev. 19:15–19 are, at least sometimes, to be interpreted with reference specifically to courtroom behavior (as if all are elaborations on Lev. 19:15, "You shall do no injustice *in judgment*"); indeed, we have seen that these and yet other sources all seem to share one of two ancient approaches to the reading of Lev. 19:17. The understanding of Gen. 49:22, *banot saʿadah ʿalei shur,* as referring to Egyptian women standing on high walls and casting down their jewelry is known not only to Jerome and various rabbinic sources, but to the author of the first-century Greek romance *Joseph and Aseneth,* and the motif's garbled form in this last source (for its exegetical import is clearly not understood by the author) suggests an even earlier *terminus a quo. Jubilees,* the *Testaments,* and Targum Pseudo-Jonathan all know that Joseph desisted from sin because he suddenly remembered his father's earlier teachings. Similarly, not only rabbinic sources but *Joseph and Aseneth* are aware of the tradition that reads Gen. 49:24 as referring to a sudden appearance of Jacob's "portrait" or face. That Joseph's bones were actually hidden away by the Egyptians is known to the *Testaments, Tebat Marqa,* and various tannaitic sources.

This catalogue could be extended, but I trust that its point is clear. For in almost all of the cases cited, the resemblances between one exegetical source and another can hardly be explained by direct influence. The Rabbis did not derive their interpretive traditions from a careful reading of *Joseph and Aseneth,* nor did they mine *Jubilees* or the *Testaments* for such light as they might shed on the Pentateuchal narrative, no more than they learned legal interpretation from the Qumran sect or the "Testament of Gad." Nor can such resemblances—and myriads like them, catalogued in great detail by scholars over the last century and more—be merely coincidental, the result of ancient exegetes independently arriving at precisely the same solution to the same biblical crux. On the contrary, such resemblances can only indicate a common store of biblical exegesis inherited by diverse, and in some cases clearly antagonistic, Jewish groups and circles that flourished in Palestine and elsewhere in the centuries just before and after the start of the common era. In other words, all this evidence of shared exegetical motifs suggests the existence of precisely what we do not have, an ancient Jewish *Glossa Ordinaria.*

And so, putting these observations together, one can only conclude that such a *Glossa Ordinaria* must have existed, but that it did not survive. For only if one postulates its existence can one explain all the precise resemblances between diverse sources just catalogued. And only if one postulates its existence can one understand why it is that the vast majority of our *other* ancient sources never set out systematically to expound Scripture, verse by verse, but only seem to *allude* to such an expounding in offhand fashion as they retell scriptural stories or recount their teachings. Yet such a hypothesis *per se* solves very little. For if indeed such an important document existed, how could it have happened that it was not preserved? Indeed, why is it that there is not a single allusion to such a text in all of our ancient sources?

The solution is only too obvious: the "document" in question was not a written text at all, but a somewhat amorphous, ever-expanding, oral one. In other words:

9. **Early exegetical documents of various sorts seem to argue, by their very form as well as by the overwhelming store of exegetical motifs shared among them—and this despite their highly diverse origins and orientations—that there existed well before the common era a substantial body of standard explanations of various problems and peculiarities in the biblical text. These explanations were apparently not gathered and passed down in written form, since no such document has survived or is even alluded to. Instead, they were passed on orally, perhaps taught to schoolchildren as part of their study of Scripture in literacy education, and/or communicated along with the public liturgical reading/translation/exposition of Scripture.**

No doubt to formulate things in this fashion is to invite a grimace from two rather different groups. For this last "thesis" sounds very much like a version of the rabbinic doctrine of the "Oral Torah" that postulates the existence of a fixed body of teachings passed on orally from generation to generation from the time of Moses to that of the Rabbis themselves. To arrive, then, at a similar-sounding conclusion will no doubt strike many as merely a reinventing of the wheel, while others may on the contrary find in it an apologetic for a standard piece of rabbinic doctrine which, therefore, ought to be rejected out of hand. The very existence of the second group should at least soften the criticisms of the first: for if to argue as I have is to reinvent the wheel, then it is a wheel apparently in need of reinvention, or reformulation, at least in the eyes of adherents of this second group. But how indeed can one answer the accusation of those who see in such an argument mere apologetics? The only answer I have is this: the peculiarities presented above do demand some explanation, and whoever would reject the one just set forth must come up with an alternative solution. I can think of none. Indeed, everything we have seen above (and much that has not been mentioned) implies what might in any case have merely been supposed: that as the place of Scripture became solidified in the life of Second Temple Judaism—serving as its very foundation document, and (in varying degrees at different times) the basis of its laws, education, political aspirations and spiritual life—a growing body of interpretations of specific biblical verses and pericopes came to be promulgated across a broad swath of the population. These interpretations were not of course merely passed on unaltered to subsequent generations: they were elaborated, and at times some were abandoned or even polemically attacked with new interpretations. Nevertheless, a corpus of methodological assumptions, as well as a good many specific interpretations, came to be shared even by the warring groups whose names and works we know from the end of this period. And it is this common inheritance—communicated orally, as suggested, perhaps through the instruction of children and/or the public reading and translation or exposition of Scripture—that is responsible for the common assumptions, and much common material, that we have seen to characterize the written sources that have survived from those early times. Finally, since the oral transmission of these interpretations already had (it is theorized) its own institutionalized place in the life of the community, there was scarcely any point to committing them to writing, unless that writing was done (as was the case with Qumran *pesher* or, in another sense, with Philo's running allegorical commentary) as part of an extended, polemical departure from the common tradition.[12]

Beyond this, though, there is a further point to be made about the place of narrative expansions and their study with regard to specifically this matter of an "Oral Torah." For most discussions of this issue have centered on matters of *halakhah*. And rightly so: no doubt legal issues must have formed the heart of early exegetical traditions, not only because so much of the Pentateuch is taken up with matters of law, but because such matters are of immediate practical consequence in daily life and therefore must have demanded both precise resolution and wide dissemination. Therefore such matters as the beginnings of legal exegesis;[13] real and inferential resemblances between the halakhic teachings of rabbinic Judaism (specifically, the Mishnah) and earlier sources like the Temple Scroll and other Qumran documents, Philo, Josephus, and so forth; Mishnah-type versus midrash-type of learning and the question of precedence[14]—such matters of legal exegesis have largely provided the raw material for this debate.

Yet there is in fact a certain perspective gained by examining the "Oral Torah" issue via nonlegal exegesis. That advantage lies in the fact that while, for example, the Qumran sect apparently disagreed with the forerunners of rabbinic Judaism precisely on matters of *halakhah*—and, as a consequence, areas of agreement between the legal exegesis of Qumran and that of the Rabbis are relatively scarce and frequently only inferential—the two groups, as well as others represented by various documents of the Second Temple period, apparently found far less to disagree about when it came to matters of a nonlegal nature.[15] Therefore, studying this common store of exegetical motifs with regard to biblical narrative may in fact be more indicative of the real nature and extent of the common heritage of biblical exegesis to which these diverse groups were heir than concentrating merely on their differing stances with regard to legal matters. For this reason too, the vast heritage of narrative expansions present in the diverse writings of the end of the Second Temple period—and the exegetical motifs that they embody—deserves the sustained attention of anyone interested in the history and development of Judaism in these formative centuries.

Notes

1. The roots of this approach, incidentally, go back to the earlier "legends" approach, itself tied to the rekindling of Jewish national self-consciousness in the nineteenth and twentieth centuries, and its (frequently secularist) attempts to find in rabbinic "legends" the Jewish equivalent of a national

literature—such literature representing, along with a national language and national homeland, the basis for Jewish political claims.

2. Perhaps it should be noted here that the pseudodistinction between *exegesis* and *eisegesis* (the latter meaning reading some meaning *into*, rather than out of, a text) has been quite purposely avoided throughout this study. The whole point of the present discussion is that such an either-or approach is quite wrongheaded with regard to midrash.

3. No doubt the well-worn Exod. 4:16 ("You shall be . . . as God") could have served for the former, or perhaps, Exod. 33:11 (i.e., "face to *face*"), or Deut. 34:10 ("And there has not *arisen* in Israel . . ."), etc., etc.; for Abraham perhaps Gen. 12:2 ("I will make your name great") or Isa. 41: 8–9 ("Abraham my beloved . . . you whom I *took* from the *corners* of the earth") could have been used.

4. Indeed, this appears to be precisely the tactic adopted by gnostic exegetes. See thus "The Secret Book (Apocryphon) According to John," in B. Layton, *The Gnostic Scriptures* (Garden City, NY: Doubleday, 1987), 39. For other manifestations of this idea in rabbinic texts, see Y. F. Baer, *Israel Among the Nations* (Jerusalem: Bialik, 1955), 86–88.

5. See my "Two Introductions to Midrash," *Prooftexts* 3 (1983):131–55 (reprinted in G. Hartman and S. Budick, *Midrash and Literature* [New Haven: Yale University Press, 1986], 77–103).

6. This in itself, incidentally, is another good instance of "impure" exegesis of the sort discussed in Thesis 1 above, for clearly with all of these above-cited verses the rabbinic exegete went out of his way to "solve" the difficulty of the verse via a doctrine that, however absurd, was one that he was pleased to promulgate.

7. I. Heinemann, *Darkhei ha-Aggadah* (Jerusalem: Magnes, 1970).

8. See thus *Mekhilta*, "Beshallah—Petihta" (Horovitz-Rabin edition, p. 80); *Genesis Rabba* 100 (Vat. Ms. 101), 11; etc. The question is: why does Gen. 50:25 read "take up my bones from here" and Exod. 13:19 read "take up my bones from here *with you*"?

9. We saw that the Mishnah's discourse "Buried by One Greater" in fact constituted an answer to the question of why Joseph did not request immediate reburial. How significant, then, that it ends up being presented as a discourse on the ever-greater rewards received by the virtuous, so that its old answer to the "plot" question was no longer even perceived as such in its present context.

10. One case in which this does happen—and one which is relevant to our overall subject of Joseph—is Amos 2:6, which speaks of Israel's sin "in their selling a righteous man for money, and a poor man for some shoes." That this verse was taken as referring to Joseph is witnessed by the "Testament of Zebulun" in the *Testaments of the Twelve Patriarchs*, which recounts that the brothers "took what was paid for Joseph and bought sandals for themselves and for their wives and children." The same theme appears in *Pirqei R. Eli'ezer* 38, *Midrash ha-Gadol* (*ad loc.*), etc. and later fused with the tradition of the Ten Martyrs. See Ginzberg, *Legends*, 5:329–30 n. 50–52.

11. It is true that the canonical status of Ecclesiastes and other books was still discussed within this period (on which see S. Z. Leiman, *The Canonization*

of Scripture [Hamden, CT: Shoestring Press, 1979]), but this is quite irrelevant to our point.

12. It seems to me that *Jubilees,* while not a running commentary proper, is a similarly polemical document and may therefore be assimilated to this group.

13. One recent study worthy of mention in this regard in M. Fishbane, *Biblical Interpretation in Ancient Israel* (Oxford: Clarendon, 1985).

14. On both of these see the recent discussion by D. Weiss-Halivni, *Mishnah and Midrash* (Cambridge: Harvard University, 1986).

15. Here I am thinking, in the context of Qumran, about a document such as the "Genesis Apocryphon" and the exegetical similarities it bears to rabbinic texts dealing with the same material.

Glossary of Sources, Terms, and Abbreviations Used in this Book

Amoraic, Amoraim: See *Rabbis, the.

Apocrypha (Gk: "hidden things," i.e. things to be hidden away):   A collection of writings, mostly from the end of the biblical period, that were accepted by early Christians as Scripture but which, because they were eventually excluded from the Jewish canon, came to be regarded by many later Christians as belonging to a special category. They were included in the Bible of Western Christianity, but under the name "Apocrypha"; later, many Protestant churches excluded them in part or in toto from their canon. These books, along with the *Pseudepigrapha, are particularly interesting to biblical scholars, since many of them contain retellings of biblical stories or reflections on particular passages or people in the Bible, and thus can provide us with a snapshot of how parts of the Bible were being interpreted from the third century B.C.E. onward. Among the best known books of the Apocrypha are *Ben Sira (= Sirach, Ecclesiasticus), Judith, 1 Baruch, Susanna, 1 and 2 *Maccabees, 1 and 2 Esdras, and Tobit.

b.:   An abbreviation for *Babylonian Talmud, followed by name of tractate.

Babylonian Talmud: A compendium of Jewish learning and biblical exegesis redacted in Babylon in the fifth and early sixth century C.E.. Organized in the form of a digressive commentary on the Mishnah, it ends up citing and explaining much of the Hebrew Bible, and is thus a valuable collection of Jewish interpretive traditions. It is quite lengthy; the English translation edited by I. Epstein (London: Soncino Press, 1938–52) runs to some thirty-four volumes.

Back-referencing: The practice of reading verses from such books as Psalms, Proverbs, Job, the Song of Songs, and Ecclesiastes as if they referred to people or events set forth in the historical narratives of the Hebrew Bible, and in particular in the Pentateuch.

Ben Sira (also known as: Sirach or Ecclesiasticus):   A book of wisdom sayings and other material written in Hebrew by Joshua (Jesus) son of Sira[ch], probably ca. 180 B.C.E.. Although it was ultimately excluded from the Jewish Canon and classified by Western Christianity among the *Apocrypha, Ben Sira was nonetheless long treasured by both Jews and Christians. It contains many reflections of Jewish exegesis as it existed in the second century B.C.E., including the well known and lengthy catalogue of biblical heroes, "Let us now praise famous men . . ."(chaps. 44–49).

Baruch, Fourth Book of (also: IV Baruch, "The Rest of the Words of Jeremiah," or *"Paraleipomena Ieremiou"* ["The Things Omitted from the book of Jeremiah"]):   A pseudepigraphic work (see: *Pseudepigrapha) purporting to be an account of the destruction of Jerusalem and subsequent events. It was probably written in the early second century C.E..

B.C.E.:   "Before the Common Era," i.e., "B.C."

C.E.:   "Common Era," i.e., "A.D."

Chronicles of Yerahme'el: Authored by El'azar ben Asher ha-Levi (late thirteenth–early fourteenth century C.E.), this book takes the form of a history of ancient times and contains much midrashic material, some of it otherwise unattested.

Damascus Document (or: "Damascus Covenant"):   A text that derives from the same sect known to us via the *Dead Sea Scrolls but which—through means not entirely clear—ended up in the storeroom ("Geniza") of a Cairo synagogue, where it was discovered by Solomon Schechter at the very end of the nineteenth century. Although it was quickly identified as the work of a Jewish sect living at the end of the biblical period, the Damascus Document's full significance could not, therefore, begin to be understood until the *Qumran documents began to appear some fifty years later.

Dead Sea Scrolls: A collection of biblical manuscripts and other writings that for the most part belonged to a sect of ascetic Jews who had retreated to the area of *Qumran along the Dead Sea. The sect seems to have existed there from the second century B.C.E. until 68 C.E., and may be identified with the Essenes, a Jewish sect described by *Philo, *Josephus, and others. This library of texts, preserved by dint of the area's dry climate and discovered in various caves of the region during the 1940s and 1950s, has properly been described as the greatest manuscript find of modern times. The Dead Sea Scrolls have provided a wealth of information about the history and development of the biblical text itself, about first-century Judaism and the roots of Christianity, and about biblical interpretation as it existed just before and after the start of the C.E.. In this last category, such texts as the *Damascus Document (or "Damascus Covenant"), the Genesis Apocryphon, and various examples of what the sect called *pesher* (interpretation) have proven to be of great importance.

Eikhah Rabba (or: Rabbati):   A midrashic collection on the book of Lamentations (Hebrew: 'Eikhah) put together in Palestine, probably in the fifth century.

element: A minor detail or piece of wording that may distinguish one version of a motif from another. In this study, elements are referred to in quotation marks, but left in lower case (to distinguish them from the names of *exegetical motifs). Thus: "citrons," "pebble," "wonder-working speech."

Ephraem Syrus (ca. 306–373): Christian scholar, the author of biblical commentaries, hymns, and other writings in Syriac.

Eusebius of Caesarea (ca. 260–ca. 340): Bishop of Caesarea, an important Christian thinker and early church historian. He is the author of *Preparation for the Gospel* and other works.

Exegesis: Interpretation, especially biblical interpretation.

Exegetical motif: The underlying idea about how to explain a biblical text that becomes the basis, or part of the basis, for a *narrative expansion. Motifs tend to become elaborated over time, and often come to be joined with other motifs to form a new motif. A motif can thus exist in different **variants** or **versions**; the common source of two or more variants may be spoken of as the **basic motif**. Motifs in this study are identified by tag-lines, capitalized and put in quotation marks—thus, the basic motif "Assembly of Ladies" is found in such variants as "Cut Their Hands" and "Forgot Their Wine."

Exodus Rabba: An early medieval composite of two distinct exegetical works. The first part of the book, consisting of sections 1–14, is a straightforward collection of exegetical remarks to the beginning of the book of Exodus; the remaining part is written in the style reminiscent of *Midrash Tanhuma* and other works of the "*Tanhuma-Yelammedenu*" type.

Fathers According to R. Nathan, the: A midrashic collection organized around a section of the *Mishnah known as the "Sayings of the Fathers" (*Pirqei Abot*). This collection, although not put into its final form until relatively late, basically contains material from the pre–200 C.E. *Rabbis and is a valuable compendium of early interpretation.

Genesis Rabba: A midrashic collection on the book of Genesis that was compiled (much of it from far earlier material) at the end of the fourth or early fifth century C.E..

Gospel of John: The fourth canonical gospel in the New Testament. Most modern scholars agree that it could not have been composed much before the end of the first century C.E..

Jerome (ca. 342–420 C.E.): Christian biblical scholar and exegete. Jerome's great achievement is the Vulgate, a translation of the Bible into Latin which became the standard Old Testament of the Roman Catholic Church. Jerome spent much time in Rome, was possessed of a thorough classical education, and served for a time as secretary to Pope Damasus. He is the author of various commentaries, introductions, and numerous letters, all of which shed light on his own understanding of Scripture as well Jewish biblical interpretation as it existed in and around Bethelehem, where he settled starting in 386 C.E..

Jerusalem Talmud: A compendium of Jewish learning and biblical exegesis completed in Palestine at the end of the fourth or early fifth century C.E..

Like the *Babylonian Talmud, it takes the form of a highly digressive commentary on the *Mishnah, but the Jerusalem Talmud is considerably shorter than the Babylonian Talmud. It has exercised somewhat less influence within later Judaism.

Joseph and Aseneth: A novella-like text probably composed near the beginning of the first century C.E. It elaborates the Bible's passing mention of Joseph's marriage to "Asenath, the daughter of Potiphera, priest of On" (Gen. 41:45) into a full-scale love story, marriage, and adventure. Aseneth, here the daughter of "Pentephres," is so smitten with Joseph that she ultimately repents of her idolatrous ways and undergoes some mystical conversion. This text, reminiscent of Hellenistic romances of the period, was probably originally composed in Greek, but by an author who was apparently quite familiar with some early Jewish exegetical traditions.

Josephus, Flavius (ca. 37 C.E.–ca. 100):   Jewish general, historian, and biblical exegete. His *Jewish Antiquities* provide a wealth of information about how the Bible was understood in the first century C.E..

Jubilees, Book of: An early (mid-second century B.C.E.?) retelling of Genesis and the first part of Exodus, presented in the form of a secret revelation given to Moses on Mt. Sinai. *Jubilees* was originally written in Hebrew, but only survives in translations. It shows some affinities with the ideology of the Jewish sect at *Qumran that produced the *Dead Sea Scrolls.

"The Ladder" or "The Ladder of Jacob":   An independent work, or part thereof, now incorporated into the *Tolkovaya Palea*, a midrashic retelling of much of Genesis and other biblical books, extant in Greek and Slavonic. "The Ladder" most likely goes back to a Hebrew or Aramaic original whose approximate time of composition is the first century C.E..

Lamentations Rabba: see Eikhah Rabba.

m.:   Abbreviation for *Mishnah, followed by name of tractate.

Maccabees, Book of: Four different books bear this name, known respectively as 1, 2, 3, and 4 Macc. **1 and 2 Macc.** actually have something to do with the events surrounding the Maccabees (the Jewish leaders of a successful revolt against Syrian domination in the second century B.C.E.), each retelling the story of the revolt from a somewhat different perspective; they were probably written in the late second or early first century B.C.E.. **3 Macc.** is a historical romance, originally written in Greek in the first century B.C.E., and set in the third century B.C.E.. **4 Macc.** is treatise devoted to the theme of Reason's domination of the passions. Written in Greek in the first century C.E., it uses biblical persons and incidents to illustrate its ideas.

Mahzor Vitry: A collection of prayers and other liturgical compositions, as well as halakhic rulings and discussions, apparently compiled in the eleventh century by Simhah b. Samuel of Vitry, a contemporary (and possibly a student) of Rashi. Mahzor Vitry was widely circulated and exists in dif-

ferent forms in various manuscripts. There is as yet no critical edition of
this work.

Manual of Discipline: A book of rules and regulations found in various
copies at *Qumran; it is among the more important of the *Dead Sea
Scrolls. It differs significantly from another rule-book associated with the
Qumran sect, the *Damascus Document.

Mekhilta of Rabbi Ishma'el: A midrashic collection on the book of Exodus.
Since the rabbis cited within it are all *tannaim* (see *Rabbis, the), it is generally assumed to have been compiled around 200 C.E. or shortly thereafter.

Memar Marqa: See Tebat Marqa.

midrash: A Hebrew term meaning interpretation or exegesis. The term is
used nowadays to designate specifically the sort of exegesis practiced by
the *Rabbis and contained in such works as the *Babylonian and
*Jerusalem Talmuds as well as various collections of rabbinic exegesis, such
as the *Mekhilta of R. Ishma'el, *Sifra, *Sifrei Deuteronomy, *Genesis (Exodus,
Leviticus, etc.) Rabba, *The Fathers According to R. Nathan, and dozens of
others. "Midrash" is also often used as the title of such collections of exegesis, e.g. "Midrash ha-Gadol," "Midrash Tanhuma," etc.

Midrash ha-Gadol: A late medieval midrashic anthology on the Pentateuch.
This collection, of Yemenite origin, often freely reworks its sources, sometimes interpolating material from Maimonides or other medieval scholars.
At the same time, it also preserves much ancient material, some of it otherwise quite unattested or at least unknown in that particular form.

Midrash Sekhel Tob: A late midrashic compilation on the Pentateuch, drawn
from various earlier sources by Menaḥem b. Solomon (early twelfth century) and completed, according to him, in the year 1139.

Midrash Tanḥuma: An early medieval midrashic collection on the Pentateuch
extant in various forms. In addition to the standard ("printed") *Tanḥuma*,
a significantly different text was published in the last century by S. Buber,
who mistakenly believed his to be the "ancient" *Tanḥuma*. Subsequently
numerous *Tanḥuma-Yelammedenu* fragments have been published from
manuscript. The various texts do all seem to derive ultimately from a common source, a Palestinian midrash on the Torah that achieved wide circulation and, in the process, acquired many additions, rewritings, and
deletions.

Midrash Tehillim: A late and composite collection on the book of Psalms, not
completed in its present form before the late Middle Ages, although containing much earlier material.

Mishnah: A codification of Jewish law and practice put into its final form ca.
200 C.E.. It fleshes out the details of many things treated only cursorily in
biblical law, as well as treating a number of entirely new matters.

MT (abbrev. for "Masoretic Text"):   The text of the Bible as handed down in
Hebrew by Jews from generation to generation. It was standardized in its

basic form by about 100 C.E.. The Masoretes, who gave this text its present scholarly name, were a school of Jewish biblicists active in the early Middle Ages; they developed and transmitted a set of increasingly sophisticated systems of annotation and punctuation for preserving the slightest details about the text's traditional pronunciation, meaning, and conventions of public reading.

narrative expansion: one of the most characteristic features of ancient biblical scholarship, whereby all manner of "extras" not found in the biblical text itself—additional actions performed by someone in the biblical narrative, or words spoken by him—are inserted in a retelling of the text by some later author or in a commentary upon it. Such narrative expansions are, by definition, *exegetical* because they are ultimately based on something that *is* in the text—an unusual word or turn of phrase that sets off the imagination of the exegete, or simply some problem in the plot that required resolution. Narrative expansions may be said to be based upon one or more *exegetical motif.

narrative resumption: The practice of restating or resuming something said earlier in a text. Most typically, this is done when an editor or later writer has inserted something into an existing text. By repeating the sentence or phrase that just preceded his insertion, he is in effect returning things to where they were before, so that the text can now flow smoothly on to the next thing as if no interruption had taken place.

Numbers Rabba: A late and composite midrashic collection on the book of Numbers. Sections 1–14 of this collection form one distinct unit, dated to the twelfth century C.E., while the latter part of the book is virtually identical with the corresponding section of our *Midrash Tanḥuma.*

Origen (ca. 185–264):   Biblical scholar and commentator, the author of numerous philosophical and exegetical works, many of which, however, have been lost. He was a champion of allegorical exegesis.

Pentateuch: The first five books of the Hebrew Bible—Genesis through Deuteronomy—also known by the Hebrew word *Torah ("teaching").

Pesiqta deR. Kahana: A collection of homilies created for festivals and other special occasions in the liturgical year. It originated in the Land of Israel, perhaps in the fifth century C.E..

Pesiqta Rabbati: A later collection of homilies in the same form as *Pesiqta deR. Kahana and recycling some of the latter's contents as well as other earlier exegetical material.

Philo of Alexandria   (ca. 20 B.C.E. to ca. 50 C.E.; also called "Philo Judæus," Philo the Jew): A Greek-speaking Jew, the author of a multivolume commentary on the Pentateuch. Philo was a champion of allegorical exegesis. His writings exercised considerable influence among early Christian exegetes, including *Origen.

Pirqei R. Eliʿezer: A midrashic work organized thematically and containing much material otherwise unknown in rabbinic writings—some of it apparently drawn from the *Apocrypha and *Pseudepigrapha. The book was apparently written in the eighth century C.E..

Pseudepigrapha [of the Hebrew Bible]:   A somewhat loose term to describe a group of texts, mostly written between the third century B.C.E. and the second century C.E., which, although generally not attributed the same sanctity as the Bible, were nonetheless studied and preserved by early Jews and Christians. They are called "Pseudepigrapha" ("falsely ascribed" writings) because many of them purport to be the pronouncements of this or that ancient worthy known from the Hebrew Bible—Enoch, Abraham, Jacob, etc. A great many of these books retell biblical stories or seek to comment on incidents or figures known from the Bible, and thus they can tell us much about how the Bible was being read and interpreted from the third century B.C.E. on. Among the Pseudepigrapha are various "apocalypses" or revelations given to this or that ancient figure, often "foretelling" events belonging to the time in which the apocalypse in question was actually written ("Apocalypse of Abraham," "Apocalypse of Adam," etc.); "testaments," i.e., the last words (containing advice and retrospection) of biblical figures ("Test. of Adam," "Test. of Abraham," *"Testaments of the Twelve Patriarchs," etc.); and retellings and expansions of biblical tales (4 *Baruch, *Jubilees, *Pseudo-Philo, etc.). Current anthologies of the Pseudepigrapha include: R. H. Charles, *Apocrypha and Pseudepigrapha of the Old Testament*; J. H. Charlesworth, *The Old Testament Pseudepigrapha*; and H. F. D. Sparks, *The Apocryphal Old Testament.*

Qumran, Khirbet: A site near the Dead Sea, about eight and a half miles from Jericho, where, starting in 1947, a collection of ancient Jewish manuscripts, the *Dead Sea Scrolls, was found hidden away in various caves. Qumran was apparently the home-base of an ascetic sect of Jews, probably to be identified with the "Essene" sect known to us from the writings of Philo, Josephus, and others, that flourished in the closing centuries B.C.E. and on into the common era.

Qurʾan (Koran):   The sacred Scripture of Islam. Held to have been dictated by God to the prophet Muḥammad, it belongs to the seventh century C.E. and contains various reflections of early biblical interpretation.

R.:   See next entry

Rabbi: An honorific title (often abbreviated "R.") that means "my teacher." See *Rabbis, the.

Rabbinic Judaism: The tradition of Judaism championed by the *Rabbis and which has survived in some measure to the present day. Scholars nowadays say "Rabbinic Judaism" instead of just "Judaism" in recognition of the fact that, in the closing centuries B.C.E. and in the early C.E., there were various "Judaisms," i.e., different Jewish sects all advocating somewhat different sorts of Jewish belief and practice.

Rabbis, the: A group of Jewish scholars that championed an approach to Scripture and to Judaism that came to bear their name ("rabbinic exegesis" and *Rabbinic Judaism; see also *midrash). The Rabbis were so known because, starting in the first century C.E.., the teachers and leaders of this group were addressed and spoken of as "Rabbi." But as a school of exegetes and practitioners, the Rabbis are probably older than the use of this particular title; scholars of similar tendencies are known to us earlier as the "sages," "elders," *soferim* ("bookmen" or scribes), and Pharisees. A conventional distinction separates the Rabbis into two chronological groups: those before ca. 200 C.E. (see *Mishna) are called **tannaim** and those after 200 C.E. are called **amoraim**.

Seder Eliyahu Rabba (and Seder Eliyahu Zuṭa):   Also known as "Tanna deBei Eliyahu," this work of uncertain date takes the form of an extended discourse on Torah-study, the importance of the commandments, etc. Although not an exegetical work per se, it contains much midrashic material which may well stem from an early period and is unparalleled elsewhere.

Seder ʿOlam: A tannaitic collection attributed to R. Yosé b. Ḥalafta; it attempts to put the events of Scripture in precise chronological order.

Sefer ha-Yashar: A midrashic collection written in pseudobiblical Hebrew whose origins are most likely to be located in Italy, probably no earlier than the thirteenth century.

Septuagint (from Lat. "septuaginta" = seventy; abbreviated LXX):   The Old Greek translation of the Hebrew Bible, so called because of a legend that holds that the Pentateuch was first translated into Greek by seventy (or seventy-two) Jewish scholars who, though working in complete isolation, nevertheless produced identical translations. This legend, found in the Letter of Aristeas and elsewhere, was apparently created to legitimize the Old Greek translation in the eyes of its first users, the Greek-speaking Jews of Alexandria (Egypt). The name "Septuagint" later came to be applied to the entirety of the Old Greek translation of the Hebrew Bible. This translation was probably carried out over a long period of time, from the third to the second or first century B.C.E. It became the Bible of Greek-speaking Christianity, but was eventually abandoned by Greek-speaking Jews. It sometimes differs radically from the traditional Hebrew (Masoretic) text; this is not because the translators were sloppy or overly free (as was once thought), but because the translators had before them a Hebrew text of the Bible that differed, in both significant matters and trivial details, from the Masoretic text. The "Septuagint" was also the basis of the old Latin Bible ("Vetus Latina"), an awkward translation that was replaced by *Jerome's Vulgate.

Sifra (also: Sifra debei Rab, Torat Kohanim):   A midrashic collection on the book of Leviticus. Since the Rabbis cited in it are all *tannaim* (see *Rabbis, the), it is generally assumed to have been compiled around 200 C.E. or shortly thereafter.

Sifrei Deuteronomy: A midrashic collection on the book of Deuteronomy. Since the Rabbis cited in it are all *tannaim* (see *Rabbis, the), it is generally assumed to have been compiled around 200 C.E. or shortly thereafter.

Sifrei Numbers: A midrashic collection on the book of Numbers. Since the Rabbis cited in it are all *tannaim* (see *Rabbis, the), it is generally assumed to have been compiled around 200 C.E. or shortly thereafter.

Talmud: See *Babylonian Talmud, *Jerusalem Talmud.

Tannaim: See *Rabbis, the.

Targum: A general name for a translation of the Hebrew Bible, or parts thereof, into Aramaic, a Semitic language related to Hebrew and spoken widely throughout the ancient Near East from the eighth century B.C.E. on. Among the targums cited herein are **Targum Onkelos**, a targum of the Pentateuch dating from the first or second century C.E. and still the best known and most frequently printed targum; **Targum Pseudo-Jonathan** (so called because in relatively recent times it came wrongly to be ascribed to Jonathan ben Uzziel, author of a targum of the prophetic books of the Bible), a highly discursive targum of the Pentateuch which did not achieve its final form until the Middle Ages but containing much ancient material; and **Targum Neophyti**, a targum of the Pentateuch recently discovered in the Vatican library (this targum is related to Pseudo-Jonathan). Onkelos is, relatively speaking, a rather close translation of the Hebrew text, but often swerves from literal rendition in order to avoid anthromorphisms or for other doctrinal reasons; Neophyti and (even more so) Pseudo-Jonathan are far from literal translations: they often insert phrases or whole sentences in order to explain the meaning of the text as they understand it, or simply in order to pass along some traditional bit of Jewish exegesis.

Tebat Marqa: A Samaritan commentary-expansion dealing principally with items from the book of Exodus. It has been dated to the fourth century C.E..

Testament of Gad: See next entry.

Testaments of the Twelve Patriarchs: A book purporting to contain the last words of each of the twelve sons of Jacob. In its present form it is a Christian work, but probably originated in a Jewish collection of testaments, perhaps going back to the first or second century B.C.E..

Tractate Abot, etc.: See Pirqei Abot in *Fathers According to R. Nathan, the.

Torah ("teaching"): A Hebrew word used in the Bible to describe, *inter alia*, a particular statute or procedure, or a collection thereof; the phrase "Torah of Moses" or "Torah of God" that appears in later biblical books may designate the contents of the *Pentateuch as a whole. In any case, the term Torah was used in postbiblical Hebrew to designate (1) the *Pentateuch (in this sense the word Torah was translated into Greek as *nomos* [law, way of life] and appears in the New Testament phrase, "the Law and the Prophets," meaning [more or less] the Bible); (2) somewhat more loosely, the

Bible as a whole; and (3) still more loosely, the entire corpus of rabbinic learning, including Bible, *Mishnah, *Talmud, *midrash.

Vienna Genesis: A book, of Christian origin, containing texts and illustrations from the Book of Genesis; it has been dated to the sixth century C.E. It was probably made somewhere in the Eastern region of the Byzantine world.

Vulgate: See *Jerome.

Wisdom of Solomon: A Jewish work probably written close to the turn of the era but purportedly composed a millennium earlier by King Solomon of Israel. It discusses the general theme of wisdom and illustrates it with biblical examples. The book was included among the *Apocrypha.

Yalquṭ Shim'oni: A late (eleventh century ?) medieval collection of midrashic material culled from earlier sources, many of them now lost.

Index

A. SUBJECTS

B. HEBREW BIBLE

C. MOTIFS STUDIED